The Second Ottoman Empire

MW00576268

Although scholars have begun to revise the eighteenth centuries marked a decline in the fortunes of the Ottoman Empire, Baki Tezcan's book proposes a radical new approach to this period. Concurring that decline did take place in certain areas, he constructs a new framework by foregrounding the proto-democratization of the Ottoman polity in this era. Focusing on the background and the aftermath of the regicide of Osman II, he shows how the empire embarked on a period of seismic change in the political, economic, military, and social spheres. It is this period – from roughly 1580 to 1826 – that the author labels "The Second Empire" and that he sees as no less than the transformation of the patrimonial, medieval, dynastic institution into a fledgling limited monarchy. The book is essentially a post-revisionist history of the early modern Ottoman Empire that will make a major contribution not only to Ottoman scholarship but also to comparable trends in world history.

BAKI TEZCAN is Associate Professor of History and Religious Studies at the University of California, Davis. He has received research fellowships from the Mrs. Giles Whiting Foundation, the National Endowment for the Humanities, and Cornell University's Society for the Humanities. He coedited *Identity and Identity Formation in the Ottoman World: A Volume of Essays in Honor of Norman Itzkowitz* (2007) and has contributed articles to numerous books and journals.

The Second Ottoman Empire

Political and Social Transformation in the Early Modern World

BAKI TEZCAN

University of California, Davis

CAMBRIDGE
UNIVERSITY PRESS

CAMBRIDGE UNIVERSITY PRESS
Cambridge, New York, Melbourne, Madrid, Cape Town,
Singapore, São Paulo, Delhi, Mexico City

Cambridge University Press
The Edinburgh Building, Cambridge CB2 8RU, UK

Published in the United States of America by Cambridge University Press, New York

www.cambridge.org
Information on this title: www.cambridge.org/9781107411449

First published 2010
Reprinted 2011 (twice)
First paperback edition 2012

A catalogue record for this publication is available from the British Library

Library of Congress Cataloguing in Publication Data

Tezcan, Baki.
The second Ottoman Empire : political and social transformation in the early modern
world / Baki Tezcan.
    p.   cm. – (Cambridge studies in Islamic civilization)
Includes bibliographical references and index.
ISBN 978-0-521-51949-6 (hbk.)
    1. Turkey – History – 1453–1683.   2. Turkey – History – 1683–1829.   3. Osman II, Sultan of
the Turks, 1603–1622 – Assassination.   4. Janizaries – History.   5. Social change – Turkey –
History – 17th century.   6. Social change – Turkey – History – 18th century.   7. Democratization – Turkey – History – 17th century.   8. Democratization – Turkey – History – 18th
century.   9. Turkey – Politics and government.   10. Turkey – Economic conditions.   I.
Title.   II. Series.
DR511.T49   2010
956'.015–dc22   2009042403

ISBN 978-0-521-51949-6 Hardback
ISBN 978-1-107-41144-9 Paperback

In memory of Abdülbaki Tezcan
(1895, Kulfallar [Razvigorovo] – 1955, Istanbul)

Contents

ix

Figures, maps, and table

Figures

Maps

Table

Acknowledgments

The research and the writing of this book were made possible by grants and fellowships from Princeton University, the American Research Institute in Turkey, the Mrs. Giles Whiting Foundation, the National Endowment for the Humanities, the University of California, Davis, and the Cornell Society for the Humanities. I am most grateful to these institutions.

I would like to thank the administration and staff of various libraries and archives for facilitating my research: Başbakanlık Osmanlı Arşivleri (BOA), Bibliothèque nationale de France, Beyazıt Devlet Kütüphanesi, Cornell University Library, Dār al-kutub al-qawmiyya, Diyanet İşleri Başkanlığı İstanbul Müftülüğü, Gazi Husrev-begova Biblioteka, İslam Araştırmaları Merkezi (İSAM), İstanbul Üniversitesi Kütüphanesi, İzzettin Koyunoğlu Kütüphanesi, Milli Kütüphane, the National Archives, Princeton University Library, Shields Library at the University of California, Davis, Süleymaniye Kütüphanesi, and Topkapı Sarayı Arşivi ve Kütüphanesi. Special thanks are due to Durmuş Kandıra (BOA), Gülendam Nakipoğlu (Topkapı Sarayı), Jason Newborn and Adam Siegel (Shields), and Birol Ülker (İSAM). I should also thank Ahmet Evin, the founding dean of the Faculty of Arts and Social Sciences at Sabancı University, for providing me with office space during my long research stay in Istanbul (1998–2000) and the late Nejat Göyünç for introducing me to the Ottoman archives.

Bilge Criss, the late Oral Sander, Kemal Karpat, and Halil İnalcık introduced me to Ottoman history when I was an undergraduate at Bilkent University in Ankara in the early 1990s. I am grateful to them all for showing me the way.

I owe a great deal of thanks to Heath Lowry in whose office I spent many weekends, learning how to read land registers and provincial *kanunname*s. He and his wife Demet Hanım created a wonderful environment for studying the Ottoman Empire at Princeton University in the mid- to late 1990s when I enjoyed the collegiality and friendship of a large cohort of Ottoman history students, namely, Mustafa Aksakal, Berrak Burçak, Nenad Filipovic, Janet Klein, Ruth Miller, Tom Papademetriou, Milen Petrov, Christine Philliou, Michael Reynolds, Şuhnaz Yılmaz, and İpek Yosmaoğlu. Other friends who contributed to this project in invaluable ways were Shahab Ahmed, Jamie Cohen-Cole,

Eleni Gara, and Yossef Rapoport. I am grateful to Norman Itzkowitz for being a real mentor who cared for all aspects of my life and for always being there whenever I needed him. Şükrü Hanioğlu taught me late Ottoman history and introduced me to Ottoman documents, spending countless hours with me as I tried to decipher various scripts. I studied Islamic law with Hossein Modarressi, Arabic with Margaret Larkin and Andras Hamori, and Persian with the late Jerry Clinton. Peter Brown and Theodore Rabb guided me in the study of late antiquity and early modern European history. Molly Greene asked me the question that eventually transformed my dissertation into this book.

Special thanks are due to Michael Cook, who took a lot of time to teach me how to write, read everything I ever sent to him, and always provided ample comments and suggestions. He has supported both my graduate and postgraduate work, and I would not have completed this book had he not encouraged me to go ahead with it.

Rifa'at Abou-El-Haj has been most influential in the way I came to think about history. Anyone who reads this book with his work in mind might notice that mine is but an extended commentary on some of his ideas. His engagement with my work during graduate school and thereafter has given me the strength to publish it.

Although I have never been his student, Cemal Kafadar has been a constant source of inspiration for me since I read his "Janissaries and Other Riffraff of Ottoman Istanbul: Rebels without a Cause?" while I was working on my dissertation. The influence of his work on the present one will be clear to all Ottoman historians.

My colleagues at the University of California, Davis, especially Ali Anooshahr, Omnia El Shakry, Susan Miller, and Sudipta Sen; my chairs in the History Department, the late Dan Brower, Susan Mann, Ted Margadant, and David Biale; my director in the Religious Studies Program, Naomi Janowitz; and the founding director of the Middle East/South Asia Studies Program, Suad Joseph, have been very supportive of my work since I arrived in Davis in fall 2002.

It was during my year at the Cornell Society for the Humanities (2005–6) that I returned to my dissertation and conceptualized the present work. I would like to extend my thanks to Brett de Bary, who was the director of the Society then, and the other Fellows, especially Nae-hui Kang, who provided an intellectually stimulating environment for me to go back to my graduate work in creative ways.

I have been very lucky to have Leslie Peirce as a senior colleague at Berkeley, so close to Davis. She has provided advice, constructive criticism, encouragement, and support and continued to do so even after she moved to New York. I should also express my gratitude to Virginia Aksan, who provided me with excellent opportunities to publish my work, read different versions of this book, and offered various suggestions for revisions.

Tülün Değirmenci helped me a great deal in the choice of the illustrations. The Berkeley graduate students who took my seminar on early modern Ottoman history in the fall of 2007 read the first – and much longer – draft of this book, and Leslie Peirce's students at New York University read the penultimate version in the fall of 2008. I owe thanks to them all for their comments. If I failed to improve the book by neglecting some of the many suggestions I received from such a diverse group of readers that included both graduate students and senior scholars, the responsibility is mine alone.

Marigold Acland at Cambridge University Press was the best editor I could hope to find. She made sure that the length of the book was manageable, which required me to cut various sections of the first draft that have since appeared as articles; hence, the references to my own work in the footnotes. I am thankful to Sarah Green, Amanda Smith, Shelby Peak, Larry Fox, and Peggy Rote for overseeing the production process and making sure that everything was in place. I owe special thanks to Gail Naron Chalew for copyediting the book, and thus saving me from many an embarrassment, and to Jim Farned for preparing the index.

Last but not least, I am grateful to my family. This book is dedicated to my paternal grandfather Abdülbaki Tezcan who emigrated from a small village around Şumnu (Shumen in Bulgaria) to Bursa early in the twentieth century, witnessed the collapse of the Ottoman Empire and the founding of the Turkish Republic, and eventually settled in Istanbul. During the last decade, while I was teaching and working on various research projects, my mother Emine Tezcan, my sister and brother-in-law Gülgûn and Hüsnü Terek, and my brother and sister-in-law Gökhan and Hülya Tezcan have taken care of many things in Istanbul, including my father Ayhan Tezcan, who passed away after a long illness in 2006. My in-laws in New York, Robert Sharlet, Jeff Sharlet, and Julie Rabig, have been very supportive and understanding throughout the research and writing of this book. Finally, my wife Jocelyn Sharlet and I have been very lucky to have Teoman Jonah (b. 2002) and Kayhan Elijah (b. 2008) to remind us that there is more to life than writing books.

Notes on abbreviations, dates, pronunciation, and transliteration

I use the following abbreviations:

Bnf: Bibliothèque nationale de France
BOA: Başbakanlık Osmanlı Arşivleri
KK: Kamil Kepeci
MM: Maliyeden Müdevver
NA: The National Archives, London
SP: State Papers
İA: *İslâm Ansiklopedisi*
İA2:   *Türkiye Diyanet Vakfı İslâm Ansiklopedisi*

The dates are mostly given in CE (Common Era) although most of the relevant primary sources are dated according to the *hijri* calendar. That calendar has twelve lunar months in a year of about 354 days, with the year 1 AH (after *hijra*) corresponding to 622 CE when Muhammad and his followers left Mecca for Yathrib. When a given *hijri* date does not have enough precision to convert it to a single year in CE, then I supply the *hijri* year first and indicate which CE years it corresponds to, such as 1007/1598–9. Rarely, such as in publication dates of books published in the Ottoman period, I only indicate the *hijri* year.

I use the Anglicized versions of most Ottoman Turkish and Arabic words rather than writing them in italics or transliterating them, the criterion being inclusion in the *Oxford English Dictionary*; hence, agha, bey, ghazi, kiblah, mufti, pasha, Sharia, timar, ulema, vizier, wakf – but efendi instead of effendi and kadi instead of cadi. In place names I prefer English spellings as well, except for place names that constitute part of the name of a publisher in the footnotes; hence, Istanbul, but İstanbul Üniversitesi.

When I transliterate Ottoman terms, I try to stay as close as possible to modern Turkish spellings. In the main body of the text and in the identification of authors, I avoid all the diacritics associated with transliteration, except for ʿ*ayn* and *hamza* when they appear in the middle of a word, which I indicate with an apostrophe [']. In reproducing titles of references in the footnotes, however, I use the circumflex to indicate long vowels in Ottoman Turkish. Because the orthography of modern Turkish is still in flux and sometimes

xvii

differs from the transliteration of Ottoman Turkish, readers may find that the same word is spelled differently in different footnotes, such as *Tarih, Târih,* and *Ta'rîh.* If a work did not originally have a title, I write the retrospectively given title in square brackets. In transliterating Arabic and Persian names and titles, I follow the conventions of the *International Journal of Middle East Studies.*

There are some Turkish letters that do not appear in the English alphabet and others that are pronounced differently from their English counterparts:

C, c: "j" as in "joy"

Ç, ç: "ch" as in "check"

Ğ, ğ: When preceded or followed by e, i, ö, ü, the "soft g" sounds like "y" as in "lawyer;" when preceded and followed by a, ı, o, u or it is in final position, it lengthens the preceding vowel; thus *dağ* is pronounced "daa."

I, ı: "e" as in "halted"

İ, i: "i" as in "bit"

Ö, ö: "eu" as in French *"deux,"* or "ö" as in German *"hören"*

Ş, ş: "sh" as in "shade"

Ü, ü: "ü" as in German *"über"* or "u" as in French *"tu"*

Introduction

Ottoman political history in the early modern period

On the morning of Wednesday, May 18, 1622, the imperial pavilion of the Ottoman sultan and many other tents were to be carried over to Üsküdar, across from Istanbul, on the Asian shores of the Bosporus (see Fig. 1). Osman II, the seventeen-year-old emperor of vast lands stretching from modern Hungary and Ukraine to Eritrea and Yemen to the south, and from Iraq to Algeria to the west (see Map 1), was about to leave his imperial capital for a pilgrimage to Mecca. However, most jurists and the overwhelming majority of the members of the army corps were opposed to the departure of the emperor as they suspected that the young sultan's pilgrimage was a cover for other plans that would have consequences detrimental to their own interests. The next day, before Osman II could even set foot outside his palace, the opposition forces enthroned his uncle Mustafa I. On Friday evening, Osman was strangled at the Seven Towers where he was being held prisoner. God's shadow on earth, as Osman II would be described in his imperial title, was not permitted to visit the House of God – the name given by Muslims to the Ka'ba in Mecca.

Ottoman emperors, God's shadows on earth, should not have been so easily dispensable, but apparently they were. The political history of the Ottoman Empire in the seventeenth century was marked by depositions like that of Osman II. Of the ten reigns by the nine sultans who occupied the Ottoman throne between 1603 and 1703, six ended with dethronements. In modern historiography, at least until recently, this discrepancy between the theoretical claims of Ottoman emperors to uncontested sovereignty and the practical reality of their frequent depositions has generally been interpreted as a manifestation of Ottoman decline, yet another sign of the disorders that plagued the empire beginning in the late sixteenth century. Although recent contributions to Ottoman historiography have challenged the decline paradigm from various angles, a new interpretation of these depositions has yet to appear.

In their recent book, *The Age of Beloveds*, Walter Andrews and Mehmet Kalpaklı took a step toward a new interpretation of seventeenth-century Ottoman depositions:

The movement in England from late-Tudor absolutism to an increasingly limited monarchy under the Stuarts is well defined and widely accepted. In the Ottoman Empire, there

1

Map 1. The Ottoman Empire, c. 1550. Adapted from Halil İnalcık with Donald Quataer (eds.), *An Economic and Social History of the Ottoman Empire, 1300–1914* (Cambridge Cambridge University Press, 1994), pp. xxxiv–xxxv.

0   500   1000 km
0   500 miles

Kazan

Moscow

R U S S I A

NOGAYS

Aral Sea

R. Volga

R. Dnieper

R. Don

COSSACKS

Astrakhan

CRIMEAN KHANATE

Azak (Azov)

Sea of Azov

CASPIAN SEA

DAVIA

Akkerman
Kilia

Caffa

CIRCASSIA

KABRDA

DAGHESTAN

SHIRVAN

Suhum

GEORGIA

BLACK SEA

Sinop

Trabzon

Erivan

GILAN

irne

Istanbul

Erzurum

L.Van

AZERBAIJAN

Tabriz

Bursa

Ankara

Sivas

RUM

L. Urmia

Foçalar

Kütahya

Kayseri

Diyarbekir

R.Tigris

Mosul

Hamadan

Izmir

ANATOLIA

Zülkadriye

Ayasoluk

Konya

IRAQ

IRAN

Antalya

Aleppo

R.Euphrates

Baghdad

RHODES

andia

CYPRUS
(Venice
1570)

Tripoli

Beirut

Damascus

SYRIA

Basra

Bandar-Abbas

Hormuz

SEA

Jerusalem

AL – HASA

PERSIAN GULF

Bahrain

Alexandria

Katif

Cairo

Suez

EGYPT

ARABIA

OMAN

Kusayr

RED SEA

SHARIFATE OF MECCA

Medina

R. Nile

Mecca

Jidda

Suakin

INDIAN OCEAN

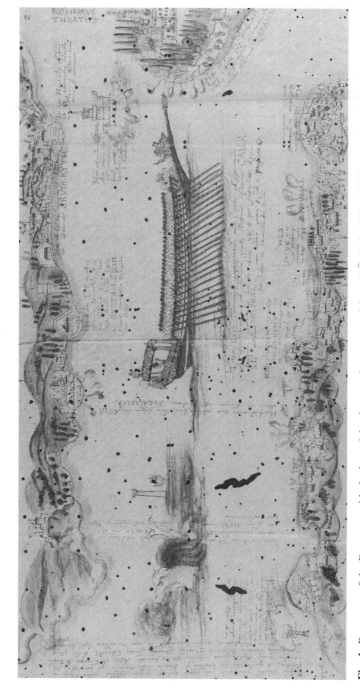

Fig. 1. Panorama of the Bosporus with the imperial palace on the extreme right and Üsküdar [Skvderith] across from it (1588); MS. Bodl. Or. 430, f. 2 (fold-out); courtesy of the Bodleian Library, University of Oxford.

appears to be a parallel to the English case in the double enthronement (1618 and 1622) of the mentally incompetent Mustafa I sandwiched around the deposition and regicide of (Genç [the Young]) Osman II.[1]

Andrews and Kalpaklı are justified in qualifying their statement with the phrase "appears to be" because as two historians of literature they could not locate a work of political history that approached the Ottoman case from an angle that would make possible a comparison with the English example. According to the prevalent scholarly view, the regicide of Osman II was nothing but a military rebellion; hence, a sign of the decline of the Ottoman Empire or a symbol of its transformation into something else that has yet to be defined. In the absence of any study on the question, Andrews and Kalpaklı hesitate to offer any suggestions about why the regicide has been viewed so negatively: "Why movements toward limitations on monarchical absolutism are seen as an advance in the one case and as a decline in the other we will leave to nonliterary historians to thrash out."[2]

Why indeed? How have we been led to believe that the English Civil War, which led to the execution of Charles I in 1649, and the "Glorious" Revolution of 1688, which dethroned Charles I's son James II, were advances in the history of limited government, whereas the regicide of the Ottoman Sultan İbrahim in 1648 and the deposition of İbrahim's son Mehmed IV in 1687, for instance, were simply signs of decline? The similarities between the events in England and in the Ottoman Empire did not pass unnoticed by contemporaries who wrote works like the "Interview between Sultan İbrahim, Emperor of the Turks, and the King of England, held in the Elysian Fields" as early as 1649 nor by modern scholars who do comparative work on a global scale.[3] Of course, there is no Ottoman parliament to compare with the English one. Yet this particular difference does not mean that the Ottoman depositions and regicides lacked any formal constitutional components and were simply results of irregular behavior on the part of some soldier-turned-bandits as mainstream twentieth-century Ottoman historiography would like us to believe. The way in which Ottoman depositions were legitimized and the presence of certain features that established links among them point to the development of an unwritten understanding of what an emperor was supposed to do and not do, when it would be legitimate to depose him, and through what means.

---

[1] Walter Andrews and Mehmet Kalpaklı, *The Age of Beloveds: Love and the Beloved in Early-Modern Ottoman and European Culture and Society* (Durham: Duke University Press, 2005), 322.

[2] Ibid., p. 323; Gabriel Piterberg's *An Ottoman Tragedy: History and Historiography at Play* (Berkeley: University of California Press, 2003) offers an insightful study of the Ottoman historiography on the regicide of Osman II. However, Piterberg does not directly engage with the question of decline in the political context of placing limitations on Ottoman royal authority.

[3] *L'Entrevue du sultan Hibraïm, empereur des Turcs et du roi d'Angleterre aux Champs Elysées* (Paris, 1649) is a short piece in verse. Jack A. Goldstone is well aware of some structural similarities related to economic crises and their social repercussions; *Revolution and Rebellion in the Early Modern World* (Berkeley: University of California Press, 1991).

A year before the Glorious Revolution took place in England, in the early morning of Saturday, November 8, 1687, the leading jurists of the Ottoman Empire convened at the Mosque of Ayasofya (the former Cathedral of Hagia Sophia) to discuss for a last time the demands of the army to depose Mehmed IV. When the grand mufti, the chief jurisconsult of the empire, asked the dignitaries present whether the sultan should be deposed, Mehmed, the chief justice of the Asian and African provinces, was the first one to give an affirmative answer. The father of this Mehmed, Abdürrahim, had issued the legal opinion that legitimized the regicide of Mehmed IV's father İbrahim in 1648 and had even overseen the execution personally. Mehmed's son Yahya was to be elected chief justice of the Asian and African provinces by the opposition forces in Istanbul in 1703 and to take part in the deposition of Mehmed IV's son Mustafa II. Thus Mustafa II came to be deposed, among others, by a jurist whose father had deposed his father and whose grandfather had deposed and executed his own grandfather.[4]

The jurists were not the only political actors involved in Ottoman depositions in the seventeenth century. The janissaries, who have been blamed for almost everything that went wrong in the Ottoman Empire after the late sixteenth century, played a consistent role in most depositions. Although mainstream Ottoman historiography has insisted on treating these political acts of the janissaries as signs of corruption and decline, according to Victor Fontanier, a Frenchman who spent many years in the Ottoman Empire in the early nineteenth century, the janissaries were defending people against the ravages of absolute power.[5] Antoine de Juchereau de Saint-Denys, another Frenchman who served the Ottomans as a military engineer in the early nineteenth century and witnessed a janissary rebellion in 1807 in Istanbul, stated that the janissaries, who were "identified with the nation," were "under the influence of popular opinion" and resembled a "populace that became sovereign."[6] For Namık Kemal, a major figure of Young Ottoman thought in the second half of the nineteenth century, the janissaries had been the "armed consultative assembly of the nation" before their destruction by Mahmud II in 1826.[7] Although the recognition of the janissaries as a political force with some popular legitimacy has been explored by Cemal Kafadar and Donald Quataert, whose works in this area have profoundly influenced this study,[8] Ottoman

---

[4] Rifa'at Ali Abou-El-Haj, *The 1703 Rebellion and the Structure of Ottoman Politics* (Leiden: Nederlands Instituut voor het Nabije Oosten, 1984), 28.

[5] Victor Fontanier, *Voyages en Orient, entrepris par ordre du gouvernement français*, vol. I: *Turquie d'Asie* (Paris: Mongie aîné, 1829), 322.

[6] Antoine de Juchereau de Saint-Denys, *Histoire de l'empire ottoman depuis 1792 jusqu'en 1844*, 4 vols. (Paris: Au comptoir des imprimeurs-unis, 1844), vol. I, 349, 355.

[7] Mehmet Kaplan, *Namık Kemal: Hayatı ve Eserleri* (Istanbul, 1948), 107.

[8] Cemal Kafadar, "*Yeniçeri – esnaf* relations: Solidarity and conflict," M.A. thesis (McGill University, 1981); C. Kafadar, "On the purity and corruption of the Janissaries," *Turkish Studies Association Bulletin* 15 (1991): 273–80; C. Kafadar, "Janissaries and other riffraff of Ottoman Istanbul: Rebels without a cause?" in *Identity and Identity Formation in the Ottoman World: A Volume of Essays in Honor of Norman Itzkowitz*, eds. Baki Tezcan and Karl Barbir (Madison: University of Wisconsin Center of Turkish Studies, 2007), 113–34, the text of

historiography in general has been very reluctant to embrace this train of thought and carry it further. It was a political scientist, Şerif Mardin, who argued that the rebellions that were attributed to the licentiousness of the janissaries or others might instead be regarded as the manifestation of a political culture that had a tradition of legitimate opposition:

> There exist a sufficient number of cases of Ottoman rebellions with a justification and of uprisings with what appears to be a tacit recourse to a theory of legitimate revolt for us to take up this thread in Ottoman history and to give it the consideration which no one has accorded it to date. One must bear in mind that in retrospect, the history of Western European democracy from its origins onwards also looks like a series of unrelated episodes of violence and intrigue.[9]

Juxtaposing a history of democracy and a history of Ottoman rebellions may sound too anachronistic for the modern reader. Some of the premodern observers of the Ottoman Empire, however, would agree with Mardin. Count Luigi Ferdinando Marsigli was one of them. Marsigli visited the Ottoman Empire in 1679–80 for eleven months in the company of the Venetian ambassador and had an opportunity to become well acquainted with some of the most renowned Ottoman men of letters, such as the historian Hüseyin Hezarfenn and the geographer Ebu Bekir. His relationship with the Ottomans continued as he was enslaved during the Ottoman-Habsburg wars in 1683. After he gained his freedom, he returned to the Habsburg service and took part in peace negotiations with the Ottomans. In the aftermath of the Treaty of Carlowitz (1699), Marsigli oversaw the actual demarcation of the 850-km-long Habsburg-Ottoman border. Thus he was one of the better informed Europeans in matters pertaining to the Ottomans. In his monumental work on the Ottoman military forces, there is a short section on the political authority of the Ottoman sultan, the grand vizier, and other pashas. After reviewing the actual sociopolitical power of the Ottoman central military organization and of the educational-judicial hierarchy, or the ulema, Marsigli implied that the Ottoman Empire merited being called a democracy rather than a monarchy or an aristocracy.[10] Taner Timur suggests that Marsigli regarded the Ottoman central military organization and the ulema as institutions whose functions paralleled the États-Généraux of France.[11]

---

which was presented at Princeton University in 1991. I am grateful to Molly Greene who brought this paper to my attention in the late 1990s; and Donald Quataert, "Janissaries, artisans, and the question of Ottoman decline, 1730–1826," in *17° Congreso Internacional de Ciencias Históricas, Madrid – 1990*, vol. I: *Sección Cronológica*, eds. Eloy Benito Ruano and Manuel Espadas Burgos (Madrid: Comité International des Sciences Historiques, 1992), 264–8.

[9] Şerif Mardin, "Freedom in an Ottoman perspective," in *State, Democracy, and the Military: Turkey in the 1980s*, eds. Metin Heper and Ahmet Evin (Berlin: W. de Gruyter, 1988), 26–7.

[10] Luigi Ferdinando Marsigli, *Stato militare dell'imperio ottomanno / L'état militaire de l'empire ottoman* (La Haye: Gosse, 1732), 31.

[11] Taner Timur, *Osmanlı Çalışmaları: İlkel Feodalizmden Yarı Sömürge Ekonomisine* (Ankara: Verso, 1989), 121.

In the eighteenth century, it was Ottoman officials themselves who described their government as more republican than the ones in St. Petersburg and Vienna because the sultan "could not offer preliminaries of peace without the concurrence of [the jurists]."[12] Sir James Porter, who served as British ambassador in Constantinople for fifteen years in the second half of the eighteenth century, asserted that the Ottoman government was "a species of limited monarchy." He went to great lengths to defend his observation to a contemporary who claimed that because of "their long residence" in the Ottoman Empire Marsigli and Porter had become so reconciled to the country and people as to make them "unwilling to admit that [the Ottoman government] should be denominated a despotism."[13] Porter regarded the Ottoman army as "a powerful check upon the Grand Signor [i.e. the sultan]" and the upper ranking jurists as the "hereditary guardians of the religion and laws of the empire."[14]

Adolphus Slade, a nineteenth-century British navy officer, agreed with Marsigli, Porter, Juchereau de Saint-Denys, and Fontanier. He argued that the Ottoman monarchy used to possess a "constitution: defective, and in a state of chronic disorder, but still a roughly balanced system."[15] As noted by Bernard Lewis, Slade saw the modernizing reforms of Mahmud II and Reşid Pasha in the first half of the nineteenth century as a "subversion of the ancient Turkish constitution" or a "subversion of the liberties of his (Turkish) subjects:"

These expressions are strikingly reminiscent of the language used by the pro-Parliament jurists during the English Civil War of the 17th century and its aftermath. The doctrine of the ancient constitution of England and the immemorial rights of Englishmen are central to the arguments which were used to justify Parliament against the King in the Civil War and, in a different way, in the ensuing struggles of the later 17th and 18th centuries.... Slade applied these characteristically English doctrines to the Turkish situation, and pursuing them in great detail, found that they fitted.[16]

For instance, it was Slade who thought that the janissaries represented the people and thus constituted a "chamber of deputies," forming the "legal opposition in the state."[17] He was justified in thinking about the janissaries in these terms as they indeed came to reflect the socioeconomic makeup of the Ottoman population as more and more lower-middle and middle-class Ottoman men

---

[12] Sir James Porter, *Observations on the Religion, Law, Government, and Manners of the Turks*, 2nd ed. (London: J. Nourse, 1771), xxxiv.

[13] Compare William Robertson, *History of the Reign of the Emperor Charles V*, 3 vols. (London, 1769), vol. I, 388–9, n. 42; and Porter, *Observations*, xiv–xxxvi.

[14] Porter, *Observations*, xxviii, xxxi.

[15] Adolphus Slade, *Turkey and the Crimean War: A Narrative of Historical Events* (London: Smith, Elder and Co., 1867), 10.

[16] Bernard Lewis, "Slade on Turkey," in *Social and Economic History of Turkey, 1071–1920: Papers Presented to the First International Congress on the Social and Economic History of Turkey (Hacettepe University, Ankara, 11–13 July 1977)*, eds. Osman Okyar and Halil İnalcık (Ankara: Meteksan, 1980), 220.

[17] A. Slade, *Turkey Greece and Malta*, 2 vols. (London: Saunders and Otley, 1837), vol. I, 303, 305, 306.

bought their way into the janissary corps in the seventeenth and eighteenth centuries. Yet, other than in a short work by Lewis that he presented to a large group of Ottoman historians more than thirty years ago, Slade's views have been practically ignored by Ottoman historiography. The present work is, in part, an effort to carry forward some of the observations offered by Marsigli, Porter, Fontanier, Juchereau de Saint-Denys, Slade, Namık Kemal, Mardin, Timur, Quataert, and Kafadar about limited government in the Ottoman Empire of the seventeenth and eighteenth centuries. However, it is very difficult to focus a revisionist lens just on the janissaries and the ulema, as well as the depositions they staged, without any regard to other dynamics of Ottoman history. That is why this book proposes an overhaul of our understanding of Ottoman history between the late sixteenth and early nineteenth centuries. Ottoman historians have produced several works in the last decades revising the traditional understanding of this period from various angles, some of which were not even considered as topics of historical inquiry in the mid-twentieth century.[18] Thanks to these works, the conventional narrative of Ottoman history – that in the late sixteenth century the Ottoman Empire entered a prolonged period of decline marked by steadily increasing military decay and institutional corruption – has been discarded. In the most recent general economic and social history of the Ottoman Empire, for instance, only one of the four contributors sees decline as a central phenomenon, which necessitates an editor's comment in the preface on the divergence of this contributor's assessment from that of others.[19] As observed by Douglas Howard, Ottoman decline became an "untrue myth."[20] Nevertheless,

---

[18] See, for instance, Gábor Ágoston, *Guns for the Sultan: Military Power and the Weapons Industry in the Ottoman Empire* (Cambridge: Cambridge University Press, 2004); Virginia H. Aksan, *Ottoman Wars, 1700–1870: An Empire Besieged* (Harlow: Pearson, 2007); Karen Barkey, *Bandits and Bureaucrats: The Ottoman Route to State Centralization* (Ithaca: Cornell University Press, 1994); Linda T. Darling, *Revenue-Raising and Legitimacy: Tax Collection and Finance Administration in the Ottoman Empire, 1560–1660* (Leiden: E. J. Brill, 1996); Cornell H. Fleischer, *Bureaucrat and Intellectual in the Ottoman Empire: The Historian Mustafa Âli (1541–1600)* (Princeton: Princeton University Press, 1986); Daniel Goffman, *The Ottoman Empire and Early Modern Europe* (Cambridge: Cambridge University Press, 2002); Nelly Hanna, *In Praise of Books: A Cultural History of Cairo's Middle Class, Sixteenth to the Eighteenth Century* (Syracuse: Syracuse University Press, 2003); Jane Hathaway, *The Politics of Households in Ottoman Egypt: The Rise of the Qazdağlıs* (Cambridge: Cambridge University Press, 1997); Dina Rizk Khoury, *State and Provincial Society in the Ottoman Empire: Mosul, 1540–1834* (Cambridge: Cambridge University Press, 1997); Leslie P. Peirce, *The Imperial Harem: Women and Sovereignty in the Ottoman Empire* (Oxford: Oxford University Press, 1993); Piterberg, *An Ottoman Tragedy*; Madeline C. Zilfi, ed., *Women in the Ottoman Empire: Middle Eastern Women in the Early Modern Era* (Leiden: Brill, 1997).
[19] Noted by Suraiya Faroqhi, *Approaching Ottoman History: An Introduction to the Sources* (Cambridge: Cambridge University Press, 1999), 197, referring to *An Economic and Social History of the Ottoman Empire, 1300–1914*, eds. Halil İnalcık, with Donald Quataert (Cambridge: Cambridge University Press, 1994), xxvi.
[20] Douglas A. Howard, "Genre and myth in the Ottoman advice for kings literature," in *The Early Modern Ottomans: Remapping the Empire*, eds. Virginia H. Aksan and Daniel Goffman (Cambridge: Cambridge University Press, 2007), 144.

the narrative of decline has not yet been replaced by a *positive* narrative that goes beyond defending Ottoman history *against* the claims of decline.[21] In short, Ottoman history of this period is lacking a grand narrative with an explanatory power that might connect well-defined short periods, themes, and topics in a coherent whole. Although some historians prefer to avoid grand narratives, others expect history to open a window onto the past that offers a larger view. This book presents an attempt to provide such a view by taking political history as its central focus. For that attempt to succeed, it is crucial that we approach the period that starts in the late sixteenth century and ends in the early nineteenth century on its own terms. When studied as such, this era acquires a character all its own, which makes it quite legitimate to call its political structures the "Second Empire."

Taking my inspiration from Rifa'at Ali Abou-El-Haj's work on the 1703 rebellion and the formation of the modern Ottoman state,[22] I argue that the Ottoman polity underwent a major socioeconomic transformation in the late sixteenth and seventeenth centuries. This transformation is so profound that one is justified in arguing that a Second Empire replaced the patrimonial empire, the perfect form of which is associated so closely with the reign of Süleyman the Magnificent (1520–66). The Second Empire came to be marked administratively by an early modern state, as opposed to a medieval dynastic institution; culturally by an early modern sensibility; economically by a more market-oriented economy; legally by a more unified legal system that came to exert some authority over the dynasty; monetarily by a more unified currency system; politically by the development of a type of limited government that grew out of the interaction between the legal developments of the time and such processes as "*civil*ization" and "proto-democratization;" and socially by a *relatively* less stratified society. I use the term "proto-democratization" to refer to the process through which a much larger segment of the imperial administration came to consist of men whose social origins were among the commoners, the very people who used to be known as "outsiders" to the previous ruling elite whose leadership was dominated by the military slaves of the emperor. Thus more and more men whose backgrounds were in finance or trade came to occupy significant positions in the government of the empire, replacing those military slaves and *civil*izing the imperial polity.

Instead of providing a detailed history of the Second Empire, this book focuses on the major political developments of the period in general and

---

[21] Serious efforts in this direction have been undertaken by, among others, Jane Hathaway, "Problems of periodization in Ottoman history: The fifteenth through the eighteenth centuries," *Turkish Studies Association Bulletin* 20/2 (Fall 1996): 25–31; and Linda T. Darling, "Another look at periodization in Ottoman history," *Turkish Studies Association Bulletin* 26/2 (2002): 19–28.

[22] R. A. Abou-El-Haj, *The 1703 Rebellion, and Formation of the Modern State: The Ottoman Empire, Sixteenth to Eighteenth Centuries*, 2nd ed. (Syracuse: Syracuse University Press, 2005 [1st ed., 1991]).

on the eventful period of 1617–22 in particular. Most of the sociopolitical transformations that produced the Second Empire can be analyzed in some detail within the historical framework of these five years; hence, that temporal focus.

The book is divided into six chapters. The first chapter explores the relationship between the development of a monetary economy in the sixteenth century and the rising political profile of jurists' law. I argue that the sixteenth century was marked by the monetization of the Ottoman economy and the political empowerment of socioeconomic groups that benefited from this process, such as merchants and financiers. These changes led to the expansion of the "political nation;" that is, the body of people who could influence or play a legitimate role in the government. Analyzing the political impact of this sixteenth-century socioeconomic transformation, I show that such feudal institutions as the timar and the *kanun*, which in many instances could be translated as fief and feudal law, respectively, lost their significance in a monetized economy. Finally, I focus on the close relationship between socioeconomic changes and the rising political profile of jurists' law, which was based on the Sharia and at times challenged the *kanun* directly; I thereby suggest that the empowerment of the Sharia and its interpreters, the jurists, was not a symptom of decline or fanaticism, but rather an outcome of the expansion of the political nation in a more market-oriented society.

How the jurists and their law came to exert control over Ottoman dynastic affairs forms the thematic focus of the second chapter, which centers on an analysis of the enthronement of Mustafa I in 1617. First, I provide a map of Ottoman politics that shows the political divide between the absolutist and constitutionalist positions. One's place in relation to that divide was determined by one's answer to the question of who had the authority to articulate the fundamentals of public law – the sultan or someone else, whether the jurists or a former sultan who had laid down a constitution for eternity. Those who would benefit from a powerful court pushed for extending the reach of royal authority deep into the domain of public law. Not surprisingly, the absolutist project of the court and its supporters had their discontents who wanted to limit royal authority within certain boundaries. The enthronement of Mustafa I in 1617 offers an opportunity to analyze the constitutionalist opposition to the absolutists and elaborate on the role of the jurists in the Second Empire. Mustafa I was the first Ottoman sultan to succeed his older brother on the throne. I argue that it was the political empowerment of jurists' law and of its most authoritative practitioners, the lords of the law, or the *mevali*, that prepared the ground for the intervention of jurists' law into the affairs of the Ottoman dynasty. I also show that the grand mufti of the time, Es'ad, played a crucial role in the constitutional act of effectively changing the rule of Ottoman succession by enthroning Mustafa I in preference to his nephew Osman II.

The Ottoman court's response to the transformation of the political structures around it forms the topic of Chapter 3, which offers an analysis of the deposition of Mustafa I and the enthronement of Osman II in 1618. In this chapter I reconstruct the Ottoman political history of ca. 1300–1580 to emphasize its transformation in the sixteenth century that was brought about by the gradual development of a market society in Ottoman realms. I argue that the feudal political relations of the formative period were instrumental in both the territorial expansion of the empire and the eventual replacement of local vassals with the members of an imperial household of slaves. Focusing on viziers, I show that these senior slaves of the emperor managed to transfer a great deal of political power from the hands of the sultan to their own, making use of the opportunities offered by a developing market economy. In response, the emperor built a closer circle of power around himself at the court by empowering court officers whose positions had either not previously existed or never had political significance before, such as the chief eunuchs and the chief gardener. A new generation of viziers who were court creatures rather than autonomous power centers followed suit. It was these new holders of power who staged the enthronement of Osman II in 1618, with the chief black eunuch Mustafa Agha at their center.

In the fourth chapter I examine the short reign of Osman II (1618–22), emphasizing his absolutist ambitions and interpreting the contemporary meaning of the project of creating a new army that has been ascribed to him. After a discussion of the influences on Osman II's upbringing, I study the grand vizierate of Ali Pasha and Osman II's military campaign against the Polish-Lithuanian Commonwealth as manifestations of Osman II's absolutist policies. To understand the contemporary connotations of Osman II's project to form a new army, I dwell upon the political developments that led to the recruitment of mercenaries, or *sekbans*, by Ottoman provincial administrators and local political leaders starting from the late sixteenth century. I argue that rather than being primarily related to military technology and long wars, as is claimed in Ottomanist scholarship, the *sekbans* and the many "rebellions" they were associated with are symbols of the sixteenth-century Ottoman socioeconomic transformation and its political repercussions in the provincial administration of the empire. Furthermore, just as *sekban* leaders crossed the line that separated legitimate holders of political authority from illegitimate rebels several times, Osman II, too, could be seen as a "rebel sultan" because of his plans to recruit a new mercenary army.

The end of Osman II, the "rebel sultan," is the topic of Chapter 5. I first provide an account of the deposition of Osman II in 1622 to establish that the sultan was not as uncompromisingly opposed to the soldiers as most of the contemporary chroniclers portrayed him to be; thus the soldiers *chose* to depose him rather than settle for a political bargain. After this emphasis on the political will of the members of the central army corps who brought about the first regicide in Ottoman history, I focus on the growing political role of the Ottoman central army, especially the cavalry forces, in the late sixteenth and early seventeenth centuries. I argue that the expansion of the army corps was not only related to military developments. Looking at the members of the army corps as economic and political agents, I suggest that the growth of the Ottoman army was closely related to the development of a market economy in the Ottoman Empire and the resulting political rivalries between the court and the viziers, as well as among the viziers themselves. I also argue that many of the new "soldiers" in the sixteenth century were primarily investors who regarded membership in the army corps as a socioeconomic privilege and political investment. Thus the Ottoman central army of the early seventeenth century was a transformed institution that should not be regarded simply as an army.

In the sixth chapter I define the most important characteristics of the Second Empire – the proto-democratization of its polity and the limitation of royal authority – that constitute it as a different political structure from those that preceded and followed it. The janissaries, who played a very important role in both features, are at the center of this chapter. I treat the janissary corps primarily as a sociopolitical corporation by discussing the diverse socioeconomic backgrounds of its members, its autonomy, and its members' involvement in various economic activities all over the empire. Finally, I substantiate my argument about the limitation of royal authority in the Second Empire by providing short analyses of selected janissary uprisings of the seventeenth century, showing how most were undertaken against absolutist policies.

The concluding chapter is devoted to a discussion of the early modern features of the Second Empire, the Ottoman decline, and their relationship to each other. Although modernity came to be closely associated with capitalism and colonialism and thus came to be seen as a European phenomenon imposed on the rest of the world, I suggest that early modernity can be defined much more globally and has to do with the relative democratization of political privileges as a result of the political empowerment of economically affluent commoners. If one were to define early modernity using these parameters, the Second Empire would definitely be an early modern polity. That does not mean, however, that it did not fall into decline. The Second Empire's future was determined by the interaction of its present with its past. The institutions it inherited from the past were truly transformed by the developments of early modernity. Yet at the end of this transformation, these institutions were no longer able to fulfill their original functions properly, which left the Ottomans vulnerable in the face of European imperialism.

One market, one money, one law

The making of an imperial market society and a law that applies to all

A group of close friends – Zübde Bey, Mirim Çelebi, Sinanbeyzade Mustafa Çelebi, Karanfilzade, Baki Beşe, and Ahmed Bey – who were all soldiers on the payroll of the Ottoman sultan in late-sixteenth-century Edirne, enjoyed drinking together. One day, while they were having drinks at the tavern, they noticed a poorly dressed dervish drinking quite a bit of wine all by himself. Ahmed Bey, the chief of the drinking party, sent him a platter of food to accompany the wine and also paid his bill. Although Ahmed Bey continued extending favors to the dervish for a few days, the latter never joined them, excusing himself by saying that he did not mingle with people. However, on the day before he was to leave the city, the dervish came to thank them. He said it was time to reward them and asked each one to make a wish. "The gate of God is open; you will attain your wishes," he added. They all laughed but being good sports, each agreed to make a wish.

Zübde Bey, probably a cavalry soldier, asked for the local command of his regiment. Mirim Çelebi, a cavalry soldier from the regiment of the sword-bearers, asked for the same position in his own regiment. Mustafa Çelebi wanted to become the superintendent of guilds and markets in Edirne. Karanfilzade requested the trusteeship of a royal foundation. Baki Beşe, the janissary, asked for 40,000 gold ducats. Then the dervish turned to Ahmed Bey and insisted that he ask for something more important than what the others had wished for. Ahmed Bey refrained and said, "You tell me whatever you consider me worthy of." After a momentary trance, the dervish prophesied: "They have given you the administration of the affairs of the Ottoman state. May your name be identical with the one on the imperial seal!"[1]

An exploration of the significance of this anecdote introduces this chapter, which proposes a connection between the socioeconomic transformation of the Ottoman Empire in the sixteenth century and the political developments of the period, including the growing influence of law in dynastic affairs. At the time Ahmed Bey was apparently a member of the imperial cavalry regiments; he was the son of Hacı Mehmed, an Albanian baker who was the head of

---

[1] Katib Çelebi, *Fezleke*, 2 vols. (Istanbul, 1286–7 AH), vol. I, 327.

the bakers' guild in Edirne, hence Ahmed's nickname Etmekcizade, the son of the baker. Subsequently Etmekcizade Ahmed Bey made enough capital for himself in the market of Edirne to become involved in the collection of the taxes imposed on Romanies. Later he became the finance director of the Danubian provinces. In 1599, he was the acting finance minister in the military campaign directed against the Habsburgs under the command of Saturcı Mehmed Pasha. Despite his close association with Saturcı, for which he was imprisoned for a short while after Saturcı was executed in 1599, Etmekcizade was able to keep his position under the new commander-general of the campaign, the grand vizier Damad İbrahim Pasha. Etmekcizade succeeded in becoming one of the rare finance ministers who enjoyed a long tenure and was made a vizier during the reign of Ahmed I. He even held the deputy grand vizierate in 1616 while the grand vizier Öküz Mehmed Pasha was engaged in a military campaign against the Safavids and thus held the imperial seal which carried the name of the sultan who happened to be his namesake. The dervish proved to be right in his prophecy.

The dervish also kept his promise to Baki Beşe, the janissary, whose father was a merchant from Aleppo. Baki himself was born in Edirne and somehow managed to get into the janissary corps. After he was promoted to the cavalry regiments, he followed in his older friend's footsteps. In 1007/1598–9, he was the collector of taxes imposed on Romanies. In 1604, he became the finance director of the Danubian provinces. Next year, he was the acting finance minister in the military campaign of the grand vizier Mehmed Pasha that resulted in the reconquest of Esztergom (in northern Hungary). In 1607, Baki accompanied the grand vizier Murad Pasha as the acting finance minister in the military campaign directed against Canpoladzade Ali, the "rebel" ruler of northern Syria. Baki Pasha was later to state that on his return from this campaign he finally succeeded in saving 40,000 gold ducats, the amount he had asked for from the dervish. Despite some occasional downturns in his later career, Baki Beşe of the tavern in Edirne became a pasha and died in 1625, while holding the finance ministry with the title of vizier.[2]

There are several significant points to note about the careers of Ahmed Pasha and Baki Pasha as well as the dervish story. First, both men came to carry the title pasha and even became viziers while they were finance ministers, which did not often occur in the fifteenth and early sixteenth centuries. The status of finance ministers had been rising since the late-sixteenth century, and Ahmed Pasha was not the first one to carry the title of vizier. In the later seventeenth century there were even grand viziers, such as Salih Pasha

[2] For contemporary sources on the lives of Ahmed and Baki pashas, see Baki Tezcan, "Searching for Osman: A reassessment of the deposition of the Ottoman sultan Osman II (1618–1622)," PhD diss. (Princeton University, 2001), 309, n. 2–3; for easier access to the notes of this dissertation that are cited throughout the book, see http://docs.google.com/fileview?id =0B9ULJyAfRPyfMWM2MTQzY2YtZGYwNi00MzZlLTkxODEtMDQwNjE3ZjQ4MjQ0 &hl=en.

(d. 1647), Hezarpare Ahmed Pasha (d. 1648), and Sofu Mehmed Pasha (d. 1649), whose backgrounds were in the finance ministry.[3] Clearly, the role of money and its prestige in politics were rising.

More important, the backgrounds of Ahmed and Baki pashas differed greatly from the traditional backgrounds of finance ministers, which were either in the educational-judicial or scribal spheres. They and their drinking companions were soldiers, albeit of a different kind. Although we do not know anything about the social backgrounds of their companions, the *–zade* ending in their names, meaning "son of" as in Sinanbeyzade, suggest that they were not *devşirme* recruits; that is, they had not been conscripted by the levy imposed upon Christian children whose paternal ancestors were usually not mentioned in their names. For instance, Sinanbeyzade was clearly the son, or perhaps grandson, of a certain Sinan Bey, who must have been a member of the political elite as suggested by his title bey. If Ahmed, Baki, and their companions were not *devşirme* recruits, one wonders why and how they had joined the military. What they aspired to become in life did not have much to do with a military career. Neither the supervision of guilds and markets in a town, nor the trusteeship of a royal foundation, would be expected to be the dream of a regular soldier.

Therefore, it is quite probable that Ahmed Pasha, Baki Pasha, and their drinking companions in Edirne, or their fathers, had entered the Ottoman central army, which at this point was about to become as much of a financial institution as it was a military one, by means of money. Since at least the mid-sixteenth century, small investors of capital had seen the Ottoman army as an institution that provided financial security and social status. In fact, some tax-farmers even demanded entry into the military-administrative personnel as a reward for their services. For instance, the tax-farmer who bid successfully for the privilege of collecting the dues of the port of Izmir – a certain Hacı Mehmed, perhaps the father of Ahmed Pasha – was enlisted in the central cavalry troops upon the completion of his contract on July 30, 1569.[4] It would be hard to believe that this investor wanted to enlist in the cavalry troops in order to fight as an Ottoman soldier. More likely he saw entrance into the Ottoman army in a way quite similar to a well-to-do Frenchman buying his way into the noblesse de robe. Hacı Mehmed and Ahmed, Baki, and their drinking companions were among the very makers of the Second Empire, which came into being through the destruction of the barriers that held commoners like

[3] Klaus Röhrborn, "Die Emanzipation der Finanzbürokratie im osmanischen Reich (Ende 16. Jahrhundert)," *Zeitschrift der deutschen morgenländischen Gesellschaft* 122 (1972): 118–39; Tezcan, "Searching for Osman," 310, n. 4; Şeyhi Mehmed, *Vakâyi'ü'l-fudalâ*, 2 vols., facs. ed. with indices in *Şakaik-ı Nu'maniye ve Zeyilleri*, ed. Abdülkadir Özcan, 5 vols. (Istanbul: Çağrı Yayınları, 1989), vols. III–IV, vol. III, 155–6, 599; Abdülkadir Özcan, "Hezarpâre Ahmed Paşa," *İA2*, vol. XVII, 301–2.

[4] For this and other examples, see BOA, KK 1767, ff. 17b, 28b, 33a, 39b, and 40a; see also Darling, *Revenue-Raising*, 149–50.

them outside the political nation, once the almost exclusive domain of the imperial slaves of mostly *devşirme* origin.

Thus the dervish story highlights a new channel of social mobility that was opening up for men who lived in the Ottoman domains: financial entrepreneurship. Men whose power came from economic and financial activities rather than military ones began to enter the privileged classes of Ottoman society in the late sixteenth and early seventeenth centuries. Around the same time money, which had always constituted the sinews of government, acquired an unprecedented significance for the Ottoman administrative-military apparatus, which seemed to need it more than ever. Most scholars usually explain this growing need by citing developments in military technology that rendered the feudal cavalry obsolete and necessitated the expansion of infantry forces, thereby creating a cash burden for salary payments. Yet the impact of technology seems to have followed the socioeconomic forces, rather than leading them, as is discussed further in Chapter 5. It was the tax-farmers who were transforming the Ottoman patrimonial polity into something else, the Second Empire.

The tax-farmers themselves were the products of an ongoing process of transformation in which a largely feudal economy, based on local economic units only loosely connected to each other from which most taxes were extracted in kind by fief holders, evolved into a primarily monetary economy relying on a wide network of markets spread over that part of the Old World where the three continents of Asia, Europe, and Africa met. The political unification of this large geographical space, finally restored by the mid-sixteenth century after an interval of a thousand years, was probably the main catalyst of this process of transformation. The unprecedented commercial links established between the Ottoman Empire and other parts of the world, such as northwestern Europe and the New World, accelerated this transformation. Just as important was the growth of Ottoman cities that created an increasing demand for market-oriented agricultural production.[5] The unification of diverse regional markets into one imperial market was symbolized by the eventual unification of Ottoman currency zones into an imperial monetary zone in the eighteenth century. The Second Empire came to being with these socioeconomic transformations.

The monumental work of Halil İnalcık on Ottoman socioeconomic history and the numerous articles and books published by Suraiya Faroqhi leave no doubt about the dynamism of Ottoman economy and society in the sixteenth century.[6] Of particular importance was the gradual unification of Ottoman

---

[5] For population estimates of Ottoman cities at different points in the sixteenth century, see Ömer Lutfi Barkan, "Essai sur les données statistiques des registres de recensement dans l'Empire Ottoman aux XVe et XVIe siècles," *Journal of the Economic and Social History of the Orient* 1 (1957): 9–36, at 27, 30.

[6] Halil İnalcık's major contributions are simply too many to count. A summary of his lifetime work may be found in his "The Ottoman state: Economy and society, 1300–1600," in *An*

currency zones as the different gold-silver ratios that marked each zone came closer to each other, despite the counter-efforts of the imperial center, which benefited from these differences that produced arbitrage profits for the imperial treasury – for example, a gold coin in Istanbul was worth more in silver currency than in Cairo.[7] During the mid-seventeenth century large European silver currencies, mostly called *guruş* (from *Groschen*) with an accompanying adjective, such as *tam* or *kamil* for the Spanish *piastre*, came to be used as a common currency in the Ottoman Empire, leading to the creation in the late seventeenth century of an Ottoman *kuruş* that was meant to be used all over the empire.[8] The *kuruş* survives to this day in some former Ottoman lands such as Egypt and Turkey.

Thus it was in the sixteenth and seventeenth centuries that the foundations of the early modern monetary system of the region we call today the Middle East were laid, as regional currencies were unified into an imperial zone mainly by indigenous dynamics and *despite* administrative interventions to the contrary. The patrimonial empire of Süleyman the Magnificent had not even made an attempt to impose a common monetary unit over Ottoman domains. It was during the age of the Second Empire, a period commonly associated with political weakness, that something like a monetary union was brought to realization in Ottoman lands. The Second Empire might have had a weaker dynastic institution, but it ended up creating a stronger state, with its legitimacy based on a relative consensus within the ruling class whose members were spread all around the empire but engaged in business using the same currency. Not surprisingly, the development of this imperial common market with a single currency and a certain degree of autonomy from political authorities went hand in hand with the empowerment of a legal system with universal claims, the source of reference for which was outside the domain of political authorities.

The first part of this chapter connects the socioeconomic transformation of the sixteenth century with the gradual demise of Ottoman timar, or fief, and *kanun*, or feudal law, and the political empowerment of jurists' law. In the second part, I sharpen my focus on the ways in which the socioeconomic transformation of the sixteenth century brought about the rise of the political profile of jurists' law and its practitioners, ultimately creating an unprecedented degree of legal supervision in dynastic affairs. Taken together, these parts lay out the framework within which the political struggles of the seventeenth century were fought and the rest of this study should be read. The Second

---

Economic and Social History of the Ottoman Empire, 9–409. A partial bibliography of Suraiya Faroqhi's work may be found in her "Crisis and change, 1590–1699," in *An Economic and Social History of the Ottoman Empire*, 627, and İnalcık, "The Ottoman state," 388.

[7] Baki Tezcan, "The Ottoman monetary crisis of 1585 revisited," *Journal of the Economic and Social History of the Orient* 52 (2009): 460–504.

[8] Şevket Pamuk, *A Monetary History of the Ottoman Empire* (Cambridge: Cambridge University Press, 2000), 149–61.

Empire was the child of a socioeconomic transformation, and its political battles were conceptually fought around legal issues. "One market, one money, one law," that is what the Second Empire was about – almost three centuries before the European Union.

The dissolution of feudal structures and the rise of jurists' law

At the same time as the market forces produced by Ottoman society were aligning the different economic zones of the Ottoman Empire, they were also dissolving the feudal structures within which the Ottoman polity had been operating since its foundation and bringing about wide-ranging social and political transformations in the empire. The consequences of these transformations had been identified as symptoms of Ottoman decline until recently. Although contemporary scholarship no longer identifies some of these as signs of decline, their interconnectedness and their strong relationship to the social changes of the sixteenth century need further exploration. In this section I focus on three such areas and demonstrate that they are signs of change, not of decline, and that they are all connected, producing a consistent image of socioeconomic change and its repercussions in political fields, such as law, which is central to a proper understanding of the Second Empire.

The first sign of change was the conversion of lands that were held as timars by provincial cavalry soldiers to lands from which tax resources were either farmed out or given as fiefs to clients. Another transformation, closely related to the first, was the move from detailed cadastral surveys of the land, which determined the exploitation of agricultural resources tied to the land, toward detailed records of tax-farms that were concerned with monetary resources. Third, there was an obvious rise in the political profile of jurists' law, or positive law based on jurists' interpretation of the Sharia, which represents for Muslims the ideal way God meant people to live. This increasing prominence of jurists' law was in sharp contrast with the decreasing role of the *kanun*, feudal law that was recorded in the compilations of customs collected and sanctioned by royal authority, on the one hand, and administrative regulations that were mostly based on precedence, on the other.[9]

The breakdown of pre- and early Ottoman social structures during the sixteenth century may best be observed through the institution of the timar, the Ottoman fief. During the conquests in Anatolia and the Balkans, the Ottomans not only integrated many local nobles into their own ranks but also inherited a number of local practices in the territories they conquered. One of the sociopolitical institutions they inherited was the Byzantine *pronoia*, literally

[9] For an example of the former category in English translation, see John Christos Alexander, *Toward a History of Post-Byzantine Greece: The Ottoman* kanunnames *for the Greek Lands* (Athens, 1985); for the latter, see Douglas A. Howard, "Ottoman administration and the tîmâr system: şûret-i kânûnnâme-i 'Osmânî berây-ı tîmâr dâden," *Journal of Turkish Studies* 20 (1996): 46–125.

"care, providence," a landed estate given to notables for them to administer and exploit its tax revenues, in return for which they had to appear for military campaigns.[10] A similar institution called *iqṭāʿ* existed in the Muslim Middle East, and it was also used in Anatolia by the pre-Ottoman dynasty of the Seljuks. Yet the Ottomans, instead of calling this institution by the Arabic term *iqṭāʿ*, adapted the Persian word *tīmār*, literally "care," that seems to translate the Byzantine *pronoia*. Whatever the origins of the Ottoman timar, it was basically a grant of rights to collect certain taxes – some in kind, some in cash – on specified land in exchange for military service, and as such, it was a medieval institution that preceded the Ottomans in Anatolia and the Balkans.

There is a heated debate on the nature of the timar. Whereas some scholars argue that the existence of this institution implies an Ottoman feudalism,[11] others emphasize the differences between the Ottoman timar and European feudalism.[12] The latter argument – that the strong centralized control of the timar grants in the sixteenth century made the Ottoman timar quite different from the European experience of feudalism – is important to consider. Yet at the same time, the early Ottoman timar might have been quite different from its sixteenth-century version. A fifteenth-century collection of letters and templates included the template text of an oath to be sworn by military-administrators not to take away any timars from their holders,[13] implying that the timar might have been conceived as an unalienable assignment. The feudal aspects of early Ottoman history require a multilayered debate, the political part of which I touch upon in Chapter 3. For the purposes of the present study, suffice it to say that feudalism in its sense of a mode of production existed in the Ottoman Empire in the late Middle Ages.[14]

However, one should reconsider the established wisdom in Ottoman economic history, which asserts that the dominant mode of production continued to be feudal in the Ottoman Empire until the nineteenth century. The *dominance* of a mode of production need not necessarily mean a statistical one, but rather can be understood in terms of its effects. Thus if market-oriented production had an impact beyond its statistical prevalence, it may well be regarded as dominant. The unification of Ottoman monetary zones strongly suggests that a market economy did indeed have a large impact on the Ottoman Empire.

[10] Douglas A. Howard, "The Ottoman timar system and its transformation," PhD diss. (Indiana University, 1987), 14–15.
[11] Vera P. Mutafcieva, "Sur le caractère du *timar* ottoman," *Acta Orientalia Academiae Scientiarum Hungaricae* 9 (1959): 5–61; Bistra A. Cvetkova, "L'évolution du régime féodal turc de la fin du XVIe jusqu'au milieu du XVIIIe siècle," *Etudes historiques* 1 (Sofia, 1960): 171–206.
[12] Ö. L. Barkan, "Feodal düzen ve Osmanlı timarı," *Hacettepe Üniversitesi Türkiye İktisat Tarihi Semineri* (June 1973): 1–32.
[13] Necati Lugal and Adnan Erzi, eds., *Fâtih Devrine âit Münşeat Mecmuası* (Istanbul: İstanbul Enstitüsü Yayınları, 1956), 101–2, no. 62, dated 1473.
[14] For a definition of feudalism in this particular sense, see Halil Berktay, "The feudalism debate – the Turkish end: Is 'tax-vs.-rent' necessarily the product and sign of a modal difference?" *Journal of Peasant Studies* 14 (1986–87): 291–333, at 311.

As is noted later, another important development of the sixteenth century was the gradual replacement of the original timar holders, who constituted a group reminiscent of a rent-collecting aristocracy, with a different stratum of economic agents. These two developments, the monetary transformation on the grand imperial scale and the political one among the fief holders, challenge the argument that feudalism was the dominant mode of production in the Ottoman Empire.

There is some evidence to suggest that a transition from a local economy, based largely on the exchange of goods and services in kind, to a monetary one was already well underway in the fifteenth century. As Halil İnalcık shows, taxes due in the form of services to one's overlord were being transformed into taxes in cash during the fifteenth century.[15] Although the feudal-royal law code of Mehmed II (1451–81) implied that the peasants could pay what they owed their lords in services either in cash or kind, during the reign of Bayezid II (1481–1512) this payment-in-lieu-of-services had a fixed name attached to it (*resm-i çift*), and there was no longer any option to pay in kind.[16]

There is evidence to indicate that a similar change occurred in taxes in kind from agricultural produce, at least in certain parts of the empire, starting from the late fifteenth century. For instance, Halil İnalcık shows that payments in kind were being converted to payments in cash in certain areas of the Balkans toward the end of the reign of Mehmed II (1451–81).[17] His work on socioeconomic history and tax law clearly suggests that the replacement of earlier taxation practices with "Ottoman law" (*kanun-ı Osmani*) symbolized the transformation from a largely feudal economy to a developing monetary economy in which taxes were collected in cash. This interpretation is supported by some East European historians as well.[18]

This transformation was gradual. The requirements of a developing monetary economy necessitated the collection of taxes in cash, yet the regulations did not always sanction this transformation wholeheartedly. Not all taxes were converted into cash payments at once, and the same rules did not apply uniformly across the empire. For instance, a provincial financial code from 1583 stated that the local authorities should *not* ask for cash payments in lieu of taxes to be paid in kind, such as the tithe. Such a negative order and its repetition later in the early seventeenth century suggest, however, that the local authorities did ask for cash payments.[19]

[15] Halil İnalcık, "The Ottoman state," 150.
[16] See, for instance, the law code of the district Tırhala (in modern Greece) dated 912/1506–7 in Ahmed Akgündüz, ed., *Osmanlı Kanunnâmeleri ve Hukukî Tahlilleri*, 9 vols. (Istanbul: Osmanlı Araştırmaları Vakfı, 1990–6), vol. II, 511.
[17] Halil İnalcık, "Adâletnâmeler," *Belgeler* 2/3–4 (1965): 49–145, at 64.
[18] Jozef Blaskovics, "XVII. asırda beylerbeyi hassaları ve tebaanın hayatı," *VI. Türk Tarih Kongresi (Ankara, 20–26 Ekim 1961): Kongreye Sunulan Bildiriler* (Ankara: Türk Tarih Kurumu, 1967), 294, # 4.
[19] Akgündüz, *Osmanlı Kanunnâmeleri*, vol. VIII, 530; vol. IX, 584.

Other developments also implied an increasing monetization of the Ottoman economy. As mentioned earlier, the unification of different monetary zones was strongly suggestive of a developing monetary economy. Another important development was demographic growth, especially in cities, which created new markets. As suggested by İnalcık, "[d]uring the period 1520–80, there was a considerable increase in the number of local markets and their development into important centers in some regions in Anatolia. This development must have been in direct relationship to the general demographic and economic development observable in the imperial survey books." In a flourishing environment for regional, interregional, and international trade, goods and services were being produced for the markets in an imperial network rather than for local consumption. This increase in trade, partially brought about by demographic growth, resulted in a growing economy that increasingly used money in transactions, rather than being based on the exchange of goods and services. Last but not least, monetization was not a phenomenon limited to the imperial center but was visible in other centers as Cairo as well.[20]

The Ottoman fief could not remain immune from this fundamental transformation of the Ottoman socioeconomic structure. As goods came to have a market value, so did the timar. There had been complaints about the assignment of fiefs to men who did not provide military service to the sultan since at least the early sixteenth century when the Şahkulu rebellion shook all of Anatolia in 1511 and cost the Ottomans the life of their grand vizier. The fief-holding provincial cavalry soldiers engaged in this rebellion claimed that their timars were sold to wealthy merchants, scholars, and servants of pashas.[21] These complaints were to be repeated throughout the sixteenth and seventeenth centuries during which one Ottoman writer after another stated that fiefs were granted not to provincial cavalry soldiers, but to the private men of provincial governors.[22] According to Douglas Howard, only 10 percent of the timars on Ottoman lands were assigned to provincial cavalry soldiers in 1600.[23]

The institution of the timar, which was a feudal legacy that the Ottomans took over in the territories they conquered, was meant to support the provincial

[20] İnalcık, "The Ottoman state," 25–32, 71–2, 179–379. Figures 2 and 3 represent two market scenes from the imperial capital. For contemporary developments in Cairo, see Nelly Hanna, *Making Big Money in 1600: The Life and Times of Isma'il Abu Taqiyya, Egyptian Merchant* (Syracuse: Syracuse University Press, 1998).
[21] Şahabettin Tekindağ, "Şah Kulu Baba Tekeli isyanı," *Belgelerle Türk Tarihi Dergisi*, 1/3 (December 1967): 34–39, 1/4 (January 1968): 54–9, at 35, 38, document # 5.
[22] Anonymous, "Kitâb-ı müstetâb," in *Osmanlı Devlet Teşkilâtına Dair Kaynaklar: Kitâb-ı Müstetâb – Kitabu Mesâlihi'l Müslimîn ve Menâfi'i'l-Mü'minîn – Hırzü'l-Mülûk*, ed. Yaşar Yücel (Ankara: Türk Tarih Kurumu Yayınları, 1988), 15; Mustafa Âli, *Mustafâ 'Âlî's Counsel for Sultans of 1581*, ed. and tr. Andreas Tietze, 2 vols. (Vienna: Verlag der österreichischen Akademie der Wissenschaften, 1979–82), vol. I, 84.
[23] Rifa'at A. Abou-El-Haj, "The Ottoman *nasihatname* as a discourse over 'morality,'" in *Mélanges Professeur Robert Mantran*, ed. Abdeljelil Temimi (Zaghouan: Publications du Centre d'Etudes et de Recherches Ottomanes, Morisques, de Documentation et d'Information, 1988), 21, n. 12.

cavalry army of the empire. Yet throughout the sixteenth century, in parallel to the development of a monetized economy, the timar turned into an opportunity for investment for those who could afford to buy it. This transformation of the very pillar of Ottoman feudal structures into a free-market investment complemented the gradual unification of distinct Ottoman monetary zones into an imperial unit as a result of the increasing connections among markets. Together these changes symbolized the slow but steady demise of a feudal society. Thus the "crisis" of the Ottoman timar is neither a cause nor a symptom of decline,[24] but rather a symbol of a profound socioeconomic transformation that produced the Second Empire.

I am well aware that some scholars prefer to associate the timar question with military developments that left the provincial cavalry obsolete.[25] Although I agree that the increasing significance of the infantry may indeed have played a significant role in the destabilization of the timar, the military developments themselves have to be evaluated within the socioeconomic context of the late sixteenth century. Without a relatively developed market economy, one could not imagine the growth in the number of infantry soldiers who received their salaries in cash. Rather than proposing military developments as the engine of change, I suggest that the socioeconomic changes facilitated the spread of the use of infantry soldiers throughout the empire, as is further discussed in Chapter 4.

Once this socioeconomic transformation is appreciated, one can better understand the disappearance of cadastral surveys of land, which were designed to determine the value of proceeds to be allocated to timars, larger fiefs, and the royal demesne. As more and more timars came to be leased to the highest bidders or earmarked as tax-farms, the cadastral surveys became obsolete. The question that the cadastral surveys were designed to answer was how many men bearing swords could be supported by a certain tract of land. As market forces came to challenge feudal structures, however, the fundamental question became how much money could be raised from the same land, with the marketplace determining that answer. Thus a different set of financial records that focused on tax-farming rather than fiefs gained significance in the age of the Second Empire, as suggested by the detailed work of Linda Darling on the Ottoman finance administration during the seventeenth century. Similarly, Metin Kunt's findings on Ottoman provincial administration point toward a "shift from a 'feudal' arrangement to a monetary one."[26]

As the cadastral surveys gradually disappeared, so did the *kanunnames*, the officially sanctioned compilations of feudal administrative, financial, and

[24] İ. Metin Kunt sees this process as "modernization;" see *The Sultan's Servants: The Transformation of Ottoman Provincial Government, 1550–1650* (New York: Columbia University Press, 1983), 98.

[25] Halil İnalcık, "Military and fiscal transformation in the Ottoman Empire, 1600–1700," *Archivum Ottomanicum* 6 (1980): 283–337.

[26] Darling, *Revenue-Raising*, 16–18, 81–160; Kunt, *The Sultan's Servants*, 98.

Fig. 2. The *bedesten*, or the central building of the Grand Bazaar in Istanbul; from a seventeenth century Ottoman collection of images including scenes of daily life and portraits produced for a Venetian patron and known as the Taeschner Album – named after Franz Taeschner who came to own and publish a reproduction of it before it was lost during the World War II; *Alt-Stambuler Hof- und Volksleben: ein türkisches Miniaturenalbum aus dem 17. Jahrhundert* (Hannover: Orient-Buchhandlung H. Lafaire, 1925).

sometimes penal customs that differed from region to region. These two developments were closely related to each other as the usual place of a *kanunname* was at the beginning of a cadastral survey. The surveyors would not only survey the land but also note the various customs adhered to in the area that pertained to the relations between the peasant producers and fief holders or to various taxes collected in towns and cities. Once the cadastral surveys became obsolete, the *kanunname*s were not renewed. A search for seventeenth-century *kanunname*s brings much fewer results in contrast with the rich documentation of the late fifteenth and sixteenth centuries.[27] And the few new *kanunname*s that were compiled for seventeenth-century conquests, such as Crete, contained clauses that would more appropriately be categorized under jurists' law rather than feudal customs.[28] To understand the relationship between the two legal traditions and the rise of the political profile of jurists' law during the

---

[27] Heath W. Lowry, "The Ottoman *liva kanunname*s contained in the *defter-i hakani*," *Osmanlı Araştırmaları / Journal of Ottoman Studies* 2 (1981): 43–74, at 56–74.

[28] Molly Greene, "An Islamic experiment? Ottoman land policy on Crete," *Mediterranean Historical Review* 11 (1996): 60–78.

Fig. 3. The *Avrat Pazarı*, or women's market, in the Haseki neighborhood of Istanbul; from an album known as *Memorie turchesche* that shares the same characteristics with the Taeschner Album, Museo Civico Correr, MS Cicogna 1971; photo credit: Bildarchiv Preussischer Kulturbesitz / Art Resource, NY.

Second Empire while feudal law, or the *kanun*, became gradually irrelevant, a discussion of their respective backgrounds is in order.

I use the term "jurists' law" to refer to *fiqh*. The distinction between *fiqh* and the Sharia is important to maintain. As Bernard Weiss suggests, the Sharia represents the divine intention about how human beings are supposed to live their lives. Many Muslims believe that this intention is to be found in the Qur'an and the Sunna, or the example of Muhammad. Yet it needs to be extracted from these sources: Sharia is certain but not obvious. *Fiqh*, or that which is found in the process of this extraction, is the body of rules and principles that Muslim jurists derive from both the foundational texts of Islam and the legal opinions of their predecessors. It is very real, and yet it operates in a zone of probability because jurists may well make mistakes in determining the divine intention. Thus in the continuous quest for representing the Sharia as precisely as possible, *fiqh* is by its very nature subject to change.[29] In a sense the distinction between the Sharia and *fiqh* is parallel to the distinction between natural law and positive law. Whereas natural law is supposed to reflect universally accepted moral principles, positive law is man-made. To emphasize the man-made nature of the *fiqh*, I consistently refer to it as jurists' law.

In its early stages of development, one of the primary concerns of jurists' law was to protect society from the interventions of the political authority. According to Baber Johansen, one of the ways in which this goal was accomplished was to divide legal claims into two categories: "claims of men," or *ḥuqūq al-ʿibād*, and "claims of God," or *ḥuqūq Allāh*. The Ottomans followed the Hanafi School of jurists' law in which, according to Johansen, political authority was meant to be operative mainly on issues that concern the "claims of God," which cover acts of worship, the punishment of certain crimes, and taxes. Even in these areas, however, governmental authority was relatively restricted.[30] Because "God cannot suffer loss or damage, . . . He will not suffer when His claims are not fulfilled;" hence, the difficulty in fulfilling His legal claims, which was the responsibility of the political authorities whose hands were tightly tied with procedural requirements. This was one of the ways in which men and women were protected from the vicissitudes of political authority. Moreover, incentives were provided "for the private legal persons to settle their claims privately rather than bring them to court and request justice according to the public law."[31] This was another way to keep people's lives secure from encroachments by the political authority.

Yet gradually, the political authority came to be allowed some discretionary space to inflict punishments not necessarily sanctioned in more conventional renderings of jurists' law. This additional discretion, which was called *siyāsa shar'iyya*, was meant to be limited mostly to criminal law and was aimed

---

[29] For a general introduction to these concepts, see Bernard G. Weiss, *The Spirit of Islamic Law* (Athens: University of Georgia Press, 1988).

[30] Baber Johansen, "Sacred and religious elements in Hanafite law – function and limits of the absolute character of government authority," in *Islam et politique au Maghreb*, eds. Ernest Gellner and Jean-Claude Vatin (Paris: Éditions du centre national de la recherche scientifique, 1981), 300.

[31] Ibid., 299.

at "maintaining public order and ensuring the welfare of society."[32] Jurists' law proper thus came to consist almost exclusively of the "claims of men," covering areas associated with private law most extensively and leaving areas related to administrative law to the discretion of the political authority.

By the nature of its development, then, jurists' law could very easily accommodate feudal law, which was constituted by local custom and had much more to do with administrative issues than private law. And in practice, jurists' law did accommodate feudal law for a considerable time. Feudal law perfectly fit into the space provided by the notion of the *siyāsa shar'iyya*, which happened to be adopted by the Hanafi School of jurists' law in the fifteenth century,[33] right around the time when compiling *kanunnames* was becoming prevalent. During the late fifteenth and early sixteenth centuries, several compendia of feudal customary law were in circulation throughout the empire. Some pertained to criminal law and included occasional clauses that disagreed with jurists' law;[34] these problematic clauses were brought into agreement with jurists' law during the sixteenth century.[35] In turn, jurists asserted that feudal law was operative in a number of areas.[36] The *politically* dominant legal tradition of the early Ottoman kingdom and the patrimonial empire was feudal law.

Nevertheless, this coexistence of feudal law with jurists' law did not last forever. From the second half of the sixteenth century onward, the use of and references to feudal law, or *kanun*, gradually decreased, eventually culminating in its stark denunciation. An imperial decree dated June 1696 stated that "all public and private affairs are completely and exclusively regulated" by the Sharia:

[I]n some decrees which have the character of *kānūn* [the term] noble *sharī'a* is followed by and connected with [the term] *kānūn* [such as in the formula 'in accordance with the *sharī'a* and the *kānūn*']. Not only is [the *sharī'a* thus] quoted in a place unbefitting it. It is also highly perilous and most sinful to juxtapose the [terms] *sharī'a* and *kānūn*. Therefore in firmans and decrees all matters shall henceforth be based on the firm support of the noble *sharī'a* only ... and warnings are given against the coupling of the [terms] noble *sharī'a* and *kānūn*.[37]

Ömer Lutfi Barkan called attention to this denunciation, describing it as a reflection of religious fanaticism; Richard Repp followed Barkan and ascribed

---

[32] Uriel Heyd, *Studies in Old Ottoman Criminal Law*, ed. V. L. Ménage (Oxford: Oxford University Press, 1973), 199.
[33] Baber Johansen, "The claims of men and the claims of God: The limits of government authority in Hanafite law," in *Pluriformiteit en verdeling van de macht in het Midden-Oosten* ([Nijmegen]: Vereniging voor de Studie van het Midden-Oosten en de Islam, 1980), at 87.
[34] Heyd, *Studies*, 180–3.
[35] Compare, for instance, Akgündüz, *Osmanlı Kanunnâmeleri*, vol. I, 347, with Heyd, *Studies*, 95.
[36] See, for instance, Heyd, *Studies*, 188.   [37] Ibid., 154–5.

it to the growing religious conservatism of the seventeenth century.[38] The denunciation of the *kanun* came to symbolize the defeat of "secular" law in the Ottoman Empire.[39]

Thus Ottoman scholarship came to associate the *kanun* with that which was secular-like, and jurists' law became the symbol of religious fanaticism. Not surprisingly, the former was depicted as the secret behind the rise of the empire, and the latter the cause of its decline. Strong sultans during the "classical" period were able to impose their will through the *kanun*, but later, what Barkan calls the "ulema mentality" took over and brought about the demise of the *kanun*.[40] This set the stage for the decline of the empire.

Yet there is a major problem with this interpretation of affairs. The decree that outlawed the use of the term *kanun* was made by the Ottoman sultan Mustafa II, who most certainly consulted Seyyid Feyzullah, his mentor and the grand mufti, before issuing it. Thus, Seyyid Feyzullah must be the source of religious fanaticism, according to that interpretation. As it happens, however, it would be very difficult to call Seyyid Feyzullah a religious fanatic. Feyzullah was known, among other things, to have been planning to convert the Galata Tower in Istanbul to an observatory with the help of European astronomers.[41] He was one of those Ottoman scholars who actually had a strong training in the rational sciences, something that religious fanatics are supposed to be opposed to. Feyzullah also founded several *medreses*, or colleges of law, and bequeathed thousands of books to their libraries, some of which operate to this day; for example, Millet Library in Istanbul.[42] These are not the distinguishing features of a religious fanatic.

Matters get even more complicated when one looks for religious fanatics around Feyzullah. Feyzullah's teacher, Mehmed Vani, was the kind of man whom Barkan and Repp would definitely associate with religious fanaticism as he was involved in the third phase of the Kadızadeli movement in the second half of the seventeenth century; this movement is usually cited as

[38] Ömer Lutfi Barkan, *XV ve XVI ıncı Asırlarda Osmanlı İmparatorluğunda Ziraî Ekonominin Hukukî ve Malî Esasları*, vol. I, *Kanunlar* (Istanbul: İstanbul Üniversitesi Edebiyat Fakültesi Yayınları, 1945), xix, n. 5; Richard Repp, "Qānūn and sharīʿa in the Ottoman context," in *Islamic Law: Social and Historical Contexts*, ed. Aziz al-Azmeh (London: Routledge, 1988), 132.

[39] Halil İnalcık describes *kanun* as "secular" law in "Kanun, iii.-Financial and public administration," *Encyclopedia of Islam, New Edition*, vol. IV, 559, 560.

[40] Barkan, *Kanunlar*, xx, n. 5.

[41] J. H. Mordtmann, "Das Observatorium des Taqī ed-dīn zu Pera," *Der Islam* 13 (1923): 82–96, at 85.

[42] Cevat İzgi, *Osmanlı Medreselerinde İlim*, 2 vols. (Istanbul: İz, 1997), vol. I, 101–2; Halil İnalcık, *The Ottoman Empire: The Classical Age, 1300–1600*, trs. Norman Itzkowitz and Colin Imber (London: Weidenfeld & Nicolson, 1973), 179–85; Mehmed Serhan Tayşi, "Şeyhü'l-islâm Seyyid Feyzullâh Efendi ve Feyziyye Medresesi," *Türk Dünyası Araştırmaları* 23 (April 1983): 9–100.

one of the reasons why the Ottoman *kanun* lost against the Sharia.[43] Just like Feyzullah, however, Vani, too, was well educated in the rational sciences, which contradicts the image of a religious fanatic. Vani was a Kurdish preacher, educated in the eastern provinces of the Ottoman Empire, where "in some outlying places, here and there in the land of the Kurds" one could still find some who taught rational sciences after such teachers were ousted from the *medreses* of the imperial center. Such easterners, according to Katib Çelebi, would "give themselves tremendous airs" when they came to Istanbul as few others had any training in rational sciences.[44] Although Katib Çelebi died before Vani arrived in Istanbul, his remarks could well have described Vani as he received a lot of attention at the court and became very close to some of the most powerful people of the time, including Mehmed IV; the queen mother Turhan Sultan; the eldest son of the sultan, Prince Mustafa; and Köprülü Fazıl Ahmed Pasha, who had met him in the east and introduced him to the imperial capital after he became grand vizier.[45] Thus both Vani and Feyzullah, the former's student and successor in the position of mentorship to Prince Mustafa, owed their prestigious positions in the learned hierarchy to the palace, and they both were trained in the rational sciences that had been ousted from Ottoman *medreses* in the late sixteenth century. They squarely belonged to the absolutist camp on the map of Ottoman politics, which I present in more detail in the next chapter.

This particular constellation of political forces, which suggested that the absolutists had entered the domain of jurists' law and styled themselves as champions of the Sharia in the late seventeenth century, simply does not line up with Barkan's explanation for the demise of the *kanun*, which is also supposed to function as an explanation for Ottoman decline in the seventeenth century. To give a striking example, Köprülü Fazıl Ahmed Pasha brought the glories of the old days back to the Ottoman Empire during his long tenure as grand vizier (1661–76). His tenure is usually represented as one of stability and likened to the "classical" era in various ways.[46] And yet, it was this same Köprülü who introduced Vani, supposedly a fanatic, to the palace and continued to support him. Could the symbol of the "classical" age and the cause of decline really belong in the same picture? In a similar vein, according to the prevalent understanding of Ottoman decline, strong sultans issued *kanun*s, and the reactionary members of the ulema opposed them later, championing the

---

[43] Repp, "Qānūn and sharīʿa," 131–2; for the Kadızadeli movement, see Necati Öztürk, "Islamic Orthodoxy among the Ottomans in the seventeenth century with special reference to the Qadi-Zade movement," PhD diss. (University of Edinburgh, 1981).

[44] Katib Çelebi, *The Balance of Truth*, tr. G. L. Lewis (London: George Allen and Unwin, 1957), 26.

[45] Öztürk, "Islamic Orthodoxy," 272–5.

[46] Bernard Lewis, *The Emergence of Modern Turkey* (London: Oxford University Press, 1961), 36.

cause of the Sharia and bringing about the victory of fanaticism. Yet Mustafa II, despite his clear support for the Sharia as opposed to the *kanun*, was a ruler who tried to strengthen the sultanate, which brought about his deposition in 1703. We also know that most of the ulema opposed Feyzullah just a few years after the issuance of the decree described earlier. How does one explain the opposition of the ulema, who are supposed to have brought about the demise of the *kanun*, to a man who actually championed the cause of the Sharia against the *kanun*? It seems that the conventional wisdom needs to be revised. Instead of being a sign of fanaticism, the rising profile of jurists' law at the expense of the *kanun* may well be yet another indication of socioeconomic change, just as were the demise of the timar and of cadastral surveys.

The political empowerment of jurists' law and its practitioners

In this section, I use specific examples to illustrate the relationship of some of the socioeconomic developments of the sixteenth century to the rise of the political profile of jurists' law. Then I show that, although Ottoman jurists lost some of their autonomy as they were integrated into an administrative hierarchy in return for securing certain privileges for themselves, their political impact on the highest levels of the imperial polity actually increased, contributing to the increasing role of legal discourse in imperial political processes.

The socioeconomic context of the political empowerment of jurists' law

The weakening and eventual denunciation of the *kanun* in relation to the empowerment of jurists' law were not related to a sudden increase of fanaticism among the Ottomans but instead can be seen as the product of two developments stemming from the socioeconomic transformation of the sixteenth century.

First, the gradual development of a monetized market economy created new institutions whose regulation fell into the domain of jurists' law, as it was this law that had experience in dealing with commercial transactions and other business deals. This made jurists' law too important to be ignored by the dynasty. The stricter divide between private law and public law of the earlier period had kept private law, the subjects of which mostly fell under jurists' law, more or less out of the realm of the political authority. Yet as jurists' law proved to be crucial for the developing market economy in the empire, the dynasty felt the need to intervene in it with a view to regularizing it.

The second development was not entirely separate from the first, but rather was a more overtly political expression of it. In the late sixteenth and seventeenth centuries there occurred the expansion of the Ottoman political nation that, at the time, corresponded more or less to the *askeri*, a term that literally meant "military" but actually referred to the privileged classes of Ottoman society. Many members of the *askeri* were the offspring of old noble families, early Ottoman conquerors, and *devşirmes*. As such they were distinguished from the *re'aya*, or the subjects (literally "flock"). The socioeconomic developments of the sixteenth century provided opportunities for upward mobility to many an entrepreneur who joined the Ottoman *askeri* as *ecnebis*, literally "outsiders," a designation that referred to their commoner origins. The dynasty felt the need to regulate affairs among the members of the recently expanded ruling class in order to continue its hegemony over them, an attempt that drew the dynasty more and more into the domain of jurists' law, which handled relations among individuals.

One of the most illustrative examples of the relationship between a monetary economy and the political empowerment of jurists' law was the cash wakf controversy of the sixteenth century. Wakf is a legal construct through which one could endow one's property as a source of income for a particular purpose. For instance, a store could be endowed with the specification that its rent was going to be used for the upkeep of a particular mosque or for the salary of a professor teaching at a college of law. There were also many "family wakfs," the primary beneficiaries of which were the descendants of the person who established them. Wakfs that were founded by cash endowments were first created in the the early fifteenth century.[47] The number of such endowments increased rapidly during the sixteenth century according to the register of wakfs that were founded in Istanbul in the century following the Ottoman conquest. According to this register, 1,150 wakfs were either exclusively or partially endowed with cash; of these, the date of the founding of 918 endowments was recorded: 4.5 percent were founded between 1456 and 1495, 24.4 percent between 1495 and 1520, and 71.1 percent between 1520 and 1546. A total of 13,253,736 *akçes* were endowed in the period 1520–46, which is roughly equivalent to the tax revenue of the Ottoman Empire derived from the Anatolian provinces in the fiscal year of 1547–8.[48] These figures demonstrate the gradually increasing significance of cash wakfs in the sixteenth century, and they could easily be supplemented by those from other registers from the latter part of the sixteenth as well as the seventeenth centuries.[49]

Although the increasing importance of endowments in cash should not be surprising within the context of the development of a market-oriented society during the sixteenth century, they nevertheless caused a legal controversy. Cash wakfs, or charitable trusts founded by endowments in cash, were not known in the Islamic world before the Ottomans. Moreover, the prevalent

---

[47] Jon E. Mandaville, "Usurious piety: The cash waqf controversy in the Ottoman Empire," *International Journal of Middle East Studies* 10 (1979): 289–308, at 290.

[48] Compare Ömer Lutfî Barkan and Ekrem Hakkı Ayverdi, *İstanbul Vakıfları Tahrîr Defteri – 953 (1546) Târîhli* (Istanbul: İstanbul Fetih Cemiyeti – İstanbul Enstitüsü, 1970), viii, xxxi; with Ö. L. Barkan, "954–955 (1547–1548) malî yılına âit bir Osmanlı bütçesi," *İstanbul Üniversitesi İktisat Fakültesi Mecmuası* 19 (1957–58): 219–76, at 240.

[49] Hasan Yüksel, *Osmanlı sosyal ve ekonomik hayatında vakıfların rolü (1585–1683)* (Sivas, 1998), 95–6, 118–20.

legal opinion among the jurists who followed the Hanafi School was not very permissive on this issue. The most liberal opinion, the one ascribed to the Hanafi jurist Zufar (d. 775), allowed cash wakfs only on the condition that the capital was placed in business partnerships to produce profits to be used for a charitable purpose. Yet in the Ottoman practice the capital was clearly used in lending money with interest, though usually under the cover of legal fictions called *mu'amele-i şer'iye* that were used to circumvent the formal prohibition of usury in jurists' law – to pay 10 percent interest, for instance, the borrower would sell a symbolic good to the creditor for the amount of the credit and promise that he would buy it back in a year for a 10 percent higher price. Moreover, Zufar was not deemed to be a major Hanafi jurist whose opinions could serve as the basis for an opinion of the whole Hanafi School. Nevertheless jurist after jurist approved cash wakfs by confirming foundation deeds of charitable trusts with cash endowments until Çivizade, the chief justice of the European provinces, made an attempt to outlaw them around 1546, which happens to be the date of the register cited earlier.[50]

Çivizade's opposition to the cash wakf was founded upon sound legal reasoning within the parameters of jurists' law. Yet in response, other jurists wrote letters or treatises arguing for the permissibility of the cash wakf based on the principles of *te'amül*, generally accepted practice, and *istihsan*, the welfare of the people. In May 1548, eight months after the death of Çivizade, Süleyman issued an imperial decree declaring the cash wakf legal on the basis of the legal opinions expressed in its favor by the leading jurists of the time, including Ebussu'ud, the grand mufti.[51]

Süleyman's decree has to be understood as an intervention of the political authority into the process of the articulation of jurists' law. As the work of Wael Hallaq demonstrates, a weak legal opinion could only become the definitive opinion of a legal school over time through such processes as *tashīh*, correction, and *tashhīr*, declaring an opinion to have become commonly accepted in the school.[52] These procedures were in the hands of the jurists as a collective and thus required a strong consensus to be built around the legal opinion in question. In the case of cash wakfs, such a consensus did not exist. Çivizade's opposition was continued by Birgili Mehmed (d. 1573), who in his widely read *Al-ṭarīqa al-muḥammadiyya* (The Muhammadan Path), singled out the

---

[50] Mandaville, "Usurious piety," 293–7; Ömer Lütfi Barkan, "Türkiye'de din ve devlet ilişkilerinin tarihsel gelişimi," *Cumhuriyetin 50. Yıldönümü Semineri: Seminere Sunulan Bildiriler* (Ankara: Türk Tarih Kurumu, 1975), 72–4.

[51] Mandaville, "Usurious piety," 297–300, 301–4; R. C. Repp, *The Müfti of Istanbul: A Study in the Development of the Ottoman Learned Hierarchy* (London: Ithaca Press, 1986), 255; and Tahsin Özcan, "Para vakıflarıyla ilgili önemli bir belge," *İLAM Araştırma Dergisi* 3/2 (1998): 107–12.

[52] The Hanafi School used the former process much more frequently; Wael Hallaq, *Authority, Continuity and Change in Islamic Law* (Cambridge: Cambridge University Press, 2001), 133–52.

cash wakf as "one of the great evils" of his day.[53] Thus the opinion supported by Ebussu'ud was not necessarily accepted as *ṣaḥīḥ*, or correct, within the Hanafi School: it was the imperial decree that secured its validity. Despite the affirmative opinions of some contemporary jurists, as far as jurists' law was concerned, the sultan was in effect sanctioning a weak opinion within the Hanafi School. Appointment letters of Ottoman judges clearly referred to the sultan's unusual sanction: "In matters in which there is disagreement, work from the strongest position [within the Hanafi School of law]. Do not use weak statements to support your actions except in the matter of cash waqf; do not abandon it."[54]

This political intervention indicated the close relationship between two developments: the gradual transformation of the Ottoman society from a pre-dominantly feudal to a market-oriented one and the lifting of the barrier between public and private law, which led to the increasing politicization of jurists' law. The cash wakf was first and foremost the product of a developing market society in which there was a certain degree of capital accumulation – hence, the endowed cash. The administrators of cash wakfs became credit providers for large segments of the population, injecting capital into the local economy for the benefit of both consumers and entrepreneurs.[55] As extraordinary taxes levied in cash, the *avarız*, gradually became a regular occurrence, neighborhoods began to establish cash wakfs to pay these taxes. Although the available evidence does not permit one to identify the borrowers of cash wakfs in adequate detail,[56] some may well have been tax-farmers, who financed the operations of the military-administrative apparatus of the dynasty by providing ready cash in return for tax-farms. In this way, the dynasty gradually lost some of its financial autonomy and was thus drawn further into interactions with the representatives of social forces who could finance its operations. The political authority, then, simply could not afford to wait for a consensus to be built around the cash wakf question: it had to protect this institution that was essential for the smooth functioning of the financial markets that were becoming crucially important for consumers, entrepreneurs, investors, and the dynastic institution of rule. Thus was Süleyman drawn into the sphere of jurists' law that previously had primarily governed social relations and operated mainly within the spheres of commercial and family law.

[53] Mandaville, "Usurious piety," 304–6.
[54] Ibid., 302; see also Tahsin Özcan, *Osmanlı Para Vakıfları: Kanûnî Dönemi Üsküdar Örneği* (Ankara: Türk Tarih Kurumu, 2003), 40, n. 99; Mehmet Zeki Pakalın, "Kadı," in *Osmanlı Tarih Deyimleri ve Terimleri Sözlüğü*, ed. M. Z. Pakalın, 3 vols. (Istanbul: Milli Eğitim Bakanlığı, 1946), vol. II, 121.
[55] Murat Çizakça, "Cash *waqfs* of Bursa, 1555–1823," *Journal of the Economic and Social History of the Orient* 38 (1995): 313–54; Maria Pia Pedani Fabris and Alessio Bombaci, *I "Documenti Turchi" dell'Archivio di Stato di Venezia* (Rome: Ministero per i beni culturali e ambientali, 1994), 250–51, # 984.
[56] Özcan, *Osmanlı Para Vakıfları*, 300–2, 382.

Süleyman's decree concerning cash waqfs was arguably his most significant intervention into the law. Ebussu'ud once noted that there were altogether thirty-two such cases in which the political authority expressed a preference among the competing opinions in the Hanafi School on a particular question to determine the preponderant opinion to be applied in the courts of law – unfortunately without identifying them.[57] Yet none of the other cases was apparently deemed to as radically alter the spirit of the Hanafi School of jurists' law as the one on the cash waqf which continued to be the only exception mentioned in the appointment letters of Ottoman judges. These letters instructed the appointees to follow the soundest opinion in cases where there was a disagreement among the Hanafi jurists "except for [the case of] the registration of trusts endowed with cash."[58] In that case the weak opinion was to be preferred – a truly substantial intervention into the law. Thus the most significant intervention of the political authority into the domain of jurists' law was one in which it acted to free up a process of economic change that had already been started by social dynamics. The dynastic authority was not the agent of change, but rather its client. Having become so enmeshed in jurists' law, the political authority could not then stop the jurists themselves from entering its own domain, where they would soon decide who would be the next emperor, as shown in the next chapter.

Let me now return to the second development I identified at the beginning of this section. The expansion of market networks and the related expansion of the political nation required the greater involvement of the dynasty in regulating the affairs of the members of the ruling class in order to continue its hegemony over them, which drew the dynasty more and more into the domain of jurists' law. Before the sixteenth century, the dynasty was primarily concerned with the *kanun*, which had a certain degree of autonomy from jurists' law as mentioned earlier. This made sense in a society that was strictly stratified between the rulers and the ruled. In Rifa'at Abou-El-Haj's discussion on the development of the Ottoman state, this stage would correspond to the pre-sixteenth-century "class-state" in which "there was hardly any distinction between the ruling class and the state, they were one."[59] The ruling class and the state were one and the same and consisted of the *askeri* who lived off the surplus produced by the subjects, the *re'aya*. Administrative law focused mainly on the legal organization of the *re'aya*'s exploitation by the *askeri* through various "taxes." Thus the sphere of public or administrative law, which was left to the discretion of the political authority in the tradition of jurists' law, was sufficient to organize the exploitation of the ruled by the

[57] Paul Horster, ed., "Zur Anwendung des islamischen Rechts im 16. Jahrhundert: Die "juristischen Darlegungen" (Ma'rūżāt) des Schejch ül-Islam Ebū Su'ūd (gest. 1574)," PhD diss. (Bonn: Friedrich-Wilhelms-Universität, 1935), 291; Colin Imber, *Ebu's-su'ud: The Islamic Legal Tradition* (Stanford: Stanford University Press, 1997), 169.
[58] Akgündüz, *Osmanlı Kanunnâmeleri*, vol. I, 70.
[59] R. A. Abou-El-Haj, "The Ottoman *nasihatname*," p. 18.

ruling class, which itself was identical with the administration. But once the ruling class came to include members other than those who were connected to the royal administration, public administrative law could not be sufficient to regulate its issues.

As the boundaries separating the *re'aya* and the *askeri* gradually shifted with the entry of economically powerful commoners into the ruling class using opportunities provided by market forces, the political authority that had to secure the sustainable exploitation of the ruled faced a new situation, which had an impact on its relationship with the law. It either had to expand to allow some space for all the commoners who entered the ruling class, or it had to differentiate itself from the ruling class and thus accept the position of representing it vis-à-vis the ruled, rather than being identical with it. The initial response seemed to be along the lines of expansion, as shown by the increasing numbers of Ottoman elite troops (see Chapter 5). But in the long run, the Ottoman political authority followed the strategy of differentiating itself from the ruling class as it came to recognize that it was impossible to include the entire political nation within its ranks. This process of differentiation was a gradual one, and it involved several struggles within the ruling class itself as the dynasty was reluctant to lose its dominant position in the polity. During these struggles, the jurists challenged the authority of the dynasty many times, as discussed in Chapters 2, 5, and 6. To respond to these legal challenges more effectively, the dynasty made an effort to extend its authority over the sphere of jurists and their law, as shown in Chapters 3 and 4. Whereas the legitimacy of dynastic authority had been built upon the feudal traditions represented by the *kanun* in the earlier period, the limits of royal authority in the Second Empire were negotiated with jurists' law, as discussed in Chapter 2.

The empowerment of jurists' law at the expense of the *kanun* lifted the barrier that separated public from private law and the sphere of the administration from that of the society. Now the entirety of the law was open for contestation between jurists of differing opinions and the political authority. The political authority could make attempts to intervene in the articulation of private law by jurists, and conversely, social forces could encourage some jurists to challenge the administration on its own ground. There were examples of both processes in operation. The case of the cash wakf was an example of the former process.[60]

However, the most powerful example of the royal attempt to unify public and private law and bring both under the purview of the dynasty with the aim of securing the dynasty's hegemony over the legal process was the organization of the Ottoman legal administration. Unlike any of their predecessors, the Ottomans made a great effort to institutionalize local courts all over the empire

---

[60] For other examples, see Vejdi Bilgin, *Fakih ve Toplum: Osmanlı'da Sosyal Yapı ve Fıkıh* (Istanbul: İz, 2003), 121–3.

by keeping court records in bound volumes and storing them for posterity.[61] The Ottoman *kadi* was both a judge for the people who lived in his district and also a public administrator who fulfilled various functions, thus symbolizing the merger of public and private law in his very office. The Ottomans also perfected a judicial hierarchy that determined the appointments and promotions of both professors of law and judges.[62] But making an attempt to control the law of the society they governed by merging the domains of public and private law and by regularizing the legal system by various means meant that they also had to allow that same law to govern their own actions, which brings us to the next section that focuses on jurists and how they came to have an impact on dynastic politics.

The political empowerment of the lords of the law in the sixteenth century

As suggested earlier, the need to create an empire-wide system of rule to respond to the needs of an empire-wide economic market and a relatively mobile society led the Ottoman administrative-military apparatus to consolidate the legal structures that supported the application of jurists' law. Jurists' law, with its openness to local traditions and administrative practices in many spheres of law, presented an opportunity for the Ottoman administration to offer an umbrella institution to cover the many administrative, financial, and criminal law practices that coexisted in the Ottoman realms and gradually to mold them together. Moving toward a more centralized system of jurists' law, however, made the Ottoman dynasty indebted to the jurists, who were the only legitimate interpreters and practitioners of this law. As argued elsewhere, the dynasty granted certain privileges to high-ranking jurists, the *mevali*, literally "lords," that led to the development of – what I call – the "lords of the law" as a relatively exclusive group whose members could practically pass their status to their sons.[63]

Throughout the sixteenth century the lords of the law gained political power thanks both to their positions in the imperial web of markets and the lifting of the barriers between public and private law. It would not be an exaggeration to claim that there was a direct relationship between the economic interests of high-ranking jurists and the legal developments that many of them found

[61] Wael B. Hallaq, "The '*qadi*'s *diwan* (*sijill*)' before the Ottomans," *Bulletin of the School of Oriental and African Studies* 61 (1998): 415–36, at 434.
[62] İsmail Hakkı Uzunçarşılı, *Osmanlı Devletinin İlmiye Teşkilâtı* (Ankara: Türk Tarih Kurumu, 1965).
[63] Baki Tezcan, "The Ottoman *mevâli* as 'lords of the law,'" *Journal of Islamic Studies* 20 (2009): 383–407; see also Madeline C. Zilfi, "Elite circulation in the Ottoman Empire: great mollas of the eighteenth century," *Journal of the Economic and Social History of the Orient* 26 (1983): 318–64; and M. C. Zilfi, *The Politics of Piety: The Ottoman Ulema in the Postclassical Age (1600–1800)* (Minneapolis: Bibliotheca Islamica, 1988).

permissible, such as the cash wakf. The wealth that jurists accumulated from their positions was much more secure than that of political grandees in the administrative-military hierarchy, who were subject to confiscations from the sultan. Therefore a second-generation high-ranking jurist inherited not only a privileged status that would give him a head start in the judicial hierarchy but also the wealth accumulated by the previous generation.

Let me provide a few examples of the ways in which jurists were involved in the monetary economy of the empire and benefited from it, thus developing a personal interest in some of the directions of the law they articulated. In addition to their investments in land,[64] jurists seemed to be able to generate large amounts of cash and to lend it to tax-farmers who had to make regular payments to the central treasury. For instance, in 1621, while Osman II was out of the capital engaged in a military campaign against the Poles and Cossacks, Bedik, an Armenian tax-farmer who was responsible for the collection of custom dues at the port of Istanbul, was asked to pay a large installment to the treasury to meet the salary payments of the infantry, which had remained in the capital. Probably because his cash was in short supply, he looked for loans. Ali Efendi, a judge, gave him 500,000 *akçe*s on August 17 and another 600,000 *akçe*s on October 2. Bedik was not able to pay these loans back, and he failed to produce enough cash for the treasury. Thus Murad Agha, a palace officer who was involved in tax collection, replaced him as the customs dues collector on November 19. Murad Agha paid the total sum of 1,100,000 *akçe*s owed by Bedik back to Ali on December 18.[65]

Let me put into context the value of 1,100,000 *akçe*s, which would be roughly equivalent to £ 3,437.50 at the time.[66] The salary of the grand mufti in 1622 was 750 *akçe*s per day or 22,500 per month and 270,000 a year.[67] Thus it would take more than four years for the grand mufti, who had the highest salary in the judicial hierarchy, to save 1,100,000 *akçe*s, if he could live without spending a penny. But Ali was not a grand mufti. He actually had only served in his first judicial appointment for some ten months as the judge of Mecca and since April 1620 had not held any office.

Yet Ali happened to be the brother of Ömer Efendi, who was the mentor of Osman II. Ömer was appointed to teach the sons of Ahmed I in 1609. At that point, Ali was a *kassam* in Egypt, a legal official who supervised

---

[64] See the grant of land ownership given to Es'ad Efendi, an early-seventeenth-century lord of the law, in *Münşe'ât-ı Selâtîn*, eds. Feridun Bey et al., 2nd ed., 2 vols. (Istanbul, 1274), vol. II, 365. Lesser jurists were also investing in land; see Eleni Gara, "Moneylenders and landowners: In search of urban Muslim elites in the early modern Balkans," in *Provincial Elites in the Ottoman Empire*, ed. Antonis Anastasopoulos (Rethymno: Crete University Press, 2005), 144.

[65] BOA, KK 1911, 46, 68, 124, 126.

[66] Fynes Moryson, *An Itinerary* (London, 1617), "A briefe Table . . . ," n.p., notes that an *akçe* makes "some three farthings English." Because 960 farthings make one pound, 1,100,000 *akçe*s would make £ 3,437.50.

[67] BOA, KK 1914, 238.

inheritance shares and collected dues on behalf of the chief justice of the Asian and African provinces. Soon Ali got his first teaching appointment on record. After the enthronement of Osman II, Ömer was no longer the private instructor of a prince, but the mentor of the sultan, with great influence on many decisions, including making appointments in the educational-judicial hierarchy. Thus in 1619, Ali was first appointed to the college of Süleymaniye as a professor and a month later to the judgeship of Mecca, a position that he left in 1620.[68]

Ali's ability to produce such a great amount of cash could be related to his brother's position and may be seen as exceptional. Yet all the men who occupied the summit of the judicial hierarchy were well situated at the center of imperial power. They were the ones who sanctioned the cash wakfs that produced roughly half of the revenues accrued from all charitable trusts in the empire – more than nine million *akçes* per year in a sample of 313 trusts founded during the seventeenth century.[69] It would not be surprising if Ali had borrowed the 1,100,000 *akçes* that he lent Bedik from the capital pool of a cash wakf or from several cash wakfs. Ali and other lords of the law were the ones who granted teaching licenses; their most senior colleagues – the chief justices of the European, and Asian and African provinces, the grand mufti, and the mentor of the sultan – had differing degrees of control over the appointments of the professors and judges. Thus the lords of the law had clients all over the empire who either got their teaching licenses from them or owed them their appointments. In addition, it was not only the cash wakfs, which these clients registered in the provinces, that could connect the lords of the law to monetary resources. Professors and judges were engaged in a wide range of financial activities that connected them with financial resources in the imperial network.

Judges of small towns, who were the clients of these high-ranking jurists, were responsible not only for the regular duties of a judge but also for collecting some of the extraordinary taxes in cash, such as *bedel-i kürekçiyan*, a tax that was meant to finance the navy, which by the second half of the sixteenth century had become more or less a regular tax. Mostly, it was the judges who decided the amount a household was supposed to pay and oversaw the collection of such taxes. Moreover, in times of war their duties included the supply of certain provisions or, as a substitute, some extra cash. All of these obligations involved some sort of monetary transaction. Mustafa Âli's remarks, in his advice book for sultans, suggested that the judges skimmed off their share of cash from such transactions:

Another point is the levy of army provisions (*nüzül*) and the extraordinary contributions ('*avarız*). These are fully collected from the population (*fuqarâ*) but are not spent entirely

[68] Nev'izade Ata'i, *Hadâ'iku'l-hakâ'ik fi tekmîleti'ş-şakâ'ik*, 2 vols. with continuous pagination (Istanbul, 1268) [reprinted with indices in *Şakaik-ı Nu'maniye ve Zeyilleri*, ed. Abdülkadir Özcan, 5 vols. (Istanbul: Çağrı Yayınları, 1989), vol. II], 717–8, 728–9.
[69] Yüksel, *Osmanlı*, 120.

on the needs of the army but shared between the judges and judge-substitutes.... In short, when a levy of army provisions (*nüzül*) and extraordinary levies ('*avarız*) are imposed on a province and a royal rescript [to this effect] is sent, at once men are sent by the judges to each village and [the villagers or their representatives] are summoned to the judge's court.... Thereafter the bribe-accustomed judge imposes a contribution of one *shâhî* [worth 7 *akçes*] on each household claiming that the court slave that had conveyed the imperial order had taken a handsome fee from him.... But the truth is that [the levy] never arrives in its entirety at the place where it is ordered to go; on the road, at the way stations it is an excellent object of commerce for the rentors of pack animals and for the judge-substitutes.[70]

Another way that a small-town judge could thrive was through cultivating connections with tax-farmers. Darling writes that tax-farm bidders could impose the condition that certain judges be nominated in their contracts: "Mültezims [tax-farmers] even presumed to nominate kadıs [judges]. One bidder made the condition that a dismissed müfettiş [inspector] and kadı of Halomiç, Şemseddin, be restored to his position, another that the kadı of Yanya be made kadı of Tırhala and müfettiş of all his mukataas."[71] Tax-farmers could thus have a great influence over a judge-inspector who owed his job to them. In turn, the connections of a judge in Istanbul could be of use in securing the tax-farm for the bidder. In short, such a partnership could satisfy both sides. There were also small-town judges who left their positions to become tax-farmers.[72] A judge who felt comfortable enough to resign his post and become a tax-farmer must have had a great deal of experience in tax-farming during his judicial tenure.

That a small-town judgeship might be quite lucrative was evident in the career of Lutfullah, known as Çelebi Kadı (d. 1632). Lutfullah started serving as a judge when his father, Zekeriya, later grand mufti, was a chief justice, and he left his judgeship when his brother was grand mufti. Although he had many opportunities to move up in the judicial hierarchy, he repeatedly asked for the judgeship of Filibe (Plovdiv in modern Bulgaria), which he held seven times. It is clear that this appointment was not considered a punishment because during his last term, he was granted the honorary rank of the chief justice of the Asian and African provinces and thus was able to grant ten licenses to teach.[73] The economic power of judges and other members of the ulema was visible in the local financial activities of small towns as well. Among the loans registered in Karaferye (Veria in modern Greece) between 1600 and 1650, for instance, ulema, or men associated with them, "appear in 41% of the cases" as moneylenders.[74] Clearly, because judgeships and other ulema appointments in small towns could well be lucrative, it would not hurt the jurists to have their own men there, to say the least. There was a great deal

[70] Âli, *Counsel for Sultans*, vol. II, 35–6.   [71] Darling, *Revenue-Raising*, 149.
[72] See the legal opinion issued by Es'ad on such judges in his *Fetâvâ*, Süleymaniye Kütüphanesi, Kasidecizade 277, f. 91.
[73] Ata'i, *Hadâ'iku'l-hakâ'ik*, 747–8.   [74] Gara, "Moneylenders," 145.

of room for patron–client relationships to develop within the hierarchy of the educational-judicial institutions as high-ranking jurists were in a position to distribute favors to men in the lower ranks of the hierarchy who were looking for a license to teach or an appointment.

In short, the jurists themselves were beneficiaries of the sixteenth-century socioeconomic transformation and the resulting more monetized economy that functioned under the purview of jurists' law. They thus had a double personal stake in increasing the political profile of the law of which they were the only legitimate interpreters: their market relations depended on it, and their political power would be augmented by it.

The primary characteristic that distinguished the Ottoman lords of the law from earlier Muslim judicial elites was their diminished autonomy vis-à-vis the administrative-military apparatus of the dynasty. This loss of autonomy, however, brought the Ottoman lords of the law unprecedented political influence over the dynasty as they used the door, through which the political authority had entered their domain, in the other direction and entered the political sphere of the dynasty, which rendered them arguably one of the most powerful judicial nobilities of the Islamic world in the premodern era, as explained in this section. To illustrate this argument, I compare the Ottoman lords of the law with their Mamluk predecessors.

As persuasively argued by Michael Chamberlain, the jurist-scholars of late medieval Syria were not very different from their Ottoman successors in terms of the practically hereditary nature of their positions.[75] There was fierce competition for positions among the elite of Damascus in the thirteenth and fourteenth centuries. Teaching posts were a means of preserving the elite status of one's family, and fathers worked hard for their sons to succeed them in their posts. Consider the careers of a father and son from Syria, 'Imād al-Dīn 'Alī bin Aḥmad (d. 1348) and Najm al-Dīn Ibrāhīm bin 'Alī al-Ṭaraṣūṣī (d. 1357).

'Alī started his teaching career in Damascus in 1320 at the Qal'a Mosque. In 1322, after the death of his father-in-law, Shams al-Dīn bin al-'Izz, the deputy of the Hanafi chief judge of Damascus, 'Alī succeeded him in office. He then succeeded the chief judge after his death in 1327. In addition to his judicial post, he taught law at a number of Damascene colleges.[76] In 1334, 'Alī's son Ibrāhīm began teaching at a college of law when he was only 15 years old. A widely used method in late medieval Syria for securing the tenure of one's intimates was the "resignation" of the office holder in favor of them while he "had the power to do so."[77] That is exactly what 'Alī did in 1346, resigning as the chief judge. Thus Ibrāhīm, after serving as the deputy of the Hanafi chief judge of Damascus for about two years, became the chief Hanafi judge of Damascus and succeeded his father in his teaching position as well.[78]

[75] Michael Chamberlain, *Knowledge and Social Practice in Medieval Damascus, 1190–1350* (Cambridge: Cambridge University Press, 1994).
[76] Baki Tezcan, "Hanafism and the Turks in al-Ṭarasūsī's *Gift for the Turks* (1352)," forthcoming in *Mamluk Studies Review* 15 (2011).
[77] Chamberlain, *Knowledge*, 93–4.   [78] Tezcan, "Hanafism."

The striking similarity between late medieval Syria and the Ottoman Empire in the late-sixteenth and early-seventeenth centuries is the significance of family ties in the hierarchy of jurist-scholars. Furthermore, as noted by Ira Lapidus, there were several areas in which the jurists and the administrative-military apparatus of the Mamluks cooperated,[79] reminding one of the relationship between Ottoman jurists and the dynasty. But there are also some differences between the Mamluk jurists and their Ottoman successors. Although family ties were also important in the hierarchy of Ottoman jurist-scholars, the Mamluk jurists were more autonomous than their Ottoman successors. For instance, an Ottoman judge could not resign his position in favor of his son. Even a professor of law was not able to do that, at least not at those colleges that produced the professorial and judicial elite.

Yet, although the Ottoman jurists may have enjoyed less autonomy from the administrative-military apparatus of the Ottoman dynasty, they were at the same time more influential on the functioning of that apparatus, as well as on the dynasty itself. Modern scholarship has often made the former point while overlooking the latter one. For instance, Ebussu'ud, the grand mufti of Süleyman the Magnificent, did make certain choices in his interpretation of jurists' law that brought the law closer to the interests of the Ottoman dynasty as discussed earlier. Yet, it was his very work that brought simultaneously "moral, legal, and institutional restrictions on the military-administrative cadres," as Engin Akarlı notes.[80] As suggested earlier, the strict distinction between public – or administrative – and private law started disappearing as the political authority entered the domain of private law more forcefully than ever in the sixteenth century. This entry, however, was not a one-way process. The lifting of the barrier between the legal domains of the administration and that of society, first and foremost the result of the socioeconomic transformation of the empire, opened public law to the scrutiny of jurists to a degree never seen before. The question of succession was one of those topics of public law in which jurists intervened.

The more autonomous Mamluk jurists were less influential on dynastic politics than their Ottoman successors in the mid-sixteenth and seventeenth centuries. Examples that illustrate the involvement of jurists within dynastic affairs in Mamluk history are very rare.[81] Jo Van Steenbergen goes so far as to state that the Mamluk ulema had "little room for any serious political involvement of their own."[82]

[79] Ira Marvin Lapidus, *Muslim Cities in the Later Middle Ages* (Cambridge, MA: Harvard University Press, 1967), 134–6.
[80] Engin Deniz Akarlı, "Review of *Ebu's-Su'ud: The Islamic Legal Tradition* by Colin Imber," *Islamic Law and Society* 6 (1999): 284–8, at 287.
[81] Lapidus, *Muslim Cities*, 134–5; Susan Jane Staffa, *Conquest and Fusion: The Social Evolution of Cairo, A.D. 642–1850* (Leiden: E. J. Brill, 1977), 140.
[82] Jo Van Steenbergen, *Order out of Chaos: Patronage, Conflict and Mamluk Socio-Political Culture, 1341–1382* (Leiden: E. J. Brill, 2006), 18; see also Robert Irwin, "Factions in medieval Egypt," *Journal of the Royal Asiatic Society* (1986): 228–46. I would like to thank Adam Sabra for bringing these sources to my attention.

The Ottoman case is quite different, especially after the mid sixteenth century, as exemplified in the question of fratricide. Although the compilation of regulations pertaining to Ottoman administrative law ascribed to Mehmed II suggested that dynastic fratricide was sanctioned by "most of the jurists," actual legal opinions proving this claim do not exist.[83] The fact that the authenticity of this compilation is questioned and that the compilation only started circulating when some of the ideas in it were being openly challenged place further doubt on this particular claim.[84] Mehmet Akman suggests that there was only one case of fratricide in early Ottoman history that was carried out with judicial sanction: the murder of Murad I's brothers. As it turns out, however, Akman's claim is based on a misrepresentation of the statements in the sources.[85] Thus before the sixteenth century, Ottoman sultans either did not need the legal sanction of jurists for fratricide, or this sanction was not deemed to be significant enough to be reported. The extant order of Bayezid II from December 1482 for the execution of his nephew Oguz Han, which had no reference to the legality of the decision, supports the former hypothesis: a prince's blood did not require legal justification to be spilled if the emperor issued the order to do so.[86]

However, in the mid-sixteenth century during the reign of Süleyman, the Ottoman dynasty seemed to lose this immunity from the law as the involvement of Ottoman jurists in dynastic politics clearly increased. Süleyman did not have to deal with any brotherly threats to his rule as he was the only surviving son of his father Selim I. Yet later on in his reign he executed his own sons, Prince Mustafa (d. 1553) and Prince Bayezid (d. 1561); the latter execution cost the Ottomans dearly as Bayezid had taken refuge with the Safavid Shah Tahmasp, who asked for a fortune in return for releasing him to Ottoman authorities. The Habsburg ambassador to the court of Süleyman, Ogier Ghiselin de Busbecq, who arrived in Constantinople about a year after the execution of Prince Mustafa, wrote that Süleyman had consulted the mufti of Istanbul, Ebussu'ud, on this execution.[87] Although there is no record of such a consultation in Ottoman sources, a collection of legal opinions on the execution of Prince

[83] Mehmet Akman, *Osmanlı Devleti'nde Kardeş Katli* (Istanbul: Eren, 1997), 173.
[84] Baki Tezcan, "The 'Kânûnnâme of Mehmed II:' A different perspective," in *The Great Ottoman-Turkish Civilisation*, eds. Kemal Çiçek et al., 4 vols. (Ankara: Yeni Türkiye, 2000), vol. III, 657–65.
[85] Compare Akman's source, İsmail Hakkı Uzunçarşılı, "Murad I," *İA*, vol. VIII, 588, with the primary sources cited there: Şükrullah, "Bahjat al-tavārīkh," partial ed. and tr. Theodor Seif, in "Der Abschnitt über die Osmanen in Şükrüllāh's persischer Universalgeschichte," *Mitteilungen zur osmanischen Geschichte* 2 (1923–26): 63–128, at 90; Mehmed Neşri, *Kitâb-ı Cihan-nümâ: Neşrî Tarihi*, eds. Faik Reşit Unat and Mehmed A. Köymen, 2 vols. (Ankara: Türk Tarih Kurumu, 1949–57), vol. I, 190; Mustafa Âli, *Künhü'l-ahbâr*, 5 vols. (Istanbul, 1277–86), vol. V, 66–7; Ruhi, "Rûhî Tarihi," eds. Halil Erdoğan Cengiz and Yaşar Yücel, *Belgeler* 14/18 (1989–92): 359–472, at 387.
[86] Topkapı Sarayı Arşivi, E. 11983/1, published in *Topkapı Sarayı Müzesi Arşivi Kılavuzu*, 2 vols. (Istanbul, 1938–40), vol. I, document 12.
[87] Noted by Repp, *The Müfti of Istanbul*, 284.

Bayezid and his followers included Ebussu'ud's affirmative opinion on Prince Bayezid's execution, as well as many others that confirmed him.[88] I must note that the execution of Bayezid was not simply a dynastic matter as Bayezid had a considerable following and a civil war between his brother Prince Selim and him was imminent at the time the legal opinions were sought – and it eventually took place in 1559 on a battlefield around Konya. Nevertheless, by asking the opinion of jurists in a matter that essentially pertained to his family, Süleyman was offering an opportunity to them that could eventually be used to regulate the dynasty's affairs, as Es'ad was going to attempt in the early seventeenth century, which is discussed in the next chapter.

Süleyman, the sultan whose political authority invaded the sphere of jurists' law in various instances, thus also invited the representatives of this law into his own domain, which had until that time been regulated by codified Ottoman royal and feudal customs, or the *kanun*. Ebussu'ud's attempts to bring the feudal customs that constituted Ottoman land law in line with jurists' law, which also took place during the reign of Süleyman,[89] was another example of the same dynamic. As Süleyman entered the sphere of jurists' law to regulate affairs that were not part of public law, as in the case of the cash waqf controversy, he was at the same time opening up public law to the regulation of jurists. Although Ebussu'ud's attempts did not significantly alter Ottoman land law at the outset, they made it possible for jurists' law to become increasingly more involved in this area, leading to the adoption of quite different principles in Crete in the second half of the seventeenth century.[90] The Ottoman jurists thus were much more influential in politically significant issues in the long term.

Conclusion

Having established the connection between the socioeconomic transformation of the sixteenth century and the political empowerment of jurists' law at various levels, let me return to the discussion of the denunciation of the *kanun* in the late seventeenth century. This denunciation was an attempt by the dynasty to control the domain of jurists' law. Erasing the *kanun* from legal discourse by royal decree was not meant to be a concession against "ulema mentality," as Barkan represents it. It was rather an attempt to claim a different type of legitimacy for the dynasty that would be anchored completely in the sphere of jurists' law, thus pulling the carpet out from under the feet of the ulema who took their authority from their competence in jurists' law. Feyzullah's unprecedented high profile during the reign of Mustafa II, who issued the royal decree denouncing the *kanun*, was similarly not a symbol of the "ulema

---

[88] These opinions are reproduced in Şerafettin Turan, *Kanuni Süleyman Dönemi Taht Kavgaları*, 2nd ed. (Ankara: Bilgi, 1997), 180–2.
[89] See Imber, *Ebu's-su'ud*, 137.   [90] See Greene, "An Islamic Experiment?"

mentality" in political authority. To the contrary, Mustafa II was entering into an alliance with a competent jurist who supported the sultan's absolutism and could thus facilitate the expansion of the role played by the dynasty in the articulation of jurists' law that was crucial for controlling the affairs of the ruling class.

The close relationship between the expansion of the ruling class and the royal authority's claim to the entire sphere of the law to enable itself to keep controlling that class was most apparent in the timing of the stark denunciation of the *kanun* in 1696. A year earlier, in 1695, the Ottoman administration had adopted the "life-term revenue tax farm (*malikane muqata'a*) [that] was a contract on state revenues which gave the tax contractor rights to collect taxes on the basis of established rates from the time of the award until the contractor's death."[91] At the outset, any Ottoman subject, whether *askeri* or *re'aya*, could enter the bidding process for a *malikane* and actually come to own it. Although eligibility to bid came to be restricted with certain qualifications after 1714, any Ottoman who had the financial means could still enter the business of running a life-long tax-farm through subleasing or be involved in it by financing the prepayment. A large number of people who had no official position in the state administration had actually been involved in these activities since the second half of the sixteenth century. But now they were being guaranteed life-long membership in the ruling class. To safeguard the interests of the ruling class and, more importantly, to keep its hegemonic position within it, the dynasty had to be able to manipulate all areas of the law, and not just the administrative law. The limited sphere of the *kanun* was not sufficient for that goal; hence, the full-fledged claim on the Sharia in 1696. Yet the 1703 rebellion and the deposition of Mustafa II made it clear that the dynasty could neither have a monopoly on the articulation of the law nor keep controlling the ruling class.

During the eighteenth century, the political authority centered at the court recognized that it had lost its bid for absolute control of the newly enlarged ruling class and contented itself with being the main representative of it; at this point the early modern Ottoman state actually became stronger because it learned to rule by consensus rather than imposing the dynasty's will, as elaborated on in Chapter 6. The eighteenth century was going to be the century of the *a'yan*, or local notables, who came to develop a considerable degree of local political autonomy in the regions they were established in.[92] While the *a'yan* represented the state in their regions, the state legitimized the satisfaction of the interests of the *a'yan* who benefited from life-long tax-farms. Another relevant event to complete this picture is the end of the *devşirme*, the levy of Christian children who after their compulsory conversion came to staff

---

[91] Ariel Salzmann, "An ancien régime revisited: 'Privatization' and political economy in the eighteenth-century Ottoman Empire," *Politics & Society* 21 (1993): 393–423, at 401.

[92] Dina Rizk Khoury, "The Ottoman centre versus provincial power-holders: An analysis of the historiography," in *The Cambridge History of Turkey*, vol. 3: *The Later Ottoman Empire, 1603–1839*, ed. Suraiya N. Faroqhi (Cambridge: Cambridge University Press, 2006), 135–56.

the central armies and the administration of the empire; this occurred around 1703.

The rise of local notables, the practical alienation of taxable resources to private third parties, and the loss of the royal prerogative in choosing conscripts for the imperial elite symbolized the victory of social forces over the dynasty and its allies. A new ruling class – most members of which had not distinguished themselves in military prowess – had effectively replaced the feudal elite of the provinces and the slave elite of the imperial center, both of which had been involved with military conquests. In contrast, the new ruling class was made up of men who knew how to make money in the market or who owed their success to such men in their retinue. The state was now theirs to run. As is well known, market relations were primarily organized by jurists' law. It is not surprising, then, that jurists' law became more and more important during the Second Empire. The rising political profile of jurists' law and its interpreters, the jurists themselves, should be analyzed within these parameters, and not in terms of an anachronistic opposition between secular and religious law. As Abou-El-Haj points out, the tension between the *kanun* and Sharia is "social in origin."[93]

[93] Rifa'at A. Abou-El-Haj, "Power and Social Order: The uses of the *kanun*," in *The Ottoman City and Its Parts: Urban Structure and Social Order*, eds. Irene A. Bierman, Rifa'at A. Abou-El-Haj, and Donald Preziosi (New Rochelle, NY: Aristide D. Caratzas, 1991), 77.

- Soldier were Paid in Cash
- money System was unified
- winning became more Cash based
- Jurist law allowed for a building of wealth.

CHAPTER 2

The question of succession

Bringing the dynasty under legal supervision

On December 8, 1617, the English resident ambassador Paul Pindar wrote the following to the British secretary of state from Istanbul:[1]

Righte Honble

Maie it please you with occasion of an extraordinarie dispatche from the Venice Bailo, the 12th of this moneth, I wrott a breefe advertizem^te unto your honor, to informe of the death of the late Gr. S.^r [Grand Seignior] Sultan Achmet, and the succeeding of his Brother in the Empier, whoo the same daie was proclaymed, named Sultan Mustapha, being of the Age of 23 yeares, whereof he hath spente 14 in close keeping, and in confine wall feare, and expectacon of stranglinge according to the custome of theis Ottoman princes, and now *contrarie to all former coorses wth out anie precedente* is come to the Empire, and yett 5 sonnes of the deceased lyeinge, the oldest beinge 13 the second 11 yeares oulde.

Let me draw your attention to the italicized phrase, *contrarie to all former coorses wth out anie precedente*. In the more than three hundred years since the Ottoman dynasty began its rule around 1300, a sultan had never been succeeded by his brother. On the contrary, when a sultan died, his sons, who were often granted governorships in the provinces, fought each other to succeed their father. Once one of them overcame the others, he would make sure that all of his brothers were killed. In the sixteenth century, these brother wars were waged even while their fathers were still reigning as sultan, as exemplified by Prince Selim's fights against his brothers in the early sixteenth century during the reign of Bayezid II, as well as his namesake Prince Selim's fight against Prince Bayezid in the mid-sixteenth century during the reign of Süleyman. Brother wars ceased in the late sixteenth century because by that time only a single prince, the oldest one, served as governor in the provinces while others remained in the imperial palace. Yet the end of the wars of brothers did not bring about an end to fratricide. Upon his accession to the throne in 1574, Murad III executed all five of his younger brothers, who were living in the palace. In 1595 Mehmed III, who had nineteen brothers, did the same.

[1] NA, SP 97/7, f. 174a; emphasis is mine.

In 1603, however, when Ahmed I acceded to the throne, he did not kill his younger brother Mustafa, who eventually succeeded him in 1617. Exceptional as it was, this practice became the general rule of Ottoman succession, and the Ottoman throne came to belong to the eldest male member of the family, whether or not he was the son of the former sultan. As a result, Ottoman sultans could no longer assert that they had proved themselves in a fight to assume the throne; they were now "seated" on the throne simply by virtue of being the eldest surviving male of the family.

This significant revision in the Ottoman practice of succession was principally the work of a jurist, Sa'deddinzade Es'ad, the grand mufti, who carried jurists' law right into the heart of Ottoman dynastic succession, thus attempting to bring the very institution of the sultanate under legal supervision. Es'ad's tenure as grand mufti came at a time when the upper ranks of the Ottoman judiciary, the *mevali* or lords of the law,[2] had evolved into a sort of aristocracy that acquired a great deal of political capital through their networks of power and the increasing political significance of the law they represented. In this chapter I argue that Es'ad's power, which stemmed both from his position among the lords of the law and the political weight of his office, which represented the highest authority to interpret jurists' law, brought about the survival of Mustafa during his elder brother's reign and then his subsequent enthronement.

This peaceful succession was a major victory for the constitutionalists, whose goal was to secure the supremacy of the law over the dynasty. Es'ad's role as a king-maker and the political empowerment of the lords of the law, the *mevali*, were made possible by the rise of the political profile of jurists' law; in turn, this rise was made possible by the demise of the *kanun* and other feudal institutions, such as the timar and the cadastral surveys, as a market-oriented network of social relations developed in the empire. It was within this larger context that the most profound Ottoman political struggles shifted from military confrontations around competitions for succession to debates about the source of legitimate authority in public law, especially as it pertained to the dynasty and the limits of royal authority.

Arguably, the most significant legal-political debate of the early modern Ottoman Empire was not between the *kanun* and jurists' law as such, but rather between the absolutist and constitutionalist positions which had the authority to articulate public law. This chapter starts with a map of the Ottoman polity on which these two positions are placed. In the second part, I focus on the political significance of the office of the grand mufti – the leader of the lords of the law – in general, and of Es'ad and his family in particular. I argue that when Es'ad became a king-maker in 1617, this was a major step in bringing the Ottoman dynasty under legal supervision, a victory for the constitutionalists.

Big Chain

[2] Tezcan, "The Ottoman *mevâlî*."

Absolutists and constitutionalists

Let me confess at the outset that the two political groups – the absolutists and the constitutionalists – did not exist as such in the seventeenth-century Ottoman Empire and are my invention. Yet, in his history of China, R. Bin Wong asks whether the linguistic absence of certain notions should imply their historical absence as well.[3] The answer to this question must be no. The Ottomans never talked about "patriarchal family structures" or "gender," yet the predominant family structure of the period was patriarchal, and issues of gender played a major role in Ottoman society and politics. Similarly, although not a single contemporary Ottoman man or woman used the terms "absolutist" or "constitutionalist," it is possible to delineate two distinct political positions in the late sixteenth and seventeenth centuries with regard to Ottoman royal authority and its limits. The first position – absolutist – is based on the idea that public law, the law that defines how the Ottoman polity is supposed to function, recognizes the royal prerogative, a sovereign right with no restrictions. The second position is built upon the denial of such an unlimited source of authority to the sultan; it is constitutionalist for it aims at limiting the royal prerogative by strengthening the power of the law. Although the political agents whom I call constitutionalists may have had different ideas about the constitutional features of the Ottoman polity, their common interest in limiting the royal prerogative constitutes sufficient ground to bring them under the same umbrella. The struggle between these two political positions may be better understood in the context of other legal-political discussions that have been better studied in modern Ottoman historiography.

Three significant political questions were raised – explicitly or implicitly – about public law in the late sixteenth century at the dawn of the Second Empire. The first two have received a lot of scholarly attention in the twentieth century. The first question is about the connection of public law with sociopolitical change. Should the law be liberal and thus adapt itself to social change, acknowledging the expansion of the Ottoman political nation by recognizing the new members of the political elite? Or should the law be conservative and arrest social change, keeping political privileges in the hands of those who hold them because of their inherited status as members of the Ottoman imperial institution of rule?[4] The second question concerns the proper relationship between the divine and the worldly in the making of public law, which may

---

[3] R. Bin Wong, *China Transformed: Historical Change and the Limits of European Experience* (Ithaca: Cornell University Press, 1997), 5.

[4] The conservative answer to this question is a common theme of the Ottoman *nasihatname* (book of advice) genre; Douglas Howard, "Ottoman historiography and the literature of 'decline' of the sixteenth and seventeenth centuries," *Journal of Asian History* 22 (1988): 52–77, at 62; Pál Fodor, "State and society, crisis and reform, in 15th-17th century Ottoman mirror for princes," *Acta Orientalia Academiae Scientiarum Hungaricae* 40 (1986): 217–40, at 239.

also be read as a question of legal authority, of who is authorized to articulate what the law is. Is it the jurist who is competent to interpret the divine intention or an administrator of the imperial institution of rule who collects local and royal traditions?[5] The third question, although it has received less scholarly attention, may be the most significant one politically: can a ruler change the law at will, or is he bound by the existing laws in such a way that he is not capable of changing them?

Looking at these three questions in interaction is very instructive. Although the last one is fundamental for the political struggle that I cast between the absolutists and the constitutionalists, it is very important to understand the first question in order to realize that the two sides – the absolutists and the constitutionalists – did not correspond to conservatives and liberals: it is possible to find representatives of each current of thought in each group. The interaction of the second question with the first and third reminds us that the divine could be co-opted by mutually exclusive sociopolitical projects as demonstrated later in this chapter.

I start with the first question about the relationship between law and social change, because the conservative response – that the law should arrest social change – had such a negative impact on our understanding of the late sixteenth and seventeenth centuries that, until recently, it was almost impossible to study this period without presupposing the existence of decline. For the sake of simplicity, I first set aside the law that is believed to be divinely inspired – that is jurists' law – and deal with its worldly counterpart, the *kanun*; I introduce the question of the divine only after I focus on the differences between the conservative and liberal positions in how they conceive of the *kanun*.

The word *kanun*, which in modern Turkish has the meaning of law, had quite different connotations in the mid-sixteenth century. Its more common usage then was in the sense of "habitual practice, customary procedure or action." In more formal settings it could mean "permissible, lawful, legal," or "regulation."[6] This cluster of meanings suggests that the basis of the legality of a *kanun* was custom. This seemed to be the case even for the regulations compiled by Ottoman officials, the *kanunnames*. Ömer Lutfi Barkan, the most eminent scholar of the sixteenth-century Ottoman *kanuns*, states that "determining the real age of various rules of Ottoman *kanuns*, and thus understanding when they became effective, becomes a quite difficult task. However much earlier we go back in time, we find ourselves in the depths of a law of customs and precedence which is always based on an older tradition." As an example, Barkan points out the possible relationship between the abolition of a certain

[5] This question has been discussed mostly in the context of criminal law; see Uriel Heyd, *Kānūn and Sharī'a in Old Ottoman Criminal Justice* (Jerusalem: Israel Academy of Sciences and Humanities, 1967), 15; and Heyd, *Studies*, 180–3.
[6] Tezcan, "The Kânûnnâme of Mehmed II," 658–60.

practice in the *kanunname* of Ankara district from 929/1522–3 and a similar proclamation found on an inscription in Kırşehir, not too far from Ankara, dating from the late thirteenth century.[7] However, the trouble with customs is that just as they are "always immemorial," they may also be "perfectly up-to-date," a point made by J. G. A. Pocock.[8] That is to say, customs change as the society that produces them changes. A mid-sixteenth-century political tract, for instance, announced that "old customs are not useful for the people of these days," where "customs" could well be read as "*kanuns*."[9] The Ottoman *kanun* was open to change, and it did change. For instance, take the question of who could be granted a fief. It is quite possible to find during the reign of the same sultan two contradictory orders on the same issue. An order from 1530 declared that commoners were the subjects of the sultan in the same way as were the members of the elite, so they could well be granted fiefs. This order also forbid to refer to them as "outsiders" from then on – commoners had been called "outsiders (*ecnebis*)" by the members of the ruling elite because they were outside the circles from which the ruling elite were drawn, such as the *devşirme* and the descendants of the conquerors.[10] Fourteen years later, yet another order from the same reign, however, prohibited the granting of fiefs to "outsiders."[11]

It had probably been customary practice to grant fiefs only to the members of the *askeri*, the Ottoman privileged class the members of which included the offspring of old noble families and early Ottoman conquerors, as well as *devşirmes*. However, the rules of entering this class were in flux during the sixteenth century in parallel with the monetization of the Ottoman economy and the translation of monetary wealth into political power. Thus one could well find those who bought their way into the Ottoman gentry by becoming tax-farmers and securing fiefs for themselves in return.[12] This would be the "perfectly up-to-date" custom that reflected the changes in society. Yet one could also find strong reactions to such newcomers from among the old elite, who understood the rules that governed access to the privileged class as a custom that had not changed since time immemorial and should never change. The field of customary law, then, became a battlefield to determine what the "real" custom was.

---

[7] Barkan, *Kanunlar*, lxvi.

[8] J. G. A. Pocock, *The Ancient Constitution and the Feudal Law: A Study of English Historical Thought in the Seventeenth Century: A Reissue with a Retrospect* (Cambridge: Cambridge University Press, 1987), 15.

[9] Anonymous, "Kitâbu mesâlihi'l-Müslimîn ve menâfi'i'l-mü'minîn," in *Osmanlı Devlet Teşkilâtına Dair Kaynaklar*, 115; compare the usage of *kanun* with that of *adet*, 93, 111, 118, 120–1.

[10] Akgündüz, *Osmanlı Kanunnâmeleri*, vol. IV, 564.

[11] Ibid., vol. VI, 349–50. For another example of changing *kanuns*, see Selaniki Mustafa, *Tarihi Selânikî*, ed. Mehmed İpşirli, 2 vols. (Istanbul: İstanbul Üniversitesi Edebiyat Fakültesi Yayınları, 1989), vol. II, 593.

[12] Aşık Çelebi, *Mi'râcü'l-iyâle ve Minhâcü'l-'adâle*, Süleymaniye Kütüphanesi, Reisülküttab 1006, f. 146a.

One could read a large part of the political literature of the late sixteenth century as arguments for or against a particular definition of the *kanun*. Because custom was ever changing while supposedly ever the same, immemorial yet perfectly adapted to new needs, this fluidity presented a serious problem for those Ottoman writers of political tracts who opposed the entry of newcomers into the political elite. Feeling the imminent danger of losing their privileged status to some "outsiders," they argued that society consisted of classes and everyone had to know one's place. As noted by Rifa'at Ali Abou-El-Haj, the language of decline that is found in most of the late-sixteenth-and seventeenth-century political tracts was the product of this conservative attitude toward social change.[13] The conservative take on public law in the Ottoman context was that it was supposed to arrest social change by defending the boundaries between the different classes. If public law could not fulfill this function, for instance, by preventing the commoners from entering the political elite, then society would be in crisis. Indeed, conservative political tracts mostly presented the entry of commoners, the "outsiders," as the chief disaster responsible for the decline of the empire.[14] In contrast, the liberal approach found in some political literature of the period suggested that the old *kanun*s were no good for the new times.[15]

Having presented the conservative and liberal arguments on the adaptability of public law to social change, let me introduce the second question that interacts with this one; that is, the proper relationship between the divine and the worldly – or the jurist and the administrator/ruler – in the making of public law. As argued earlier, some of those who discussed the law mostly in terms of the *kanun* were liberal, at least on certain issues, and thus believed that the law needed to adapt to social change. Others were conservative and suggested that if the law was not able to arrest social change, then decline was definitely impending. A different set of writers, who approached the law mostly in terms of jurists' law, were similarly divided in their understanding of the adaptability of the law. Let me provide a conservative viewpoint.

Kınalızade Ali, a celebrated Ottoman scholar and jurist whose *Sublime Ethics (Ahlak-ı Ala'i)* was *the* most popular work among the Ottoman reading public for centuries on practical philosophy, which consists of ethics, economics – to be understood as household management – and politics, exemplified the jurist who interpreted conservatively what he believed to be the divine intention. A common denominator of many political tracts (*nasihatnames*) of the late sixteenth and seventeenth centuries, the concern about class

---

[13] Abou-El-Haj, "The Ottoman *nasihatname.*"

[14] Hasan Kafi Akhisari, "Hasan Kâfî el-Akhisarî ve devlet düzenine ait eseri *Usûlü'l-hikem fî nizâmi'l-âlem*," ed. by Mehmet İpşirli, *Tarih Enstitüsü Dergisi* 10–11 (1979–80): 239–78, at 253; Koçi Bey, *Koçi Bey Risalesi*, ed. Ali Kemali Aksüt (Istanbul: Vakıt, 1939), 38, 45; Hasanbeyzade Ahmed, *Usûlü'l-hikem fî nizâmi'l-âlem*, İstanbul Üniversitesi Kütüphanesi, T 6944, f. 4b.

[15] Tezcan, "The Kânûnnâme of Mehmed II," 661.

boundaries, was articulated in *Ahlak-ı Ala'i* in the most elaborate fashion
through the intricate relationship among ethics, economics, and politics. In the
larger scale of society, the boundaries separating different classes become a
natural extension of the boundaries between the members of the household and
those between one's three souls – the royal (rational), the savage (irascible),
and the bestial (concupiscent) souls.[16] To reach perfection and equilibrium,
both individually and socially, these boundaries had to be protected. So far
Kınalızade was not any different from more worldly conservatives who argued
the same point by using the *kanun* as the instrument of legal control for the
protection of class boundaries.

What made Kınalızade a conservative jurist – in the sense of a *divine
law*yer – as opposed to a conservative supporter of the *kanun* was his lack
of confidence in the ability of the *kanun* to keep a society in order; that is,
to maintain the political hegemony of the current political elite. He was well
aware that social life is an arena in which conflicting interests face each other
continuously. Everyone has particular desires, and everyone, "especially the
common people whose appetites are not well-refined and are marked by evil,"[17]
may pursue these individual desires without regard for others. The presence
of incompatible interests may well bring about situations in which people use
force to obtain what they want. Hence the need for a supreme government
run by a potent arbitrator or ruler. However, a potent ruler cannot guarantee
the longevity of the social order by himself. This ruler *has to* rule by divine
law. But why, one might ask, could a potent ruler not rule by a different kind
of law? How about, for instance, a potent king who lays down laws, such as
Genghis Khan and his *yasa*, or law? Kınalızade asserted that such man-made
laws inevitably pass away as the power of the state declines, as did the laws of
Genghis Khan, which disappeared after about the late 1440s. In contrast, the
divine law of Islam has been in force "for almost a thousand years."[18] Thus a
government should be based upon the law of God if it is to last. It is not hard to
see that Kınalızade invoked God's law to prevent "the common people whose
appetites are not well-refined and are marked by evil" from entering the ruling
class, a conservative cause in the late sixteenth century.[19]

Divinely inspired jurists' law, however, did not have to be conservative. Vejdi
Bilgin demonstrates in a recent study that Ottoman jurists, who legitimized
their legal opinions always in reference to divine law, actually displayed a
great degree of adaptability toward social change in the late sixteenth and
seventeenth centuries. This adaptability was evidenced in matters pertaining

---

[16] On this division and other aspects of Kınalızade's work, see Baki Tezcan, "The definition of
sultanic legitimacy in the sixteenth century Ottoman Empire: The *Ahlâk-ı Alâ'î* of Kınalızâde
Ali Çelebi (1510-1572)," MA thesis (Princeton University, 1996).

[17] Kınalızade Ali, *Ahlâk-ı 'Alâ'î* (Bulak, 1248), book II, 73.   [18] Ibid., book II, 74.

[19] Baki Tezcan, "Ethics as a domain to discuss the political: Kınalızâde Ali Efendi and his
Ahlâk-ı Alâî," in *Proceedings of the International Congress on Learning and Education in
the Ottoman World, Istanbul, 12–15 April 1999*, ed. Ali Çaksu (Istanbul: IRCICA Publications,
2001), 109–20, at 117–18.

to economic issues, whereas their prevalent attitude on family issues was conservative.[20] Thus jurists were selective in their legal attitude toward social change, which may well have been true for those Ottoman writers who worked mostly in the worldlier domain of the *kanun* as well.

The last question I mentioned at the beginning of this section is the one that occupies us throughout the rest of this study. Can a ruler change public law at will, or is he bound by the existing laws in such a way that he is not capable of changing them? A simple example that would connect this theoretical question with the Ottoman historical experience would be whether a ruler could abolish the privileges of established institutions, such as the janissaries. For instance, Osman II, as an absolutist, thought that he could; others, the constitutionalists, disagreed. For them, the sultan had certain rights and obligations that included the "protection of privileges and entitlements of those who were thought to deserve them."[21] He could not simply declare them null and void as these were foundational bonds that held the Ottoman political structures in place.

Let me emphasize again that the groups I label absolutists and constitutionalists did not dovetail with conservatives versus liberals. Thus there were both conservative and liberal constitutionalists in the sense that some supporters of the limitation of royal authority were actually interested in arresting social change, whereas others were inclined to affirm it. Similarly some conservatives supported absolutism because they believed it would help them limit the impact of social change, whereas some liberals did the same in order to encourage change. This complexity arises from the simple fact that social change produces complex results. The age of the Second Empire was marked by two closely related developments: (1) the expansion of the political nation and the subsequent tension that developed between the old elite and the new and (2) the reconfiguration of the role of the dynasty within the expanding political nation, which created the two positions of the absolutists and constitutionalists. The expansion of the political nation did not place every newcomer in the same sociopolitical space. For instance, many upwardly mobile commoners attempted to enter the provincial political elite in the late sixteenth century. However, others tried to join the elite entrenched in the imperial capital, leading to the inflation of the number of personnel of the ruling institution, which is discussed in Chapters 5 and 6. Both the commoners who joined the provincial elite and those who found a position in the imperial capital had the same objective – ensuring the confirmation of their privileged status – but at times they had to fight each other to achieve it, as in the case of the Jalali rebellions discussed in Chapter 4.

Similarly, one's particular ideas about the proper relationship between the divine and the worldly in the making of public law did not correspond to any particular place in the absolutist–constitutionalist divide. It was quite possible

[20] Bilgin, *Fakih ve Toplum*, 71–167.
[21] Boğaç A. Ergene, "On Ottoman justice: interpretations in conflict (1600–1800)," *Islamic Law and Society* 8 (2001): 52–87, at 52.

to make a case for the supremacy of jurists' law and yet allow a proper place for the royal prerogative within it, as was done frequently in the sixteenth century.[22] Alternatively, this supremacy could be constructed in such a way as to curb the sultan's authority, as was done in the military rebellions of the late sixteenth and seventeenth centuries that are analyzed in Chapters 5 and 6. Or one might construct an ancient constitution based on worldly sources of law, yet use this constitution to limit the authority of the sultan, as is discussed shortly. Finally, one could also argue that the royal prerogative is a right granted by the ancient constitution, as an Ottoman author suggested to Murad III when he claimed that for Selim I anything that a sultan did was *kanun*.[23]

The fact that the groups on either side of the absolutist–constitutionalist divide did not dovetail with those on the two sides of the debate about the proper place of the *kanun* in Ottoman law may be problematic for the secular-minded modern reader who might be conditioned to associate constitutionalism with *kanun* and absolutism with jurists' law. Yet one has to remember that the *kanun* could well be used for an absolutist project as in the autocratic policies of Mehmed II (1451–81).[24] And the Islamic tradition, from which the jurists' law originates, has been a rich source for alternative political systems from the anarchism of the early Kharijites in the seventh century to the totalitarian dictatorship of some Wahhabis in the twentieth; thus it should not be surprising that Ottoman jurists could give their support to different political projects.

What seems more troublesome was the lack of correspondence between the constitutionalists and liberals, on the one hand, and the absolutists and conservatives, on the other. After all, traditional political history has a tendency to lump such categories together, as exemplified in the description of the Whigs as constitutionalist liberals. Yet we do know, for instance, that much before the rise of the Whigs as a group, the royalist and antiroyalist forces of the English Civil War were not divided along class lines, which would have facilitated an argument for the liberal upwardly mobile gentry supporting the antiroyalists and the conservative wealthy peers defending the royalty. Although more peers joined the royalists, some did join the antiroyalists, and others were neutrals or turncoats.[25] According to one historian, "[t]he gentry were equally divided, without any clearly marked divisions on lines of wealth."[26] Had Oliver Cromwell not been on the losing side of a political struggle between two factions in his home town of Huntingdon in 1630, he might have continued to hold office there and could well have been a royalist during the Civil War, instead of beheading Charles I whose father James I was frequently entertained

---

[22] Bilgin, *Fakih ve Toplum*, 111–23.

[23] Anonymous, "Hırzü'l-mülûk," in *Osmanlı Devlet Teşkilâtına Dair Kaynaklar*, 175.

[24] Halil İnalcık, "Mehemmed II," *Encyclopedia of Islam, New Edition*, vol. VI, 978–81.

[25] Lawrence Stone, *The Crisis of the Aristocracy, 1558–1641*, abridged ed. (London: Oxford University Press, 1967), 353.

[26] Lawrence Stone, *The Causes of the English Revolution, 1529–1642*, 2nd ed. (London: Routledge, 1986), 55.

by his uncle and namesake, Oliver Cromwell, the "Golden Knight."[27] If one's support of a particular party in the Civil War was not a derivative of one's class or social standing, how could we be sure that it was a product of one's ideas pertaining to social change?

The absence of a perfect correspondence between such categories as constitutionalists and liberals, on the one hand, and absolutists and conservatives, on the other, does not, however, mean that the struggle between the absolutists and the constitutionalists was simply a power struggle among the Ottoman elite without any connection to social change. Failing to recognize this significant distinction may lead one to dismiss the seventeenth-century rebellions in the Ottoman Empire as merely an expression of elite infighting. The socioeconomic changes that took place in the Ottoman Empire throughout the late fifteenth and sixteenth centuries led to the development of a new social group, which consisted of people who were successful both in using the monetization of the economy to their own advantage and in translating this economic advantage to political status by demanding, for instance, that tax-farming should be rewarded by *askeri* status. The entry of such newcomers into the political elite in the late sixteenth century led to the expansion of the political nation. It was these new players who challenged the political domination of the old elite and forced its members either to form alliances with them or to take an active stance against them. At the end, the political struggle took place along the boundaries of royal authority between parties that included members of both the old and the new elite. Thus, as is demonstrated in some detail in the following chapters, the struggle was brought about by the socioeconomic forces that forged the new elite in the first place.

Having made all the necessary qualifications, it is time to focus on how the constitutionalist case was made by one of its most eloquent defenders, Mustafa Âli,[28] against Murad III, the sultan who instigated a number of projects with absolutist agendas. Murad III was keen on changing the role of the sultan on the Ottoman political stage. When he came to Istanbul to succeed his father Selim II, very late on Tuesday night, December 21, 1574, he almost kissed the hand of Sokollu Mehmed Pasha, who, as grand vizier for the past nine years, had nearly controlled the empire all by himself.[29] Sokollu's powerful grip on politics was not lost on Murad III's consultants. The anonymous author of the *Castle of Kings*, for instance, urged the sultan to take the initiative in making appointments to the imperial administrative and bureaucratic structures:

The pleasure of the sultanate is in bestowing [offices]. Since quite a few years bestowal [of offices] has left [the domain of] the sultans and fallen under the control of the grand viziers. For today all offices are given to those who are protégés of the grand vizier and put forward

[27] Peter Gaunt, *Oliver Cromwell* (Oxford: Blackwell, 1996), 31–2; Pauline Gregg, *Oliver Cromwell* (London: J. M. Dent, 1988), 4–5.
[28] On this figure, see Fleischer, *Bureaucrat and Intellectual.*
[29] İbrahim Peçevi, *Ta'rîh-i Peçevî*, 2 vols. (Istanbul, 1281–83), vol. I, 26–8; see Chapter 3, 97–8.

by him [for office]. Thus those who get an office are under the impression that all power of disposal [over] appointments and dismissals is in the hands of the grand vizier. Under these circumstances, those who are appointed to a post feel they must not act against his consent, and must follow his orders, whether good or evil.[30]

The sultan did follow these suggestions and started to use his own discretion in making appointments. Instead of letting his viziers run the imperial network of clients, Murad III attempted to control the reins himself. At some point in 1580, he even entertained the idea of dispensing altogether with the office of the grand vizier.[31] Murad III's tendency toward absolute control led his critics, such as Mustafa Âli and Selaniki, to complain about his accepting bribes, making many appointments personally, and not leaving the viziers and the jurists any independence.[32] Murad III later came to be remembered as the sultan during whose reign respect for the *kanun* disappeared and the decline of the empire started.[33]

The significance of the reign of Murad III in the construction of the Ottoman decline narrative cannot be overstated. Many contemporary accounts as well as several modern studies have identified either 1574, the year of his accession to the Ottoman throne, or 1579, when Sokollu Mehmed Pasha was assassinated, leading to Murad III's more direct control of state affairs, as the beginning of the empire's degeneration or decline. Murad III's personal style of government, the increasing influence of royal women and palace officials in imperial government during his reign, the sale of offices, and even his character traits are invoked in the literature to make a case for his responsibility for the Ottoman decline.[34]

Clearly, Murad III was attempting to change the way the empire was run. All the complaints made about his ruling style add up to a portrait of a monarch who wanted to have absolute control of his empire from within the walls of his palace; hence, my suggestion that one can talk about absolutism and absolutists in the late sixteenth century. Obviously, the palace had been a very significant center for imperial administration before Murad III. However, as described in Chapter 3, the patrimonial rule of Süleyman was to a large extent based on the delegation of authority to military slaves. Murad III, in contrast, came to suspect most of them.[35]

It was in response to Murad III's absolutist political projects that authors such as Mustafa Âli made an attempt to anchor the concept of *kanun* in more stable ground than the elusive field of custom and then to fortify it with legal

[30] Anonymous, "Hırzü'l-Mülûk," 188.   [31] Selaniki, *Tarih*, vol. I, 128.
[32] Ibid., vol. II, 427–8, 431–2; Fleischer, *Bureuacrat and Intellectual*, 296.
[33] Mehmet Öz, *Osmanlı'da "Çözülme" ve Gelenekçi Yorumcuları* (Istanbul: Dergah, 1997), 63 [n. 28], 69.
[34] For a contemporary account, see Fleischer, *Bureuacrat and Intellectual*, 300; for a modern study, see Yaşar Yücel and Ali Sevim, *Türkiye Tarihi*, 4 vols. (Ankara: Türk Tarih Kurumu, 1990–92), vol. III, 32.
[35] Murad III's absolutist policies are discussed further in Chapter 3.

perfection so that its alteration would become a sacrilege. One such ground could be the legislation of a founding father, a man who conquered the land and laid down its laws once and for all. Who would be a better candidate for this role than Mehmed II, known as "The Conqueror"? Some already regarded Mehmed II as the founder of several Ottoman institutions. For instance, in Idrīs Bidlīsī's Persian work of history, *Hasht Bihisht* (the Eight Paradises), which covered the reigns of the first eight Ottoman sultans (Osman through Bayezid II), a section was devoted to the military organization of the empire at the beginning of its account of the reign of Mehmed II.[36] Mustafa Âli seemed to have been inspired by this section, yet what he wrote went far beyond Bidlīsī's presentation. In his major world history entitled the *Essence of History*, Âli created in the person of Mehmed II a founding father of Ottoman laws that could be regarded as once-and-for-all enactments. Mustafa Âli did this by devoting a lengthy section in his account of the reign of Mehmed II to the organization of the higher Ottoman administration, right after describing the conquest of Constantinople and the sultan's construction activities in his new capital. Thus he created the impression that Mehmed II conquered the city that became the capital of the empire, built the imperial palace and a number of major mosques that turned the city into a Muslim capital, and then laid down the laws of his state.[37]

Mustafa Âli kept working on this historical portrait and revisited the topic in a later work in which he buttressed the argument for the impeccable Ottoman laws legislated by Mehmed II. In this work, he narrated a conversation that Mehmed II was supposed to have had with his grand vizier Mahmud Pasha. After stating that Mehmed II and his vizier Mahmud Pasha laid down the *kanun-ı kadim* (the ancient constitution), Âli wrote that Mehmed II asked Mahmud Pasha what could possibly destroy their kingdom:

Mahmud Paşa answered, "Only the Eternal King does not pass away. However, among poor earthly rulers there is no path surer or firmer than this *kanun* we have established. Despite its strength, there are still two ways in which the kingdom and state could be destroyed. One is the case in which one of your noble descendants might not observe the *kanun*, saying that *kanun* is whatever he decrees. The second way [of destruction] is the entry of unauthorized [*ecnebi*] people into the military, which will destroy the order of the servitors [*kul*] of the state.[38]

As far as I know, this conversation, which would have had to take place before Mahmud Pasha died in 1474, is not to be found in any source until Âli recorded it some time around 1598.

---

[36] Idrīs Bidlīsī, *Hasht bihisht*, Nuruosmaniye Kütüphanesi 3209, ff. 358a–364b.
[37] This part of the *Essence of History* is available in a critical edition by M. Hüdai Şentürk, *Künhü'l-ahbār, c. II: Fātih Sultān Mehmed devri, 1451–1481* (Ankara: Türk Tarih Kurumu, 2003), 9–103.
[38] Translated by Fleischer, *Bureuacrat and Intellectual*, 178.

Quite significantly, Âli attributed to Mehmed II social conservatism – that is, opposition to the entry of commoners into the elite – in parallel with constitutionalism, which was meant to tie the hands of the sultan vis-à-vis the law. As suggested earlier, it was the entry of a new social group into the ruling elite that had started the political struggles between the absolutists and the constitutionalists. It is not a coincidence that this presentation of the *kanun* as an unchanging law enacted once and for all by an ideal sultan, the Conqueror, came at the conclusion of a work that started with an introduction giving special emphasis to the execution of regulations on fixed prices.[39] After all, commercial and financial activities were the forces creating a new group of commoners who, using their economic power, were buying the privileged status of an *asker*, a member of the Ottoman political elite. To close the doors of legitimacy on these new practices, which could well assume the status of law had the *kanun* kept its elusive nature associated with custom, the *kanun* had to be frozen so that even future sultans could not change it. That was what Âli did in his presentation of Mehmed II as the founder of Ottoman *kanun*s, which he made sure to portray as definitive constants. In Âli's presentation, it was Murad III who was really responsible for the alterations in the ancient constitution; thus his constitutionalist critique of Murad III's absolutism coexisted with a conservative attitude toward social change.

Mustafa Âli's construction of Mehmed II as the founder of Ottoman laws was so successful that many later scholars assumed that the historian actually had seen the document known as the "*Kanunname* of Mehmed II," or the "Law-Book of Mehmed II."[40] This document is a collection of regulations that mainly governed issues related to precedence and promotion within the higher levels of the state administration. It was thought to have been produced during the last years of the reign of Mehmed II, who died in 1481. Yet as argued elsewhere, a comparison of the relevant section in the work of Mustafa Âli with the "Law-Book" suggests that he had not seen it.[41] What is interesting, however, is that Mustafa Âli's construction of Mehmed II as the founder of Ottoman law became a successful project. The oldest extant copy of the "Law-Book of Mehmed II" dates from the early seventeenth century, almost 150 years after its supposed production. Whether or not the document is a forgery,[42] it only became relevant after Mehmed II was successfully constructed as the founder of Ottoman laws by Mustafa Âli and his likes.

Mustafa Âli was not alone in making a case for founding fathers and the unalterable nature of the laws enacted by them. Earlier during the reign of Murad III, an anonymous translator produced a Turkish translation of the

[39] Mustafa Âli, *Fusûl-i hall u 'akd fî usûl-i harc u nakd*, Princeton University, Islamic Manuscripts MS 106B, f. 2b.
[40] See, for instance, Abdülkadir Özcan, ed., *Fatih Sultan Mehmed: Kânunnâme-i Âl-i Osman (Tahlil ve Karşılaştırmalı Metin)* (Istanbul: Kitabevi, 2003), xxxv.
[41] Tezcan, "The Kânûnnâme of Mehmed II," 658.
[42] There is not enough evidence to pass conclusive judgment on this question; ibid., 662–3, n. 1–3.

Book of China, a Persian work of the early sixteenth century by ʿAlī Akbar. Although the *Book of China* had a certain emphasis on the notion of law, the Turkish translation, tellingly entitled the *Law-Book of China*, made this emphasis the center of the work, arguing that Chinese rulers cannot change their ancient laws even one iota. Should they try doing so, they would be deposed.[43] As it happens, the *Essence of History*, the work of world history in which Mustafa Âli constructed Mehmed II as the founder of Ottoman laws, described, among other things, the history of China. His section on China was based to a large extent on the *Book of China* and included a reference to the custom of deposing rulers who did not abide by their laws,[44] which was much more of an Ottoman construct than a Chinese tradition. The anonymous translator of the *Law-Book of China* and Mustafa Âli were equally impressed by the emphasis on law that they found in the China that ʿAlī Akbar created.[45] The *Law-Book of China*, which was translated around 1582; the *Essence of History*, which Mustafa Âli wrote in the 1590s; and the "Law-Book of Mehmed II," which started to circulate around the beginning of the early seventeenth century, are examples of the constitutionalist trend in Ottoman politics, which was to have a powerful impact on dynastic traditions in the early seventeenth century.[46]

Circumscribing dynastic traditions by legal principles

Arguably the most significant constitutional issue in any monarchy is the question of succession. For instance, the first and only Ottoman written constitution of 1876 addressed this issue in its third article, directly after stating in its first two articles that the Ottoman Empire is indivisible and its capital is Istanbul.[47] Therefore the change in Ottoman succession that was brought about by Sa'deddinzade Es'ad's enthronement of Mustafa I in 1617 should

---

[43] ʿAlī Akbar, *Tercüme-i Taʾrîh-i Nevâdir-i Çîn-i Mâçîn*, anonymous translation (Istanbul, 1270), 5–6; Baki Tezcan, "The multiple faces of the One: the invocation section of Ottoman literary introductions as a locus for the central argument of the text," *Middle Eastern Literatures* 12 (2009): 27–41, at 35–8.

[44] Mustafa Âli, *Künhü'l-ahbâr*, Milli Kütüphane, A 68, f. 139b; compare Akbar and anonymous, *Tercüme*, 38; ʿAlī Akbar, *Khitāy-nāme*, ed. İraj Afshār, 2nd ed. (Tehran, 1372), 93.

[45] Yih-Min Lin, the only scholar who attempted a thorough comparison of the information provided by ʿAlī Akbar with Chinese sources, believes that Akbar had probably never made it to China himself; see his *Ali Ekber'in Hitayname adlı eserinin Çin kaynakları ile mukayese ve tenkidi* (Tai-Pei, 1967).

[46] For an exploration of the literary expressions of Ottoman absolutism, see Baki Tezcan, "The politics of early modern Ottoman historiography," in *The Early Modern Ottomans: Remapping the Empire*, eds. Virginia H. Aksan and Daniel Goffman (Cambridge: Cambridge University Press, 2007), 171–80; B. Tezcan, "Law in China or conquest in the Americas: competing constructions of political space in the early modern Ottoman Empire," forthcoming in *Journal of World History*; and B. Tezcan, "Some thoughts on the politics of early modern Ottoman science," in *Beyond Dominant Paradigms in Ottoman and Middle Eastern/North African Studies: A Tribute to Rifa'at Abou-El-Haj*, eds. Donald Quataert and Baki Tezcan (Istanbul: İSAM, forthcoming).

[47] *Kânûn-ı Esâsî – Meclis-i Meb'ûsân Nizâmnâme-i Dâhiliyesi – Meclis-i A'yân Nizâmnâme-i Dâhiliyesi – İntihâb-ı Meb'ûsân Kânûnu* (Istanbul: Matba'a-ı 'Âmire, 1328), 1.

be regarded as a major constitutional development in Ottoman history, an important step toward the circumscription of dynastic authority by legal principles. In this section I briefly describe the Ottoman dynastic traditions of succession and then analyze Es'ad's enthronement of Mustafa I in the context of the growing authority ascribed to the office of the mufti at the beginning of the seventeenth century.

The survival of Prince Mustafa

Obviously, it was Prince Mustafa's survival during the reign of Ahmed I (1603–17) that made possible his enthronement upon the death of his brother. For those who are not familiar with traditional means of Ottoman succession, the survival of a younger brother during the reign of his elder brother may not seem to be a significant fact. Yet the royal custom of Ottoman rulers had been to kill all their brothers because, in the words of Leslie Peirce, all princes regardless of their age were legitimate "candidates for the throne, no matter how slim the odds of their becoming sultan."[48] Thus fratricidal wars were a regular feature of Ottoman history, especially in the fifteenth and sixteenth centuries – for instance, there were wars between the sons of Bayezid I, Mehmed II, Bayezid II, and Süleyman I.

Acquiring the throne at the end of a fatal competition functioned as an ordeal for Ottoman princes that determined the one who had the divine mandate to rule. Halil İnalcık traces the importance of this divine mandate to rule to Central Asia where Turkish rulers would attribute their position to divine grace and their personal *kut*, which may be translated as auspiciousness, fortune, luck, and felicity. Not surprisingly, the Arabic word *dawla*, which is related to change and rotation and evolved to have the meaning of "state" in Arabic, Persian, and Turkish (*devlet*), has the same range of connotations in the sense of representing a turn of fortune. Thus the *devlet* of a certain Ottoman prince was both his fortune and his turn in political power; the two were inseparable. If he did not have *devlet* in the sense of fortune, he would not have his turn in power either. In a sense, then, in a fratricidal struggle, princes would be testing each other's fortunes, an act for which there is even an idiomatic expression in Turkish, *devlet sınaşmak*, literally, testing one another's *devlet*. For example, the inhabitants of Edirne in the early fifteenth century demanded such a test when two Ottoman princes claimed sovereignty over the city, which was the Ottoman capital at the time. Whoever proved to have *devlet* on his side would take control of the state capital.[49] The sacred connotations of such a charismatic source of authority should be obvious.

---

[48] Peirce, *Imperial Harem*, 96.
[49] Halil İnalcık, "The Ottoman succession and its relation to the Turkish concept of sovereignty," tr. Douglas Howard, in H. İnalcık, *The Middle East and the Balkans under the Ottoman Empire: Essays on Economy and Society* (Bloomington: Indiana University Turkish Studies, 1993), 37–69; Ömer Asım Aksoy and Dehri Dilçin, *Tarama Sözlüğü*, 8 vols. (Ankara: Türk Dil Kurumu, 1963–77), vol. V, 3434; Mehmed Neşri, *Kitâb-ı Cihan-nümâ*, vol. II, 509.

After the establishment of the rule of seniority, however, Ottoman princes no longer had to prove their *devlet*; they just had to wait their turn, which did not leave much room for imagining a sacred source of authority or ascribing charisma. In contrast to the earlier practice in which they would serve in a provincial governorship that would both prepare them for the sultanate by providing some experience in government and offer them an opportunity to build a following, all princes were now kept in the imperial palace. The caliber of teachers assigned to their education fell dramatically, and they were denied mobility outside the residential part of the palace where they had to live in an apartment that came to be known as the "cage," or *kafes*.[50] Not surprisingly, the Ottoman dynasty produced much weaker sultans in this period. Although many a historian identified this weakness as one of the reasons for the Ottoman decline,[51] its political implication, that is, leaving more room for other actors in the polity and thereby implicitly limiting royal power, has not been adequately explored.[52]

This shift – from a race that was open to all princes and only ended when one undisputed winner murdered all of his brethren, to the rule of seniority – did not happen overnight. After the Ottoman civil war between Princes Bayezid and Selim during the later years of the reign of Süleyman, only one Ottoman prince, who became practically the crown prince, remained in the provinces during the reigns of Selim II (1566–74) and Murad III (1574–95). However, Murad III in 1574 and Mehmed III in 1595 still murdered their brothers. Why then did not Ahmed I order the execution of his younger brother Mustafa?

Elsewhere, I suggest that Prince Mustafa survived the accession of his brother most probably because their father had died too young. Ahmed I became sultan at the age of thirteen, thus risking the continuation of the Ottoman dynastic line. Mustafa was left alive during the early years of Ahmed I's reign because, first, even though Ahmed fathered two sons within almost a year, his sons were too young to ensure the dynasty's future, and second, Mustafa was most probably much younger than it is generally assumed and thus did not present a serious political threat. Yet his survival during the last years of Ahmed I's reign after the sultan's sons had become teenagers and Mustafa had grown into adulthood is another matter that needs further consideration.[53] One wonders, for instance, whether Ahmed could have

---

[50] Tezcan, "Searching for Osman," 189, 373–4; Aga Dede, *Ta'rîh-nâme*, Gazi Husrev-begova Biblioteka, R-9724, 34.
[51] Bernard Lewis, "Some reflections on the decline of the Ottoman Empire," *Studia Islamica* 9 (1958): 111–27, at 112–13.
[52] For a significant exception, see Abou-El-Haj, *The 1703 Rebellion*, 12.
[53] Baki Tezcan, "The debut of Kösem Sultan's political career," *Turcica* 40 (2008): 347–59; for the limits of the case made there, see Tezcan, "Searching for Osman," 98; for new evidence on Mustafa's age, see Günhan Börekçi, "İnkırâzın eşiğinde bir hanedan: III. Mehmed, I. Ahmed, I. Mustafa ve 17. yüzyıl Osmanlı siyasî krizi," *Dîvân: Disiplinlerarası Çalışmalar Dergisi* 14/26 (2009): 45–96.

considered his brother as a successor to himself as some European contemporaries claimed in their explanation of Mustafa's succession in 1617.[54]

The ultimate source for the dynastic history of the reign of Ahmed I was Mustafa Safi, the sultan's imam, or prayer leader. In his writings, Safi never mentioned the name of Mustafa, thus practically denying his existence.[55] Although he did refer to princes in general a few times while describing some of the trips undertaken by Ahmed, Safi only once mentioned their names in a public ceremony: in February 1614, while Ahmed was about to enter Istanbul on his return trip from Edirne, he ordered that the princes Osman and Mehmed be mounted on horses.[56] Thus the public, probably for the first time, got an opportunity to see the sons of Ahmed riding horses. But what is more important to note was the absence of the name of Mustafa at this point. Moreover, although all of the extant Venetian reports from the reign of Ahmed talked about his brother, they never mentioned his name. Though the public knew that a brother of the sultan was alive,[57] Ahmed did nothing to present him as his successor. Therefore it might be safe to conclude that, as far as Ahmed was concerned, his younger brother Mustafa was not a real option for succession.

However, we do not know whether Ahmed could easily have gotten away with executing Mustafa, had he decided to do so. When Murad III and Mehmed III ordered the execution of their brothers at the time of their respective accessions, these acts were seen as unfortunate but still in line with Ottoman tradition.[58] Yet when Osman II decided to execute his younger brother Mehmed before leaving the capital for a military campaign in 1621, he apparently could not secure an affirmative legal opinion from the grand mufti and then asked for one from the chief justice of the European provinces, who granted it.[59] What is significant is not simply that the mufti declined to justify the execution; more importantly, an Ottoman sultan had to ask for an affirmative legal opinion to execute his brother. Apparently in the early seventeenth century fratricide was no longer regarded as a basic custom of the Ottoman dynasty that the sultans

[54] Richard Knolles and Edward Grimston, *The General Historie of the Turkes*, 3rd ed. (London: Adam Islip, 1621), 1372; anonymous, "The strangling and death of the Great Turk," reprint of the original edition of July 15, 1622, with revised spelling in *The Harleian Miscellany*, vol. 4 (London, 1745), 34.

[55] In contrast, Ahmed's elder brothers, who had died before Ahmed was enthroned, are mentioned; Mustafa Safi, *Mustafa Sâfî'nin Zübdetü't-tevârîh'i*, ed. İbrahim Hakkı Çuhadar, 2 vols. (Ankara: Türk Tarih Kurumu, 2003), vol. I, 22.

[56] Ibid., vol. II, 150, 204, 245, 304.

[57] Maria Pia Pedani-Fabris, ed., *Relazioni di ambasciatori veneti al senato*, vol. XIV: *Constantinopoli, Relazioni inedite (1512–1789)* (Padova: Bottega d'Erasmo, 1996), 514; Nicolo Barozzi and Guglielmo Berchet, eds., *Le relazioni degli stati europei lette al senato dagli ambasciatori veneziani nel secolo decimosettimo: Turchia*, 2 vols. (Venice, 1871–2), vol. I, 131, 292.

[58] See, for instance, Mustafa Âli, *Künhü'l-ahbâr*, İstanbul Üniversitesi Kütüphanesi, TY 5959, f. 497a.

[59] Hasanbeyzade Ahmed, *Hasan Bey-zâde Târîhi*, ed. Nezihi Aykut, 3 vols. (Ankara: Türk Tarih Kurumu, 2004), vol. III, 927; Peçevi, *Ta'rîh*, vol. II, 375.

could apply at their discretion. For instance, Murad IV could only order the execution of his two brothers after he established his political charisma with the reconquest of Yerevan in 1635, suggesting that even a sultan known for his iron fist could not easily afford to carry the political burden of fratricide.[60] Later in 1669, an alleged plot to execute the brothers of Mehmed IV led to large-scale popular protests in the capital.[61] It is probably not a coincidence that the oldest extant manuscript of the *"kanunname* of Mehmed II," in which fratricide was declared to be legal, was copied in 1029/1620, around the time when a mufti opposed the practice for the first time. Clearly, the legitimacy of fratricide, a fundamental question of Ottoman public law, was then being debated in Ottoman politics. Thus the process that had started when Süleyman asked for the opinions of the high-ranking jurists about the execution of his son Bayezid was reaching its final destination: judicial scrutiny of the royal prerogative.[62]

The grand mufti who opposed the execution of Prince Mehmed in 1621 was Es'ad, a powerful lord of the law and one of the sons of Sa'deddin, a former mufti who had served Murad III and Mehmed III as mentor. Es'ad had also held the position of the grand mufti during the last two years of Ahmed I's reign. He was preceded by his elder brother Mehmed, who was mufti from 1608 to 1615 and enjoyed the political prestige of his family, just as much as would his younger brother. Thus there is some ground to argue that, even if Ahmed I had intended to execute his brother Mustafa, he might not have been able to back his decision with the legitimizing opinion of his chief jurists, a point I reiterate later with additional examples. Perhaps it was this awareness that led Ahmed I to let his younger brother live. Whether this was indeed the case, it was definitely Es'ad who enthroned Mustafa I in 1617 in opposition to the established Ottoman dynastic traditions, thus, in effect, denying the dynasty the authority to decide on a fundamental aspect of public law.

Es'ad and the office of the grand mufti at the beginning of the seventeenth century

In this section I underline the political independence of Es'ad and other muftis during the reign of Ahmed I and chart the political empowerment of the office of the mufti at the turn of the seventeenth century. During most of the reign of Ahmed I, the brothers Mehmed and Es'ad monopolized the office of the grand mufti (the mufti of the imperial capital Istanbul). Mehmed was appointed to this post for the second time in June 1608 and continued to hold it until his death in July 1615. His uninterrupted tenure of seven years in the office of

---

[60] Katib Çelebi, *Fezleke*, vol. II, 178.
[61] Evliya Çelebi, *Evliya Çelebi Seyahatnamesi*, 10 vols. (Istanbul, 1314–1938), vol. VIII, 429; Silahdar Fındıklılı Mehmed Ağa, *Silahdâr Ta'rîhi*, 2 vols. (Istanbul, 1928), vol. I, 510; Mehmed Raşid, *Ta'rîh-i Râşid*, 2nd ed., 5 vols. (Istanbul, 1282), vol. I, 160.
[62] See Chapter 1, 42–3.

the mufti was the longest since the death of Ebussu'ud in 1574. Upon the death of Mehmed, his younger brother Es'ad succeeded him and held the position continuously until the deposition of Osman II in May 1622. Es'ad was appointed mufti once again in October 1623 and died in office in May 1625.

Both Mehmed and Es'ad were powerful actors on the political stage of the imperial capital as they had inherited the political legacy of their father Sa'deddin, who had served two sultans as mentor and also held the office of the mufti. Some of their decisions were quite critical for the interests of the dynasty. For instance, Mehmed seemed to have played an important role in the execution of Nasuh Pasha, the grand vizier and son-in-law of the sultan, in 1614. As for Es'ad, narrative sources related two significant legal cases in which he made decisions to the detriment of the dynasty's interests. In the first case, Es'ad was instrumental in denying Mehmed III a great sum of money from the tribute of Egypt, which used to be the sultan's own "pocket money." In the second one, he forced the Queen Mother Safiye Sultan to dismiss her representative, who was handling the construction of the mosque she had endowed.[63] Thus Es'ad was independent enough to act in defiance of the will of the Ottoman royal family.

In short, both Mehmed and Es'ad, with the immense political influence and wealth they inherited from their father Sa'deddin, definitely had the prestige to lead the lords of the law, or the *mevali*, as grand muftis. Moreover they did not seem to mind going against the interests of the most powerful members of the Ottoman polity, such as the dynasty and a grand vizier like Nasuh Pasha. Thus they were at least strong enough to attempt to defy the will of the sultan, as Es'ad did in 1621 when Osman II asked him to affirm his decision to execute his brother Prince Mehmed. We do not know whether Ahmed I ever consulted Mehmed or Es'ad about the question of fratricide. But if he did so, they were in a position to oppose the idea, not simply because they were powerful and courageous lords of the law but also because the position they occupied and the law they represented had gained tremendous political capital throughout the sixteenth century.

As argued in the first chapter, the intervention of the political authority into the domain of jurists' law had also opened the way for the jurists to be actively involved in the highest circles of dynastic politics. This development may be illustrated well by discussing the role of the grand mufti in some of the revolts staged by the political opposition in the capital in the early years of the seventeenth century. I first show how the court and the imperial administration used symbols of jurists' law to portray themselves as zealous guardians of law and order. Then I suggest that the opposition was able to do the same by forming an alliance with the grand mufti. As a result of these developments

---

[63] Tezcan, "The Ottoman *mevâlî*," 397–406.

the emperor found himself unable to attend to his own family affairs without the sanction of the grand mufti.

At the turn of the seventeenth century the Ottoman sultanate faced one of its most serious crises of legitimacy. The army had been engaged in a long war against the Habsburgs in Central Europe since 1593, and the Jalali rebellions had just started in Anatolia with the rise of Abdülhalim Karayazıcı, bringing the court of Mehmed III under heavy attack from all corners. In November 1599, the first news of Karayazıcı's political ambitions for an independent kingdom reached the capital. Apparently he was issuing orders with an imperial seal that read "Halim Shah, may he be victorious." His orders, some examples of which were sent to Istanbul by Mehmed Pasha, who was besieging him in Urfa, were penned by his *nişancı*, or seal-bearer, Zeydi, an Ottoman officer who had previously aspired to become a secretary in the imperial administration but had failed. Moreover, Karayazıcı had appointed a number of judges; made Hüseyin Pasha, an Ottoman pasha turned "rebel," his grand vizier; and was organizing his new recruits in the Ottoman imperial fashion as janissaries, *bölük halkı* (cavalry divisions), *acemiyan* (janissary cadets), and *çavuşes* (heralds). Finally Karayazıcı was reportedly claiming that his genealogy went back to former – unidentified – shahs and that the Prophet had appeared to him in a dream and granted him the right to rule.[64]

While the provinces were in turmoil, in Istanbul the people close to the court of Mehmed III were being constantly accused of corruption. As is touched upon in Chapters 3 and 5, the absolutist political posture of the court was drawing much criticism. These criticisms soon turned into violent confrontations. In the last days of March 1600, Esperanza Malchi, the Jewish *kiera* (lady in Greek) known to have been very close to the Queen Mother, was lynched by the cavalry soldiers who believed that the debased coins, with which they were paid, had been received from her tax-farm payments. The soldiers also demanded the heads of the chief gardener and the chief white eunuch of the sultan, but were appeased after they had lynched Malchi and her son.[65] A year later, in March 1601, the cavalry soldiers staged yet another confrontation. Once again they insisted on the execution of the chief white eunuch, Gazanfer Agha. The troops threatened the sultan by stating that "[t]hey would accept and obey him as their loyal Prince, if not, they would depose him and put up some other in his place, that would govern according to their ancient and

[64] Selaniki, *Tarih*, vol. II, 834, 846–7; Katib Çelebi, *Fezleke*, vol. I, p. 143; see also Mustafa Akdağ, *Celâlî İsyanları, 1550–1603* (Ankara: Ankara Üniversitesi Dil ve Tarih-Coğrafya Fakültesi Yayınları, 1963), 199, 246–9; and Michael A. Cook, *Population Pressure in Rural Anatolia, 1450–1600* (London: Oxford University Press, 1972), 36 n. 6.
[65] Her other son saved himself by converting to Islam and promising to pay their debts to the treasury. He apparently became known as Aksak Mustafa Çavuş and died during the reign of İbrahim (1640–8); Selaniki, *Tarih*, vol. II, 854–7; Na'ima, *Ta'rîh-i Na'îmâ*, 6 vols. (Istanbul, 1281–3), vol. I, 231, 247; the English ambassador Lello's dispatch on March 29, 1600; NA, SP 97/4, f. 77; on the term *kiera*, see J.H. Mordtmann, "Die jüdischen Kira im Serai der Sultane," *Mitteilungen des Seminars für orientalischen Sprachen* 32 (1929): 1–38.

canon laws."[66] At the turn of the seventeenth century, not only had the concept of deposition entered the Ottoman political vocabulary but also the members of the central cavalry troops had already developed an articulate language of legitimate opposition that made references to a constitutional tradition. This time they were appeased by the intervention of Cıgalazade Sinan Pasha and the dismissal of the chief gardener of the sultan.[67]

One of the ways in which the Ottoman government responded to this crisis of legitimacy was to use legal symbols of public order and social discipline. By emphasizing the strict application of jurists' law in the Ottoman domains, the sultan tried to respond to the criticisms directed against his court. Probably the most illustrative examples suggesting that the turn of the seventeenth century was a time of legal displays of social discipline were the orders regarding the clothing of non-Muslims and alcohol consumption, conservative regulations that had been very rarely enforced in Ottoman history. In 1600 and 1601 orders were issued that, among other things, banned Christians and Jews from wearing silk.[68] In April 1601, right after the March 1601 incident involving the cavalry soldiers and concurrently with the dispatch of an army against Karayazıcı under the leadership of the vizier Hacı İbrahim Pasha, the use of alcohol was strictly prohibited, all taverns closed (see Fig. 4), and the office of the finance ministry that collected taxes from the sale of alcohol abolished – all of which were reinstated once the political stage seemed to be under control in the fall of 1602 for, needless to say, taxes mattered much more than the strict application of conservative interpretations of jurists' law that became popular during political crises.[69]

It was not only the government, however, that embraced symbols of a zealous adherence to law and order. The political opposition was also aligning itself with jurists and jurists' law by creating an alliance with the grand mufti Sun'ullah Efendi, who seemed to have been involved in the revolts of 1600 and 1601 as a supporter of the cavalry troops.[70] On Monday, January 6, 1603, the members of the elite cavalry units finally succeeded in forcing Mehmed III

---

[66] The dispatch of the English ambassador Lello on March 25, 1601; NA, SP 97/4, f. 131a (in modernized spelling).

[67] Hasanbeyzade, *Târîh*, vol. III, 640; *Calendar of State Papers and manuscripts relating to English affairs, existing in the archives and collections of Venice, and in other libraries of northern Italy*, 38 vols. [in 40] (London: H. M. Stationery Office, 1864–1947), vol. IX, 450; Tezcan, "Searching for Osman," 348, n. 178.

[68] *Calendar of State Papers – Venetian*, vol. IX, 444.

[69] Abdül'aziz Karaçelebizade, *Ravzatü'l-ebrâr* (Bulak, 1248), 490; Katib Çelebi, *Fezleke*, vol. I, p. 143; Cengiz Orhonlu, ed., *Osmanlı Tarihine Âid Belgeler: Telhîsler, 1597–1607* (Istanbul: İstanbul Üniversitesi Edebiyat Fakültesi Yayınları, 1970), 27, # 32; *Calendar of State Papers – Venetian*, vol. IX, 457, 461, 463–6.

[70] Sun'ullah's alliance with the cavalry soldiers is suggested by Na'ima in the context of the Jewish *kiera* incident, *Ta'rîh*, vol. I, 231. This suggestion is indirectly confirmed in a dispatch of the English ambassador Lello on April 12, 1600; NA, SP 97/4, f. 81a. Sun'ullah was mufti during both the 1600 and 1601 incidents. A few months after the latter one, he was dismissed. Yet in the first days of January 1603, he was reinstated in accordance with the demands of the cavalry soldiers.

Fig. 4. "The destruction of a wine tavern"; from the Taeschner Album.

to execute his chief white and black eunuchs, for the soldiers held them responsible for misinforming the sultan about the "rebels" by underestimating their strength in Anatolia and not responding forcefully to the political turmoil. According to Hasanbeyzade, who received the news while he was in the Balkans in the company of the grand vizier Yemişçi Hasan Pasha, the soldiers were about to depose the sultan and enthrone the mufti Sun'ullah on the grounds that the ruler of the Muslim community should be chosen according to his virtues.[71]

Hasanbeyzade's account suggests that the elite cavalry soldiers were as capable of using the mechanisms of jurists' law as the administration had been doing recently. Not only did they use the concept of deposition but they also made an argument about the qualities that a legitimate ruler should possess, which they found in a jurist rather than in the sultan. Although in this instance the soldiers did not in fact depose the sultan, they did use another

[71] Hasanbeyzade, *Târîh*, vol. III, 692.

mechanism of jurists' law by securing the legal opinion of the mufti Sun'ullah confirming that the grand vizier Yemişçi Hasan Pasha deserved execution. Hasan Pasha could only save his head by mobilizing the janissaries after his return to Istanbul, storming the capital, and executing the main representatives of the elite cavalry units. Sun'ullah was then dismissed.[72] Yet Yemişçi Hasan Pasha himself was eventually executed in October 1603, whereas Sun'ullah continued to receive his salary on the sultan's payroll, suggesting that a mufti, by virtue of the political prestige of the law he represented, was untouchable even after dismissal on grounds of political opposition to the court.[73]

Thus, by the beginning of the seventeenth century, jurists' law had become the default venue for any political actor to justify his actions. The emperor himself was not immune from this requirement even when the relevant action involved his family business. For example, in late May or early June 1603, Mehmed III was informed that his son Prince Mahmud might have been involved in some political plot to depose him. According to the English ambassador Lello, the sultan decided to consult with his grand vizier and the mufti on this issue. From the wording of Lello's report, it was clear that Mehmed III demanded a legal opinion as to whether he could execute his son from Ebulmeyamin Mustafa Efendi (see Fig. 5), the man who succeeded to Sun'ullah's position in February 1603. Mustafa's first response was apparently negative:

> In this councell the Muftie was of opinion that by there lawe wthout witnesses he could not be put to death: yet p[er]ceavinge that nothing but his death would satisfie the father condiscended & gaue sentence that the sonne were depriued of his lief then the father to liue in feare & ielosie.[74]

Clearly there was some room for negotiation. Had Mehmed III faced a mufti who was more independent of the court, he would have received a different response.

That Mehmed III demanded a legal opinion from the mufti of the imperial capital on the execution of Prince Mahmud demonstrated that the office of the grand mufti had acquired the potential power to limit the political will of the sultan in a matter pertaining to his very own family. Mustafa did not dare use his position to limit the political will of the sultan in 1603. Yet a more powerful mufti, who did not owe his position to the dynasty to the same degree that Mustafa did, could well have responded differently. In comparison with Es'ad, who was teaching at the Süleymaniye College of Law, the summit of a teaching career in law, at the age of twenty-two thanks to his father's backing,

---

[72]   Ibid., vol. III, 692–722.

[73]   Mehmed Rumi (bin Mehmed), *Nuhbetü't-tevârîh ve'l-ahbâr* (Istanbul, 1276), III, 216; Ömer Lütfü Barkan, "İstanbul saraylarına ait muhasebe defterleri," *Belgeler* 9/13 (1979): 1–380, at p. 175, notes his retirement salary of 550 *akçes* per day, which started right after his dismissal in February 1603 and was as much as the salary of the incumbent grand mufti.

[74]   Henry Lello, *The Report of Lello: Third English Ambassador to the Sublime Porte – Babıâli nezdinde üçüncü İngiliz elçisi Lello'nun muhtırası*, ed. and tr. Orhan Burian (Ankara: Ankara Üniversitesi Dil ve Tarih-Coğrafya Fakültesi Yayınları, 1952), 16.

Fig. 5. Ebulmeyamin Mustafa Efendi (grand mufti, 1603–4, 1606) at his home with peti-
tioners asking for fetwas, or legal opinions; manuscript illustration from Ganizade Nadiri,
Dîvân-ı Nâdirî, Topkapı Sarayı Kütüphanesi, H. 889, f. 18b; courtesy of the Topkapı Palace
Museum.

Mustafa did not come from a family of jurists and thus could not reach the same post until he was forty-nine years old. Mustafa then entered the circle of jurists under the patronage of the Queen Mother Safiye Sultan in whose endowed college of law he became the first professor to teach in 1598. His career advancement accelerated after this appointment at what was later to be called the "catapult" college for the speed of promotions of the professors teaching there. Mustafa was appointed mufti of the imperial capital only three years after receiving his very first judicial appointment, the judgeship of Edirne, in 1600.[75] Without the backing of Safiye Sultan, he would most likely not have attained the position of the grand mufti. Because of his debt to the imperial family, he gave in to Mehmed III in June 1603, giving him judicial approval to execute his son. In contrast, Es'ad, who had proven his independence by making decisions detrimental to the royal family in the past, said no to Osman II eighteen years later on the question of the execution of Prince Mehmed. He would most probably have done the same if Ahmed I had ever consulted him about Prince Mustafa.

The reign of Ahmed I started in December 1603 while the memory of the events of March 1600, March 1601, and January 1603, which had seriously threatened the court of the sultan, were still quite fresh. One of Ahmed I's first acts was to send his grandmother Safiye Sultan, who had been one of the major targets of criticism directed against the court of Mehmed III, to the Old Palace. Ahmed I attempted to create a very pious image of himself throughout his reign, as best symbolized by building the last great imperial mosque in the Ottoman capital, the one known as the Blue Mosque where Pope Benedict XVI faced the kiblah some four hundred years later. It was also during his reign that large investments were made in the Muslim pilgrimage sites of Mecca and Medina. These pious acts of the sultan and many others were duly recorded by Ahmed's official historiographer, Safi Mustafa Efendi, who was his personal prayer leader or imam, a quite telling choice.[76]

Sun'ullah, the former grand mufti whom the cavalry troops seemed to consider for the throne in 1603, first got a raise in his retirement salary during the reign of Ahmed I in April 1604 and was then reappointed grand mufti in June 1604. Thus even though he gave support to the protests of the cavalry forces, Sun'ullah still was able to return to his powerful position. He was recorded as being the only one to dare oppose the sultan's opinion in a consultation in the summer of 1606 at which all of the viziers were present. Although he was dismissed soon after this meeting because the grand vizier Derviş Pasha came to regard him as a serious threat, upon the death of the next mufti, Ahmed I reappointed him in November 1606. Right after this final reappointment of Sun'ullah, Derviş Pasha was executed; not surprisingly, Sun'ullah was said to have played a role in this decision. He was also thought to be influential in the choice of the next grand vizier, Kuyucu Murad Pasha. When Sun'ullah

[75] Ata'i, *Hadâ'iku'l-hakâ'ik*, 511–13.   [76] Safi, *Zübdetü't-tevârîh*, vol. I, 46–55, 109–24.

was finally dismissed in June 1608 because of his failure to analyze Crimean politics accurately, at which his successor was apparently better, his retirement salary was increased once again.[77]

In short, the political confrontations at the turn of the century had increased the power of the office of the grand mufti because parties to those conflicts were using jurists' law as the medium for their arguments. Although the government tried to present itself as the champion of jurists' law in response to a serious legitimacy crisis, critics of the government also turned to the same law and embraced the grand mufti as a center of opposition to the power of the court. The grand mufti, the chief representative of jurists' law and the lords of the law, thus came to be a focus of legitimate opposition against the Ottoman court. As exemplified by the reappointments of Sun'ullah and the raises in his interim retirement salaries, the mufti had become too powerful a person for the sultan to alienate categorically. Whereas with court creatures like Ebulmeyamin Mustafa, the sultan could count on favorable legal opinions, others like the brothers Mehmed and Es'ad who monopolized the office between 1608 and 1622 could be much more independent.

Given this background, one would be justified in assuming that Sun'ullah, Mehmed, or Es'ad, who occupied the office of the grand mufti during most of Ahmed I's reign, would have the independence to resist the sultan if ever asked for a favorable legal opinion to execute his younger brother Prince Mustafa. As the representatives of the lords of the law and potential leaders of legitimate opposition to the court, the grand muftis had an interest in circumscribing the powers of the sultan. Keeping the brother of the sultan alive would serve this purpose in two ways. Obviously, having an alternative sultan at the palace was a point of leverage against the incumbent sultan. If necessary, a sultan could be deposed but the political system would still survive with the enthronement of his brother; and the sultan, being aware of this, would not exceed certain limits. For instance, Ahmed I knew that his father's court had exceeded those limits and that three rebellions had resulted. The third rebellion cost the heads of two men, the chief white and black eunuchs, who symbolized the palace both in its public and private spheres – the white eunuchs were more visible in the public parts of the palace, whereas the black ones were mostly employed in the residential part. Therefore Ahmed I started his reign by banishing his grandmother Safiye Sultan, another target of the political opposition, to the Old Palace, which was a tacit offer of peace to the forces of opposition.

Second, on a more general level, the existence of an alternative sultan would make the nature of the sultanate more institutional than charismatic. Up to the mid-sixteenth century, the Ottoman sultans came to the throne by proving themselves on the battlefield against their brothers. They showed that as possessors of *devlet* in the sense of fortune, which was proven by their victory over their brothers, they deserved to rule. But in the latter half of the

---

[77] Ata'i, *Hadâ'iku'l-hakâ'ik*, 554; Hasanbeyzade, *Târîh*, vol. III, 846–56.

sixteenth century, all they could prove at the time of their accessions was that they could execute their brothers, some poor unarmed boys who had never left the palace. The survival of their brothers, in contrast, would mean that the *devlet* of a particular sultan was totally accidental and not necessarily deserved. More importantly, the survival of brothers would also mean that the *devlet* in the sense of state was now more institutional, as it would no longer depend on the success or failure of the incumbent sultan to produce male heirs, but would rather continue with the next available member of the dynasty. There were then good reasons to keep all princes alive and thus weaken the political power of the person of the sultan while rendering the sultanate itself impersonal, which, in the long term, would professionalize the administrative institution of the dynasty and lengthen its life. We do not know whether any one of these points ever crossed the mind of Es'ad when he was informed of the death of Ahmed I. Yet his decision to enthrone Prince Mustafa set a very important precedent for the establishment of the rule of seniority in Ottoman succession.

Accession to the throne versus enthronement by virtue of seniority

In this section I analyze the significance of the enthronement of Mustafa I in 1617 and argue that it was Es'ad who brought him to the throne, most probably using an argument from jurists' law. Let me start with the term used to describe this event by three contemporary authors, Hasanbeyzade, Hibri, and Peçevi. They explicitly used the word "to enthrone," in contrast to the Ottoman term that signifies accession to the throne, which is *cülus*, literally "sitting." Thus until then the Ottoman sultans used to seat themselves on the throne. Yet, this time others enthroned an Ottoman sultan; thus "they seated him (*iclas*)."[78] This telling difference in terminology may best be understood by recalling how Ahmed acceded to the throne in 1603.

Early on Sunday morning, December 21, 1603, just at the beginning of the imperial council meeting, the superintendent of the ushers brought an imperial rescript, an order personally written by the emperor himself, which was handed to him by the chief white eunuch to be conveyed to Kasım Pasha, the deputy grand vizier. The poor vizier could not decipher the illegible handwriting. All he could read was the word *babam*, my father, which made Kasım Pasha all the more suspicious as the father of Mehmed III had passed away eight years ago. Kasım Pasha gave the rescript to Hasanbeyzade, a senior secretary, who was good at deciphering illegible handwriting. Thanks to Hasanbeyzade's chronicle, we know that it read as follows: "You, Kasım Pasha! My father is gone by God's will, and I have taken my seat on the throne. You had better

---

[78] Peçevi, *Ta'rîh*, vol. II, 360; Abdurrahman Hibri, *Defter-i Ahbâr*, Beyazıt Kütüphanesi, Veliyüddin 2418, f. 4b; Hasanbeyzade, *Târîh*, vol. III, 915; see also Katib Çelebi, *Fezleke*, vol. I, 385.

keep the city in good order. Should sedition arise, I will behead you!"[79] Kasım Pasha was taken by surprise because he did not even know that Mehmed III had been sick. He sent a note to the chief black eunuch asking whether the imperial rescript he received was a trick to test his loyalty to Mehmed III. In response, Kasım Pasha was called to the audience hall in private, where he saw Ahmed I, a thirteen-year-old boy, sitting on the throne. Then he gave orders for the preparation of the public ceremony in which all major officials of the state, who thought they were going to see Mehmed III, were to pay their allegiance to the new sultan.[80]

There was one striking difference between the two successions of 1603 and 1617. In 1603 the new sultan had literally taken his seat on the throne before any public figure even knew about the death of the former sultan. The question of succession was already resolved within the private compounds of the palace by the time public officials were notified that Ahmed I had acceded to the throne.[81] Thus the dynasty had taken care of its own business. In 1617, however, the major statesmen, the *ashab-ı hall ü akd*, or the men who have the authority to "loose and bind," as Katib Çelebi wrote,[82] were apparently notified of the death of Ahmed I before any action took place regarding the succession. These statesmen were the ones who chose to enthrone the brother of the late sultan instead of one of his sons. Thus Mustafa I did not accede to the throne, but was *en*throned by public officials.

The circumstances surrounding the enthronement and the testimony of the contemporary sources suggest that it was Es'ad who made the crucial move for Mustafa's enthronement. Ahmed I had most probably died on Tuesday, November 21, 1617, the night before the enthronement of Mustafa, although it is possible that he may have died a few days earlier.[83] The grand vizier Halil Pasha was in Diyarbekir, wintering there in preparation for a new military campaign against Safavid Persia the next spring. If Ahmed had really died on Tuesday night, the grand vizier was definitely not consulted about the enthronement as he could not have provided any meaningful input overnight while he was so far away.[84] It would be safe to assume that the major statesmen were notified of Ahmed's death immediately, and they met to discuss what to

---

[79] Hasanbeyzade, *Târîh*, vol. III, 800.   [80] Ibid., vol. III, 801–3.

[81] Of course, this was itself a novelty as, for the first time, the prince who succeeded was not in a provincial post. Yet even in 1595, when the oldest prince was in Manisa at the time of Murad III's death, he was notified by his mother with a letter and invited to the capital before the deputy grand vizier found out about the death of the sultan; Selaniki, *Tarih*, vol. I, 426.

[82] Katib Çelebi, *Fezleke*, vol. I, 385.

[83] Ibid., compare BnF, fr. 16148, 157a; NA, SP 97/7, f. 174a.

[84] An anonymous chronicle (attributed to Vasfi) written for and about Halil Pasha suggests that the grand vizier was informed of the death of Ahmed and the enthronement of Mustafa by a messenger, who brought him the new sultan's orders, which confirmed his grand vizierate and commander-generalship; *Gazânâme-i Halîl Paşa*, Österreichische Nationalbibliothek, H. O. 72, ff. 173b–174a.

do. The viziers present in the capital at the time, according to a contemporary chronicle, were the deputy grand vizier Sofu Mehmed Pasha, Gürcü Hadım Mehmed Pasha, Etmekcizade Ahmed Pasha, Davud Pasha, Nakkaş Hasan Pasha, and Cıgalazade Mahmud Pasha. Among the six, the only one with a personal interest in the enthronement of the brother of Ahmed I was Davud Pasha because he was Mustafa I's brother-in-law. As for the high-ranking ulema, Zekeriyazade Yahya and Ahizade Hüseyin were chief justices of the European, and Asian and African provinces, respectively. Finally, the mufti was Sa'deddinzade Es'ad. Among these statesmen, Es'ad was the most senior one in governmental affairs. Although all of the viziers present in the capital were appointed to the imperial council during the reign of Ahmed I, Es'ad had been chief justice of the Asian and African provinces during the reign of Mehmed III and was appointed to the same position for the European provinces by Ahmed I in February 1604, before any of those viziers had joined the imperial council.[85] Moreover, as the heir to both the social power of his family, which was arguably only second to that of the dynasty in the early seventeenth century, and the political power of his office, which had competed with that of the sultan at the turn of the seventeenth century, Es'ad had all the credentials that a king-maker would need to have.

Apparently Es'ad did make the king, most probably using an argument derived from jurists' law. Rumi, a contemporary author, stated that "[w]hile it was not customary [for the brothers to inherit the sultanate], that is to say, while it was established that the inheritance of the sultanate was reserved for the noble sons and not for the brothers [of sultans]," Es'ad insisted on the succession of Mustafa. Rumi's point was going to be reiterated by Osman II himself after he claimed the throne in 1618 when he wrote to his grand vizier Halil Pasha that "the throne of the sultanate was restricted to my imperial majesty in accordance with the ancient Ottoman *kanun*." Yet "the viziers and the pillars of the state" followed Es'ad, and they enthroned Sultan Mustafa. Another contemporary, Hasanbeyzade, confirmed Rumi's account by stating that in accordance with the "opinion of the chief of the ulema," Mustafa I was enthroned. Unfortunately, there is no elaboration as to why Es'ad might have preferred Mustafa I to one of Ahmed I's sons. Peçevi and Hibri claimed that the decision to enthrone Mustafa was made on the basis of the youth of Ahmed's sons and the relatively older age of his brother Mustafa; Osman II's letter to Halil Pasha implied the same.[86] Given that Mustafa may have been

[85] The list of incumbent viziers comes from Abdülkadir, *Topçular Kâtibi 'Abdülkādir (Kadrî) Efendi Tarihi (Metin ve Tahlil)*, ed. Ziya Yılmazer, 2 vols. (Ankara: Türk Tarih Kurumu, 2003), vol. I, 663; for biographies of these viziers and the two chief justices, see Tezcan, "Searching for Osman," 338–9, n. 87–8; 351–2, n. 200–4; for Es'ad, see Ata'i, *Hadâ'iku'l-hakâ'ik*, 690–2.
[86] Mehmed Rumi (bin Mehmed), *[Ta'rîh]*, Süleymaniye Kütüphanesi, Lala İsmail Efendi 300, f. 8b; anonymous, *Gazânâme*, f. 175b; Hasanbeyzade, *Târîh*, vol. III, 915; Peçevi, *Ta'rîh*, vol. II, 360; Hibri, *Defter*, f. 4b.

only a few years older than Osman, that no Ottoman sultan had ever succeeded his father by virtue of being older than his brothers, and that Osman was as old when his father died as the latter had been when he succeeded his own father, this claim may seem spurious at first.[87] Yet if one were to consult jurists' law, there is indeed a point related to a ruler's age that would have provided Es'ad with a legal basis for his choice.

Although we do not possess a treatise specifically devoted to the question of succession in relation to this event, there was a treatise of advice authored in 1623 for Murad IV, most probably by a preacher, that is very suggestive of the way in which Es'ad may have brought up the issue of age in the enthronement of Mustafa I in 1617. The anonymous author counted himself among the *meşayih ü suleha* – that is, the "sheiks and righteous/pious ones" – which is the way Sufi sheiks and preachers were referred to in this period. This sheik devoted a short chapter to the qualities that a Muslim ruler should possess. At the beginning of the chapter he listed the ten conditions of imamate, which he used interchangeably with *padişahlık*, the first two conditions being maturity and reason. The remainder of the chapter was devoted to the significance of the second condition. "Although maturity is the first condition," stated the sheik, "reason comes to existence after maturity, and yet reason is comprehensive of all the [ten] conditions." The sheik also compared reason with sanctity (*velayet*): "the world is not run with sanctity, but rather, it is run with reason."[88] There were attempts undertaken to legitimize the sultanate of Mustafa I by reference to his sanctity during his second reign in 1622–3, including the use of the epithet "saint" (*veli*) in reference to him.[89] Clearly, the sheik was responding to these attempts by arguing that sanctity is of no use for worldly government.

What can also be discerned in this anonymous treatise is the association of Mustafa I with maturity because he was older than Murad IV, who was only eleven years old when he was enthroned in 1623. The anonymous author was at pains to argue that maturity does not mean anything without reason, suggesting that the maturity argument had been used to legitimize the sultanate of Mustafa I. Es'ad must have used this point about maturity in 1617 when Prince Osman was thirteen years old. Mustafa's age would have given Es'ad

---

[87] On Mustafa's age, see n. 53; and Tezcan, "Kösem Sultan," 353–4. Both Osman and his father Ahmed were thirteen years old when they lost their respective fathers.

[88] Anonymous, [*Ta'rîh-i Sultân Murâd Hân*], Dâr al-kutub al-qawmiyya (Cairo), 191 Ta'rīkh Turkī, ff. 5b-6a, 7b. Other conditions of legitimate rulership listed include freedom; manhood; descent from the tribe of the Quraysh, on which, the author adds, scholars disagree; hearing and eyesight; courage; competence; knowledge; and piety; compare Ann K. S. Lambton, *State and Government in Medieval Islam: An Introduction to the Study of Islamic Political Theory – The Jurists* (London: Oxford University Press, 1981), 76, 79–80, 89, 105–6; and Hamilton A. R. Gibb, "Luṭfî Paşa on the Ottoman Caliphate," *Oriens* 15 (1962): 287–95.

[89] See Baki Tezcan, "The history of a 'primary source:' The making of Tûghî's chronicle on the deposition of Osman II," *Bulletin of the School of Oriental and African Studies* 72 (2009): 41–62, at 53–15; and Tezcan, "The multiple faces of the One," 30–5.

the leverage to build a legal argument on his behalf based on the requirement of maturity for legitimate rule. As suggested by this treatise, it was precisely this point that was used after the regicide of Osman II to keep Mustafa I on the throne as opposed to enthroning Prince Murad.

Whether or not Es'ad indeed used the argument of maturity derived from jurists' law on Mustafa's behalf in 1617, that this argument was clearly used a few years later and that counter-arguments were also derived from jurists' law in these years suggest that there was a legal discourse in the making about the question of succession in the Ottoman Empire of the early seventeenth century. Jurists' law was rich enough to supply arguments and counter-arguments for parties supporting different candidates for the throne. But more importantly, jurists' law was accepted as the proper medium to discuss this issue rather than letting the princes fight it out among themselves to determine whose *devlet*, or fortune, was stronger. In 1617, then, Es'ad, the most prestigious interpreter of jurists' law in the empire and the most powerful man among the lords of the law, took a crucial step to replace the accidental *devlet* (fortune) of the Ottoman sultan with the *devlet* as an institution, the state. The principle on which he enthroned Mustafa was later to be the third article of the first Ottoman written constitution in 1876; it stipulates that the Ottoman sultanate belongs to the eldest prince of the House of Osman in accordance with "ancient principles."[90] In this sense, Es'ad's enthronement of Mustafa I was a constitutional act for what I call the Second Empire.

Conclusion

The enthronement of Mustafa I by Es'ad in 1617 was a very significant moment in the history of political development in the region we call the Middle East today. However closely Es'ad may have been connected to the court through his father, he was not a *kul* – that is, a royal slave – or a military-administrative delegate of the political power personified by the sultan. Es'ad was the most powerful representative of the law that governed the lives of Ottoman subjects and that protected them from the possible encroachments of political authority into their lives. Therefore, despite being the leader of the lords of the law, hence a noble man of sorts, Es'ad was at the same time a representative of Ottoman society. His direct involvement in the Ottoman succession, most of the previous crises of which were handled by the *kul*, was an important step in the *civil*ization of the Ottoman polity, which was to continue enlarging its base to include more representatives from nonmilitary segments of society.

More importantly, Es'ad was opposing royal tradition, or *kanun*, which preferred sons over brothers of sultans, and in effect denying the dynasty the authority to legislate in the most fundamental area of public law. The jurists and their law were thus entering the dynasty's own backyard. Es'ad's

[90] *Kânûn-ı Esâsî*, 1.

enthronement of Mustafa I in 1617 was a potent symbol of the process of the limitation of dynastic political authority in the Ottoman Empire, which is the most fundamental condition of proto-democratization. Within the framework drawn in the first part of this chapter, this enthronement could be interpreted as a moment of victory for the constitutionalist cause in its political struggle against the absolutist one.

This enthronement dealt a heavy blow to the charismatic nature of royal authority and thus to the absolutist camp centered at the court. One of the central tenets of this authority was the unbroken chain of Ottoman succession from father to son since the late thirteenth century. At the death of each sultan, the next one was supposed to prove himself by acceding to the throne by his own merits, which included a demonstration of his fortunes with a victory in a fratricidal war or some experience in provincial government. In 1617, however, the sultan did not accede; he was rather *en*throned by the most powerful representative of the law without any regard to established royal tradition. Yet as is demonstrated in the next chapter, this heavy blow did not prove to be a decisive victory for the constitutionalists because Mustafa I was deposed the next year by a palace coup. Nevertheless, 1617 was a significant point in the history of the development of Ottoman limited monarchy as it provided a reference for the eventual stabilization of the rule of Ottoman succession, the very regulation of which by an outside force was in effect a constitutional check on the dynastic prerogative.

It should be emphasized, however, that not all jurists belonged to what I call the constitutionalist camp, nor was jurists' law inherently opposed to absolutism. As discussed earlier, the Ottoman court actively supported certain jurists so it could have some influence among the lords of the law.[91] This should not be surprising for not all of the social groups that owed their empowerment to the socioeconomic transformation of the sixteenth century were constitutionalist. What is important to recognize, however, is that the increasing political significance of jurists' law at the expense of feudal law and dynastic traditions facilitated the gradual formation of a common legal-political ground on which a struggle between such groups as absolutists and constitutionalists could take place. This new ground was a byproduct of the sixteenth-century socioeconomic transformation that brought the market and that which is economic right into the heart of the political. The law that used to govern market relations followed suit and entered the domain of the political authority to regularize it. Eventually, the same law was used to depose sultans as is discussed in Chapters 5 and 6.

In short, by the early seventeenth century at the latest, the legitimacy of political authority came to be a question discussed through the language of jurists' law, leaving a long-lasting legacy in Ottoman politics. This Sharia-based legacy has been disowned by the secular Turkish Republic as a symbol

---

[91] See this chapter, 68–70.

of reactionary politics. Ironically, however, the Turkish word used to this very day to denote "legitimate" is *meşru* (Ar. *mashrū'*), literally "that which is enacted as law," where the law stands for the Sharia. Clearly, the practical meaning of the Sharia for those who have used it as a frame of reference in political debates for centuries was simply "the law," without any other attribute, such as divine or Islamic. For Ottoman political actors of the early modern period, there was no other legal system in comparison to which the Sharia could be qualified with an adjective. This was the law they used to fight their political battles with, gradually bringing royal authority under legal supervision.

- Absolutist vs. Constitutionalist
- Impact of Mustafas's enthronement
  More of a constitutional move since Ebas really made the choice

CHAPTER 3

The court strikes back

The making of Ottoman absolutism

On Monday, February 26, 1618, Istanbul woke up to a surprise. As the resident French ambassador Baron de Sancy put it, it was a time of miracles.[1] It had just been three months since Ahmed I had died and had been succeeded by his brother Mustafa I on Wednesday, November 22, 1617. This Monday, however, the town criers were wandering around the city announcing the enthronement of Osman II, the eldest son of Ahmed I. Yet Mustafa I had not died; he was deposed.

A deposition of this kind had never happened in Ottoman history. Selim I (1512–20) had forced his father Bayezid II (1481–1512) to retire in 1512, but he was a prince with broad military support that included the elite infantry divisions of the central army, the janissaries.[2] There had been many bloody fights for the throne in the past, yet the contenders had always been adult princes who enjoyed some kind of military support. In contrast, Osman II was a thirteen-year-old boy whom the people had only had a few opportunities to see on ceremonial occasions during the later years of his father's reign. With the exception of accompanying his father on his journeys to Edirne in Thrace, Osman had never left the capital. He was too young to have had any kind of opportunity to build a loyal following. Thus he was not in a position to strategize for the deposition of his uncle and his own succession. This was another case of *en*thronement in which an Ottoman sultan was brought to the throne as a result of certain political dynamics that were not under his own control. However, this time it was not the mufti of the imperial capital who was at the center of these dynamics; Osman II owed his throne to Mustafa Agha, an African eunuch who was the superintendent of the residential part of the imperial palace.

That Osman II had a right to rule was beyond question, yet he had been considered to be too young to do so just three months earlier, when his father died. As suggested in the last chapter, Es'ad, the grand mufti, most probably

---

[1] BnF, fr. 16148, f. 285a.
[2] Çağatay Uluçay, "Yavuz Sultan Selim nasıl padişah oldu?" *Tarih Dergisi* 6/9 (1954): 53–90, 7/10 (1954): 117–42, 8/11–12 (1955): 185–200.

using a legal argument based on the requirement of maturity for a ruler, had instead brought Mustafa to the Ottoman throne. However, just three months later, Mustafa was declared incapable of ruling, most probably based on the legal requirement that a ruler should have the capacity to reason, and he was replaced by his oldest nephew, Osman.[3] As is discussed later in this chapter, Mustafa might have been mentally imbalanced, yet there is not enough evidence to establish this beyond a reasonable doubt. One thus wonders whether Mustafa could have become mentally incapable within such a short period as three months or whether the signs taken as evidence for his mental incapacity had been there all along but were interpreted opportunistically; that is, he had been deemed able to rule by some who would prefer having a weak monarch, but not so by others who would rather operate within a powerful court.

This chapter analyzes the deposition of Mustafa I and the enthronement of Osman II within the larger context of the gradual transformation of the Ottoman court into a major locus of political power. This transformation began in the last quarter of the sixteenth century in response to the development of other loci of power in the Ottoman polity, such as the vizier households and the lords of the law. These developments were taking place in the context of the gradual demise of feudal social structures and the slow but steady development of a market society.

When the Ottoman Empire was a predominantly feudal society, the primary object of power was to control agricultural land resources through a chain of military-administrators in a hierarchical pyramid, which reached all the way from the village level to the summit at which stood the monarch. Although land did not lose its importance overnight, the gradual development of a market society shifted the primary locus of political power toward the control of monetary resources through a network of patron–client relationships in a weblike structure that did not have a single center. The political actors whom I call the constitutionalists wanted to place the monarch at the symbolic center of this web, which, not unlike the center of some spider webs, was devoid of any real significance. In contrast, the absolutists preferred having the sultan control the very spinning of the web. Mustafa I would quietly sit at the empty center, but Osman II was groomed by the absolutists to become a spinner.

In the first part of the chapter, I provide an overview of the evolution of pre-sixteenth-century Ottoman political structures to underline the novelty of the kind of political power that was competed for in the late sixteenth century. In the second part, I first discuss the development of vizier households as alternative loci of political power in the late sixteenth and early seventeenth centuries. Then I argue that beginning with the reign of Murad III (1574–95) the Ottoman court evolved into a new locus of political power that included

---

[3] See Chapter 2, 75–6. Official correspondence about Osman II's enthronement did not refer to any problems with Mustafa but simply stated that he withdrew from the matters of the sultanate as he was always accustomed to retire in seclusion; anonymous, *Gazânâme*, f. 175b.

new actors introduced onto the political stage, who were empowered by the sultan to act as power brokers and whose influence was intended to undermine the standing of the viziers. In the third part, I demonstrate that the enthronement of Osman II was brought about by these new political actors whose interests were in absolutism.

The transformation of feudal vassals into patrimonial emperors

No one in his right mind would call Süleyman (1520–66) "Süleyman Bey," as the ancient Turkic title bey, or "lord,"[4] would be an insult for this emperor who came to be known as Süleyman the Magnificent in Europe. The same could be said for his father, Selim I (1512–20), who conquered Eastern Anatolia, Syria, and Egypt and who was recognized as the sovereign of the Hejaz, including the two holiest cities of Islam, Mecca and Medina. Yet the grandfather of Selim I, Mehmed II – the conqueror of Constantinople, the man who brought the Roman Empire to an end and thus inherited the title of Caesar by virtue of his sword – was known as Mehmed Bey among his people. This was attested to by Georgius de Hungaria, who lived in Ottoman lands for a long time and also saw the sultan, whom he called "Mechemetbeg," as Mehmed II was on his way to a bathhouse. Georgius himself referred to him regularly as the "king (rex)."[5] So "bey" was used not to diminish his authority, nor was it Mehmed II's official title. This popular usage, however, must have had a certain ring to the ears of Anatolians and the inhabitants of the Balkans for whom the memory of many other beys or lords sharing the rule of the land as vassals of distant Bulgarian, Mongol, or Serbian kings was very fresh. Moreover, the Ottomans continued to use the same titles, transforming the meaning of lord to an officer: most of the Ottoman officers serving as district governors or large fief holders were called beys. What distinguished Mehmed II was his claim to be the greatest bey, as expressed in his official title, Sultan Mehmed, *el-emir el-kebir*, which contemporary sources translated as "megas amiras" or "magnus admiratus" (the "great bey" or "great lord").[6]

The transformation of a warlord that Osman Bey (Osman I) was in the late thirteenth century, first, into a great lord in the fifteenth century and then into an emperor in the sixteenth century, symbolizes the transformation of Ottoman political structures in that period. In this section I first discuss the earliest period of Ottoman rule (ca. 1300–1453) during most of which the Ottoman lords were just one of many groups of lords. I use Benno Teschke's conceptual model for international politics during the European Middle Ages

---

[4] See M. Fuad Köprülü, "Bey," *İA*, vol. II, 579–81.

[5] Georgius de Hungaria, *Tractatus de moribus condictionibus et nequicia Turcorum: Traktat über die Sitten, die Lebensverhältnisse und die Arglist der Türken*, ed. and tr. Reinhard Klockow (Köln: Böhlau, 1993), 24, 149.

[6] Kate Fleet, "Early Ottoman self-definition," *Journal of Turkish Studies* 26/1 (2002): 229–38, at 237–8.

to highlight the fundamentally feudal nature of Ottoman political relations and structures in this era.[7] Then I argue that from the mid-fifteenth to the mid-sixteenth centuries the feudal relationship between Ottoman lords and their vassals evolved into a patriarchal one between master and slave as the *kuls* of the sultan gradually took the place of his vassals in the administration of the empire. This was an ingenious Ottoman response to the political challenges associated with the centrifugal forces of feudalism; it was also prompted by the social forces unleashed by the unification of the Anatolian and Balkan markets under the political umbrella of the Ottomans, as evidenced by the spread of the *akçe* as a common currency all over the territories of the empire by the reign of Mehmed II. Because this was only one of the several stages that Ottoman political structures went through, there is no justification for privileging it as the "classical" period as has been often done in Ottomanist scholarship.

From Osman, the lord, to Mehmed II, the great lord

Teschke's model for international politics during the European Middle Ages is especially useful in understanding the political structures of the early Ottoman period because it points out that "the economic" and "the political" were inseparable then. As such it proves to be very helpful in understanding the expansionist pressures on medieval polities and especially the swift series of conquests during the early Ottoman period, which are usually treated under the heading of the "rise" of the Ottoman Empire, a concept that has failed to receive the revisionist attention paid to its "decline."

   Teschke shows that the economic and the political in the Middle Ages were intimately connected through the mediation of extra-economic surplus appropriation, such as taxes in kind paid to a fief holder whose economic and political power over his peasants were inseparable. This fusion of the economic and the political produced the institution of lordship as the basic feudal unit. Yet no lord "owned" the land. As the late Harold Berman put it, "land, in fact, was not 'owned' by anyone; it was 'held' by superiors in a ladder of 'tenures' leading to the king or other supreme lord."[8] The fief holder could only enjoy the exploitation of his land under certain conditions such as providing certain services to his lord. Not only was property conditional but rival lords also competed for the "conditional property." To compete successfully, lords had to engage in what Robert Brenner calls "political accumulation," which included

---

[7] Benno Teschke, "Geopolitical relations in the European Middle Ages: History and theory," *International Organization* 52 (1998): 325–58; for a slightly more elaborate discussion of Teschke's model, see Baki Tezcan, "The Second Empire: The transformation of the Ottoman polity in the seventeenth century," *Comparative Studies of South Asia, Africa and the Middle East* 29 (2009): 556–72, at 559–60.

[8] Harold Berman, *Law and Revolution: The Formulation of the Western Legal Tradition* (Cambridge, MA: Harvard University Press, 1983), 312, quoted by Teschke, "Geopolitical relations," 339.

strategies that in one way or another implied an investment in the means of violence, such as conquering neighboring regions either to colonize and settle in the lands there or to establish client states that would provide annual tribute payments.[9]

The lords had to engage in such violent strategies, which produced conflict among the ruling class, not because of the autonomy of the sphere of politics as the Weberians would maintain, but rather as a result of the pressures produced by the peasant strategies of farming the land. Because feudal property structures and class relations dictated that the peasant surplus was to be extracted from them via extra-economic means, the peasants did not have any serious incentives to invest in productivity beyond the necessary level for their own sustenance. Their farming practices included the diversification of agricultural production and reduced hours of work, both of which set limits on productivity. Should their lords squeeze them further to extract a greater surplus of their labor, they always had the option of flight, which deprived the lords of a labor supply. Feudal conditions of social action, then, set limits to exploitation by their lords. Because the lords were competing with other lords over a basically stagnant peasant surplus, there was "a systemic pressure to build up military power. Unsurprisingly, development of agricultural technology was relatively lethargic, whereas military innovations based on systematic investment in the means of violence were, throughout the Middle Ages and beyond, spectacular."[10] The violence of the Middle Ages, then, cannot be theorized without incorporating the social relations of lordship.

The conditional, nonabsolute nature of property brought about a political organization based on a series of interpersonal bonds among the members of the lordly class. Yet a vassal who paid homage to an overlord could also opt to join the following of another lord or aspire to become an overlord himself. In this sense, the sovereignty of the overlord was never absolute but conditional, very much in the same sense as medieval property was conditional. This was especially so in the marches, or frontier regions:

Ethnic, religious, natural-topographical, or linguistic aspects were secondary in determining the "demarcation" of frontier regions. The extension of medieval territory followed the opportunities of military conquest, that is, political accumulation.... To the degree that marcher-lords had to be invested with special military powers of command to deal effectively with unruly neighbors, they became semiautonomous. More often than not, they abused their privileges for the buildup of regional strongholds.[11]

The early Ottoman historical experience fit Teschke's model perfectly. Osman, or perhaps Atman as suggested by the earliest extant spellings of

---

[9] Teschke, "Geopolitical relations," 339, 340–1; Robert Brenner, "The agrarian roots of European capitalism," in *The Brenner Debate: Agrarian Class Structure and Economic Development in Pre-industrial Europe*, eds. T. H. Aston and C. H. E. Philpin (Cambridge: Cambridge University Press, 1985), 236–42.
[10] Teschke, "Geopolitical relations," 342.   [11] Ibid., 345–6.

his name in contemporary Byzantine sources,[12] was a marcher-lord of this kind who most probably recognized as his sovereign Ghazan Khan (d. 1304), the Mongol ruler of the Il-khanate centered in western Persia. Coins struck in the name of Mongol khans in the early Ottoman period, as well as quasi-archival and literary evidence from the fourteenth and early fifteenth centuries, suggest that the Ottomans recognized the suzerainty of Mongol overlords well into the mid-fourteenth century and later.[13]

Although Osman would be a vassal in his relationship with his suzerain, the Mongol Il-khan, he was an overlord in his relationship with his *alps*, or knights, who had their own subservient companions. In his analysis of a chapter found in an early-fourteenth-century Anatolian Turkish Sufi text, the *Garibname* by Aşık Pasha, Halil İnalcık emphasizes the close resemblance between the relationship of an *alp* with his companions and that of a feudal lord with his vassals. In this chapter Aşık Pasha wrote about what it took to be an *alp*. The first three qualities of an *alp* were bravery, strength, and zeal. He should have a horse, preferably an armored one. Fifth, an *alp* himself must be armored. The next three conditions pertained to his weapons: a proper *alp* must carry a bow and arrows, a sword, and a spear. According to Aşık Pasha, even if a man had all those personal qualities and military paraphernalia, he would not qualify to be an *alp* if he lacked a comrade. Aşık Pasha also referred to an oath taken on one's sword, which İnalcık explains as "a ritual for establishing blood brotherhood or war companionship." İnalcık compares this bond to a vassal's promise of homage and fealty to his lord, the *commendatio*, which was "one of the strongest social bonds the [European] feudal period has ever known."[14]

According to Fuad Köprülü, who was the first to draw attention to the same passage in Aşık Pasha, the *alp*s constituted the nobility of the medieval nomadic society of the steppes:

When the chief of a tribe takes various tribes under his authority and establishes a political system of a confederate nature, around him there would be an aristocratic class constituted by *alp*s. These *alp*s, some of whom may be chiefs of the subordinated tribes, would be tied

---

[12] Gyula Moravcsik, "Türklüğün tetkiki bakımından Bizantolojinin ehemmiyeti," in *İkinci Türk Tarih Kongresi (İstanbul, 20–25 Eylül 1937)* (İstanbul: Türk Tarih Kurumu, 1943), 496; Georges Pachymérès, *Relations historiques*, vol. IV, ed. and tr. Albert Failler (Paris: Institut français d'études byzantines, 1999), 346, n. 15.

[13] Aydın Ayhan and Tuncer Şengün, "Anadolu beyliklerinin ve Osmanlı Beyliği'nin İlhanlılar adına kestirdiği sikkeler," in *XIII. Türk Tarih Kongresi, Ankara, 4–8 Ekim 1999: Kongreye sunulan bildiriler*, 3 vols. in 5 (Ankara: Türk Tarih Kurumu, 2002), vol. III, part II, 1161–71; Ahmet-Zeki Validi [Togan], "Economic conditions in Anatolia in the Mongol period," tr. Gary Leiser, *Annales Islamologiques* 25 (1991): 203–40; İsmail Hakkı Uzunçarşılı, *Osmanlı Tarihi*, 4 vols. (Ankara: Türk Tarih Kurumu, 1947–59), vol. I, 30–1.

[14] Halil İnalcık, "Foundation of Ottoman State," tr. Metin Yeğenoğlu, in *The Turks*, eds. Hasan Celal Güzel, et al., 6 vols. (Ankara: Yeni Türkiye, 2002), vol. III, 60–2; and Aşık Paşa, *Garib-nâme: tıpkıbasım, karşılaştırmalı metin ve aktarma*, ed. Kemal Yavuz, 2 vols. (İstanbul: Türk Dil Kurumu, 2000), vol. II, part II, 548–79.

to the great chief with a personal bond that is reminiscent of the bond of vassalage we see in western European feudalism. . . .

The mutual relationships between the great chief and other chiefs, on the one hand, and between the lesser chiefs and their *alps*, on the other, were ordered and determined according to the rules of customary law. Nonobservance of these rules by either one of the parties would bring about a sudden break in the relationships, that is to say, it would cause internal revolutions and rebellions. . . . The chiefs had to give general banquets to their own *alps* at certain times in accordance with certain ceremonial rules that would be followed by a looting of the goods of the chief by his *alps*. . . . A chief who would not do this would easily lose his rule over his *alps*. [The *alps* lived in an] era during which raid and plunder were means of production.[15]

The age of the *alps* "during which raid and plunder were means of production" extended well into the thirteenth and fourteenth centuries, if not later, as this nomadic society migrated westward into Byzantine Anatolia. The *Book of Dede Korkut*, a collection of epic stories in Turkish, was a product of this age in which a leader of *alps* "used to have his tents plundered at gatherings."[16] The extant written version of this collection seems to originate from the second half of the fifteenth century. Although some of its stories went way back to the pre-Islamic period in Central Asia, others had a more contemporary ring to them.

It was not only in epics, though, where one finds the *alps*, who were described by Aşık Pasha with such precision in the early fourteenth century. Right around the time when the *Garibname* was composed, the company of Osman, the founder of the Ottoman dynasty, included names such as Ayghud Alp, Dündar Alp, Hasan Alp, Turgut/Durkut Alp, and Konur Alp. In the Ottoman chronicle that supplied some of these names, Osman said the following to his son Orhan as the last statement of his will: "Bestow abundant favors on your comrades (*nökers*) – for your benevolence towards them is the trap [that keeps them] in their condition."[17] In other words, as long as one satisfied his vassals, they would remain loyal; to put it the other way around, if one did not satisfy them, they might look for other leaders. Thus benevolence was not a disinterested ethical goodness but rather a political requirement to secure a vassal's homage to his overlord. The sense of mutual obligation that was invoked by Köprülü in reference to a somewhat earlier period in his

---

[15] M. Fuad Köprülü, "Alp," *İA*, vol. I, 382–3.
[16] *The Book of Dede Korkut: A Turkish epic*, eds. and trs. Faruk Sümer, Ahmet E. Uysal, and Warren S. Walker (Austin: University of Texas Press, 1972), 168; see also Geoffrey Lewis' note that cites historical cases in which such plunders took place, *The Book of Dede Korkut*, tr. Geoffrey Lewis (Harmondsworth: Penguin, 1974), 210, n. 135.
[17] Aşıkpaşazade Ahmed, "Tevârîh-i âl-i Osman," in *Osmanlı Tarihleri*, ed. Çiftçioğlu N. Atsız (Istanbul: Türkiye Yayınevi, 1949), 112; for Ayghud Alp, see Sa'deddin, *Tâcü't-tevârîh*, 2 vols. (Istanbul, 1279–80), vol. I, 21; for Dündar Alp, who might have been Osman's uncle, see Hüseyin Bosnavi (called Koca Mü'errih), *Bedâyi'ü'l-vakâyi'*, ed. A. S. Tveritinova, 2 vols. (Moscow, 1961), vol. I, 34, 78–79; for the other *alps* mentioned, see the index of Aşıkpaşazade.

discussion of the banquets, then, was very much alive around the time that Osman was engaged in the conquest of Byzantine Bithynia.

Although raiding someone else's territory might be productive in the short term and satisfy one's companions, the long-term good of the Ottoman ruling class, which at this point might be construed to consist of Osman, his comrades, and the comrades of their comrades, lay in the sustainable exploitation of the peasantry. This idea was expressed by Ghazan Khan, the Mongol Il-khan of Persia and the overlord of all former Seljuk territories in Anatolia; hence, Osman's ultimate suzerain. Ghazan Khan was said to have addressed the Mongol-Turkish military and nomad aristocracy in the following manner:

> I am not on the side of the [Iranian subjects]. If there is a purpose in pillaging them all, there is no-one with more power to do this than I. Let us rob them together. But if you wish to be certain of collecting grain and food for your tables in the future, I must be harsh with you. You must be taught reason. If you insult the [subjects], take their oxen and seed, and trample their crops into the ground, what will you do in the future? . . . The obedient [subjects] must be distinguished from the [subjects] who are our enemies. How should we not protect the obedient, allowing them to suffer distress and torment at our hands.[18]

Osman may or may not have said anything of this sort to his comrades. It is, nevertheless, important to demystify the formation of the Ottoman political enterprise. Whether the Ottomans believed that they were fighting in the name of their faith or they styled themselves as benevolent lords, they were living off the land, not unlike the other conquerors of the medieval world. Just as the Middle Ages in Europe "could not live on Catholicism," in Karl Marx's words, the late medieval Ottomans could not live on Islam.[19] When Osman's comrade Turgut Alp conquered İnegöl, Osman is supposed to have given the area to him as a timar. In due course, the area consisting of "his villages" was called Turgut Eli, or the Land of Turgut. Similary, Hasan Alp received Yar Hisar.[20] Thus the heroic knights (*alps*) were becoming feudal landlords whose livelihoods, as well as that of their retinue and other dependents, were dependent on the extra-economic appropriation of the surplus produced by their peasants.

This feudal nature of the Ottoman polity in the fourteenth and fifteenth centuries created two related sources of political tension; this tension in turn brought about the series of conquests, the narrative of which constitutes the "rise" of the Ottoman Empire, and led to the development of the patrimonial political system in the sixteenth century. The source of the first tension, which may be called the horizontal one, was the fact that the Ottoman ruler was not the

---

[18] Quoted by I. P. Petrushevsky, "The socio-economic condition of Iran under the Il-khans," in *The Cambridge History of Iran*, vol. V: *The Saljuq and Mongol Periods*, ed. J. A. Boyle (Cambridge: Cambridge University Press, 1968), 494.

[19] "One thing is clear: the Middle Ages could not live on Catholicism, nor could the ancient world on politics;" Karl Marx, *Capital: A Critique of Political Economy*, vol. I, tr. Ben Fowkes, reprint (London: Penguin, 1976), 176; quoted by Teschke, "Geopolitical relations," 325.

[20] Aşıkpaşazade, "Tevârîh-i âl-i Osman," 105.

only political power in the region. Because he was only one of many overlords who competed for the support of the vassals, he had to earn and sustain their homage by securing their satisfaction. If Orhan did not show himself to be the more capable and promising ruler, his men would start shifting their allegiance toward the neighboring lordly families, such as the House of Aydın, Germiyan, or Karasi or even the Byzantine Empire.

There were historical moments at which one could imagine that political entities like Osman and his retinue could have been integrated into the Byzantine Empire the way many Balkan polities lived under Byzantine suzerainty for centuries. Turkish mercenaries who joined the Catalans in the service of the Byzantine Empire against other Turkish warlords in Anatolia are well known.[21] A more striking example of cooperation was the meeting of Demir Khan, the leader of the House of Karasi, with the Byzantine Emperor Andronicus II (1282–1328) at Pegai, around modern Karabiga on the southern shore of the Marmara Sea. At this meeting a Turkish contemporary of Orhan kissed the foot of the Byzantine Emperor in acknowledgment of his superiority.[22]

The marriage of Orhan to Theodora, the daughter of John VI Cantacuzenus, in 1346 was represented in similar terms by Byzantine sources, which gave the impression that Orhan asked for her hand, "promising thereafter to serve [John VI] as a vassal with his whole army."[23] Interestingly, Gregoras Nikephoros, a contemporary of Orhan, started calling him Hyrcanus in his chronicle from the moment this marriage proposal was mentioned. This name change suggested that once Orhan became part of a civilized family, he gave up his barbarian name and took a Greek one; this act was not unlike that of John, the king of Judaea, who had taken the same name, Hyrcanus, upon his accession to power in the late second century BCE as a symbol of the Jewish recognition of Hellenistic culture.[24] Obviously one should read this marriage as John VI's attempt to ally himself with Orhan to gain military strength in his political struggle for the Byzantine throne.[25] Yet it is clear that whether one was from Constantinople or Bursa determined whom one identified as the senior partner in the relationship between John VI Cantacuzenus and Orhan.

[21] Ramón Muntaner, *The Chronicle of Muntaner*, tr. Lady Goodenough, 2 vols. (London: Hakluyt Society, 1920–21), vol. II, 542–4, 578–9.
[22] John VI Cantacuzenus, *Geschichte*, trs. Georgios Fatouros and Tilman Krischer (Stuttgart: A. Hiersemann, 1982-), vol. II, 20.
[23] Donald M. Nicol, *The Last Centuries of Byzantium, 1261–1453*, 2nd ed. (Cambridge: Cambridge University Press, 1993), 204.
[24] Nikephoros Gregoras, *Rhomäische Geschichte*, tr. Jan Louis van Dieten (Stuttgart: A. Hiersemann, 1973-), vol. III, 154; compare vol. II, part II, 224, 282.
[25] That is exactly how a Turkish historian of the Byzantine Empire recounted the event; Şerif Baştav, *Bizans İmparatorluğu Tarihi: Son Devir (1261–1461)* (Ankara: Türk Kültürünü Araştırma Enstitüsü, 1989), 42. A more detailed analysis of this marriage is offered by Anthony Bryer, "Greek historians on the Turks: The case of the first Byzantine-Ottoman marriage," in *The Writing of History in the Middle Ages: Essays presented to Richard William Southern*, eds. R. H. C. Davis and J. M. Wallace-Hadrill (Oxford: Clarendon Press, 1981), 471–93.

Orhan, then, had to perform well to keep his men on his side and not lose them to another warlord like himself or to the Byzantine emperor himself. The trouble with this pressure was that its successful resolution only brought more pressure. A victory on the battlefield or a conquest attracted more men to the Ottoman enterprise, creating further pressures to keep their allegiance under conditions of limited agricultural resources. The creation of new resources was only possible through further conquest as agricultural productivity was limited for reasons presented earlier in the discussion of Teschke's model. Thus the Ottomans *had to* conquer new territories for political survival in a world of limited agricultural productivity. Fortunately, for them, and unfortunately for many others, they had a competent leadership that delivered on its promise of satisfaction to its vassals through a swift series of conquests. As noted by Teschke, "strong unifying forces are discernible wherever a competent warlord set out to lead his co-ruling nobles into successive cycles of campaigning and the subsequent redistribution of conquered land and the wider spoils of war (slaves, women, hostages, treasure, tributes, armaments) among his contented warriors."[26]

These unifying forces brought the Ottomans to the heart of southeastern Europe and eastern Anatolia rather quickly. Yet their unity always remained fragile because the feudal ties that the Ottomans established with their vassals were by their very nature vulnerable. This vulnerability had nothing to do with religious differences between the suzerain and his vassals. To give a striking example, Stefan Lazarević, the Orthodox Christian Prince of Serbia and an Ottoman vassal, apparently tried to free his suzerain and brother-in-law, Bayezid I, by entering into battle three times after the latter was caught by Timur's soldiers at the Battle of Ankara in 1402.[27] What made these personal ties even more vulnerable was the ease with which a suzerain could fall from power and become a vassal. Ya'kub II, the Lord of Germiyan, had lost his territories to Bayezid I, but after the Battle of Ankara, he became the senior ally of Mehmed I, who was much weaker than his father had been, as evidenced by the oath he took to be loyal to Ya'kub II.[28]

By the second half of the fifteenth century, however, Ottomans had already started replacing their vassals with governors. One after the other, all the Anatolian and Balkan principalities, including the Byzantine capital Constantinople, were annexed to the Ottoman Empire, leaving Mehmed II the one and only great lord of the lands stretching from the Danube to the Euphrates. This period corresponds to the second stage of Ottoman conquests in the analysis of Halil

[26] Teschke, "Geopolitical Relations," 343.
[27] John V. A. Fine, Jr., *The Late Medieval Balkans: A Critical Survey from the Late Twelfth Century to the Ottoman Conquest* (Ann Arbor: University of Michigan Press, 1987), 499.
[28] Şinasi Tekin, "Fatih Sultan Mehmed devrine ait bir inşa mecmuası," *Journal of Turkish Studies* 20 (1996): 267–311, at 296–7, 307–8; Dimitris J. Kastritsis, tr., "Çelebi Mehemmed's letter of oath (*sevgendnāme*) to Ya'kūb II of Germiyan: notes and a translation based on Şinasi Tekin's edition," *Şinasi Tekin'in Anısına: Uygurlardan Osmanlıya* (Istanbul: Simurg, 2005), 442–4.

İnalcık, who argues that the Ottomans did not intervene in local affairs in the first stage of their conquests and only engaged in centralization efforts later.[29] Although İnalcık leaves one with the impression that this two-tiered approach to conquests was a conscious policy choice on the part of the Ottomans, the analysis offered here suggests that the first stage of the conquests in İnalcık's framework could not have happened any other way because of the political limitations imposed upon a "great lord" by the nature of feudal relations. The "great lord" was the suzerain of his vassals who were lords in their own areas. Thus it was impossible for him to intervene in their internal affairs. It was only after Mehmed II formed the *akçe* zone, thereby securing a rich treasury, that the second stage marked by centralization ensued.

From Mehmed II, the great lord, to Süleyman I, the emperor

As shown in the first chapter, already in the fifteenth century there was the beginning of a gradual move toward a monetary economy in the Ottoman realms.[30] A very significant indication of this shift was the development in the mid-fifteenth century of the *akçe* zone between the Danube and the Euphrates, an area in which many different currencies had been in place. The various Byzantine denominations, the South Slav monetary systems that had been in use in the late thirteenth and early fourteenth centuries,[31] and all the different examples of coinage among the Anatolian principalities were replaced by a single currency throughout the geographical unit that roughly corresponded to the Byzantine territories of the eleventh century. The lands of the Ottoman Empire were well integrated monetarily without much effort, suggesting that such an integration might well have been underway long before Mehmed II brought about political integration. Although there is little available evidence to show the social dynamics that made the monetary integration possible, it is quite clear that the socioeconomic move toward a market-oriented economy created monetary resources that allowed Mehmed II to transform the Ottoman political structures once he secured the charisma to execute this transformation with the conquest of Constantinople in 1453. This first wave of monetization was to be repeated in the sixteenth century over a larger geographical area.

As suggested earlier, two inherent political tensions arose from the nature of Ottoman feudal political relations. The first one, which I called the horizontal one, created pressures on the suzerain to make territorial conquests to satisfy his vassals so they would not work for another overlord. The second inherent tension in the system was the ever-present possibility that an Ottoman vassal would become an overlord in his own right and so would compete with the

[29] Halil İnalcık, "Ottoman methods of conquest," *Studia Islamica* 2 (1954): 103–29.
[30] See Chapter 1, 21.
[31] D. M. Metcalf, *Coinage in the Balkans, 820–1355* (Thessaloniki: Institute for Balkan Studies, 1965), 200.

Ottoman ruler himself. The Ottomans were well aware of this risk as they themselves had been vassals of superior powers, such as the Mongols, in their early history. These two fundamental sources of political tension, the horizontal competition between suzerains over the allegiance of vassals and the vertical competition between the suzerain and the vassal to sustain the hierarchical relationship of power, were further complicated by their interaction with each other. Whereas strengthening a vassal with a view to securing his continuing loyalty in the face of overlords competing for his homage could encourage him to become independent, weakening him to prevent his independence could encourage him to look for an alternative overlord.

These tensions shaped the formative period, about 1300–1453, of the Ottoman Empire in two fundamental ways. Whereas horizontal competition between overlords culminated, as suggested earlier, in the series of conquests that created the Ottoman Empire, the vertical tension between the Ottoman overlord and his vassals was eventually resolved in a patrimonial political system (1453–1580) in which feudal relations were replaced by artificial ties of kinship constructed by real as well as fictive bonds of what I call "political slavery."[32] I use the term "political slavery" to distinguish the slavery of, let's say, a grand vizier, from that of an African laborer in North America in the eighteenth century. In contrast to slave owners in the American South, an Ottoman sultan owed very expensive obligations toward his slaves; in the case of a grand vizier, his compensation might well exceed the combined treasury revenue of several small contemporary kingdoms in Europe.

Thus the difference between feudalism and Ottoman patrimonialism, as I use these terms, is not a qualitative one. In the final analysis, both were based on mutual obligations created by a political bond that defined a power relationship between two parties, one of which was cast as superior to the other. The difference between the two systems *seems to be* related to the question of stability. Feudalism was inherently instable as the political bond between the overlord and the vassal could not be taken for granted. The vassal of today could aspire to become the suzerain of tomorrow, or the vassal of a certain king could shift his allegiance to another one. Ottoman patrimonialism, however, was supposed to be a system in which the bond between the master and his servant, or slave, could not be broken. Thus Ottoman patrimonialism transformed one of the defining characteristics of feudal social relations, vassalage, which basically meant being "the 'man' of another man," into a seemingly more stable bond—that of artificial kinship through slavery.[33]

Contemporary sources documented well the transformation of feudal political relationships into bonds of slavery. As is well known, from the reign

---

[32] For patrimonialism, see Halil İnalcık, "Comments on 'sultanism:' Max Weber's typification of the Ottoman polity," *Princeton Papers in Near Eastern Studies* 1 (1992): 49–72, at 56.

[33] For the quote, see Marc Bloch, *Feudal Society*, tr. L. A. Manyon, 2 vols. (Chicago: Chicago University Press, 1961), vol. I, 145.

of Mehmed II on, Ottoman grand viziers and other high-ranking military-administrative personnel began to be drawn more from the household of the sultan and less from the ranks of the Anatolian and Balkan nobility. The reasoning behind this shift was symbolically explained in a dream attributed to Murad II, the father of Mehmed II; an anonymous Greek chronicle from the early sixteenth century placed this dream within the course of the events of about 1445:

They say that Murad had a dream one night, which he then related and the Turks believed it to be prophetic: he saw a man dressed in white garments, like a prophet, who took the ring that his son was wearing on his middle finger and transferred it to the second finger; then he took it off and put in on the third; after he had passed the ring to all five fingers, he threw it away and he vanished. Murad summoned his hodzas and diviners and asked them to interpret this dream for him. They said: "Undoubtedly, the meaning is that only five kings from your line will reign; then another dynasty will take over the kingdom." Because of this dream it was decided that no members of the old, noble families, i.e. the Turahanoğlu, the Mihaloğlu, or the Evrenos, would be appointed beglerbegs or viziers and that they should be restricted to the office of the standard-bearer of the akıncı, i.e. the horsemen who owe military service and receive no salary when they form the vanguard during campaigns. There is another family of this kind, called Malkoçoğlu. These standard bearers are under the command of the beglerbeg. All these families had hoped to reign but, because of Murad's dream, they were deprived of their former considerable authority.[34]

This transition from a leadership based on local nobility to one drawn from the slaves of the sultan in the mid-fifteenth century could not have happened in the absence of a strong monetary economy that financed it. It was the monetary resources that Mehmed II amassed that made it possible for him to keep a larger slave household and a strong central army. While his slave household members staffed the uppermost ranks of the Ottoman administration, their authority was secured by the central army, which also consisted of royal slaves of *devşirme* origin. The expenses of both were financed by the gradually increasing production for the market without which neither taxes in cash could be expanded nor former feudal ties be broken. For instance, soon after the conquest of Trabzon from the Byzantine Comnenos dynasty in 1461, fiefs in the area were distributed to the slaves coming from the household of the sultan.[35] The sultan could not have maintained these slaves without a market economy that created the cash tax resources for their upbringing and education in the central army. In addition, as men stationed in the imperial capital Istanbul, they would not have been able to use revenue from a tract of land in Trabzon without engaging in monetary transactions in the marketplace.

[34] Marios Philippides, tr. *Byzantium, Europe, and the Early Ottoman Sultans – 1373–1513: An Anonymous Greek Chronicle of the Seventeenth Century (Codex Barberinus Graecus 111)* (New Rochelle: Aristide D. Caratzas, 1990), 59–60; quoted by Heath W. Lowry, *The Nature of the Early Ottoman State* (Albany: State University of New York Press, 2003), 140.

[35] Ö. L. Barkan, "Timar," *İA*, vol. XII/I, 299–300.

Thus slowly but steadily, the growth of a monetary economy allowed the slaves of the sultan to replace feudal vassals on various levels in the exploitation of agricultural resources. This transformation could not be better symbolized than in the shift of meaning attached to the term *nöker*, which lost its primary connotation relating to Mongol nobility and came to mean a servant or slave.[36] The slave-servants of the sultan became the new nobility of the land, the members of which were supposed to be replaced by the next generation of slaves, thereby making it impossible to build strong bases of opposition to royal authority.

Süleyman the Magnificent, then, was not the suzerain of many vassals but rather the emperor of his slaves.[37] The patrimonial system seemed to have reached such a level of perfection toward the end of his reign that one did not need to wonder about who was going to be the next grand vizier. Everything functioned like clockwork. The promotion system in place selected the gifted servants of the sultan and raised them in the hierarchy through proper steps up to the second vizierate. Whoever happened to be the second vizier at the time of the dismissal or death of a grand vizier replaced his predecessor in office. Ayas Pasha (grand vizier, 1536–9), Lutfi Pasha (1539–41), Hadım Süleyman Pasha (1541–4), Rüstem Pasha (1544–53, 1555–61), Kara Ahmed Pasha (1553–5), Semiz Ali Pasha (1561–5), Sokullu Mehmed Pasha (1565–79), and Semiz Ahmed Pasha (1579–80) were all former royal servants who were appointed as viziers to the imperial council during the reign of Süleyman and were promoted to the grand vizierate in due course after serving as second vizier.[38]

The only remaining source of political tension appeared to be the one among the royal princes. Whereas in the feudal age the Ottoman sultan had to be wary about losing his men to a competing overlord in the region, in the age of patrimonialism, the central concern was not to divide the allegiance of the political slaves among royal princes. Thus during the reigns of Bayezid II (1481–1512) and Süleyman I (1520–66), the competition among royal princes for imperial succession began happening already during the lifetime of their fathers. During the reigns of Selim II (1566–74), and Murad III (1574–95), only one prince held a governmental post in the provinces, thus making it

[36] See Halil İnalcık's comments in Ahmet Caferoğlu, "Türk tarihinde 'nöker' ve 'nöker-zâdeler' müessesesi," *IV. Türk Tarih Kongresi – Ankara, 10–14 Kasım 1948* (Ankara: Türk Tarih Kurumu, 1952), 260.

[37] There were, however, parts of the empire of Süleyman where one might be able to talk about vassalage, such as the Ottoman Kurdistan; see Baki Tezcan, "The development of the use of 'Kurdistan' as a geographical description and the incorporation of this region into the Ottoman Empire in the 16th century," in *The Great Ottoman-Turkish Civilisation*, eds. Kemal Çiçek et al., 4 vols. (Ankara: Yeni Türkiye, 2000), vol. III, 540–53.

[38] For biographies of these grand viziers except Semiz Ahmed Pasha, see the relevant entries in *İA* and *İA2*. Semiz Ahmed Pasha, for whom no entry is provided in reference works, was third vizier in the mid-1570s, whereas Piyale Pasha was second vizier. The latter died in 1578; thus Semiz Ahmed must have been the second vizier in 1579 when Sokullu died; Selaniki, *Tarih*, vol. I, 113, 125; Şerafeddin Turan, "Piyâle Paşa," *İA*, vol. IX, 566–9.

impossible for any factions to be formed around competing princes.[39] In theory, this system created a unity of purpose among the members of the extended family of the emperor that included, first and foremost, his slaves. As articulated by Kınalızade Ali around 1565, it was this unity that ensured the successful exploitation of the empire's subjects:

[As long as] the union that is concluded among the masters of the *devlet* lasts, the supremacy and domination, which are inseparable from that union, continue. It is an established fact that each *devlet* begins with a group of men entering an alliance and acting like the members of one body . . . in helping and supporting each other. Each individual has a certain degree of power, yet once their power is assembled together in one place, it becomes more than [the sum of] each one's power. Thus a small group of allied men prevails over many groups that are disunited. Is it not obvious that the number of men who are in possession of a *devlet* does not even amount to one hundredth of the number of that *devlet*'s subjects? And yet since these men are allied and the subjects are not, the former become victors and rulers while the latter are defeated and ruled.[40]

However, a major contradiction was about to create serious problems for the Ottoman political system. The perfected system of the imperial exploitation of agricultural resources had developed in response to the inherent vertical tensions of feudal political relations, which in turn, were a reflection of feudal socioeconomic relations. Yet the patrimonial political system was very much the product of a market economy as argued earlier. Not surprisingly, new socioeconomic forces were to create new kinds of political tensions to which the patrimonial system was going to respond ineffectively.

The development of the court as a center of political power

The patrimonial political system that the Ottomans developed in response to the inherent tensions of feudal political relations produced new challenges, such as powerful vizier households, to which the dynasty reacted by transforming the court into a new center of political power. As pointed out earlier, while the Ottomans were responding to tensions associated with feudal political relations, they had already started operating under a new socioeconomic setting, that of a market society in the making. The patrimonial response to some of the most essential political tensions of a bygone age had uncalculated consequences in a new era that was to be defined by the slow but steady growth of a market society. Producing for the market provided incentives for peasants and others to maximize their profits, leading to an increase in labor productivity from the fifteenth to the sixteenth centuries.[41] As the age of "political

---

[39] See Chapter 1, 46.
[40] Kınalızade, *Ahlâk-ı 'Alâ'î*, book III, 2; cf. Süleymâniye Kütüphanesi, Hamidiye 626, f. 408a.
[41] Metin M. Coşgel, "Agricultural productivity in the early Ottoman Empire," *Research in Economic History* 24 (2006): 161–87, at 171.

accumulation" was coming to a close, the quintessential resource to be controlled became cash flows rather than agricultural resources. By the end of the sixteenth century, the Ottoman sultan came to realize that he was about to lose his grip on the reins of imperial power; that is, the control of cash flows in his domains. His competitors were not other suzerains who commanded the allegiance of his vassals or one of his vassals who had become independent, but his very own slaves.

The Ottoman centralist policies, which attempted to hinder the formation of alternative loci of power in the provinces by appointing palace school graduates who did not have local power bases, had the unwanted effect of creating other alternative loci of power. The palace graduates took the opportunity to build clienteles of their own, using their powerful offices as a base from which to distribute lesser positions. In the end, the imperial servants gradually replaced the provincial notables of the conquered territories in local power structures. As a result there developed a web of personal relations running all over the empire, with Istanbul as the center where all the ties came together. In this type of a centralized state, the timar was transformed from being a salary substitute for a provincial cavalryman into a commodity in the market of patron–client relationships.[42]

The power of the vizierial political patronage centered in Istanbul was immense. While the viziers were building their clienteles, they were not bestowing their favors for free. The practice of the sale of offices was widespread.[43] The Venetian ambassador Giacomo Soranzo, who was in Istanbul around 1575, noted the riches of the grand vizier Sokollu and stated that he controlled all appointments and sold everything publicly.[44] The sale of offices was not the only source of income enjoyed by the grand vizier. For instance, Sokollu also profited from international trade by selling the produce of his lands to Venice and other European countries.[45] In fact, he was so involved in trade that he was actively engaged in developing a new port on the Eastern Mediterranean coast slightly to the north of İskenderun (Alexandretta) in ancient Baiae, or Payas (modern Yakacık).[46]

How could one quantify the power of a vizier? One way is to establish the extent of his wealth. Fortunately we have an inventory of the estate of Rüstem Pasha, the son-in-law of Süleyman the Magnificent who had served him for some fifteen years as grand vizier (1544–53, 1555–61).[47] At the time of his death, Rüstem Pasha's wealth, most probably excluding his generous

---

[42] For examples, see Chapter 1, 22; Tezcan, "Searching for Osman," 145–6.

[43] In the early seventeenth century, this practice was so commonplace that a small town imam/teacher and former warden in Bosnia was to declare in his own work that he sold his office of the warden, converting it into cash; Aga Dede, *Ta'rîh-nâme*, 27.

[44] Pedani-Fabris, *Relazioni*, 209.   [45] Anonymous, "Hırzü'l-mülûk," 178.

[46] M. Fatih Müderrisoğlu, "Osmanlı İmparatorluğu'nun Doğu Akdeniz'deki iskelesi Payas ve Sokullu Mehmed Paşa Menzil Külliyesi," in *9th International Congress of Turkish Art – 23–27 September 1991, Istanbul*, 3 vols. (Ankara: Kültür Bakanlığı, 1995), vol. II, 513–24.

[47] Âli, *Künhü'l-ahbâr*, TY 5959, f. 241b; Peçevi, *Ta'rîh*, vol. I, 23.

endowments that supported a number of mosques, hospices, and colleges all over the empire, was far greater than the annual revenues of the Ottoman central treasury. In the fiscal year of 1547, the total of the revenues that reached the treasury from all sources of cash was 128,608,946 *akçes*,[48] whereas the value of the silver, gold, and jewelry in the list of Rüstem Pasha's possessions, the three items for which cash estimates were made, added up to 155,660,000 *akçes*,[49] which only accounts for a portion of the estate.

Although we do not know the monetary value of most of the items in Rüstem Pasha's estate inventory, the 815 farms and 476 water mills that were located in various parts of Anatolia and Rumelia, as well as the 1,700 slaves, 2,900 horses, and 1,106 camels, show the extent of the economic activities in which a grand vizier could engage. The estate inventory also suggested that Rüstem Pasha either had an immense group of clients in the empire who kept presenting him gifts or that he was involved in trade of luxury goods. Otherwise it would be hard to account for the following items, only some of which could have been used by him and his slaves: 80,000 turbans (*dülbend*), 5,000 caftans, 1,100 golden "bonnets" (*üsküfs*), 2,000 suits of armor, 600 silver saddles, 500 jeweled golden saddles, 1,500 silver helmets, 130 golden stirrups, 760 jeweled swords, and 1,000 silver halberds. Rüstem Pasha probably did not buy 8,000 manuscript copies of the Qur'an either, 130 of them with jeweled covers, although he might have bought some of the 5,000 other manuscripts.

Thus, the men who were well situated at the imperial center accumulated fortunes as well as large groups of clients. Despite the royal policy of confiscations, or *müsadere*, of large amounts from deceased military-administrators' estates, viziers and high-ranking administrators were able to pass their status to their sons. During his long tenure in office, Sokollu Mehmed Pasha appointed quite a number of his family members to important positions, and after his death, his son Hasan Pasha continued to climb the hierarchy, receiving the title of vizier early in 1593. A younger relative of Sokollu, Lala Mehmed Pasha, was to become grand vizier during the reign of Ahmed I.[50] Finally, another son of his, İbrahim Pasha, held the governorship of Bosnia in the early seventeenth century and founded the family referred to as the İbrahimhanzadeler, the sons of İbrahim Khan, who were at some point considered as a possible substitute for the Ottoman dynasty should it die out.[51] When the son of Lala Mustafa Pasha, who had been the acting grand vizier of Murad III in 1580, died at the age of thirty, he had already attained the governorate of Aleppo.[52] Osman Pasha,

[48] Barkan, "954–955 (1547–1548)," 237.
[49] 780,000 gold ducats at 57 *akçes* per ducat would make 44,460,000 *akçes* (for the exchange rate, see ibid., 246–7); 32 pieces of jewelry were estimated to be worth 11,200,000 *akçes*. The total value of silver ingots and coins was 100,000,000 *akçes*. For the wealth of Ali Pasha, another grand vizier, see Tezcan, "Searching for Osman," 148.
[50] Selaniki, *Tarih*, vol. I, 304; Peçevi, *Ta'rîh*, vol. II, 353.
[51] Feridun Emecen, "Osmanlı hanedanına alternatif arayışlar: İbrahimhanzadeler örneği," in *XIII. Türk Tarih Kongresi*, vol. III, part III, 1877–86.
[52] Âli, *Künhü'l-ahbâr*, TY 5959, ff. 463b–464a.

the grand vizier of Murad III, was the son of Özdemir Pasha, the governor of Yemen and Ottoman Ethiopia during the reign of Süleyman. Sinan Pasha, five times grand vizier to Murad III and Mehmed III, had two siblings both of whom reached governorates.[53] His son, Mehmed Pasha, attained the title of vizier in 1594 while Sinan Pasha himself was grand vizier, which violated the dynastic tradition that restricted sons of viziers and governors from reaching high-ranking posts during the lifetime of their fathers.[54] Mahmud Pasha, the son of Cıgalazade Sinan Pasha, one of the grand viziers of Mehmed III, also attained the title of vizier.[55] Mehmed Pasha, both of whose grandfathers were grand viziers,[56] himself became the grand vizier of İbrahim in 1644.[57]

Taken together, such examples suggest that in the latter part of the sixteenth century Ottoman administrators of high rank were able to pass their political influence to their families, creating alternative loci of power.[58] Thus replacing local aristocracies with the slaves of the sultan did not eliminate the formation of alternative power centers. These alternative centers of power, however, did not challenge the Ottoman ruling family's right to the sultanate, nor did they make an effort to undermine the prestige of the sultanate. After all, their own power derived from the powers and privileges of the sultan, which they enjoyed as his legitimate delegates. Rather, they tried to enlarge the powers delegated to them, which, in practice, meant a transfer of power from the person of the sultan to his delegate. Thus their challenge to the Ottoman sultanate was an indirect, yet real one.

Not surprisingly, the political advice literature that was produced in the sixteenth century mainly addressed the viziers. Lutfi Pasha's *The Book of Asaph* was meant to be a handbook for grand viziers – Asaph was Solomon's vizier.[59] The anonymous author of *The Book on the Affairs of Muslims and the Interests of the Believers*, written in the mid-sixteenth century, saw the grand vizier as the man who was to implement his reform proposals and addressed

---

[53] His elder brother Ayas Pasha was governor-general of Erzurum during the reign of Süleyman; his other brother, Mahmud Pasha, became the governor-general of Anatolia in 1591, while Sinan Pasha himself was grand vizier, Selaniki, *Tarih*, vol. I, 236.

[54] Selaniki, *Tarih*, vol. I, 381; Klaus Röhrborn, "Osmanlı İmparatorluğunda müsadere ve mutavassıt güçler," in *I. Milletlerarası Türkoloji Kongresi, İstanbul, 15–20.X.1973: Tebliğler*, vol. I: *Türk Tarihi* (Istanbul: Tercüman, 1979), 255.

[55] Tezcan, "Searching for Osman," 338, n. 87.

[56] His paternal grandfather was Semiz Ahmed Pasha, grand vizier of Murad III in 1579–80, and his maternal grandfather was Cıgalazade Sinan Pasha, grand vizier of Mehmed III in 1596.

[57] For another vizier whose father was a vizier, examples of marriage alliances of viziers with jurists, and of the transformation of royal slaves into local power holders in provinces, see Tezcan, "Searching for Osman," 149–50, 356, n. 44.

[58] For later and stronger manifestations of these dynamics, see Rifa'at Ali Abou-El-Haj, "The Ottoman vezir and paşa households, 1683–1703: a preliminary report," *Journal of the American Oriental Society* 94 (1974): 438–47.

[59] See Lutfi Pasha, "Lütfi Paşa Âsafnâmesi: yeni bir metin tesisi denemesi," ed. Mübahat S. Kütükoğlu, in *Prof. Dr. Bekir Kütükoğlu'na Armağan* (Istanbul: İstanbul Üniversitesi Edebiyat Fakültesi Tarih Araştırma Merkezi, 1991), 49–99.

him at the end of almost every chapter, whereas in the later part of the sixteenth century, the author of the *Castle of Kings* urged the sultan to stop the transfer of power to the grand vizier.[60]

The grand vizier in whose person this transfer of power was best symbolized was Sokollu Mehmed Pasha. When Murad III acceded to the Ottoman throne, Sokollu Mehmed Pasha had been grand vizier for nine years and had already accumulated great wealth and a large network by appointing his men to various posts and selling offices to others.[61] Murad III's absolutist tendencies, which were introduced in the last chapter,[62] developed, at least partially, in response to his uneasiness with the political power of his grand vizier.

There is an interesting episode narrated by Peçevi that demonstrates the relative power of the grand vizier Sokollu vis-à-vis Murad III at the outset of the sultan's reign. Very soon after Selim II died on December 15, 1574, Sokollu sent a letter to the court of Prince Murad in Manisa, inviting him to the capital to assume the throne. A galley was then sent to the southern coast of the Marmara Sea to meet the prince and bring him to Istanbul. However, when Murad and his retinue reached the coast, they could not find the royal galley, so instead they boarded a commercial carrier of wheat, which happened to belong to Feridun Bey, the chief secretary of the imperial council (*nişancı*). Murad and his retinue, which included three prospective viziers and a future grand mufti, were caught in a storm and had a rather unpleasant trip, so much so that Murad, the new sultan, was apparently seasick, laid himself down, and put his head on the lap of one of his men, Tiryaki Hasan, for him to pat his head and wipe his face. Very late on Tuesday night, December 21,[63] they arrived at one of the coastal gates of the capital on the Marmara Sea, Ahurkapu; there the guards refused to let them in, stating that they had strict orders to send any galleys to Bagçekapu, another coastal gate located at the Golden Horn.

Murad had not had much experience of the imperial capital. He was born in 1546 in Manisa, while his father, Prince Selim, was governor of the province of Saruhan. In 1558 Murad moved to Konya, as Selim was transferred to the governorship of Karaman that year. In 1559, Murad became an eyewitness to the battle between his father and his uncle, Prince Bayezid, who were fighting for their future inheritance on the Konya plain, after which he briefly visited his grandfather Süleyman in Istanbul;[64] he then returned to Kütahya, the governorship of which was assigned to his father. In 1561 his grandfather appointed him to the governorship of Manisa, where he stayed until the death of his father in 1574. If Murad had ever had a chance to meet Sokollu, it must have been during the latter's visit to Selim in 1559 when Sokollu helped the prince against his brother. Murad may have seen Sokollu once again during

---

[60] Anonymous, "Kitâbu mesâlihi'l-Müslimîn," in passim; anonymous, "Hırzü'l-müluk," 188. For the correct dating of the former work, see Tezcan, "The Kânûnnâme of Mehmed II," 658–9.

[61] Pedani-Fabris, *Relazioni*, 209.   [62] Chapter 2, 56.

[63] Selaniki, *Tarih*, vol. I, 99.   [64] This short visit is noted by Rumi, [*Ta'rîh*], f. 2a.

his short visit to the capital around 1560, when Sokollu was third vizier at the imperial council. Since then, Sokollu had married Murad's sister Esma Han, had become grand vizier in 1565, and had been practically ruling the empire since the death of Süleyman in 1566.

It was this powerful man who came to welcome Murad that cold December night in 1574. Probably having been notified by the guards of Ahurkapu, Sokollu came to Bagçekapu in his boat, landed on the shore, ordered a small carpet to be spread out on the ground for Murad, and invited the new sultan to disembark from the commercial vessel. Murad was worried. One of his five brothers could have been enthroned during the past week; he could be walking to his death. However, he did leave the boat. In a moment of hesitation about how to handle the situation, Prince Murad, by then practically a sultan, bowed down when his hand met Sokollu's. An Ottoman sultan was about to kiss the hand of his grand vizier! Sokollu did not let him do that and quickly kissed the sultan's hand instead.

This anecdote related by Peçevi on the authority of Tiryaki Hasan Pasha, who as a member of Prince Murad's retinue was an eyewitness to the encounter, suggests that a powerful grand vizier could be intimidating enough to make a fresh sultan fall into sycophancy.[65] This incident raises the question of who really ruled and places into context the remarks of the anonymous author of the *Castle of Kings*, whose main target was the very grand vizier Sokollu.[66] At the outset of the reign of Murad III, the reins of power were clearly in the hands of the grand vizier.

Selaniki, another contemporary, also suggested that the sultan was but a symbolic ruler, noting the difference between those who knew how things were actually run and the inexperienced newcomers who had been in the retinue of Murad III in Manisa. He described the scene on Friday, January 14, 1575, the first day of the Muslim feast that marked the end of Ramadan, the month of fasting; on that day, a throne was set up in the courtyard of the palace so that all the major officials in the capital could come to greet Murad III, who was enjoying his first month as sultan:

[When] that untruthful, inconstant, and ungrateful trickster, which they call the throne of the sultanate and the caliphate, was set in front of the Gate of Happiness in the courtyard, the old servants, who have seen that while in a short time two eminent and grand . . . emperors [i.e. Süleyman I and Selim II] said "[the throne] is mine" it actually was in the disposal of others, knew that it was in swift decadence [and thus] moaned and groaned with heartache. And those [servants], who came from the other side [i.e. Manisa] with the prince of [the throne, i.e. Murad III] and saw the throne of the sultanate, became arrogant from the comfort and joy of it, not having seen [the past].[67]

Murad III, however, turned out to be more diligent in making the throne really his own. In a reply to one of the writs of his grand vizier Sinan Pasha, who

[65] Peçevi, *Ta'rîh*, vol. I, 26–8.   [66] Anonymous, "Hırzü'l-mülûk," 177–8; see also Chapter 2, 55–6.
[67] Selaniki, *Tarih*, vol. I, 109.

Fig. 6. Murad III's favorite mute, late sixteenth century; Österreichische Nationalbibliothek, Cod. 8626, fol. 41; courtesy of the Austrian National Library.

apparently showed some reluctance in executing one of his orders regarding the assignment of a large fief to a Circassian mute in the palace, Murad III asserted that the "sultanate is supposed to mean that the sultan's order must be taken as an order [to be executed]" (see Fig. 6).[68] Both Murad III's statement and his order to grant a large fief to a palace favorite illustrate the essentials of the framework within which the power struggle between the sultan and the viziers took place in the late sixteenth and the early seventeenth centuries. Frustrated with the prevalence and strength of the networks centered on the households of the viziers, the Ottoman sultan started to create his own network of patron–client relationships in which his – and not the viziers' – orders were to be obeyed.

Many came to perceive Murad III as a sultan who crossed the proper boundaries of royal authority because of his actions and policies in seizing the reins of power. Selaniki, the author of the comments mentioned earlier on the Ottoman throne and its occupants, had quite different things to say about

---

[68] Sinan Pasha, [*Telhîsât*], Süleymaniye Kütüphanesi, Esad Efendi 2236, f. 70b.

the sultanate of Murad III twenty years later, when he wrote a rather critical summary of the sultan's reign on the occasion of his death in January 1595. According to Selaniki, the sultan had not allowed any independence to his viziers and the *mevali*; he kept dismissing them and appointing new ones.[69] Murad III had clearly reclaimed the Ottoman throne for the sultan.

Whether or not the self-inflicted intimidation by his grand vizier Sokollu on coming to Istanbul, which was described by Peçevi, had a deep, lasting impact on Murad III, the sultan did follow the policy suggested by the author of the *Castle of Kings* and started to use his own discretion in making appointments. That is why Mustafa Âli complained about the sultan accepting bribes and making many appointments himself. In addition, Sokollu's power was curbed because many of his men lost their positions.[70] Instead of letting his viziers run the imperial network of clients, Murad III attempted to control the network himself. In 1580 after the death of Semiz Ahmed Pasha, the last grand vizier whose initial appointment to the imperial council was made by Süleyman I (1520–66), Murad III even entertained the idea of dispensing with the office of the grand vizier altogether;[71] hence, my suggestion of dating the beginning of the Second Empire, which was shaped by a fierce struggle between the absolutists and their opponents, in 1580.

Although Murad III did not dispense with the office of the grand vizier, he did manage to destabilize the position by frequently dismissing its occupants. After the death of the grand vizier Semiz Ahmed Pasha in 1580, the sultan appointed five viziers to the grand vizierate for a total of nine terms within fifteen years, and only one of the appointees died in office.[72] While destabilizing the position of the grand vizier, the sultan found other ways to create alternative loci of stable power that were centered within the court. One of these ways was the empowerment of a new office at the imperial court, that of the chief black eunuch (*darüssa'ade ağası*, or *kızlar ağası*), who was the chief officer of the harem, which was in the residential part of the palace. It is not exactly clear whether Murad III created this office; it might well have existed earlier. Yet even if it did, its significance must have been minimal because one does not find many references to it in earlier sources (compare Figures 13 and 14 in Chapter 4).[73]

---

[69] Selaniki, *Tarih*, vol. I, 427–8, 431–2.
[70] Âli, *Künhü'l-ahbâr*, TY 5959, ff. 501b, 503b–504b, 506b–507b.
[71] Selaniki, *Tarih*, vol. I, 37, 128.
[72] The five grand viziers appointed between 1580 and 1595 and their terms in office were Sinan Pasha (1580–2, 1589–91, 1593–5, dismissed by Mehmed III), Siyavuş Pasha (1582–4, 1586–9, 1592–3), Özdemiroğlu Osman Pasha (1584–5, died in office), Hadım Mesih Pasha (1585–6), and Ferhad Pasha (1591–2).
[73] Ahmed Resmi, *Hamîletü'l-küberâ*, ed. Ahmet Nezihi Turan (Istanbul: Kitabevi, 2000), 44, states that there are some references, which he does not identify, to the existence of the office during the reigns of Süleyman I (1520–66) and Selim II (1566–74). Yet, Resmi adds, it is known that during this earlier period the supervision of the harem was under the control of other officers.

Eunuchs had probably been employed at the Ottoman court since the four-teenth century.[74] Many were eventually appointed to positions in the imperial administration, just like the graduates of the palace school, and some of them even reached the grand vizierate, as did Ali Pasha (d. 1511), Sinan Pasha (d. 1517), Süleyman Pasha (d. 1547), Mesih Pasha (d. 1589), Hasan Pasha (d. 1598), and Gürcü Hadım Mehmed Pasha (d. 1626). Ottoman sultans preferred to appoint eunuchs to the governorship of Egypt, the tribute of which was earmarked for their personal treasury because, as Âli noted, "they are free of the care for wives and children, and all their possessions in the end revert to the Sultan."[75] Of the more than thirty governors of Egypt in the century follow-ing the Ottoman conquest (1517–1618) the three with the longest tenure were eunuchs: Süleyman Pasha (1525–36, 1537–8), Davud Pasha (June 1538–April 1549, died in office), and Mesih Pasha (January 1575–June 1580).[76]

Yet it was more lucrative to remain in the palace than to get an appointment in the imperial administration. The chief officer of the administrative part of the Ottoman palace was the chief white eunuch (babüssa'ade ağası, or kapu ağası), who enjoyed the privilege of direct access to the sultan. This privilege was an extremely important asset for the person who occupied the position, but it could also be used as a channel through which the sultan could grant offices to men who were not among the clients of the viziers. The chief white eunuch could procure positions and thereby create his own clients. Thus, through his chief eunuch, the sultan could develop alternative networks whose loyalties would be to him, rather than to the grand vizier.

Gazanfer Agha, who served Selim II, Murad III, and Mehmed III, was the first chief eunuch to become an imperial power broker.[77] Although it is usually assumed that he occupied the position of the chief white eunuch during the reigns of those three sultans, he must have only assumed this office during the reign of Murad III: when Murad III acceded to the throne, this position was occupied by a certain Mahmud Agha.[78] Gazanfer Agha became arguably the most well-known chief white eunuch in Ottoman history, and he created a strong political network that competed with those of the viziers. His political influence was exemplified in the move against the grand vizier Sokollu and in

[74] A manumitted eunuch of Orhan, the second ruler of the Ottoman dynasty, appeared as the administrator of a wakf established by Orhan in the oldest extant Ottoman document, dated 1324; see İ. Hakkı Uzunçarşılı, "Gazi Orhan Bey vakfiyesi, 724 Rebiülevvel – 1324 Mart," Belleten 5 (1941): 277–88, at 279–81.
[75] Mustafa Âli, Mustafâ 'Âlî's Description of Cairo of 1599: Text, Transliteration, Notes, ed. and tr. Andreas Tietze (Vienna: Verlag der österreichischen Akademie der Wissenschaften, 1975), 73.
[76] Ibid., 70–1; Muḥammad Ibn Abī al-Surūr, Al-minaḥ al-raḥmāniyya fī al-dawla al-'uthmāniyya, ed. Laylá al-Ṣabbāgh (Damascus: Dār al-Bashā'ir, 1995), 160, 233.
[77] Gazanfer was born a Venetian; see Maria Pia Pedani, "Safiye's household and Venetian diplomacy," Turcica 32 (2000): 9–31, at 14.
[78] Fleischer, Bureaucrat and Intellectual, 72; anonymous, "Kitâb-ı müstetâb," 25–6; Âli, Description of Cairo, 73, suggested that he was holding this position at the end of the reign of Selim II as well.

Fig. 7. Murad III and his chief black eunuch Mehmed Agha with the sultan's sword-bearer and water-carrier; manuscript illustration from Seyyid Lokman, *Zübdetü't-Tevârîh* (1583), Türk ve İslam Eserleri Müzesi, MS 1973, f. 88b; courtesy of the Museum of Turkish and Islamic Arts.

the appointment of Özdemiroğlu Osman Pasha to the grand vizierate in 1584 and that of Cığalazade Sinan Pasha to the same post in 1596 – in all these three actions the sultans in power, Murad III and Mehmed III, seem to have followed the advice of Gazanfer who was a supporter of Sokollu's rivals as well as of Osman and Sinan pashas.[79]

However, one powerful eunuch was not enough for Murad III, who had to compete with the powerful grand vizier Sokollu Mehmed Pasha at the beginning of his reign. That is why he appointed Mehmed Agha, an African eunuch allegedly from Ethiopia (see Fig. 7),[80] to the position of the chief eunuch of the harem, a post that, as mentioned earlier, he either created or strengthened in 1575.[81] As the superintendent of the harem, Mehmed Agha had access to

[79] Fleischer, *Bureaucrat and Intellectual*, 73, 114, 169.
[80] Ali el-Habeşi, *Râfi'ü'l-gubûş fî fezâyili'l-hubûş*, Süleymaniye Kütüphanesi, Fatih 4360, f. 9b, marginal note.
[81] Âli, *Künhü'l-ahbâr*, TY 5959, f. 94b; Selaniki, *Tarih*, vol. I, 229; Resmi, *Hamîletü'l-küberâ*, 44–5.

the private life of the sultan and was in a position to build relationships with Nurbanu Sultan, the queen mother; Safiye Sultan, the favorite of Murad III; as well as his unmarried daughters, such as Ayşe Sultan, the future wife of İbrahim Pasha, a prospective grand vizier. Just like the chief white eunuch, who was given the privilege of keeping a house outside the palace, Mehmed Agha, too, had a residence in Istanbul.[82] He was also assigned the additional duty of the supervision of the pious endowments whose revenues were earmarked for Mecca and Medina.[83] Thus with his influential office at the palace, his residence in the capital, and his financial responsibilities, Mehmed Agha was in a position to forge powerful connections that could compete with those of the viziers and to sponsor careers for future viziers.[84]

Mehmed Agha soon developed strong connections with the Ottoman ulema as well. In 1582, he endowed a college and secured a teaching position for the brother of Nevali Efendi, who was appointed to teach Prince Mehmed in the same year. Other professors who taught at Mehmed Agha's college during his lifetime and thus entered his network, such as Memikzade Mehmed and Azmizade Mustafa, were all to attain high ranks in the Ottoman educational-judicial hierarchy.[85] Furthermore, some of his protégés among the ulema eventually entered the finance department, such as Tophaneli Mahmud Efendi, who became a minister of finance during the reign of Mehmed III.[86] Thus Mehmed Agha had forged the connections necessary to sponsor careers among the ulema as well, a telling example being Mullah Ali, an African slave, who eventually became the chief justice of the European provinces in 1621.[87] Chief black eunuchs of sultans who succeeded Murad III continued to create alternative networks of power centered in the imperial court. Mustafa Agha, the chief black eunuch of Ahmed I and Osman II, for instance, was regarded as so indispensable that he was called back from his retirement in Egypt to serve Murad IV in 1623. Mustafa Agha sponsored the careers of such men as the future grand vizier Tabanıyassı Mehmed Pasha, the vizier and finance minister Hasan Pasha, and two other viziers, Sarrac Hasan Pasha and Hamidi Mustafa Pasha.[88]

It is hard to pinpoint the exact standing of the chief eunuchs within the Ottoman polity. Yet by the end of the sixteenth century, within the context of the

---

[82] Selaniki, *Tarih*, vol. I, 230.

[83] Hüseyin Hüsameddin and Mahmud Kemal, *Evkâf-ı hümâyûn nezâretinin ta'rîhçe-i teşkîlâtı ve nuzzârın terâcim-i ahvâli* (Istanbul, 1335), 14–15, n. 2.

[84] Resmi, *Hamîletü'l-küberâ*, 45, stated that most of the men "educated" by Mehmed Agha eventually became viziers.

[85] Ata'i, *Hadâ'iku'l-hakâ'ik*, 390, 407, 448, 739.   [86] Ibid., 304; Orhonlu, *Telhîsler*, 73.

[87] Baki Tezcan, "*Dispelling the Darkness*: The politics of 'race' in the early seventeenth-century Ottoman Empire in the light of the life and work of Mullah Ali," in *Identity and Identity Formation in the Ottoman World: A Volume of Essays in Honor of Norman Itzkowitz*, eds. Baki Tezcan and Karl Barbir (Madison: University of Wisconsin Madison Center of Turkish Studies, 2007), 81; see Chapter 4, 129–31, Fig. 11.

[88] Rumi, [*Ta'rîh*], f. 41a, 61a, 64a, 67b.

absolutist policies of Murad III, which were continued by his son Mehmed III (1595–1603), the chief eunuchs came to be situated on the boundary between officialdom and the dynasty, with privileged access to both. Gradually they came to be regarded as an extension of the dynasty. In 1595, for the first time in Ottoman history, a college that was endowed by someone outside the Ottoman dynasty was treated in terms of professorial promotions as an imperial college; that is, a college endowed by a member of the dynasty. Not surprisingly, this was the college of Gazanfer Agha, the chief white eunuch (see Fig. 8).[89] This change in the status of Gazanfer Agha's college during his lifetime was a telling symbol of the strong alliance between the dynasty and certain court offices created to restore the political initiative to the hands of the sultan.

In addition to the empowerment of the eunuchs, another office situated within the palace gained increasing importance during the same period, that of the *bostancıbaşı*, literally the chief gardener. In a certain sense, the young gardeners were the men most loyal to the sultan because they were employed within the palace, and their chief officer was one of the few who had direct access to him. During the reigns of Mehmed III and Ahmed I, the office of the chief gardener evolved into a power brokerage. In 1601, the Venetian ambassador reported with great joy that the chief gardener of the sultan had been dismissed as a result of a military rebellion that was directed against the court. The reason for the ambassador's joy was that the chief gardener had been lobbying on behalf of English interests at the palace.[90] In 1606, Ahmed appointed his former chief gardener Derviş Pasha as grand vizier. Hüseyin Agha, the chief gardener of Ahmed later in his reign, was to attain the grand vizierate during the reign of Osman II. Ahmed's last chief gardener, Receb Agha, later became the grand vizier of Murad IV.

This rise of the court as a center of administrative power was also reflected in the role that royal women were playing in politics. Leslie Peirce's study deals quite extensively with the political role of royal women, such as queen mothers, wives and concubines of sultans, and princesses.[91] I simply point out a few examples here of how the deeds of royal women created new channels of patronage in the educational-scholarly hierarchy of the empire. Although Murad III himself did not engage in large-scale construction in Ottoman capital cities the way his father did in Edirne and his grandfather in Istanbul, his mother Nurbanu Sultan surpassed all previous royal women in the prestige accorded to her pious endowments. In 1579, the college she endowed in Üsküdar, the Asian suburb of Istanbul, opened its doors. This imperial college was even more prestigious than the Süleymaniye. Some of the professors who taught there received judicial appointments to the cities of Bursa and Edirne, which were usually reserved for judges who had already served in the provincial capitals of Aleppo, Damascus, and Cairo, to which the professors of the

[89] Tezcan, "Searching for Osman," 359, n. 81.
[90] *Calendar of State Papers – Venetian*, vol. IX, 450.   [91] Peirce, *Imperial Harem*.

Fig. 8. The college of law endowed by Gazanfer Agha; manuscript illustration from Nadiri, *Dîvân-ı Nâdirî*, f. 22a; courtesy of the Topkapı Palace Museum.

Süleymaniye had been appointed.[92] Safiye Sultan, the mother of Mehmed III, followed her predecessor in the same path. The professors of the college of Safiye Sultan, rightly called the "catapult college," were given the opportunity to bypass the troublesome route of advancement through holding various provincial positions in the judiciary. Safiye Sultan's college was opened in February 1598; its first professor was Ebulmeyamin Mustafa, a protégé of Sa'deddin Efendi, the mentor of the sultan. Mustafa was appointed to the judgeship of Edirne after teaching two years there, and in 1603, he became grand mufti. In that position, Mustafa was later to legitimize Mehmed III's wish to execute his son whom he suspected of scheming to depose him.[93] Thus by providing privileged patronage to legal scholars, the court was trying to gain the loyalty of future *mevali*.

Providing rapid advancement for scholars of law through the colleges endowed by royal women was not the only mode of intervention in the *mevali* aristocracy. Another method was the appointment of scholars from within court circles to influential positions. The most telling examples of this kind of favor were the careers of two men closely related to a female courtier, Raziye Hatun (d. 1597), the *musahibe*, or confidante of Murad III since the days of his princely governorship in Manisa.[94] Raziye Hatun had two sons and a daughter as well as a husband. Her known husband Yahya was probably her second husband and not the father of her children, yet just like her children, Yahya took advantage of his wife's connections at the court. Thanks to those connections, Yahya was favored by the queen mother and personally received by Mehmed III. Although Yahya entered the educational profession quite late in life, he made up for this late start by bypassing all the typical procedures of advancement in the Ottoman ulema hierarchy, causing resentment among the ulema; hence, his epithet "the bird," which referred to his unusually quick rise through the ranks.[95] In 1597, while he was the judge of Mecca, Yahya was appointed chief justice of the Asian and African provinces, bypassing the typical route of serving several years in the judgeships of Bursa, Edirne, and Istanbul. In the same year, he was promoted again to become chief justice of the European provinces, replacing Mehmed, known as Damad Efendi, literally Mr. Son-in-Law. Mehmed had acquired this title by being the son-in-law of Raziye Hatun, the wife of Yahya.[96] Thus at the end of the sixteenth century, the apex of the judicial hierarchy was under the control of two men, both of whom had direct ties to the same female courtier at the court.

Yet, the court sought to secure closer control of other governmental institutions in addition to the judicial hierarchy. Beginning with the reign of Murad III, Ottoman sultans jumpstarted the careers of a number of viziers, from both within and outside the palace school, to strengthen their control of the

[92] For examples, see Tezcan, "Searching for Osman," 359, n. 84.
[93] Ata'i, *Hadâ'iku'l-hakâ'ik*, 448, 512, 569–70, 755–7; Selaniki, *Tarih*, vol. II, 724, 846; see Chapter 2, 68–70.
[94] Âli, *Künhü'l-ahbâr*, TY 5959, f. 502b.   [95] Selaniki, *Tarih*, vol. I, 419.
[96] Ata'i, *Hadâ'iku'l-hakâ'ik*, 520, 561.

imperial administration. The careers of İbrahim Pasha, the brother of Canfeda Hatun, who was the stewardess of the harem during the reign of Murad III, and of Raziye Hatun's son Mustafa Pasha showed how the court initiated alternative paths of advancement in the administrative hierarchy. In addition, the rapid promotion to vizierates in the late sixteenth century of a number of men who were known to be close to the court indicated the court's efforts to dominate the imperial council. For instance, Mehmed, an Armenian *devşirme* graduate of the palace school and a *musahib*, or a close companion, of Murad III, was promoted to the command of the janissaries in 1583, to the governorship of Rumelia the next year, and to a vizierate in 1587. As is described in Chapter 5, this vizier was the one who became the target of the 1589 rebellion of the imperial cavalry soldiers, the first of a series of confrontations between the army and the court. Mehmed III's promotion of Mehmed, his *lala*, or princely adviser, first to a vizierate without any previous administrative appointment, and soon after to the grand vizierate, illustrates the same royal attempt to create loyal viziers. Ahmed I's quick promotion of Derviş Pasha from the office of chief gardener to the grand admiralty, and then to the grand vizierate, was yet another example.[97] These men were given positions that others could only reach after many years of service, mostly in the provinces.

Another sphere that the court tried to control more directly was the financial administration. With the intermediacy of Esperanza Malchi, the Jewish *kiera*, or lady, who was a close companion of the Queen Mother Safiye, control of some of the most lucrative sources of taxation, such as customs duties, were farmed out to people who were close to the court, such as the very sons of the *kiera*. Just as Murad III's favorite vizier Mehmed Pasha became the target of a rebellion in 1589, another "military rebellion" was aimed at the *kiera* and her sons in 1600, as described in Chapter 2.[98]

All of these cases may be seen as examples of nepotism or corruption. Indeed, some contemporaries referred to them that way. Yet they instead should be seen as a conscious effort to increase the political authority of the court in response to other independent loci of political power, such as the households of the viziers, pashas, and the *mevali*. Through the newly empowered offices of the chief eunuchs and the chief gardener, and the financial resources assigned to royal women for them to build networks of clients, as well as the unusual promotions granted to some select graduates of the palace school, the Ottoman sultan aimed to create his very own clientele. The purpose seemed to have been the same as what motivated Mehmed II in the mid-fifteenth century to replace the Anatolian and Balkan aristocracy with the *devşirme* graduates of the palace school. Yet this time, it was the networks that these very *devşirme* graduates had been building over the sixteenth century at which the court took aim. Another major difference was the challenge faced by the dynasty. In the mid-fifteenth century, the local noblemen could still emerge as viable political

---

[97] Selaniki, *Tarih*, vol. I, 140, 150, 179–80; vol. II, 437, 447, 537; Rumi, [*Ta'rîh*], f. 23b.
[98] Chapter 2, 65.

alternatives to the Ottoman enterprise. In the late sixteenth century, however, the issue at stake was not the identity of the dynasty but simply the limits of royal authority, the debates on which were examined in the last chapter. The empowerment of the court vis-à-vis the viziers should be understood within this political context.

By the early seventeenth century, the court had achieved some success in its moves against the established vizier families, as illustrated by a comparison between two grand viziers from the Sokollu family. A relative of the senior Sokollu, also a Mehmed Pasha,[99] became grand vizier in 1604. Yet the way he was treated by the sultan was quite different from how Murad III treated Sokollu Mehmed Pasha in 1574 when he arrived in Istanbul.[100] The younger Mehmed Pasha reconquered Esztergom (in northern Hungary) in 1605, which he had lost to the Habsburgs ten years earlier. In the spring of 1606 Ahmed I ordered his victorious grand vizier, who had just returned from the Habsburg front, to lead a military campaign against the Safavids who, in the last two years, had reconquered most of the territories they had lost to the Ottomans during the long war of 1578–90. Mehmed Pasha was not pleased with this order, preferring to send a commander-general to the east so that he could stay in Istanbul and strengthen his position as grand vizier on the political stage of the imperial capital. Yet far from being able to persuade the sultan to change his mind, Mehmed Pasha could not even obtain an audience with the sixteen-year-old Ahmed I.[101] Clearly things had changed quite a bit since Ahmed I's grandfather Murad III had attempted to kiss the hand of Mehmed Pasha's elder cousin some thirty years earlier.

In summary, responding to the evolution of the vizier households into independent loci of power and the empowerment of the judiciary in the hands of the *mevali*, the Ottoman sultans of the late sixteenth and early seventeenth centuries attempted to reassert their authority through a redefinition of the roles of various palace officers as well as the creation of new ones. As argued in the last chapter, however, the enthronement of Mustafa I in 1617 marked a defeat for the court in that the authority of the grand mufti overrode the will of the previous sultan, and a younger brother followed his elder sibling on the throne for the first time in Ottoman history. In the final part of this chapter, the deposition of Mustafa I and the enthronement of Osman II are discussed within the context of this conflict between the court and other loci of power.

The deposition of Mustafa I and the enthronement of Osman II

The deposition of Mustafa I in 1618 was very much a product of the political structures built during the late sixteenth century. It could not have occurred

---

[99] Peçevi, *Ta'rîh*, vol. II, 353.   [100] See this chapter, 97–8.
[101] See the memoranda of Mehmed Pasha submitted to Ahmed I; Orhonlu, *Telhîsler*, 101, no. 118, 107, no. 128, 116, no. 146.

in the absence of the politically empowered office of the chief black eunuch, which was a product of the absolutist policies adopted by the Ottoman court starting from around 1580. In this sense, the deposition of Mustafa I and the enthronement of Osman II should be seen as a victory for Ottoman absolutism.

The conventional explanation for the deposition of Mustafa I – his mental incapacity – may well have some validity, but we do not have sufficient sources on his three-month-long reign in the winter of 1617–18 to assess the claim that he was mentally incompetent. Mustafa's lack of education suggested that he did not grow up the way other princes did; that is, in contact with teachers who came from outside the palace. Some sources indicated that Mustafa's imperial rescripts, which are supposed to be written by the hand of the reigning sultan, were actually written by a female servant. This female servant may well have been the high-ranking servant of the harem who was appointed to the position of the "teacher of the sultan" during the second sultanate of Mustafa (1622–3), two months after his accession.[102] None of the Ottoman sultans before him had a harem servant as a teacher. Yet, the fact that Mustafa had such a teacher was not surprising for, as argued elsewhere, he was too young to receive a proper education during the reign of his father, Mehmed III.[103] Furthermore, as demonstrated in the last chapter, Ahmed I did not think of his younger brother as a viable successor to himself,[104] so he did not invest in Mustafa's education. Instead, he assigned Mustafa a private apartment within the residential part of the palace that came to be known as a "cage," or *kafes*.[105] In short, Mustafa's contact with the outside world had been more limited than that of any previous Ottoman prince who eventually became a sultan. Whether or not the rumors about his elder brother Ahmed trying to have him executed were true, Mustafa may well have led a terrorized life, constantly in fear of a fratricidal death, as he was the first Ottoman prince to survive his elder brother's reign in the palace.

Nevertheless, all of this evidence does not establish that Mustafa I was mentally imbalanced when he came to the throne in 1617. The only piece of information about his short first reign provided by an Ottoman chronicler who did not have any reason to be biased suggested that Mustafa made a number of excursions to the arsenal and the navy docks, examining various sorts of arms and taking an active interest in the munitions supply of the army and the navy.[106] Moreover, one of the dispatches of Baron de Sancy, the resident French ambassador, suggested that Mustafa was interested in leading the Safavid campaign himself and was entertaining the idea of wintering in Konya for that purpose.[107] These were not the kind of acts that justify the claim of mental incapacity.

---

[102] See BOA, MM 6147, 78–9; Pedani-Fabris, *Relazioni*, 514; M. Münir Aktepe, "Mustafa I," *İA*, vol. VIII, 694.
[103] Baki Tezcan, "Kösem Sultan," 352–4.   [104] Chapter 2, 62.
[105] Aga Dede, *Ta'rîh-nâme*, 34.   [106] Abdülkadir, *Tarih*, vol. I, 669–70.
[107] BnF, fr. 16148, f. 246a, dated January 10, 1618.

Interestingly enough, the one plausible explanation given for the palace coup that deposed Mustafa I and enthroned Osman II did not have much to do with the alleged mental incapacity of Mustafa. On March 10, 1618, twelve days after the deposition of Mustafa I, the French ambassador Baron de Sancy seemed to have acquired some information that was not available to him on February 26, when he had reported the deposition of Mustafa I and the enthronement of Osman II. According to this later dispatch, rumors were definitely circulating in the capital about the mental incapacity of Mustafa I. Mustafa Agha, the chief black eunuch, was the man who vigorously worked to spread these rumors as widely as possible. These two pieces of information were also supported by Ottoman narrative sources.[108] How Mustafa Agha turned his political campaign to discredit Mustafa into a successful deposition was not made clear in the Ottoman sources.

Yet Baron de Sancy had a plausible explanation. Mustafa Agha's main ally seemed to have been Ali Pasha (1581–1621), a relatively young man who was the grand admiral of the navy at the time of Mustafa's enthronement in 1617. Although Ali Pasha was the son of a pasha, his rise to power had more to do with his own connections at the court, rather than his father's. His father, Ahmed Pasha, a corsair turned naval captain from the island of Cos (İstanköy in Ottoman usage, now in Greece), had become governor of Tunis and married the daughter of a certain Kaya Pasha.[109] In 1590, while dealing with a local uprising in Tripoli (in modern Libya), Ahmed Pasha was killed by an explosion of gunpowder in a magazine.[110] In consolation, his nine-year-old son Ali seemed to have been rewarded with the governorship of Damietta, on the Mediterranean coast of Egypt. During his long years of service in this position, Ali visited the capital quite a number of times, as he was charged with the delivery of the yearly tribute of Egypt, which was earmarked for the personal treasury of the sultan. In November 1605, when Ahmed decided to move to Bursa with his court to underline his commitment to deal with the Jalali rebels, it was Ali's ship that carried the sultan to the southern coast of the Marmara Sea.

Ali's subsequent rise to power was an excellent example of the growing powers of the chief black eunuch and hence a consequence of Ottoman absolutist policies. A special relationship developed between Mustafa Agha, Ahmed's new chief black eunuch, and Ali in the first decade of the seventeenth century. Mustafa Agha had served Mehmed III as a eunuch in the harem, but was sent to Egypt for retirement in 1011/1602–3 for unspecified reasons. After performing a pilgrimage to Mecca, Mustafa Agha returned to Istanbul upon the invitation of the new sultan, Ahmed I, who must have known Mustafa

[108] Hasanbeyzade, *Târîh*, vol. III, 919.   [109] Ata'i, *Hadâ'iku'l-hakâ'ik*, 657.
[110] Selaniki, *Tarih*, vol. I, 222–3; a more detailed account of the uprising was provided by Âli, *Künhü'l-ahbâr*, Süleymaniye Kütüphanesi, Esad Efendi 2162, ff. 575–576. Although Âli referred to Ahmed Pasha as governor of Tripoli, I follow Selaniki's designation of him as governor of Tunis.

Agha from his childhood. Mustafa Agha remained very close to Ahmed who appointed him in 1605, shortly before the Bursa campaign, to the office of the chief black eunuch.[111] Mustafa Agha may have known Ali from his exile in Egypt or from Ali's previous trips to the capital, in which case the choice of Ali's ship for the journey to Bursa may not have been an accident. In any event Ali was said to have been adopted by the black eunuchs of the palace as a son, suggesting a close relationship between Ali and Mustafa Agha.[112] Probably with the intermediacy of Mustafa Agha, Ali was offered the governorship of Yemen as a reward for his services during the Bursa campaign, but he declined it. Ahmed I then bestowed on him the governorship of Damietta with lifelong tenure.

Ali's later career continued to be shaped by his connections to the Ottoman court. Shortly after his appointment to Damietta with lifelong tenure, the grand admiral Cafer Pasha took Ali away from Damietta and lobbied for his appointment to the governorship of Magosa in Cyprus. Ali declined this appointment, came to the capital, and secured the governorship of the province of Tunis, the office of his father. Ali Pasha stayed in Tunis for some two years and was transferred to the governorship of the Morea around 1609, when the construction of the imperial mosque of Ahmed I was started.

The Venetian ambassador Contarini explained how this transfer came about. Apparently, the site of Ahmed I's mosque was occupied by two palaces, one of which belonged to Ali's mother. The sultan bought it for 30,000 ducats, which Ali Pasha seemed then to contribute toward the construction of the mosque.[113] In return for his donation, Ali Pasha was rewarded with the governorship of the Morea, which he did not personally assume but sent a deputy instead. Ali Pasha played an active role in the building of the mosque by employing his own galley slaves in the construction. After three years, Ali Pasha was appointed to the governorship of Cyprus and then to that of Tunis with a vizierate. Finally, through the intervention of Mustafa Agha, he was appointed to the grand admiralty in the winter of 1616–17, replacing Halil Pasha, who had just become grand vizier.[114] When Ahmed I died in November 1617, Ali Pasha was still the grand admiral of the Ottoman navy.

Mustafa Agha and Ali Pasha were both creatures of the political structures built around the Ottoman court in the late sixteenth century in response to the growth of alternative power structures centered around the households of viziers; it was their cooperation that brought Osman II to the throne and secured the dynasty another chance at absolutism. Ali Pasha, who early in Mustafa I's reign was replaced as grand admiral by Davud Pasha, the sultan's brother-in-law, had good reason to support Mustafa Agha's plans. The two men coordinated their efforts to discredit the new sultan as incompetent.

[111] Safi, *Zübdetü't-tevârîh*, vol. I, 80–1; Rumi, *Nuhbetü't-tevârîh*, III, 231.
[112] Rumi, [*Ta'rîh*], f. 31b.   [113] Barozzi and Berchet, *Relazioni*, vol. I, 180.
[114] Rumi, [*Ta'rîh*], f. 32a.

In addition, Mustafa Agha could easily enlist the support of Cafer Pasha, whom Baron de Sancy described as a protegé of Mustafa Agha. Cafer had graduated from the palace as a *çaşnigir* (taster). He became *kapucılar kethudası* (the steward of the doorkeepers at the palace) in 1604, at the beginning of the reign of Ahmed I. Around 1606, Cafer was promoted to the post of the First Master of the Horse (*mirahor-ı kebir*). Soon after, in September 1606, he was appointed to the governorship of Ottoman Ethiopia. Cafer Pasha did not seem to stay in Ethiopia for long, becoming governor of Yemen with the title of vizier in 1607, a position that he kept until 1616. Then, after a short stay in Egypt, Cafer Pasha returned to Istanbul in September 1617 and probably became a vizier in the imperial council. As a reward for his support in the enthronement of Osman II, Cafer Pasha was appointed to the governorship of Egypt by the new sultan in 1618.[115]

Although Cafer Pasha had much to gain from a new sultan in whose enthronement he would be playing a role, others were more reluctant to provide support for a coup. The grand vizier Halil Pasha was in the east at the time, commanding the Ottoman armies against the Safavids, so he could not really play an active role even if he was indeed interested in bringing Osman II to the throne. Gürcü Hadım Mehmed Pasha, an experienced vizier during the reign of Ahmed I, refused to get involved. Es'ad, the grand mufti, who was instrumental in the enthronement of Mustafa I, was opposed to his deposition.

But then, according to Baron de Sancy, Ali Pasha, the dismissed grand admiral, found out something that would make the deputy grand vizier Sofu Mehmed Pasha join their ranks, which, in turn, influenced the grand mufti as well. Davud Pasha, the brother-in-law of the new sultan, had apparently just managed to obtain an imperial rescript from Mustafa I appointing him to the deputy grand vizierate. Since he was not going to need the office of the grand admiralty any more, Davud Pasha offered the latter office, which he himself was occupying, to Ali Pasha for 50,000 ducats. Thus having learned that Davud Pasha was about to replace Sofu Mehmed Pasha in the deputy grand vizierate, Ali Pasha rushed to tell him the news. In addition to giving him this information, Ali Pasha also took the opportunity to solicit Mehmed Pasha's support for the deposition of Mustafa I by promising him that he could keep his position if he were to serve Osman. According to Baron de Sancy, Ali Pasha even had a letter written by Osman empowering him to promise the deputy grand vizier in the prospective sultan's name such change and recompense as he pleased.[116] Ali Pasha might have had access to such a letter through the chief black eunuch Mustafa Agha, who must have been in contact with the young prince at the palace.

---

[115] For contemporary sources on Cafer Pasha's life, see Tezcan, "Searching for Osman," 361–2, n. 109–15.

[116] BnF, fr. 16148, f. 294a.

According to Baron de Sancy, the deputy grand vizier Sofu Mehmed Pasha was easily persuaded and took 24,000 ducats to the mufti the very same day to secure his allegiance. Es'ad initially declined to support the coup, but changed his mind later, probably because he saw that there was not much he could do to stop the deputy grand vizier from becoming involved. Mustafa Agha and Ali Pasha did not try to persuade anyone else because they had already drawn to their side the two men who mattered most, the deputy grand vizier and the grand mufti. Yet Ali Pasha did not forget the janissaries and made a deal with the *sekbanbaşı* Kara Hasan Agha, a janissary officer and their deputy general in the absence of Hüseyin Agha, the general of the janissaries, who was engaged in the military campaign against the Safavids. In return for a promise to appoint him to the position of the general of the janissaries and to provide some money for distribution among the janissaries, Ali Pasha secured Kara Hasan Agha's loyalty and involvement in the deposition of Mustafa and the enthronement of Osman. Baron de Sancy claimed that it was the night following the day when Ali Pasha cut his deal with Kara Hasan Agha that Es'ad, the grand mufti; Sofu Mehmed Pasha, the deputy grand vizier; Ali Pasha, the former grand admiral; and Cafer Pasha, the former governor of Yemen succeeded in overthrowing Mustafa I by locking him into a small apartment in the palace with the help of Mustafa Agha, the chief black eunuch, and other eunuchs of the harem. Thus was Osman II enthroned at night in the residential part of the palace; others paid him allegiance the next morning, Monday, February 26, 1618.[117]

Ottoman narrative sources do not support this story directly, yet most agreed that the chief black eunuch Mustafa Agha was the architect of the deposition of Mustafa I and the enthronement of Osman II.[118] Apart from some inaccuracies regarding personal information on the royal family, the ambassadorial reports of the time tended to be reliable sources of information because the ambassadors made sure to enlist informants who had access to the circles of power.[119] The information they provided was usually confirmed by local sources. Whether or not one regards the specific story about the coup as credible, Ottoman sources confirmed that an Ottoman sultan was deposed and a new one enthroned through the strategies of the chief black eunuch, a position that had no major political influence before the reign of Murad III. Mustafa I may well have been mentally unbalanced, yet one wonders whether that could be a sufficient reason for the deposition had someone like Mustafa Agha not done his best to expose the behavior of the sultan to the public. After all, the empire could well have been run by an able grand vizier without much recourse to the sultan, as had been more or less the case during the reign of Selim II, whose grand vizier Sokollu ran the empire with his own men. Yet

---

[117] Ibid., ff. 293b–294a.
[118] See, for instance, Peçevi, *Ta'rîh*, vol. II, 360–2; Hasanbeyzade, *Târîh*, vol. III, 919–20.
[119] See, for instance, *Calendar of State Papers – Venetian*, vol. XI, 117.

Mustafa Agha, the occupant of a position founded by an absolutist sultan in the late sixteenth century, did not let that happen.

The deposition of Mustafa I lends itself to different interpretations. It might be seen as a symbol of the weakening of the institution of the sultanate in the late sixteenth and early seventeenth centuries as a result of the development of alternative loci of power. Apparently, it did not matter much who was ruling for most of the people, as the deposition of Mustafa did not create much public reaction. The soldiers who were at the capital did not seem to engage in opposition, as they were pleased to receive yet another set of accession benefits in cash within three months.[120] The soldiers at the army camp in Diyarbekir expressed discontent – not about Osman II per se but rather about the way his predecessor had been deposed and he himself enthroned at the pleasure of the deputy grand vizier and the chief black eunuch – yet they too seem to have been appeased after receiving their accession benefits.[121] Although contemporary sources did not record any discontent among the population at large, the "sanctification" of Mustafa might be an indication of people's silent resentment of the deposition.[122]

Although the ease with which an Ottoman sultan was deposed behind closed doors seems to suggest that the sultanate had become a weak institution in the early seventeenth century, the enthronement of Osman II may also be regarded as a victory for the institution of the sultanate, at least retrospectively. As was argued in the last chapter, the enthronement of Mustafa I in 1617 symbolized a victory for the lords of the law who, in the person of Es'ad, the grand mufti, interfered with the established Ottoman system of succession, which had always been from father to son. Although Mustafa Agha was probably acting in his own interests while preparing his plot to depose Mustafa I, his office was a symbol of the late-sixteenth-century Ottoman court that was reconfigured to become a center for absolutist politics. The very fact that a court officer, whose office had either not existed or not made it into the contemporary narrative sources until the late sixteenth century, could engineer a deposition in 1618 suggests that the efforts of Murad III, Mehmed III, and Ahmed I to promote the court as a center of power did bear fruit. Brought to the throne by an officer of his court rather than by an outside force, after having been originally bypassed by the grand mufti, Osman II was now going to make an effort to further empower the sultanate vis-à-vis the lords of the law and the vizier households with a new absolutist agenda, which is the subject of the next chapter.

[120] Baron de Sancy suggested that Davud Pasha tried to organize some opposition with the help of the soldiers, but they were appeased as soon as they received their accession donations; BnF, fr. 16148, f. 294b.
[121] Ibid., f. 341b, dated April 21, 1618.
[122] Ibid., f. 440a, from October 1618; Chapter 2, 75.

CHAPTER 4

A new empire for a second Osman

Osman II in power (1618–1622)

In the early morning of November 4, 1604, a group of palace officers led by the chief black eunuch were riding their horses swiftly to the Rumelian gardens in the outskirts of Istanbul where Ahmed I was having an outing. They had some great news to convey to the fourteen-year-old sultan. He had acceded to the throne almost a year ago, on December 21, 1603. More or less forty weeks ago, on January 23, 1604, he had become the first Ottoman sultan to be circumcised *after* his succession to the throne (see Fig. 9).[1] The news Ahmed I received that November morning confirmed that his reproductive activities that he engaged in after his circumcision had borne fruit: his concubine Mahfiruz had given birth to a boy the night before.[2] Ahmed I was now the youngest Ottoman sultan to become a father, and his newborn son was the first Ottoman firstborn prince to be born in Istanbul, the imperial capital.[3] Since the conquest of the city in 1453, every firstborn prince had been born in a provincial capital where their fathers served as prince-governors because princes would not engage in biological reproduction until after they were sent out to govern a province, which usually followed their circumcision.[4] Ahmed I's son was also the first Ottoman firstborn prince to be born in the second *hijri* millennium, which had started in 1591. The young emperor marked the occasion by naming his son Osman, after his ultimate ancestor, the feudal lord who some three hundred years earlier in Byzantine Bithynia began a political enterprise that became the Ottoman Empire. This was indeed a new beginning for the dynasty that was entering a new stage: a second Osman for the second millennium, or the Second Empire.

Osman, this firstborn prince, was to be at the age of sixteen the youngest Ottoman sultan to lead a military campaign. Moreover the area to which he led his armies, Khotin (in modern Ukraine), was the northernmost target the Ottoman armies had ever attacked in a military campaign led by a sultan.

---

[1] Rumi, *Nuhbetü't-tevârîh*, III, 221; Safi, *Zübdetü't-tevârîh*, vol. I, 19–21.
[2] Rumi, [*Ta'rîh*], f. 9; Safi, *Zübdetü't-tevârîh*, vol. II, 23–4; Na'ima, *Ta'rîh*, vol. II, 156.
[3] Selim II (1566–74) and most probably Mustafa I (1617–8, 1622–3) were born in Istanbul as well, yet neither was a firstborn prince.
[4] Peirce, *Imperial Harem*, 53.

Fig. 9. "Circumcision"; from the Taeschner Album.

Osman II was also the first Ottoman sultan to announce his intention of undertaking the Muslim pilgrimage to Mecca, more than 2,000 miles away from Khotin as the bird flies – but still within the same empire (see Map 4). Unfortunately, before he could leave his capital for this pilgrimage at the age of seventeen, he became the first victim of regicide in Ottoman history.[5] Although he could not build the new empire he aspired to, his ambitions set the stage for the struggle that was going to define the Second Empire.

The tragic end of Osman II's reign has been interpreted in several different ways.[6] The prevalent twentieth-century interpretation of Osman II was as a reformer because of his efforts to recruit a new army, which recent historians regarded as a major reform initiative. Rather than trying to find out whether he was a reformer or not, however, this chapter aims to place Osman II and his plans within a dynamic context in which the sultan is one of the parties contending for political power. I argue that he and his supporters were the absolutist party, aiming at centralizing political power at the court, in opposition to the constitutionalists, who shared the goal of limiting royal authority. I also suggest that his plan of creating a new army was seen as a rebellious act by the contemporary establishment in the imperial center rather than as a reform measure.

Before analzying the implications of Osman II's policies, especially those of the new army he intended to create, this chapter first discusses Osman II as a young ruler. Osman II was a teenaged monarch who was very eager to alter the course of certain developments that had been shaping the empire, such as the empowerment of the lords of the law and the transformation of the janissary corps into a public corporation; this latter development is discussed in Chapter 6. His ambitions were shaped by the absolutist policies of some of his ancestors and the resultant configuration of political power at the court, as well as a relatively new emphasis on social discipline – all of which were related to the sixteenth-century Ottoman socioeconomic transformation.

In the first part of this chapter I analyze the possible influences that Ömer Efendi, the tutor of Osman, may have had on the intellectual and political formation of the sultan. In the second part, I focus on the short reign of Osman II, especially on the grand vizierate of Ali Pasha and on Osman II's military campaign against the Polish-Lithuanian Commonwealth, which I interpret as manifestations of Osman II's absolutist ambitions. Finally, I discuss the idea of a new *sekban* army to be constituted of mercenaries that is ascribed to Osman II and argue that his contemporaries in the political establishment

[5] Bayezid II might have been poisoned on the orders of his son Selim, who deposed him in 1512. He spent a month in Istanbul in peace and died while he was on his way to Dimetoka where he intended to spend the rest of his life; see Şerafettin Turan, "Bayezid II," *İA2*, vol. V, 237.
[6] Baki Tezcan, "The 1622 military rebellion in Istanbul: a historiographical journey," *International Journal of Turkish Studies* 8 (2002): 25–43.

viewed the sultan as a rebel rather than a reformer. I also conclude that the pro-
liferation of the *sekbans* in the late sixteenth and early seventeenth centuries,
which has traditionally been explained by developments in military technology, was actually a product of the sixteenth-century Ottoman socioeconomic
transformation and its impact on the provincial administration of the empire.

Osman, his youth, and Ömer Efendi

Osman II was a thirteen-year-old boy when he was enthroned in February
1618. In today's world it is hard to imagine a teenager running an empire. Yet
the Ottomans did not seem to have had much trouble with the idea. Although
they might have forgotten their young Safavid adversary Ismail in the early
sixteenth century, the early reign of Osman II's father Ahmed I was quite fresh
in everyone's mind. Although the Ottomans did not have a formal institution
of regency, a thorough analysis of the sources suggests that it was Mustafa
Efendi, the tutor of Ahmed I, who was the most influential personality around
the minor sultan.[7] Therefore, it might follow that Ömer, the tutor of Osman II,
must have had a significant influence on the formation of Osman, first as a boy
and then as a young sultan.

Before focusing on Ömer, however, an introduction to what is known about
Osman's childhood is in order. Osman's mother most probably died while
Osman was a young child, certainly no older than age five.[8] In the absence of his
mother, Osman likely spent time with his stepmother Kösem Sultan, Ahmed I's
favorite. But later on Ahmed I is reported to have kept his son away from her.[9]
Although one cannot be sure why Osman was kept away from his stepmother,
it is possible that Ahmed I may have been worried about Kösem's stake in her
own son, Prince Mehmed, who was only four months younger than Osman.[10]
The only consistent source of motherly affection Osman received probably
came from his foster mother, whose name was not recorded in the sources.[11]

About Osman's private life, we do not know much. As a boy he seemed
to be fond of riding horses; his first public appearance on horseback was
probably in February 1614 when he was only nine years old.[12] Like more or
less every Ottoman sultan, he wrote some poetry, using the pen name Farisi (the
adjective form of *fāris*, "rider" in Persian),[13] which reflected his fascination
with horses. Osman's love of horses is well attested by a rare artifact: the
tombstone for his horse, which he apparently buried within the grounds of a

---

[7] Baki Tezcan, "The question of regency in Ottoman dynasty: The case of the early reign of
Ahmed I," *Archivum Ottomanicum* 25 (2008): 185–98.
[8] Tezcan, "Kösem Sultan," 348–50.   [9] Barozzi and Berchet, *Relazioni*, vol. I, 133, 292.
[10] Tezcan, "Kösem Sultan," 350–1.
[11] A privy purse register from 1622, after the deposition of Osman II, recorded her continuing
salary; BOA, MM 6147, 78; see also Peirce, *Imperial Harem*, 233.
[12] Safi, *Zübdetü't-tevârîh*, vol. II, 304.
[13] For his poems, see *Sultan II. Osman*, ed. Esra Keskinkılıç (Istanbul: Şûle Yayınları, 1999).

royal palace in Üsküdar.[14] His interest in horses inspired Kadızade Mehmed – most probably the preacher who gained great fame during the reign of Murad IV and after whom the Kadızadeli movement was named – to write a treatise on horses, which included a short section on political advice, and to present it to Osman II.[15] Some of the most popular portrayals of Osman II in Ottoman paintings were on horseback.[16]

Like his father Ahmed I, Osman II seemed to enjoy hunting. Just a week after his enthronement, he went to Üsküdar for a royal hunt,[17] and in the first months of his reign he had an accident in which he fell off his horse and injured his head. In fact, people were spreading rumors in early August 1618 that he had died and been replaced by one of his brothers without any public acknowledgment to avoid the payment of yet another series of succession donations.[18] Osman II's active interest in riding and hunting was accompanied by an appreciation of the arts of war. An interesting treatise on military dexterity by a master of Ottoman martial arts that was commissioned by the court of Osman II suggested that the sultan patronized masters who provided training in traditional forms of warfare.[19] Osman II was also interested in heroic epics, such as the *İskendername*, the Book of Alexander,[20] and the *Shahname*, the Persian Book of Kings, a Turkish prose rendering of which was being produced for him under the guidance of his first chief black eunuch, Mustafa Agha, who had also served his father Ahmed I.[21]

---

[14] Halil Edhem [Eldem], "Bir atın mezâr taşı kitâbesi," *Türk Ta'rîh Encümeni Mecmû'ası* 15/9 [86] (1341/1925): 196–9; Hüseyin Ayvansarayi, *Mecmuâ-i Tevârih*, eds. Fahri Ç. Derin and Vâhid Çubuk (Istanbul: İstanbul Üniversitesi Edebiyat Fakültesi Yayınları, 1985), 369.

[15] See *Kitâb-ı makbûl der hâl-i huyûl*, Süleymaniye Kütüphanesi, Kadızade Mehmed 420 (probably an autograph), especially f. 8b–12b; for a modern Turkish edition, see Kadızade Mehmed, *Kitab-ı Makbul: Atalarımızın Gözüyle At*, ed. Tahir Galip Ser'atlı (Istanbul: Uğur Yaraman, 1986). There is yet another Kadızade Mehmed (known as Sofyalı), who was a contemporary preacher and the predecessor of the better known Kadızade at the mosque of Ayasofya; see Tezcan, "Searching for Osman," 370, n. 57; Derin Terzioğlu, "Bir tercüme ve bir intihal vakası: Ya da İbn Teymiyye'nin *Siyāsetü'ş-şer'iyye*'sini Osmanlıcaya kim(ler), nasıl aktardı?" *Journal of Turkish Studies* 31/2 (2007): 247–75, at 266; see also this chapter, 125, n. 43.

[16] See, for instance, Harvard University Art Museums, the Edwin Binney 3rd Collection, 1985.0238; Topkapı Sarayı Kütüphanesi, Hazine 2169, f. 13a; and British Library, or. 2709, f. 3a. I would like to thank Tülün Değirmenci for bringing these portraits to my attention.

[17] Topkapı Sarayı Arşivi, D. 73, f. 1b, records the 2,000 *akçe*s that were spent during this outing.

[18] BnF, fr. 16148, ff. 431, 440a.

[19] Necib Asım [Yazıksız], "Fevâ'id-i gazâ: On birinci 'asrda hayât-ı cündiyâne," *Ta'rîh-i 'Osmânî Encümeni Mecmû'ası* 1 (1329/1911): 542–50; Jan Schmidt, *Catalogue of Turkish Manuscripts in the Library of Leiden University and Other Collections in the Netherlands* (Leiden: Leiden University Library, 2000-), vol. I, 239–43, 279–82.

[20] There is a copy in St. Petersburg that probably came from his library; see Boris Andreevich Dorn and Reinhold Rost, *Catalogue des manuscrits et xylographes orientaux de la Bibliothèque impériale publique de St. Pétersbourg* (St. Pétersbourg: Imprimerie de l'Académie impériale des sciences, 1852), 513–4, no. 566. The likely ascription to "Osman II bin Moustafa," however, is problematic and makes one wonder whether it was Osman III who was meant here. Unfortunately, I have not examined this manuscript myself.

[21] Tülün Değirmenci, "Resmedilen siyaset: II. Osman Devri (1618–1622) resimli elyazmalarında değişen iktidar sembolleri," PhD diss. (Hacettepe Üniversitesi, 2007), forthcoming

Thus Osman II likely was groomed to become a warrior sultan in the style of Mehmed the Conqueror or Süleyman the Magnificent. Yet this was not an obvious path for an Ottoman sultan to take in the late sixteenth and early seventeenth centuries. Since the death of Süleyman I in 1566, only one sultan, Mehmed III, had personally led his armies into battle, doing so in 1596. Ahmed I had seemed to be developing a charismatic warrior profile at the beginning of his reign,[22] yet later on he became preoccupied with courtly pleasures and played an important role in the move of the dynasty to residences at the Bosporus, which led to further residential developments alongside the Bosporus and brought the Asian and European sides of this waterway closer to each other.[23] In contrast, Osman II, despite widespread opposition from the lords of the law and other statesmen who suggested that he should stay in Istanbul, did enter the field of combat in person at the age of sixteen as will be explained in Chapter 5.

A last point about Osman II's personal history is that he most probably felt cheated out of the throne at the time of his father's death. The imperial communications sent out to announce his accession after the deposition of his uncle in 1618 implied that Mustafa I's reign had not been in line with the "ancient Ottoman constitution (kanun-ı kadim-i osmani)."[24] Moreover, works of history written for him made an obvious effort to erase the short reign of Mustafa from the history of the empire. For instance, Mehmed Rumi referred to Osman II as the fifteenth Ottoman sultan and thus did not count Mustafa, whom he also failed to include in the Ottoman family tree.[25] Ganizade Nadiri, after mentioning the death of Ahmed, referred to the reign of Mustafa as the "false dawn," in contrast to the "real dawn" – the enthronement of Osman II.[26]

When he was enthroned, Osman II had two close advisers, the chief black eunuch Mustafa Agha and his tutor Ömer. Mustafa Agha's significant role in Ottoman politics during the reign of Ahmed I and in the enthronement of Osman II was described in the last chapter.[27] Although Mustafa Agha continued to play an important role in the early reign of Osman II, he was sent

---

as a book from Kitap Yayınevi; Firuza Abdullaeva, "A Turkish prose version of Firdawsi's *Shahnama* in the manuscript collection of the St. Petersburg University Library," *Manuscripta Orientalia: International Journal for Oriental Manuscript Research* 3 (1997): 49–57.

[22] In 1605, Ahmed made a journey to Edirne and another one to Bursa on short notice with the aim of showing his commitment to dealing with the Jalalis; Rumi, *Nuhbetü't-tevârîh*, III, 231. In 1606, he was planning to lead his armies in person against them, a plan he never realized; Comte Théodore de Gontaut Biron, ed., *Ambassade en Turquie de Jean de Gontaut Biron, Baron de Salignac, 1605 à 1610: Correspondance diplomatique & documents inédits* (Paris: H. Champion, 1889), 78.

[23] Pietro della Valle, *Reiss-Beschreibung in unterschiedliche Theile der Welt* (Genff, 1674), 25; Gontaut Biron, *Ambassade en Turquie*, 28, 102.

[24] Anonymous, *Gazânâme*, f. 175b.

[25] Rumi, *Nuhbetü't-tevârîh*, I, 3, II, 74–5, compare II, 70.

[26] Ganizade Nadiri, "Ganî-zâde Nâdirî: Hayâtı, edebî kişiliği, eserleri, dîvânı ve Şeh-nâmesinin tenkidli metni," ed. Numan Külekçi, PhD diss. (Atatürk Üniversitesi, 1985), 326.

[27] See Chapter 3, 103, 110–13.

to retirement to Egypt and replaced by Süleyman Agha as chief black eunuch in 1620 (see Fig. 13).[28] In contrast, Ömer remained very close to Osman II throughout his reign with the exception of a short episode in 1620.[29]

Not much is known about Ömer's family background. He was born in Amasya in 962/1554–5. His father was a certain Mehmed, and their family was apparently known as İğnecizade. Ömer had at least three brothers. Two of them, Sarı Ali and Karabaş Abdurrahman, followed him in ulema careers, whereas the third one, Ahmed, became a military administrator. Ömer got his teaching license from Mazlum Melek Ahmed, the tutor of the younger sons of Selim II (1566–74), who were executed by their elder brother Murad III. It is not clear whether Ömer was with Ahmed when he was still in Istanbul during the reign of Selim II. Ata'i stated that Ömer accompanied his patron to Medina while Ahmed served as the judge of that city (1577–80). After teaching at a college in Amasya for a while Ömer came to Istanbul in 1582 in the hope of obtaining an appointment to another provincial college in Niksar. But his fortunes rose when an upper ranking pasha granted him the professorship of the college he had just founded in Eyüp. Thus Ömer was able to stay in the capital and married into the family of Vahyizade, a famous preacher. Vahyizade was not only a famous preacher in his own right but was also a relative of Ali Bey, a former fief-holder-turned-sheik from the family of Edebali, the Sufi sheik who, according to early Ottoman lore, had blessed Osman, the founder of the Ottoman dynasty, by letting him marry his daughter.[30] It was Ali Bey who girded Ahmed I's sword in the first recorded enthronement-related sword-girding ceremony of Ottoman history.[31]

What changed Ömer's life was his second career as a preacher, which he may well have embarked on following the example of Vahyizade, his

[28] Mustafa Agha was later invited back from Egypt during the reign of Murad IV, just as he was invited back at the beginning of the reign of Ahmed I; Resmi, *Hamîletü'l-kübera*, 48–9; Chapter 3, 110–11.
[29] BnF, fr. 16149, f. 39b; fr. 16150, ff. 42b, 64a.
[30] Hüseyin Hüsameddin [Yaşar], *Amasya Tarîhi*, 4 vols. (Istanbul, 1328–1928), vol. IV, 7, 35; Ata'i, *Hadâ'iku'l-hakâ'ik*, 263, 598, 717–8, 728–9, 763. On Edebali, see Cemal Kafadar, *Between Two Worlds: The Construction of the Ottoman State* (Berkeley: University of California Press, 1995), 128–9.
[31] Cemal Kafadar, "Eyüp'te kılıç kuşanma törenleri," in *Eyüp: Dün / Bugün (Sempozyum, 11–12 Aralık 1993)*, ed. Tülay Artan (Istanbul: Tarih Vakfı Yurt Yayınları, 1994), 55; and Colin Imber, "Die Thronbesteigungen der osmanischen Sultane: die Entwicklung einer Zeremonie," in *Investitur- und Krönungsrituale: Herrschaftseinsetzungen im kulturellen Vergleich*, eds. Marion Steinicke and Stefan Weinfurter (Köln: Böhlau Verlag, 2005), 300, rely on Safi, who stated that the incumbent grand mufti girded the sultan's sword; *Zübdetü't-tevârîh*, vol. I, 16. Nicolas Vatin and Giles Veinstein, *Le sérail ébranlé: Essai sur les morts, dépositions et avènements des sultans ottomans, XIVᵉ–XIXᵉ siècle* (Paris: Fayard, 2003), 310, refer to a later chronicler, Müneccimbaşı, who provided the same information, most probably relying on Safi as well. Although Safi was very close to Ahmed I after December 1608 when he became his imam, he probably was not present at the girding ceremony that took place in January 1604 when he was the imam of a mosque in Istanbul. Therefore I prefer the testimony of Ata'i who must have used a larger network of informants for his vast biographical dictionary than Safi did for his chronicle; *Hadâ'iku'l-hakâ'ik*, 598.

well-connected father-in-law. Sometime in the late sixteenth century, Ömer became the preacher of the Zal Pasha mosque in Eyüp. In the first decade of the seventeenth century, apparently thanks to his father-in-law, Ömer was appointed to preach at the Ayasofya, the famous cathedral-turned-mosque of the city, right in the vicinity of the imperial palace. Ahmed I must have met him at this mosque and found him worthy of the position of princely tutor. In January 1609, Ömer became the preceptor of the two sons of Ahmed I, Osman and Mehmed, both of whom were about four years old.[32] In this capacity he must have played a significant role in the formation of Osman. The fact that Osman II was to name his only known son after Ömer Efendi supports this hypothesis.[33] Unfortunately, however, Ömer did not leave any writings behind that could help us draw a picture of his worldview, which presumably had an impact on Osman. Yet his professional background, if examined within the context of early seventeenth-century Istanbul, may actually provide some clues.

Although Ömer had been a professor, he was better known as a preacher, which was quite unusual for a preceptor of princes. In the past half-century, preceptors had usually been chosen from among professors who had passed the middle stages of their careers. Starting with Ömer, however, the nature of the position of the princely tutor changed, as imams of sultans and preachers came to monopolize this position in the seventeenth century.[34] The unprecedented prestige of the imams of sultans, which was in stark contrast with the Süleymanic era, might be seen as a defensive reaction of the court directed against the *mevali*, as imams of sultans usually came from modest backgrounds and were not related to the lords of the law.[35] In addition, the increasing representation of preachers among the tutors of princes reflected their growing importance in the political life of the capital at the turn of the seventeenth century.

Ottoman narrative sources clearly reflected the increasing importance ascribed to preachers at the turn of the seventeenth century (see Fig. 10). These sources were relatively silent with regard to preachers of the sixteenth century, but definitely not for the seventeenth century.[36] Some of the anecdotes related in those sources suggest that the preachers enjoyed great popular respect in their capacity as representatives of moral authority in this period. One was about Va'iz Emir Abdülkerim (d. 1015/1606–7), who used to preach at the Süleymaniye Mosque at the end of the sixteenth century. Apparently,

---

[32] Gontaut Biron, *Ambassade en Turquie*, 258; compare Ata'i, *Hadâ'iku'l-hakâ'ik*, 728; Karaçelebizade, *Ravzatü'l-ebrâr*, 512.
[33] Katib Çelebi, *Fezleke*, vol. II, 23.   [34] See Tezcan, "Searching for Osman," 373–4, n. 77–8.
[35] Some *imams* of sultans even became grand muftis and chief judges in this period; see, for instance, Şeyhi, *Vakâyi'ü'l-fudalâ*, vol. III, 61–2, 409–10, 651–3. For a comparison with the Süleymanic era; see Fleischer, *Bureaucrat and Intellectual*, 17–18.
[36] See the comparison of sources on this issue in Tezcan, "Searching for Osman," 374–5, n. 81–2.

Fig. 10. "Preachers"; from the Taeschner Album.

after delivering his sermons he would respond to questions from the people in his audience, who would write their questions and leave them at his seat. His responses came to draw larger audiences than his sermons. They were apparently so popular that men would wait in the coffeehouses around the Süleymaniye for the sermon to end and show up when Va'iz Emir started his responses.[37] The usual Muslim practice was for Muslims to direct their questions regarding the legality of their various practices in daily life to the mufti. However, this anecdote suggested that the preachers had become a kind of "muftis of the people" in the Ottoman capital at the turn of the seventeenth century.

---

[37] Ata'i, *Hadâ'iku'l-hakâ'ik*, 597; Hasanbeyzade, *Târîh*, vol. III, 418–9, 793, 913–4; Peçevi, *Ta'rîh*, vol. II, 359.

Hand in hand with their growing popularity, preachers in the late sixteenth and early seventeenth centuries seemed to be voices of opposition in the imperial capital. They were expected to relate prophetic traditions and comment on the verses of the Qur'an. For instance, the preacher at the mosque of Ayasofya, which was the summit of a preacher's career, was referred to as the "chief of the commentators [of the Qur'an] and the crown of the traditionists [of the Prophet]."[38] Depending on the choice of a verse and/or tradition a preacher picked to share with his congregation and the interpretation he made of them, commenting on the Qur'an and traditions, however, could be quite political. As suggested by some of their critics in the 1580s, the preachers apparently took the liberty of going beyond covertly political sermons and made more explicit references to the problems of their days, implicitly attacking the powerful people of the capital.

Mustafa Âli devoted a section to preachers in his *Counsel for Sultans*, which was originally written in 1581. In this work, he presented preachers as a threat to the Ottoman political order and asked the sultan to stop "the insolent and slanderous preachers who in their sermons become abusive and scold people:"

Now, how come these enemies of the state should grouch in the guise of reforming zeal, should attract thousands and thousands of simple-minded people to their gatherings and, seemingly preaching virtue, should commit acts of rebellion by starting a chain of mischief and disorder? . . .

These men, these mischief-makers who claim to be spiritual leaders, are each one of them without doubt a secret rebel [*celâlî*] right inside these well-protected lands, perhaps even right in the ancestor-inherited capital, kindling the flames of sedition with their perversive speeches and blowing it into a strong blaze with their foul-mouthed breaths.[39]

Contemporary accounts suggested that the preachers' critical stance actually gained significant popular support, which was very easily translatable into political influence and financial power. When, for instance, the earlier mentioned Va'iz Emir was exiled because of a sermon he gave that touched some sensitive nerves in the imperial capital, his followers engaged in protests that succeeded in bringing him back. Had he not returned, the janissaries were apparently going to attack people in the circle of the queen mother, whom they held responsible for the exile.[40] Most probably because of this support, during the reigns of Murad III and Mehmed III the preachers were consulted for advice on such important matters as the appointment and the dismissal of grand viziers.[41] At least in some cases, the preachers also succeeded in

---

[38] Ata'i, *Hadâ'iku'l-hakâ'ik*, 759.   [39] Âli, *Counsel for Sultans*, vol. I, 55–6.
[40] Selaniki, *Tarih*, vol. II, 679; Ata'i, *Hadâ'iku'l-hakâ'ik*, 597.
[41] Mustafa Âli, *The Ottoman Gentleman of the Sixteenth Century: Mustafa Âli's* Mevâ'idü'n-nefâ'is fî Kavâ'idi'l-mecâlis – *Tables of Delicacies Concerning the Rules of Social Gatherings*, tr. Douglas S. Brookes (Cambridge, MA: Harvard University, Department of Near Eastern Languages and Civilizations, 2003), 172.

translating their political influence into financial power; for example, Yah-nikapan Abdülkerim Pasha started his career as a preacher and ended it as a finance minister with a vizierial title.[42]

Contemporaries used the words preacher (va'iz) and [moral] counselor (nasih) interchangeably, which made sense as preachers advised people on how they should live their lives. But when some preachers started to receive the personal attention of sultans at the end of the sixteenth century, their advice evolved into counsel for sultans, written examples of which appear first in the early seventeenth century, around the same time that Ömer became the preceptor of Osman.[43]

It was also in this period that two very influential preachers, Kadızade Mehmed and Sivasi Abdülmecid, made their preaching debuts. The social life of the Ottoman capital in the seventeenth century was marked by heated debates led by them and their successors around a number of issues.[44] At least one of these issues, that of the permissibility of smoking, was most probably a matter of public debate already during the reigns of Ahmed I and Osman II, as is described shortly. The appointment of Ömer by Ahmed I to tutor his sons around the same time may well have been related to these social developments.

Unfortunately there is no direct evidence to relate Ömer to either of the two factions represented by Kadızade or Sivasi, though they probably started to develop during the reign of Osman II. Yet certain attitudes of Osman II, as well as some of his actions, easily align with the ideas associated with Kadızade later on in the century. As noted by Leslie Peirce, one of the qualities of Osman II that bothered some people was his preference for wearing light and simple clothes and not caring about a majestic appearance as his forefathers did.[45] Osman II's preference for humility and simplicity also affected his relationships with women. At the end of his reign, Osman II made legal marriages with two free women of high social standing; the second one was the daughter of Es'ad, the grand mufti. Ottoman sultans had not married any free women for more than a century and only reproduced with concubines of slave origin, whom they rarely took as legal wives. Osman II may even have considered dismantling the harem and living modestly with legal wives rather than concubines.[46] Finally, his last major decision was to perform the Muslim pilgrimage to Mecca, which cost him his throne and life. These clues suggest, among other things, that Osman preferred piety and simplicity to

---

[42] Rumi, [Ta'rîh], ff. 63b–64a; Na'ima, Ta'rîh, vol. II, 355–6.
[43] Ata'i, Hadâ'iku'l-hakâ'ik, 468; Selaniki, Tarih, vol. II, 531; for written counsels for sultans by preachers, see Kadızade Mehmed (Sofyalı), Nushü'l-hükkâm ve sebebü'n-nizâm, Süleymaniye Kütüphanesi, Aşir Efendi 327; and Mesmû'atü'n-nakâyih mecmû'atü'n-nasâyih, Süleymaniye Kütüphanesi, Husrev Paşa 629, both of which were presented to Kuyucu Murad Pasha initially.
[44] For a list of these issues, see Katib Çelebi, Balance.   [45] Peirce, Imperial Harem, 183.
[46] BnF, fr. 16150, f. 109a, 116a; A. D. Alderson, The Structure of the Ottoman Dynasty (Oxford: Oxford University Press, 1956), Table xxx.

pomp and lavish displays of power, a preference with which the Kadızadelis would wholeheartedly agree.

A more significant clue that ties Osman II to the ideas that were to be identified with the Kadızadelis is that, starting from the very first year of his reign, Osman II issued a number of orders prohibiting the cultivation, sale, and use of tobacco.[47] All of these orders referred to previous orders to the same effect, suggesting that the smoking ban must have been proclaimed some time during the reign of Ahmed I (1603–17). English merchants introduced tobacco into the Ottoman realms around 1600.[48] In the first years of the seventeenth century, the use of tobacco must have become so widespread in the Ottoman capital that the death of the grand mufti Ebulmeyamin Mustafa in 1606 was interpreted by some people as the result of his heavy smoking.[49] The ban on its use was likely proclaimed in the next few years.[50] The prohibition must have been taken seriously as its effects were apparently felt by English merchants, who seem to have persuaded their king, James I, to protect their tobacco exports to the Ottoman realms. It is interesting to note that James I, who championed the cause of tobacco in his correspondence with Ottoman emperors, was himself an ardent opponent of the use of tobacco in his own country.[51]

Some of the arguments used against tobacco by the Ottomans, such as the claims that it led to laziness, which kept people from work, and to prodigality, which resulted in the wasteful use of monetary resources,[52] point in

---

[47] *82 Numaralı Mühimme Defteri (1026–1027 / 1617–1618): Özet – Transkripsiyon – İndeks ve Tıpkıbasım*, ed. Hacı Osman Yıldırım, et al. (Ankara: Başbakanlık Devlet Arşivleri Genel Müdürlüğü, 2000), 228; Kadı Sicilleri, Rodoscuk (modern Tekirdağ), no. 1570, f. 84b; Manisa, no. 48, 120–1. The Mühimme collection at the Ottoman archives includes only one register from the reign of Osman II, which partially covers the orders sent from the center to the provinces in 1618. For the remaining years of his reign, I tried to reconstruct these orders by checking extant registers of provincial district court records that included copies of central orders sent to the districts.

[48] Peçevi, *Ta'rîh*, vol. I, 365; cf. Katib Çelebi, *Balance*, 51. Peçevi's passage on tobacco is translated by E. Birnbaum, "Vice triumphant: the spread of coffee and tobacco in Turkey," *Durham University Journal* (December 1956): 21–7, at 24–6; I would like to thank Norman Itzkowitz for drawing my attention to this article.

[49] Ata'i, *Hadâ'iku'l-hakâ'ik*, 512.

[50] *Calendar of State Papers – Venetian*, vol. XI, 505–6; Birnbaum, "Vice triumphant," 26; Katib Çelebi, *Fezleke*, vol. II, 154.

[51] See "King James his letter to the Greate Turke," NA, SP 97/8, ff. 312b–313a. This copy of the letter is undated, but the references in it suggest that it must have been written during the second reign of Mustafa (1622–3). James, who described tobacco as beneficial for the preservation of one's health in this letter, was actually opposed to its use in England; see his "Counterblaste to Tobacco" (first published anonymously in 1604), in *Workes of... Iames... King of Great Britaine* (London, 1616), 221, 222; cited by Birnbaum, "Vice triumphant," 26.

[52] The orders prohibiting the cultivation and use of tobacco did not provide an elaborate explanation of why the government engaged in this prohibition. What they stated was that the use of tobacco took people's time from work; Yıldırım, *82 Numaralı Mühimme*, 228. A certain Kadızade, most probably the well-known one from Balıkesir, devoted a section to tobacco in a treatise that seemed to be the written version of one of his sermons in the last years of his life. Among other things, he claimed that every day 100,000 *guruşes* are spent on smoking.

the direction of a Puritan work ethic that is very much in line with revivalist movements like that of the Kadızadelis – one should add that there are also obvious connections between the development of a market society and a new attentiveness to the way in which monetary resources are spent. Other arguments, such as claims that its use was tantamount to apostasy because it involved an imitation of non-Muslims who smoked and brought the habit to Ottoman realms,[53] are suggestive of anxieties about Ottoman self-confidence, which had recently been shaken by the long and inconclusive wars with the Habsburgs and the Safavids, as well as the Jalali rebellions. Moreover, the unprecedented inflation and devaluation of the late sixteenth century had created numerous economic problems. Social discipline was seen as a way to cope with this problematic economic situation and to adapt to the requirements of a developing market society. Within this framework, the preachers assumed a new role within society. In addition to their traditional function of providing guidance on how to live a righteous life, they had now become counselors whose help was needed to rectify society and set the right example to follow in this new and threatening age.

Within this context, "enjoining good and forbidding evil," a controversial principle of Islamic law,[54] gained a new currency. For instance, the anonymous author of the *Treasury of Justice*,[55] which was dedicated to Ahmed I, concluded his chapter on this principle with a conversation that was supposed to have taken place between the Prophet and Abū Bakr, his successor. Abū Bakr asks the Prophet whether there is any holy war other than fighting the infidels. The Prophet responds positively and states that there are people on earth who carry out holy war, God takes pride in them, and heaven is adorned for them. When Abū Bakr asks who these people are, the Prophet states that "they are those who enjoin good and forbid evil."[56] Thus the rectification of society is presented to Ahmed I as a form of holy war, implying a new conception of the *ghazi*, or the holy warrior, as a champion of enjoining good and forbidding evil. Ömer's appointment as the tutor of Ahmed I's sons may well be seen as a reflection of this increasing interest in the practice of "enjoining good and forbidding evil." Although there is no direct evidence that Ömer educated

By engaging in this profligate expenditure, Muslims became brothers of the Devil; Kadızade, *Câmi'ü'l-'akâ'id*, Princeton University Library, 2012Y, f. 15b.

[53] Ibid., ff. 14a, 16b.

[54] For a short synopsis of the concept, see Katib Çelebi, *Balance*, 106–9; for a thorough historical analysis, see Michael Cook, *Commanding Right and Forbidding Wrong in Islamic Thought* (Cambridge: Cambridge University Press, 2000).

[55] This is yet another Ottoman Turkish adaptation of 'Alī Hamadānī's *Dhakhīrat al-mulūk* with additional material. For the Persian work, see the edition by Maḥmūd Anwārī (Tabriz: Mu'assasa-i Ta'rīkh wa Farhang-i Īrān, 1358/1980); for its earlier Turkish editions, see Seyyid Ali Hemedani, *Zahîratü'l-mülûk: Hadisler ışığında yönetim ilkeleri, yönetici nitelikleri*, tr. Muhammed b. Hüseyin, ed. Necdet Yılmaz (Istanbul: Dârulhadis, 2003). This Ottoman Turkish adaptation, entitled *Gencîne-i 'adâlet*, revised some of the original chapters and also included new material; see Topkapı Sarayı Kütüphanesi, Bağdat 348.

[56] Anonymous, *Gencîne-i 'adâlet*, f. 75a.

Osman by emphasizing this principle, it is interesting to note that Katib Çelebi in his world history that he wrote in Arabic described Osman II as a sultan who cared for "forbidding evil."[57]

To sum up, Osman II was the first Ottoman sultan to be educated by a preacher. Regardless of whether or not this preacher, Ömer, was an ardent supporter of the principle of "enjoining good and forbidding evil," Osman grew up in an environment where this principle had gained a new currency as exemplified by the rising profile of preachers, the earlier mentioned treatise Treasury of Justice, and the ban on tobacco. Some of Osman II's actions, such as his preference for simplicity, his commitment to continuing the ban on tobacco, the execution of certain Sufi sheiks with Shiite leanings in Istanbul during his reign,[58] and his later decision to dismantle the harem, suggest that this environment of social discipline may well have had an impact on the way he envisioned himself as a sultan.

Absolutist ambitions

Although the early-seventeenth-century emphasis on social discipline in the Ottoman capital seemed to have an impact on Osman II, the evolution of the court into a new center of power starting from the late sixteenth century was the political context within which his reign started. Both of these developments set the stage for Osman II to attempt to reshape the role of the sultan in the Ottoman polity through absolutist policies that were meant to circumscribe the power of the *mevali* and the vizier households. The intellectual foundations for this new role of the sultan were laid down in the aforementioned anonymous work authored for Ahmed I, the *Treasury of Justice*.

The *Treasury of Justice* contains a conception of the caliphate that had been mostly discarded in the medieval Islamic world: the caliph understood not as the successor of the Prophet but of God Himself.[59] The second chapter of the work opens with the following quotations:

O David, We have made you Caliph on the earth. So judge between men equitably, and do not follow your lust lest it should lead you astray from the way of God. Surely for those who go astray from the way of God, is severe punishment, for having forgotten the Day of Reckoning [Qur'an, 38:26].

The sultan is the shadow of God, for everyone oppressed by the calamity of the raging events of time goes to him for refuge [attributed to Muhammad].

[57] Katib Çelebi, *Fadhlakat al-tawārīkh*, Beyazıt Kütüphanesi, 10318, f. 229b.
[58] See Hibri, *Defter*, f. 6a; Karaçelebizade, *Ravzatü'l-ebrâr*, 538; M. A. Danon, "Un interroga-toire d'hérétiques musulmans (1619)," *Journal Asiatique* 11ème Série 17 (1921): 281–93; Andreas Tietze, "A document on the persecution of sectarians in early seventeenth-century Istanbul," *Revue des Études Islamiques* 60 (1992): 161–6.
[59] See Patricia Crone and Martin Hinds, *God's Caliph: Religious Authority in the First Centuries of Islam* (Cambridge: Cambridge University Press, 1986).

The attribution to Muhammed of the statement that the sultan is the "shadow of God" is spurious, but that does not change the fact that this idea had a large following since, at least, the eleventh century.[60] Although the "shadow of God" was generally meant to be a humbler concept than the Caliph of God, the anonymous author of the *Treasury of Justice* equated the two concepts and thus declared that the sultanate and the caliphate were one and the same:

Being a sultan, being an emperor, is [being] the Caliph of God . . . and being His regent on earth. The Teacher [i.e. Muhammad] . . . said that the sultan is the shadow of God . . . That, too, carries the meaning of caliphate.

More importantly, the author claimed that the caliphate was inclusive of prophethood:

God . . . decreed thus: "*I am setting in the earth a Caliph* [from Qur'an 2:30, referring to Adam]." That is to say, He said "I am bringing a Caliph in the earth; I am setting up a regent in the kingdom of the world." He did not say "I am bringing a prophet," or "a scholar," or "a servant." That is so because these [qualities] existed in the caliphate. Likewise, He decreed to David, the Prophet, may peace be upon him: "*We have made you Caliph on the earth* [from Qur'an 38:26]." That is to say He said "We made you a Caliph." He did not say "We made you a prophet," or "a scholar" because all of these befall to the caliphate.[61]

This particular conception of the caliphate would obviously be detrimental to the interests of the lords of the law, the legitimate representatives of jurists' law in the empire. Clearly, the anonymous author of the *Treasury of Justice* had them in mind when he made the sultan a caliph and added that the caliph was inclusive of the qualities of a scholar. That Osman II was inclined to circumscribe the authority of jurists was apparent from his empowering Ömer to take charge of the high-level appointments in the ulema hierarchy, which were usually under the control of the grand mufti.[62] Another example of Osman II's attempts to keep the lords of the law under closer control was his appointment of Mullah Ali – an African who had been a slave of

[60] This tradition is not found in the more respected compilations of prophetic traditions; for Arabic proverbs that carry the same meaning, see Riad Aziz Kassis, *The Book of Proverbs and Arabic Proverbial Works* (Leiden: Brill, 1999), 65–6; for a study of the idea in the context of ancient Persian traditions of kingship as well as Islamic history, see Said Amir Arjomand, *The Shadow of God and the Hidden Imam: Religion, Political Order, and Societal Change in Shi'ite Iran from the Beginning to 1890* (Chicago: University of Chicago Press, 1984), 85–100.

[61] Anonymous, *Gencîne-i 'adâlet*, f. 14b. This section did not appear in earlier adaptations of the *Dhakhīrat al-mulūk*; this work did not even mention the tradition attributed to Muhammad about the sultan being the shadow of God on earth; see the index of traditions in Hamadānī, *Dhakhīrat al-mulūk*, 793–840. The first part of the quotation is reminiscent of Jalāl al-Dīn Muḥammad Dawānī: "Such a person is truly the Shadow of God, the Caliph of God, and the Deputy of the Prophet," cited by John E. Woods, *The Aqquyunlu: Clan, Confederation, Empire – A Study in 15th/9th Century Turko-Iranian Politics* (Minneapolis: Biblioteca Islamica, 1976), 118.

[62] Hasanbeyzade, *Târîh*, vol. III, 922–3; Peçevi, *Ta'rîh*, vol. II, 370. The discontent of the ulema with the empowerment of Ömer was noted by Rumi, [*Ta'rîh*], ff. 83b–84a.

Fig. 11. Mullah Ali; from an Ottoman album produced for a western European audience, *The Habits of the Grand Signor's Court*, ca. 1620; British Museum, 1928-3-23-046, f. 9b; courtesy of the Trustees of the British Museum.

Murad III's chief black eunuch Mehmed Agha and who had received the support of powerful black eunuchs in the late sixteenth and early seventeenth centuries – to the most prestigious judgeships of the empire, promoting him quickly through the ranks all the way to the chief judgeship of the European provinces (see Fig. 11). Mullah Ali's preference for a rationalist epistemology over a traditionalist one, which was manifested in his *Dispelling the Darkness*, befitted his position as a jurist close to the court and was also in line with other works produced by jurists who frequented court circles. Such jurists made an implicit attempt to privilege reason over tradition with a view to challenging the exclusive authority of the lords of the law as the only arbiters of jurists' law in which tradition had held the epistemological upper hand for a long time.[63]

Yet however strong Osman's ambitions might have been, his power was still limited. He would have liked to get rid of his uncle Mustafa I, yet the grand mufti would not let him do that.[64] Despite the fact that Es'ad had been instrumental in the enthronement of Mustafa I in 1617, Osman II did not feel strong enough to dismiss him either.[65] In addition to his uncle Mustafa, Osman II had six younger brothers in the palace whose potential as alternative sultans was yet another factor that tied his hands. If Osman II were to strengthen his political standing, he really needed a conquest that would boost his charisma, which in turn would make him powerful enough to eliminate alternative loci of power in the capital.

Ottoman sultans had always needed the prestige of a conquest, if they were to succeed in initiating a serious change in the polity or even to make controversial decisions. One of the most significant changes in the Ottoman polity had taken place after the conquest of Constantinople in 1453, when Mehmed II felt powerful enough to deal a heavy blow to the Anatolian aristocracy by executing his grand vizier Çandarlı and confiscating legally inalienable estates that had been endowed to family trusts and foundations that were meant to support the descendants of their founders and/or local mosques, schools, and colleges. Süleyman was able to appoint his favorite İbrahim to the grand vizierate only after the conquest of Rhodes in which the sultan personally took part in 1523. Similarly, after the reign of Osman II, his younger brother Murad IV ordered the execution of his brothers only after his conquest of Yerevan from the Safavids in 1635.

The problem Osman II faced was that he did not have an army that could make such conquests possible. As is shown in the next chapter, the Ottoman army had evolved into a mainly financial institution by the beginning of the seventeenth century. Both of the two major military enterprises undertaken during the reign of Osman II ended in failure. The first of these was the Safavid war that had started during the reign of his father.

Although the long Ottoman-Safavid war of 1578–90 had ended with the annexation of large territories by the Ottomans, the Safavids had succeeded in recovering these territories in a second round of war in 1603–12.[66] On the pretext that the Safavid Shah Abbas had not sent the 200 loads of raw silk he

[63] Tezcan, "Dispelling the Darkness;" Tezcan, "Law in China."
[64] See the dispatch of the French ambassador dated February 8, 1620; BnF, fr. 16150, f. 8a.
[65] That Osman II was feeling bitter toward Es'ad was noted by Hasanbeyzade, *Târîh*, vol. III, 922.
[66] Bekir Kütükoğlu, *Osmanlı-İran Siyâsî Münâsebetleri (1578–1612)*, 2nd ed. (Istanbul: İstanbul Fetih Cemiyeti, 1993).

had promised according to the peace agreement of 1612, Ahmed I ordered his grand vizier Öküz Mehmed Pasha to undertake a military campaign against the Safavids in 1615. Although the silk in question did arrive after Mehmed Pasha left the capital with a large army, the Ottomans still pursued the war. After spending the winter of 1615–16 in Aleppo, Mehmed Pasha laid siege to Yerevan in 1616. Yet the Ottoman army failed to take the city. Ahmed I discharged Mehmed Pasha and in his stead appointed the grand admiral Halil Pasha as grand vizier and commander-in-chief of the Ottoman armies. Halil Pasha left the capital in June 1617 and spent the winter of 1617–18 in Diyarbekir.[67] It was during this winter that Ahmed I died and was succeeded by Mustafa I, who in turn was deposed and replaced three months later by his nephew Osman II. Although Halil Pasha entered Tabriz in 1618, the attack against Ardabil ended in a great failure that almost cost the life of the Crimean Khan who had joined the Ottoman army with his forces. The resulting peace, which was ratified by the Ottoman capital in 1619, reduced the amount of raw silk that Shah Abbas was to send as tribute to 100 loads. The Ottoman-Safavid border was fixed along the same line that had been agreed in the time of Süleyman in 1555.[68] If Osman II were interested in conquest, he had to look elsewhere and do it himself.

Ali Pasha: A court creature as a grand vizier

After the failure in the east, Osman II replaced his grand vizier Halil Pasha with Öküz Mehmed Pasha, his brother-in-law and the predecessor of Halil Pasha. Yet Mehmed Pasha was but an interim grand vizier and was dismissed before he had served for a full year: Osman II had not forgotten that Mehmed Pasha had failed at the siege of Yerevan in 1616. A much more promising candidate for grand vizier than Öküz Mehmed Pasha was Ali Pasha, who, as was discussed in the last chapter, was instrumental in bringing Osman II to the throne. Yet although Ali Pasha had been the grand admiral of the Ottoman navy, he was actually one of the most junior viziers; he had to prove himself worthy of the grand vizierate. Ali Pasha's successful naval campaign in 1619, the spoils of which he presented to Osman II, established him as a competent commander (see Fig. 12).[69] Thus on December 24, 1619, Osman II dismissed Mehmed Pasha and appointed the grand admiral Ali Pasha to the grand vizierate.

Ali Pasha's appointment to the grand vizierate marked the beginning both of Osman II's aggressive foreign policy and the consolidation of the court-centered absolutism that were to mark the rest of his reign. In his letter announcing the appointment of Ali Pasha, de Césy, the resident ambassador

[67] Rumi, *Nuhbetü't-tevârîh*, British Library, Or. 31, ff. 350b–352b.
[68] For Halil Pasha's Safavid campaign, see Peçevi, *Ta'rîh*, vol. II, 364–9; Abdülkadir, *Tarih*, vol. I, 655–63, vol. II, 673–83; BOA, MM 4695; Feridun, *Münşe'ât*, vol. II, 262–5.
[69] Peçevi, *Ta'rîh*, vol. II, 371.

of France, suggested that the appointment was the work of Mustafa Agha, the chief black eunuch, and Ömer, the tutor of the sultan. In his next dispatch dated January 7, 1620, de Césy noted that the replacement of the grand vizier pointed to a significant change in the way things were run at the Porte. The same dispatch also recorded the decision to make war on the Polish-Lithuanian Commonwealth,[70] suggesting that the appointment of Ali Pasha and Osman II's plans for a military campaign might well be related.

Ali Pasha's rise to power was a significant novelty in and of itself. As was pointed out in the last chapter, Ali Pasha was not a palace school graduate but rather a creature of the new power structures that had been established at the court since the reign of Murad III.[71] Another important reason for Ali Pasha's appointment was his skills in producing funds for the treasury. Ali Pasha did bring a lot of booty from his successful naval campaign in 1619, but it was not just booty that he was able to produce. Ali Pasha persuaded Osman II that he could be trusted to generate funds to finance the treasury, and his short grand vizierate proved that he indeed could do so. Ali Pasha supplied the sultan with regular payments into his private treasury and also provided funds of his own to the central treasury.[72] A look at the income and expenditures of the central treasury for the fiscal year 1620 (March 21, 1620 to March 20, 1621) shows that the treasury succeeded in ending the year without excessive recourse to the private funds of the sultan, despite the fact that preparations were being made for a military campaign against the Polish-Lithuanian Commonwealth, which speaks to Ali Pasha's financial success.[73]

Ali Pasha followed a very aggressive fiscal policy. Part of the reason for his success in generating funds was his confiscation of the property of rich statesmen. Soon after his appointment to the grand vizierate, Ali Pasha took Baki Pasha into custody in the Seven Towers and confiscated whatever he could find that belonged to this powerful finance minister.[74] Another method he employed was to force the European merchants in the capital to buy certain goods, such as the Safavid tribute silk, at prefixed prices and quantities.[75]

---

[70] BnF, fr. 16150, f. 2a, 4 a.   [71] See Chapter 3, 110–13.

[72] See, for instance, Hasanbeyzade, *Târîh*, vol. III, 924–5; Peçevi, *Ta'rîh*, vol. II, 371; NA, SP 97/7, f. 205a. That Ali Pasha was transferring funds to the private treasury of the sultan was also confirmed by Ottoman archival evidence; see, BOA, KK 1808, 6, 22, 26, recording a total of 14,400,000 *akçe*s paid to the private treasury of the sultan in March 1620. BOA, KK 1909, 86, 462, 464, 466, 467, recorded a total of 5,259,500 *akçe*s that Ali Pasha lent to the treasury in May and December 1620; see also BOA, KK 1808, 661, 678.

[73] According to my calculations based on the two registers KK 1808 and 1909 that recorded the incoming and outgoing funds of the treasury in the fiscal year 1620 on a daily basis, 470,262,064 *akçe*s entered the treasury and 497,971,710 *akçe*s left it. Part of the deficit was financed by funds from the private treasury of the sultan, which amounted to 18,800,000 *akçe*s. Yet the sultan might have received much more than he paid because already in the first few days of the fiscal year, 14,400,000 *akçe*s were paid to his private treasury, see n. 72.

[74] More than 12,000,000 *akçe*s of Baki Pasha were confiscated; see KK 1807, Sunday, 12 Rebî'ü'l-evvel 1029, # 1; KK 1808, 26; KK 1909, 165, 180.

[75] *Calendar of State Papers – Venetian*, vol. XVI, 410; NA, SP 97/7, f. 205a; BOA, KK 1909, 425, 439, 460, 470.

Fig. 12. The naval victory of Ali Pasha that precipitated his appointment to the grand vizierate in 1619; manuscript illustration from Ganizade Nadiri, *Şehnâme-i Nâdirî* (ca. 1622), Topkapı Sarayı Kütüphanesi, H. 1124, ff. 28b–29a; courtesy of the Topkapı Palace Museum.

While Ali Pasha was making the life of foreign merchants difficult, he was also protecting the rights of Ottoman merchants with great vigor. In a legal case that might well have been unprecedented in Ottoman history, Ali Pasha forced Venice to pay compensation for the losses of some Ottoman merchants

Fig. 12 (*continued*).

whose goods and monies were captured at sea despite Venetian guarantees of their safety. In 1617, twenty-two Ottoman merchants had sailed to Venice, sold their goods, bought Venetian goods, and started their return trip. On their voyage home, their goods were pillaged by a Spanish ship. They sued the state of Venice, as they claimed that their safety had been guaranteed by the Venetians. The issue grew into an international scandal in 1619–20, and after a number of hearings and a great deal of diplomatic pressure applied on Venice by the grand vizier Ali Pasha, the merchants received full compensation for their losses – partially in cash, partially in kind, and all of it delivered by the Dutch ambassador in June 1620.[76] These assertive commercial and financial policies were paralleled by an equally assertive foreign policy.

The military campaign of Osman II against Poland in 1621

As noted earlier, the decision to make war on Poland was confirmed right after the appointment of Ali Pasha to the grand vizierate. The Commonwealth of Poland and Lithuania, which I refer to here as Poland for the sake of convenience, and the Ottoman Empire had friendly relations in the late sixteenth century.[77] Yet in the early seventeenth century this peaceful picture started to change. The Ottomans and the Poles clashed over Moldavia a few times. Moreover, the Cossacks created serious troubles for the Ottomans by sacking Ottoman towns on the coast of the Black Sea.[78] For many an Ottoman statesman, however, all of this did not really require the sultan to lead a full-scale military campaign against Poland. In 1616, and again in 1620, Ottoman provincial forces proved able to deal with the Polish forces that had come to help Moldavian princes who had been dismissed by the Ottoman capital.[79] Thus some Ottoman statesmen argued that an Ottoman provincial army led by a military commander-in-chief could well deal with the job of teaching the Poles a lesson.[80]

However, Osman II was determined to take part in the military campaign personally despite the widespread opposition of the viziers and the lords of the law, whom the resident French ambassador described as being "very powerful in this country."[81] This determination seemed to be related to his need to enhance his own position through conquest. Using his prospective absence from the capital as a pretext, for instance, Osman II secured a legal opinion from Kemaleddin Taşköprüzade, the chief justice of the European provinces,

[76] BOA, D. BŞM, 8/62; Calendar of State Papers – Venetian, vol. XVI, 165–6, 167, 173, 258, 259, 294, 336; BnF, fr. 16150, f. 10b.
[77] Baki Tezcan, "Khotin 1621, or how the Poles changed the course of Ottoman history," Acta Orientalia Academiae Scientiarum Hungaricae 62 (2009): 185–98 at 188.
[78] In 1614, for instance, Cossacks attacked Sinop, burned the fortress of the town, and enslaved numerous people; Peçevi, Ta'rîh, vol. II, 342.
[79] For these two military confrontations, see Peçevi, Ta'rîh, vol. II, 346–7, 372–4. Na'ima, Ta'rîh, vol. II, 177–85, provided an eyewitness account for the second battle, which was absent in earlier sources. Xaver Liske, "Der türkisch-polnische Feldzug im Jahre 1620: nach gedruckten und handschriftlichen Quellen dargestellt," Archiv für österreichische Geschichte 41 (1869): 353–97, supplies the Polish side of the account for the second battle; see also E. Schütz, ed., An Armeno-Kipchak Chronicle on the Polish-Turkish Wars in 1620–1621 (Budapest: Akadémiai Kiadó, 1968), 40–9.
[80] Katib Çelebi, Fezleke, vol. I, 403.
[81] BnF, fr. 16150, f. 61a.

justifying the execution of Prince Mehmed, the oldest of his brothers.[82] Moreover, on his way to Poland, Osman also moved against the lords of the law by abolishing the institution of the *arpalık*.[83] *Arpalıks* were judgeships of small towns, which were granted to those *mevali* who were either retired or temporarily lacking a post appropriate to their rank. Those *mevali* would usually not reside in the town of such an *arpalık* appointment, but rather would send a deputy who would then send the dues to his patron.[84] Thus the *arpalıks* provided a steady source of income for high-ranking judges in their retirement or in the periods during which they did not hold positions. Their abolition was a major blow to the lords of the law.

As for the viziers, Osman II's preference for those closely connected to the court was once again confirmed by his appointment of Hüseyin Pasha to replace Ali Pasha, who died in March 1621. Hüseyin Pasha had been the chief gardener during the reign of Ahmed I, a position that he owed to the protection of the black eunuch Mustafa Agha.[85] Later he had become general of the janissaries and the governor-general of Rumelia. At the time he was appointed to the grand vizierate he was one of the least senior viziers in the imperial council.[86] Thus his appointment was the second blow to the autonomy of the viziers delivered by Osman II, the first one being the previous appointment of Ali Pasha, who was also relatively junior. In short, Osman II implemented policies that could well lay the foundations for a well-consolidated Ottoman absolutism, had the army delivered a victory against Poland, which the court circles had been taking for granted.[87]

Osman II's military campaign against Poland was most probably meant to be much more ambitious than what it ended up being. Circumstantial evidence points to a larger plan that involved the Protestant Bohemian nobility; the Ottoman vassal prince of Transylvania, Gabor Bethlen, who was elected king of Hungary in 1620; and perhaps the conquest of a city in southern Poland, such as Kamianets-Podilskyi (today in Ukraine) in the short term and Krakow later – the conquest of Krakow would have increased Ottoman chances for success in a future attack against Vienna, which had just been besieged in 1619 by Bohemian and Transylvanian forces that were Ottoman allies at this early stage of the Thirty Years' War (see Map 2).[88] What really happened, however, was much less breathtaking. After a long and inconclusive confrontation with the Cossack and Polish forces around Khotin (in modern Ukraine) on the Dniester, the Ottoman army withdrew, first to

---

[82] The grand mufti Es'ad refused to legitimize this decision; hence, Osman II's consultation with Taşköprüzade; Hasanbeyzade, *Târîh*, vol. III, 927; Peçevi, *Ta'rîh*, vol. II, 375.

[83] Karaçelebizade, *Ravzatü'l-ebrâr*, 541.

[84] İsmail Hakkı Uzunçarşılı, *Osmanlı Devletinin İlmiye Teşkilâtı* (Ankara: Türk Tarih Kurumu, 1965), 118–21.

[85] Rumi, [*Ta'rîh*], f. 32; Katib Çelebi, *Fezleke*, vol. II, 31.

[86] See Abdülkadir, *Tarih*, vol. II, 703.   [87] See Peçevi, *Ta'rîh*, vol. II, 378–9.

[88] Tezcan, "Khotin 1621," 190–1.

Fig. 13. Osman II, launching his military campaign against the Polish-Lithuanian Commonwealth, 1621; manuscript illustration from Ganizade Nadiri, *Şehnâme-i Nâdirî*, ff. 53b; courtesy of the Topkapı Palace Museum. Note the proximity of Süleyman Agha, the chief black eunuch, to the sultan, which is in stark contrast to the solitude of Süleyman I in the midst of his body guards in a military campaign as depicted in the next image.

Edirne and then to the capital.[89] All that Osman II accomplished was a peace agreement restoring to the Ottomans the fortress of Khotin, which

[89] Although the military campaign was officially presented as a victory, Ottoman narrative sources had no misgivings about the result; compare Peçevi, *Ta'rîh*, vol. II, 376–80, and

Fig. 14. Süleyman I on his way to the battle of Mohács in southern Hungary, 1526; manuscript illustration from Seyyid Lokman, *Hünernâme*, vol. 2 (1588), Topkapı Sarayı Kütüphanesi, H. 1524, f. 256b; courtesy of the Topkapı Palace Museum.

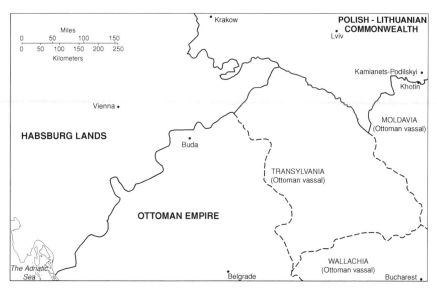

Map 2. The Ottomans in Central Europe.

had belonged to the principality of Moldavia – and hence to the Ottoman Empire – but had been ceded to Poland by a Moldavian prince a few years ago.[90] Osman II's long stay in Edirne, during which he even asked for his newly born son to be brought from Istanbul, suggested that the sultan might have been planning to winter in Edirne so he could engage in another campaign in 1622.[91] Yet the protests of the army seemed to force him to return to Istanbul on January 9, 1622.[92]

The young monarch looks for a new army

By the time Osman II arrived in the capital he had already made up his mind about the "pilgrimage campaign." However, its real target was open for speculation. Although it was announced to be a royal pilgrimage to Mecca, some claimed that the pilgrimage was a cover for the real object of the campaign, which was dealing a blow to Fakhr al-Dīn Ibn Ma'n, a local Druze ruler who had established a relatively autonomous rule in the early seventeenth century

---

Katib Çelebi, *Fezleke*, vol. II, 4, with Mehmed Halisi, *Zafer-nâme*, facs. ed. Yaşar Yücel (Ankara: Ankara Üniversitesi Dil ve Tarih-Coğrafya Fakültesi Yayınları, 1983) and Halîl Edhem [Eldem], "Sultân 'Osmân Hân-ı Sânînin Leh seferine dâ'ir Türkce bir kitâbesi," *Ta'rîh-i 'Osmânî Encümeni Mecmû'ası* 1 (1329/1911): 223–32.

[90] According to Nicolae Jorga, this had occurred in 1612; *Geschichte des osmanischen Reiches,* 5 vols. (Gotha: Perthes, 1908–13), vol. III, 366.

[91] Abdülkadir, *Tarih*, 756; Nadiri, "Şeh-nâme," 414–15.   [92] BnF, fr. 16150, f. 106a.

in the area that roughly corresponds to today's Lebanon.[93] Others believed that Osman II was leaving the capital to recruit mercenaries for a new army. This latter speculation appears to be correct and seemed to motivate the members of the army corps to depose Osman II.[94] Therefore, it is necessary to understand what it meant to recruit a new army in the context of early-seventeenth-century Ottoman politics, which is the focus of the rest of this chapter.

Modern works on Ottoman history generally see Osman II's alleged plan of recruiting a new army as a reform attempt.[95] Yet at least some of his contemporaries would have begged to differ with this interpretation. Had Osman II succeeded in accomplishing this alleged plan of recruiting soldiers for a new army in the Asian provinces, the men employed by leaders of the Jalali rebellions in the 1600s would have constituted the new Ottoman army of the 1620s. Thus I argue that, at least from the perspective of the capital, Osman II would have become a "rebel sultan" by so recruiting a new army of mercenaries, the very men who had been recruited by the rebels of the recent past. The line that separated legitimate uses of force from illegitimate ones was quite vaguely drawn in the Ottoman Empire of the early seventeenth century, and Osman II was straddling it.

To understand the contemporary perception of Osman II's plans, however, a brief discussion of the use of *sekbans* (mercenaries) is in order. The *sekban* phenomenon of the late sixteenth and early seventeenth centuries was a product of local political power struggles that took place within the context of an economy in the process of monetization. In a certain sense, Osman II was to carry these struggles onto an imperial scale with his plan of creating a new army.

The rise of the sekbans

The word *sekban* literally means "keeper of the hounds." The Ottoman army included units described with this term as early as the fourteenth century, and later in the mid-fifteenth century these units were incorporated into the janissary corps as *sekban bölükleri*.[96] Yet the *sekbans* that one comes across in the sources from the late sixteenth century onward refer to mercenaries, usually equipped with firearms and recruited by governors or commander-generals for a specific purpose, such as a military campaign or the protection of a newly conquered castle. The same term was also applied to the mercenaries recruited

[93] Ibid., f. 106b; for Ibn Ma'n and his family, see Kamal S. Salibi, "The secret of the House of Ma'n," *International Journal of Middle East Studies* 4 (1973): 272–87.
[94] In Chapter 5, I engage in a detailed evaluation of the evidence within the framework of the rebellion that brought about the deposition of Osman II. Suffice it to say here that the truth of the rumors is impossible to verify indubitably, as it was supposed to be a secret plan. Thus all references to the campaign in question in state records called it a "pilgrimage campaign," or *sefer-i hac*.
[95] See Tezcan, "The 1622 military rebellion."
[96] M. Tayyib Gökbilgin, "Sekbân," *İA*, vol. X, 325–7.

by Jalali leaders, who were regarded as rebels by the imperial center, thereby loading the term with a quite ambiguous connotation regarding the legitimate use of power.

Mustafa Âli asserted that the use of the *sekban*s in the sense of mercenaries equipped with muskets dated to the Safavid wars (1578–90). He actually singled out Hadım Cafer Pasha (d. ca. 1600), one of the influential commanders during the last phase of this war (1585–90), as the man who first used *sekban*s extensively.[97] Cafer Pasha's identification as the first one to employ *sekban*s suggests that the use of this new type of soldier was a result of the exigencies of war. The modern explanation for the rise of the *sekban*s follows the same implication when it asserts that the Ottoman government, faced with the German infantry during the Habsburg wars, increased the number of janissaries and hired *sekban* troops.[98]

Yet the development of the *sekban*s was not directly related to war. Many local governors had recourse to these new soldiers even though they were not involved in military campaigns. The first use of the term *sekban* in greater Syria occurred around the same time that Cafer Pasha was involved in the Safavid wars, suggesting that the exigencies of war may not be a proper explanation for the development of the *sekban* troops. Al-Būrīnī (1556–1615), an Arab scholar who spent most of his life in Damascus, noted that *sekban*s were unheard of until a certain Abū Sayfayn came to Syria as governor of Nablus (in the modern West Bank, Palestine, see Map 3). Abū Sayfayn apparently brought around 100 *sekban*s with him. Other governors followed suit, and soon the number of *sekban*s in greater Syria multiplied.[99] Another Damascene author, al-Ghazzī (1570–1651), mentioned Abū Sayfayn as a Turk who was appointed to the governorship of Ajlun (in modern Jordan) with the support of Sinan Pasha, who was then governor of Damascus. Soon after his appointment, however, Abū Sayfayn was killed by the forces of Qānṣūh, who seemed to have been the hereditary emir of Ajlun.[100]

Sinan Pasha was appointed to the governorship of Damascus in late 1586, and he was back in Istanbul in the spring of 1589.[101] Thus Abū Sayfayn's appointment to the governorship of Ajlun and his death would have taken place around 1587–8. Al-Būrīnī's reference to Abū Sayfayn's governorship of Nablus might be an earlier event because although they were not far from each other, Nablus and Ajlun were two separate administrative districts.[102] But in any case, the employment of *sekban*s in Syria seemed to start in the

---

[97] Âli, *Künhü'l-ahbâr*, TY 5959, 589b; Rumi, [*Ta'rîh*], f. 56a.

[98] The most elaborate statement of this view is in İnalcık, "Military and fiscal transformation."

[99] Al-Ḥasan ibn Muḥammad al-Būrīnī, *Tarājim al-aʿyān min abnā' al-zamān*, ed. Ṣalāḥ al-Dīn al-Munajjid, 2 vols. [incomplete] (Damascus: al-Majmaʿ al-ʿIlmī al-ʿArabī bi-Dimashq, 1959–63), vol. II, 259.

[100] Najm al-Dīn al-Ghazzī, *Al-kawākib al-sā'ira bi-aʿyān al-mi'a al-ʿāshira*, ed. Jibrā'il Sulaymān Jabbūr, 3 vols. (Beirut: American University of Beirut, 1945–59), vol. III, 202.

[101] Selaniki, *Tarih*, vol. I, 177, 211.   [102] Kunt, *The Sultan's Servants*, 107.

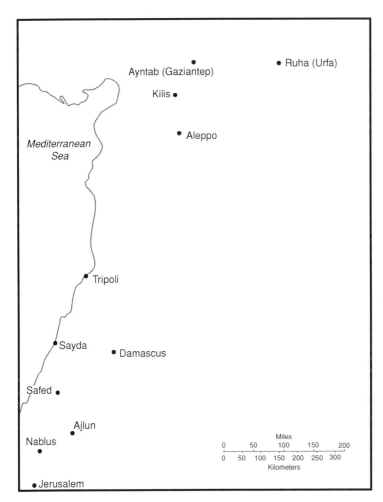

Map 3. Ottoman Syria

1580s, around the same time that Âli credited Cafer Pasha with their use. Whereas Cafer Pasha might have been forced to recruit such forces because of the exigencies of war, the use of *sekban*s in greater Syria around the same time cannot be explained in the same way.

Rather than the Safavid or Habsburg wars, it was the socioeconomic developments of the late sixteenth century that played a significant role in the rise of the *sekban*s. It was not a coincidence that the *sekban*s were first used in Syria around the same time that large fortunes were being made there in international trade and money exchange while Spanish silver was invading the Levant.[103]

---

[103] Tezcan, "The Ottoman monetary crisis," 484–90.

Moreover the same period also witnessed the founding of regional loci of power with the rise of a number of influential families, such as the Maʿns in Lebanon, that continued to have influence in the area for centuries to come. The significance of Syria and its economic resources in the development of the *sekban* phenomenon is shown by the fact that one of the best-known Jalali leaders, Abdülhalim Karayazıcı, who controlled a rebel *sekban* army, made his debut in Syria. The dynamics that led to his rise as a Jalali leader are worth discussing in some length as they demonstrate that the rise of the *sekban*s may not be simply a consequence of the Ottoman wars with the Habsburgs or the Safavids.

Derviş Bey, a *çavuş* (herald) of the Sublime Porte, had succeeded in securing his appointment as the governor of Safed (in modern Israel), probably some time after December 1593, when the governor of Damascus executed Manṣūr Ibn al-Furaykh, the previous governor of Safed.[104] Karayazıcı was the chief of Derviş Bey's *sekban*s. In response to orders sent from the capital dismissing and replacing him with a new governor, Deli Ali, probably one of the former men of Ibn al-Furaykh,[105] Derviş Bey was encouraged by Karayazıcı not to cede his position. Karayazıcı then fought against the Ottoman forces sent by the governor of Damascus Husrev Pasha to execute the imperial orders. Failing to hold on for long, Derviş Bey and Karayazıcı left Safed for Sayda (in modern Lebanon), where emir Fakhr al-Dīn Ibn Maʿn (d. 1635) supplied them with provisions but did not let them stay in his domains. Derviş Bey then went to the capital with the hope of settling the issue. Yet things did not work out as he thought they would, and he was beheaded in Şevval 1005/May–June 1597.[106] Husrev Pasha was governor of Damascus at least twice; his confrontation with Karayazıcı must have happened during his first tenure, which likely started after August 1595 and ended in February 1597.[107] Thus it was most probably in 1594 that Karayazıcı was hired by Derviş Bey and in 1596 that he made his debut as a rebellious *sekban* leader.[108]

What is most important to note about this chronology of events is that the structures in which the Jalali rebellions were to take place were in place at the beginning of the Habsburg wars (1593–1606). Thus the explanation that the increasing need for infantry troops during the Habsburg wars created the *sekban*s, who in turn intensified the scale of the Jalali rebellions, seems to

---

[104] Muḥammad Amīn al-Muḥibbī, *Khulāṣat al-athar fī aʿyān al-qarn al-ḥādi ʿashar*, 4 vols. (Cairo, 1284), vol. IV, 426–8.

[105] Ibid; Būrīnī, *Tarājim*, vol. II, 260–1.

[106] Būrīnī, *Tarājim*, vol. II, 259–61; Selaniki, *Tarih*, vol. II, 688.

[107] Muḥammad Ibn Jumʿa, "Al-bāshāt waʾl-qudāt," in *Wulāt dimashq fī al-ʿahd al-ʿuthmānī*, ed. Ṣalāḥ al-Dīn al-Munajjid (Damascus, 1949), 24, 26; Selaniki, *Tarih*, vol. II, 461, 498, 500, 669.

[108] Turkish narrative sources did not refer to Karayazıcı's early career in Syria; see Tezcan, "Searching for Osman," 384, n. 158; there is, however, a vague reference in a modern study, see William J. Griswold, *The Great Anatolian Rebellion, 1000–1020/1591–1611* (Berlin: Klaus Schwarz, 1983), 25.

be inadequate. The context in which the *sekban*s were first noted in Syria suggests that the rise of this new military group was related to competition for local political power. Karayazıcı's last assignment before he became a well-known Jalali leader supports this suggestion. After his patron Derviş Bey left Sayda for the capital, Karayazıcı first followed the coastline and reached Tripoli (in modern Lebanon) and then went inland and came to Kilis (in modern Turkey), where a similar fight for the local governorship was going on between Canpoladzade Hüseyin Pasha, the Ottoman descendant of a pre-Ottoman local power magnate, and Dev Süleyman, the newly appointed governor of Kilis. Karayazıcı seemed to have been employed by Canpoladzade who eventually succeeded in holding on to his governorship.[109]

The fact that Canpoladzade, whose Kurdish forefathers had ruled Kilis in the early sixteenth century, could still hold on to his ancestral lands almost a century after the Ottoman conquest, suggests that the local holders of political power in greater Syria were able to retain their political influence in the area even after their "Ottomanization."[110] In the late sixteenth century, when the central government attempted to appoint new governors, the local power holders were able to offer resistance using *sekban*s, whom they could only have hired if they had had sufficient funds to do so, a point to be discussed further. Yet it was not just the local magnates who had recourse to *sekban*s. As suggested by the identities of Karayazıcı's first patron and his opponent, governors sent from the center employed *sekban*s against local magnates as well. Thus *sekban*s emerged within the context of local power struggles that took place in the late sixteenth century while the Ottoman economy was in a process of monetization, which enabled contenders to hire mercenaries and buy their administrative positions using their connections in the capital.

Thus, although some of the local players in politics belonged to old local families, it is important to note that the means by which political struggles were pursued were new. Market forces created cash resources that made it possible to hire mercenaries. It was the control of these forces that the representatives of local nobles and the appointees from the imperial capital were fighting for. Thus recent socioeconomic developments made possible the political rivalries in the context of which the *sekban*s were employed.

The fine line between vizier and rebel, or legitimate and illegitimate armies

I suggested earlier that Osman II could well have been perceived as a "rebel sultan" by some of his contemporaries because of his alleged plans to recruit

---

[109] For a short biography of Hüseyin Pasha based on several contemporary sources, see Tezcan, "Searching for Osman," 384–6, n. 159.
[110] Thus the empire of Süleyman the Magnificent that was mostly run by slaves had certain limits of reach; see Chapter 3, 92, n. 37.

mercenaries for a new army. In this section I substantiate this argument by exploring the vague line that separated legitimate uses of force from illegitimate ones.

Was Abdülhalim Karayazıcı, whose early career has already been described, a rebel or a governor? In the fall of 1599, he appeared to be a very serious rebel. Karayazıcı had taken Ruha (Urfa in modern Turkey) under his control and was issuing orders with an imperial seal that read, "Halim Shah, may he be victorious." As mentioned in Chapter 2, in his provincial area, he was imitating the practices of Ottoman central institutions – issuing orders penned by a seal-bearer, appointing judges and a grand vizier, and organizing his new recruits in the Ottoman imperial fashion as janissaries, *bölük halkı*, and so on.[111] These reports that portrayed Karayazıcı as a rebel are perplexing if one considers the future course of events. Mehmed Pasha, the Ottoman general sent to the area, and Karayazıcı came to an agreement at Ruha in December 1599, according to which Karayazıcı handed over Hüseyin Pasha, who, before becoming Karayazıcı's grand vizier, had been an Ottoman pasha. In return, Karayazıcı secured the governorship of Ayntab.[112] Thus a "rebel" became a "governor." Karayazıcı was to be labeled a "rebel" again in 1600, then recognized as a "governor," and finally die as a "rebel" in March 1602.[113]

An interesting story mentioned by al-Būrīnī illustrates the relationship between the "rebel" and legitimate authority. In the winter of 1601–2, Hasan Pasha, the commander-in-chief of the Ottoman armies that were fighting Karayazıcı, sent Hoca Hasmı Osman Pasha, who was the governor of Erzurum at the time, to pursue the "rebel" to the mountains. Osman Pasha then found himself surrounded by Karayazıcı's men, who took him to their leader. Osman Pasha spent some time with Karayazıcı as an honored prisoner and witnessed the movements of Karayazıcı and his men from place to place in the mountains for some forty days. Al-Būrīnī's source for this story was a financial secretary in the Damascene army, Behram Agha, who met Osman Pasha after his release by Karayazıcı. Apparently, during his "imprisonment," Osman Pasha was taken care of by his former officers and soldiers, who had served him in the past but had then joined Karayazıcı. Thus at least some of Karayazıcı's men were former "Ottoman" officers in the service of provincial governors.

At some point during Osman Pasha's journey with Karayazıcı, a group of 200 men wanted to see the Jalali leader. He permitted fifteen representatives to come and talk to him. It turned out that they were provincial soldiers from Erzurum, most probably timar holders, who asked him not to enter their territories. But the way they worded this request is interesting. They conceded the fact that Karayazıcı did not oppress his subjects, yet they were afraid that

---

[111] See Chapter 2, 65.   [112] Selaniki, *Tarih*, vol. II, 842.
[113] For the last years of Karayazıcı, see the various sources cited by Tezcan, "Searching for Osman," 386, n. 163.

once he entered their territory, Ottoman soldiers would follow him and ruin the land and the people. Al-Būrīnī has these soldiers of the province of Erzurum cite this verse from the Qur'an: "Surely when kings enter a city they destroy it and despoil the honour of its nobility. So will they do (to us)" [Qur'an 27: 34].[114] They offered money to Karayazıcı to leave their land; otherwise, they said, they had some 8,000 men and would have to fight him. Karayazıcı accepted their offer and afterward let Osman Pasha go, asking him to use his good offices with the sultan.

Once in Istanbul, Osman Pasha told Mehmed III that Karayazıcı was asking for a governorship in the Balkans for himself and the governorship of the district of Çorum for his brother Hasan. Then he added that he personally believed that Karayazıcı was a traitor. Even though he appeared to be asking for the governorships in return for bringing his rebellion to an end, he was actually trying to free himself from the forces of Hasan Pasha so that he could go back to his rebellion.[115]

Both the presence of Osman Pasha's former men in the retinue of Karayazıcı and the fact that al-Būrīnī, or his source Behram Agha, if not Osman Pasha himself, reported that the soldiers of Erzurum spoke about the Ottoman army in a very critical fashion suggest that as far as the population was concerned, there was not much difference between the "rebel" and the legitimate authority in terms of oppression. As noted by Michael Cook,

tax collection and banditry collapse into the same undifferentiated activity of living off the land, so that whether or not a man is a rebel comes to depend less on what he does than on the more or less fortuitous fact that he has or has not an official authorization for his maraudings.[116]

Soldiers could work just as legitimately for the "rebel" as for the government. A soldier on the payroll of the sultan or a pasha could easily change sides and work for Karayazıcı. The English ambassador Lello noted on February 22, 1601, that "[t]he rebell his forces do greatly increase, many souldiers of Grecia flying unto him doubling their wages of that the Grand Seignor giveth them." The soldiers that Lello referred to must have been timar holders of the province of Rumelia, who were probably desperate for a decent salary, "but before their entertainment requireth them a mark or brand in the eares whereby they may be knowen to have served him, and thereby supposing they should be the unwillinger to revolt from him."[117] Later, most of these soldiers went back to Ottoman service. For instance, Peçevi related that Şahverdi, the steward (kethuda) of Karayazıcı, later joined the retinue of Lala Mehmed Pasha, who became the grand vizier of Ahmed I in 1604.[118]

---

[114] Būrīnī, *Tarājim*, vol. II, 152; the English translation is from Ahmed Ali, tr. *Al-Qur'ân*, revised ed. (Princeton: Princeton University Press, 1988), 323.
[115] Būrīnī, *Tarājim*, vol. II, 149–55, 158–9.
[116] Cook, *Population Pressure*, 40.   [117] NA, SP 97/4, f. 127a.
[118] Peçevi, *Ta'rîh*, vol. II, 253.

The government was also quite inconsistent in its dealings with the "rebels." One vizier could conceive of employing Karayazıcı as a district governor, and his successor would send an army against him. The same inconsistency was displayed in dealing with Karayazıcı's brother, Deli Hasan. In March 1602, Karayazıcı died from natural causes in Samsun.[119] Deli Hasan took over the leadership of his brother's forces and fought successfully all Ottoman forces sent against him. Among others, Hasan Pasha himself, the son of the well-known grand vizier Sokollu, was killed by Deli Hasan's men.[120] Finally the central government gave in and appointed Deli Hasan to the governorship of Bosnia in April 1603. Yet, he was executed just a few years later in 1606.[121]

Although Karayazıcı's days ended in the mountains and his brother's as a governor, the first commander sent against Karayazıcı, Mehmed Pasha, was executed as a rebel. After his military campaign against Karayazıcı, Mehmed Pasha, the son of the late grand vizier Sinan Pasha (d. 1596), was appointed to the governorship of Baghdad. He was dismissed from this post in 1604. On his way to the capital he received the governorship of Karaman as an *arpalık*, a kind of retirement benefit. Right around this time the commander-in-chief of the Safavid military campaign, Cıgalazade Sinan Pasha, was on his way to the Safavid border. Mehmed Pasha met Sinan Pasha around Konya, apparently with a private army of 3,000 men. He talked to Sinan Pasha in a "Jalali-like" manner, asserted that the revenues of the province of Karaman could not support his men, and requested the governorship of the province of Damascus.[122] Mehmed Pasha did receive the governorship of Damascus and entered the city in September 1604. But soon after, in February 1605, a new governor, Hoca Hasmı Osman Pasha, entered the city. With the help of the Damascene janissaries, Mehmed Pasha was arrested. In May he was taken out of custody and soon left for Istanbul. Once in Istanbul, he sat in the imperial council for a day, which suggests that he was brought to the capital with the promise of a vizierial appointment, and was then executed on the orders of Ahmed I.[123]

Another controversial figure around whom the line between rebel and vizier disappeared was Nasuh Pasha. Thanks to the protection of the queen mother, Safiye Sultan, Nasuh had received the governorship of Aleppo at the end of Mehmed III's reign (1595–1603). At the time he arrived in Aleppo there was a certain power structure in place that had not been challenged by previous governors. Since the Ottoman conquest of the region in 1516, the janissaries of

---

[119] Būrīnī, *Tarājim*, vol. II, 269–70.
[120] Actually there was a rumor to the effect that he might have been killed by a man sent by the sultan; ibid. vol. II, 161.
[121] For a summary of these developments, see Griswold, *Great Anatolian Rebellion*, 39–46; cf. Tezcan, "Searching for Osman," 387, n. 172.
[122] Rumi, [*Ta'rîh*], f. 54b.
[123] Najm al-Dīn al-Ghazzī, *Lutf al-samar wa qatf al-thamar min tarājim a'yān al-tabaqa al-ūlā min al-qarn al-hādī 'ashar*, ed. Mahmūd al-Shaykh, 2 vols. (Damascus, 1981–2), vol. I, 125–9; Rumi, [*Ta'rîh*], f. 55a.

Syria had been assigned, among other things, to Aleppo's protection. Yet theirs was more than a military protection. Most of these janissaries had clients in Aleppo, whom they protected against Ottoman governors. Thus the janissaries of greater Syria had evolved into moderators who acted as a buffer between some of the locals and the discretionary power of Ottoman governors.[124] Yet whereas the janissaries protected some in Aleppo, for others they were severe oppressors.[125] Nasuh Pasha knew this existing power structure very well as he had been the proxy of the queen mother for the collection of the revenues assigned to her in the region. He arrived in Aleppo at a time when the janissaries had supposedly increased their level of extortion from the local population. Nasuh Pasha took this state of affairs as an opportunity to move against them. The outcome was quite interesting: the Ottoman janissaries of Syria asked the local rulers of the region, such as Fakhr al-Dīn Ibn Maʿn, for help against the Ottoman governor of Aleppo while Nasuh Pasha was in alliance with Canpoladzade Hüseyin Pasha. After Nasuh Pasha overcame the janissaries and pushed them back to Damascus, he turned against his ally Hüseyin Pasha. Yet Canpoladzade proved to be the stronger one. He both secured his appointment to the governorship of Aleppo and succeeded in taking the city away from Nasuh Pasha, who resisted leaving it for quite a while.[126] Canpoladzade Hüseyin Pasha was later to be executed by Cıgalazade Sinan Pasha, and his nephew Ali was to create quite a bit of trouble for the Ottomans.[127]

Nasuh Pasha learnt his lesson from his experiences in Aleppo and recruited his own *sekbans*. By the fall of 1608, when Nasuh Pasha met the grand vizier Murad Pasha in eastern Anatolia, he was controlling an army of 7,000 men.[128] Rumor has it that Murad Pasha was ordered to execute Nasuh Pasha but could not afford doing so when he realized the strength of Nasuh Pasha.[129] All of these examples suggest that the boundary between legitimate and illegitimate authority was ambiguous, to say the least.

Conclusion

All of the examples discussed in the previous section reinforce the argument that the rise of the *sekbans* was a result of competition for political power in the provinces, rather than a purely military development produced by the exigencies of new types of warfare. Yet the socioeconomic background shaped the form in which this political competition took place. Had the competitors not been able to muster funds to hire mercenaries, the rise of the *sekbans* would not have been possible. Whether one talks about a provincial district governor

---

[124] BnF, Collection Dupuy 429, ff. 105b–106a.
[125] For an example of the activities of such janissaries, see Ghazzī, *Lutf al-samar*, vol. II, 612–27.
[126] Griswold, *Great Anatolian Rebellion*, 93–8.   [127] Ibid., 110–46.
[128] Katib Çelebi, *Fezleke*, vol. I, 311.   [129] BnF, Collection Dupuy 429, f. 108a.

like Abū Sayfayn in the 1580s, or a *sekban* leader like Karayazıcı in the 1590s, or a vizier like Nasuh Pasha in the 1600s, all these leaders had funds to hire soldiers, as opposed to fiefs to allocate to them. As feudal economic relations were being replaced by market relations, local lords who used to assign fiefs to their supporters, or slave-governors of the sultan who commanded fief holders in their provinces, were being replaced by local leaders who kept mercenary contingents to assert their claim to political power.

Studies devoted to this period pay a lot of attention to the relationship between the rise of the *sekban*s, on the one hand, and the long wars that the Ottomans were engaged in against the Safavids and the Habsburgs in the late sixteenth century, as well as the spread of the use of firearms, on the other. These studies overlook the relationship between the monetary crisis of the 1580s and the rise of the *sekban*s. As argued elsewhere, the integration of the different zones of the Ottoman economy into a single imperial zone played an important role in this monetary crisis. Moreover, the crisis was partially the result of the overvalued *şahi*, a regional Ottoman currency, and the profits that were being made from converting Spanish silver into *şahi*s in greater Syria,[130] precisely the region where autonomous political structures making use of the *sekban*s posed the most serious threat to Ottoman central power around the turn of the seventeenth century.

Thus the *sekban*s were first and foremost products of an increasingly monetized economy that affected the way in which political power was acquired and displayed. Local leaders like the Canpolads and Ibn Ma'ns operated in a monetary economy and thus were able to hire mercenaries in their political struggle against the Ottoman center. The socioeconomic developments of the sixteenth century enabled these leaders to use new methods in their political struggles. They were not members of a new elite; to the contrary, they came from established families of their respective regions. This fact has to be strongly emphasized, for the sociopolitical struggles of the late sixteenth and seventeenth centuries did not take place between the old elite and the new one. Rather, parties on both sides included members of both old and new elites. Whereas Canpoladzade was a member of the old ruling class, the man he hired to help him, Karayazıcı, represented the new. It is very difficult to identify Canpoladzade as a party to a political struggle between the old and the new, but he can be seen as a figure of opposition against absolutist designs that would give a free hand to the emperor in selecting whomever he wanted to rule a province; hence, my emphasis on the struggle between the absolutists and their opponents as the one that defined the period. In the aftermath of the sixteenth-century socioeconomic transformation, the Second Empire was already in place: the struggle was about who was going to control it.

[130] Tezcan, "The Ottoman monetary crisis," 484–90.

Osman II's intention of recruiting an army of *sekbans* from Anatolia and the Arab lands of the empire likewise has to be evaluated within this political framework. Rather than being seen as a reform of the existing Ottoman army, this attempt may be seen along the same lines as the "rebellion" of Karayazıcı, who wanted to build a small kingdom for himself or at least become a respectable Ottoman governor. Using mercenaries in the same way, Osman II was planning to employ *sekbans* to gain control of the Second Empire. To assert the political authority he aspired to, he had to overcome the opposition of other loci of political power in the capital, the strongest one of which in the early seventeenth century was the Ottoman army.

Osman II's prospective supporters in this enterprise were probably going to include members of the old elite as well as the new. His grand viziers were all upstarts who owed their power to him, but the forces the sultan was hoping to have recourse to in the provinces included the army of Fakhr al-Dīn Maʿn,[131] another one of those local leaders of Syria who crossed the fine line between legitimate and illegitimate power quite a few times and who belonged to an established family representing the old elite. The sultan may well have been planning to use the legacy of the Canpolads, one of whose members, Canpoladzade Mustafa, was present at the imperial palace. Mustafa, whose father Hüseyin Pasha was executed by Cıgalazade Sinan Pasha, had entered the palace when his uncle Ali Pasha was asking for a pardon in 1608. He was to become a very close companion (*musahib*) of Murad IV in the 1620s, and he must have been close to Osman II as well because he was the secretary of the internal treasury at the time of his enthronement.[132] Thus it is quite possible to imagine Osman II deriving some inspiration from a Canpolad, whose elders had rebelled against Ottoman rule.

Another indication that Osman II was interested in building alliances with local power holders and in hiring mercenaries from greater Syria was his appointment of Dilaver Pasha as his grand vizier in late 1621. Osman II dismissed Hüseyin Pasha because of his military failure in the midst of the siege of Khotin. The man who replaced him in the grand vizierate, Dilaver Pasha, had been the governor-general of the province of Diyarbekir. Although Dilaver Pasha had carried the title of vizier during his governorship, he had actually never sat in the imperial council before. Clearly, this was an extraordinary appointment in which a provincial governor was promoted to the highest administrative position of the empire, jumping over several ranks at once. What was distinctive about Dilaver Pasha was that he had been serving in the

---

[131] Although there were rumors suggesting that the pilgrimage campaign intended to deal him a heavy blow, as discussed in Chapter 5, it actually seems that Ibn Maʿn was about to become an ally of Osman II.

[132] Rumi, [*Taʾrîh*], f. 68b; Topkapı Sarayı Arşivi, D. 73, f. 1b; Canpoladzade Mustafa's occupation of this position suggested that he was highly trusted and could contact the sultan through the chief treasurer of the internal treasury, who was usually a eunuch, relatively easily.

Diyarbekir area for quite a while and was able to generate a lot of cash.[133] Thus he was an Ottoman governor of the kind that Nasuh Pasha had been: an administrator sent from the center but competent to establish local ties and use them to empower himself.

In short, Osman II was on his way to becoming a "rebel sultan" who seemed to have derived the idea of employing *sekbans* from the political structures that developed in Syria in the late sixteenth and early seventeenth centuries within the context of an economy in the process of monetization. He was a party to a political struggle that took place within a new socioeconomic context. Osman II was perceived to be turning into an Abū Sayfayn, who brought *sekbans* to Syria in the 1580s, or a Derviş Bey, the local governor who had hired Karayazıcı in the 1590s. But a sultan taking those actions would have produced quite different effects, in the sense that the stakes involved not the district of Safed or Ajlun, but the whole empire. And the sultan's opponent was not another local governor who had just bought his administrative position. Osman II was facing the central establishment, the strongest component of which had become the imperial army that developed into a center of political power in the late sixteenth and early seventeenth centuries. Ottoman absolutism was about to face its greatest challenge.

---

[133] Rumi, [*Ta'rîh*], f. 33a.

CHAPTER 5

The absolutist dispensation overturned

A regicide

During the morning of Wednesday, May 18, 1622, the royal pavilion was being loaded at the port of Istanbul on a boat that was going to carry it over to Üsküdar across the Bosporus (see Fig. 1). The sultan was about to leave the capital for a pilgrimage to Mecca (see Map 4 and Fig. 15). Soon after Muhammad and his followers immigrated to Yathrib (later to be known as Medina) in 622, pilgrimage to Mecca had become a central pillar of Muslim practice. Now a thousand years later, a young emperor, eager to renew his empire by reshaping its institutions, was going to pay his respects to the Islamic tradition with a pilgrimage. In addition to being an occasion for the recruitment of a new mercenary army, the pilgrimage was going to strengthen Osman II's credentials as a pious young man who was at the same time giving up the pleasures of a harem in return for the moral rectitude offered by lawful wives.[1] Failing to achieve the charisma of a conqueror in Central Europe, Osman II was ready to settle for that of a pious pilgrim-sultan. Renewing the sultan's hold on the empire required the kind of legitimacy sanctioned by the tradition. If there were no strong traditions of absolutism that supported unlimited royal authority, Osman II was ready to invent one in his pilgrimage.

The same morning, the members of the Ottoman central army corps gathered together in the central square of the city and moved en masse, first to the residence of the sultan's tutor Ömer, and then to that of the grand vizier Dilaver Pasha, seeking an audience with them to ask them to convey their demands to Osman II, which included the cancellation of the pilgrimage. The corps members did not find either one of them, and so a larger crowd gathered the next morning at the same square. This time they submitted their demands to influential members of the lords of the law who were going to convey them to the sultan. They were asking for the execution of some high-ranking imperial administrators who were deemed responsible for directing the emperor away from the course that an Ottoman emperor was supposed to follow. Later in the day, they entered the palace, and not being satisfied with the answer of the sultan, they found Prince Mustafa, the deposed uncle of Osman II, and

---

[1] See Chapter 4, 125.

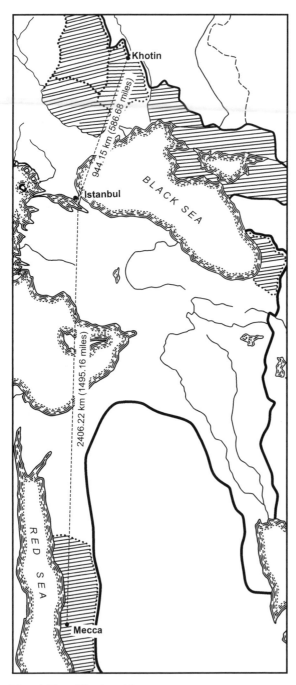

Map 4. From Khotin to Mecca

Fig. 15. Mecca, early eighteenth century; copperplate engraving from Johann Bernhard Fischer von Erlach, *Entwurf einer historischen Architektur* (Vienna, 1721), private collection; photo credit: The Stapleton Collection / The Bridgeman Art Library.

155

enthroned him. On Friday evening Osman was killed. Thus occurred the first regicide in Ottoman history. The absolutist dispensation was overturned.

This chapter examines the rebellion, which brought about the deposition and murder of Osman II, within the context of the transformation of the Ottoman central army that took place in the late sixteenth and early seventeenth centuries. First, I establish a few significant details regarding the role of the army corps members in the murder of Osman II. Then I show that in the late sixteenth and early seventeenth centuries, in parallel with the development of the Ottoman court into a new center of power, the Ottoman army increasingly became political, offering serious resistance to the absolutist tendencies of the court, especially when it came to making war. As a possible explanation for this development, I suggest that during this same period the Ottoman army came to include financial entrepreneurs, who were not interested in making war, and partisans of viziers, who were doing their best to secure the power of their patrons. The central army corps had thus assumed a political function around the turn of the seventeenth century that evolved around limiting the political authority of the Ottoman sultan.

The Shadow of God captured by his army

As pointed out in the last chapter, Osman II announced his intention of undertaking a pilgrimage to Mecca as soon as he returned to Istanbul from Edirne in January 1622. Despite their claim to be the servants of the two holy cities of Islam, Mecca and Medina, the Ottoman sultans had never performed the pilgrimage. The only Ottoman sultan to reach Mecca did so 300 years later; Mehmed VI went there after he was deposed by the Grand National Assembly in 1922, but he left the city without performing the pilgrimage rites.[2]

The fact that no reigning Ottoman sultan ever undertook the pilgrimage does not mean, of course, that the Ottoman sultans did not care about this central Muslim practice. Muslim scholars argued that it was a more important obligation for the sultan to oversee his realm from his capital and be in control of political affairs than to perform the pilgrimage.[3] The Ottoman sultans seemed to take their advice to heart. To compensate for their physical absence from the holy places, they made every effort to make their symbolic presence felt in Mecca and Medina during the pilgrimage season as well as at other times of the year.[4] They never felt comfortable enough, however, to leave the capital for a pilgrimage. Leaving the capital for a long journey without the central army would probably have been regarded as a security risk, and because of the large size of the army, it was impossible to provide the logistical support needed for a trip to Arabia.

[2] See Chapter 4, 140; Alderson, *Ottoman Dynasty*, 126.
[3] Anonymous, *Gencîne-i 'adâlet*, f. 6b.
[4] See Suraiya Faroqhi, *Pilgrims and Sultans: The Hajj under the Ottomans, 1517–1683* (London: Tauris, 1994).

Yet Osman II was not planning to take his army with him. According to Katib Çelebi, some 500 janissaries and around 1,000 *sipahis* were to accompany the sultan, and the rest of the army was to remain in Istanbul. Although we do not know who the soldiers accompanying the sultan on his pilgrimage were going to be, the fact that there was a graduation (*çıkma*) from the palace school just after Osman II returned to Istanbul in January 1622 suggests that the sultan could have been planning to take these new graduates, who would be expected to be more loyal.[5]

The aim of the pilgrimage campaign

The rebellion of the members of the central army corps was not related to their hostility toward the idea of a pilgrim-sultan per se. A pious pilgrim-sultan probably was more of a concern for the constitutionalists among the lords of the law, who would be wary of a sultan who might get a chance to represent himself as closer to the divine than they were. Their sociopolitical power depended on their monopoly of the articulation of jurists' law that was the law of the land. A pilgrim-sultan could make a better pitch for discarding tradition in the articulation of the law and pushing for a more rationalist epistemology that could potentially weaken the constitutionalist jurists. Osman II's chief justice Mullah Ali's critique of some prophetic traditions on the basis of pure "reason and intelligence" demonstrated where such an agenda could possibly lead.[6] Thus, the members of the army corps did not rebel because of the sultan's departure for a pilgrimage; they were more worried about what the emperor might return with.

Contemporary sources and modern scholars share the widely held assumption that the real aim of this "pilgrimage campaign" was to recruit a new army. However, I was not able to find direct and conclusive evidence in the archival records to support this assumption. Yet there are two points that one needs to keep in mind in evaluating this absence of evidence. First, the obvious source for such a recruitment order, the *Mühimme* registers in which copies of orders sent to the provinces were kept, is wanting: volumes for the reign of Osman II are missing, with the exception of a register that partially covers the first year of his reign.[7] In the absence of these central records, I have tried to reconstruct the orders sent to the provinces from provincial court records, some of which included copies of the orders sent from the center. Unfortunately, these provincial records are also incomplete, and my examination did not produce any conclusive results. Yet even if all of the contemporary registers were extant, I wonder whether one could ever find an order stipulating that a new army was to be recruited so that the current army could be crushed. After all,

---

[5] Katib Çelebi, *Fezleke*, vol. II, 10; BOA, KK 257, 65–70.
[6] Tezcan, "Dispelling the Darkness," 90; see also Chapter 4, 129–31.
[7] The register in question is BOA, Mühimme 82. Financial records referred to the campaign as the "pilgrimage campaign;" BOA, KK 1914, 189.

if this plan really existed, it was surely meant to be a secret one and would not have been among the official orders that were recorded in the provincial courts.[8]

Among the available archival and narrative sources produced in 1622, one finds ample circumstantial evidence clearly supporting the widely held assumption about the real aim of Osman II's campaign. Diplomatic dispatches constitute one such source. The French ambassador de Césy, for instance, wrote two letters every two weeks, one to the king of France and the other to the French secretary of state. In these letters, he suggested that the real target of the pilgrimage was Fakhr al-Dīn Ibn Ma'n, the Druze emir who was practically controlling what is today roughly modern Lebanon. In the last dispatch he sent just four days before the rebellion started, de Césy did not refer to any secret design for recruiting a new army. Yet in his dispatch of May 20, 1622, which in its postscript informed France of the murder of Osman II at the Seven Towers, de Césy referred to Osman's recently disclosed design of recruiting a new army.[9] Interestingly enough, that was also the way in which Roe, the English ambassador, presented the course of events. Only in the aftermath of the rebellion did Roe refer to the plans of Osman II to recruit a new army, although, like de Césy, he had earlier noted the discontent of everyone with the pilgrimage.[10]

According to Roe, both the pilgrimage and the attack on Ibn Ma'n were just excuses to leave the capital. The grand vizier Dilaver Pasha was arranging for Osman II a force of 40,000 soldiers to be made up of 10,000 soldiers to be recruited from around Damascus, another 10,000 from the Kurds, and 20,000 from Ibn Ma'n. The sultan was to stay in Damascus for a year and then return to Istanbul at the head of this new army. Although this story may well be true, Roe reported it only after the execution of Osman II. Thus Roe, like de Césy, was not aware of any recruitment plans of the sultan before the uprising of the army.

Consequently, the diplomatic dispatches do not conclusively establish what Osman II may have had in mind because the story may well have been fabricated to legitimize the murder of Osman II. Ottoman histories that ascribe the new army plan to the young sultan rely on another source, the chronicle of Hüseyin Tugi. Tugi was a former janissary who had retired after serving in the special *solak* contingents that used to function as bodyguards of the sultan in military campaigns and other outings. The form and contents of Tugi's

[8] Kadı Sicilleri, Bursa, B-41, f. 166, no. 1297, recorded, for instance, an order dated to early February 1622, which stated that a certain *müteferrika* named Mehmed was sent to Egypt for an important affair and asked the local authorities to make sure that he and his men would have horses ready to change at appropriate locations. It is not clear, however, what the "important affair" was about.

[9] See BnF, fr. 16149, f. 321a; fr. 16150, f. 120, 124.

[10] Sir Thomas Roe, *The Negotiations of Sir Thomas Roe in His Embassy to the Ottoman Porte* (London, 1740), 42–5, 50–1.

chronicle, the variants in its later "editions," and his very pen name, Tugi, which refers to a flag attached to a stick that storytellers used to post in a spot to delineate their space in a public square, suggest that he had become a storyteller in the janissary corps and performed his "chronicle" live to janissaries and others soon after the deposition and murder of Osman II.[11] Tugi claimed that a halberdier of the Old Palace called Eski Yusuf was sent to Aleppo to prepare for the provisioning of the pilgrimage campaign. Yet the rumors that circulated in the capital painted another picture of his real duty: they claimed that he was sent to recruit new soldiers from among the peasants and the nomads.[12]

It is actually possible to identify an individual who fit the description of this Eski Yusuf. In December 1621, while Osman II was still in Edirne, a halberdier of the Old Palace called Yusuf was promoted to the central cavalry troops as a reward for his services as the *voyvoda* (revenue collector) of Yeni İl, alongside two other halberdiers who had been employed with Yusuf in collecting the revenues of Yeni İl and the "Turkomans of Aleppo," two districts primarily defined by the tax revenues they provided, as will be explained shortly. The three colleagues received a salary increase of 5 *akçe*s per day four days after their promotion to the cavalry troops, and Yusuf seemed to have been made a *çavuş* with a large fief as well. When the sultan returned to the capital in January 1622, Yusuf received another salary increase of 5 *akçe*s per day.[13]

This archival evidence indicated that Yusuf was a trusted man in court circles; as the revenue collector of Yeni İl, he was actually serving the sultan personally. Yeni İl, literally the "new province," was an administrative district created during the reign of Süleyman by putting together a number of villages as well as winter and summer pastures used by nomads around Sivas. It did not seem to have its own governor, as no such district was listed under the administrative divisions of the province of Rum. The revenues of this district were earmarked for the endowment of a foundation established by Mihrimah Sultan, the daughter of Süleyman and the wife of Rüstem Pasha, his grand vizier. This foundation was used to construct a complex of public buildings, including a mosque, college of law, school, soup kitchen, and hotel, in Üsküdar. Later the district was attached to the endowment of Nurbanu Sultan, the wife of Mihrimah's brother Selim II and the mother of Murad III. Nurbanu Sultan established a similar foundation in Üsküdar.[14] In addition to financing these

---

[11] Tezcan, "The history of a 'primary source,'" 42–7; see also Piterberg, *An Ottoman Tragedy*, 71–90.

[12] See, for instance, Hüseyin Tugi, [*Hikâyet-i Sultân 'Osmân Hân*], İzzettin Koyunoğlu Kütüphanesi (Konya) 13316, f. 4a.

[13] BOA, KK 257, 60, 62.

[14] See Akgündüz, *Osmanlı Kanunnâmeleri*, vol. VI, 288–95; vol. VIII, pp. 443–57; Cahid Baltacı, *XV.–XVI. Asırlarda Osmanlı Medreseleri: Teşkilat – Tarih* (Istanbul, 1976), 304–6, 470; Hüseyin Ayvansarayi, *Hadîkatü'l-cevâmi'*, ed. [with additions] Ali Sati, 2 vols. (Istanbul, 1281), vol. II, 182–4, 186–7; Ayn Ali, *Kavânîn-i âl-i 'Osmân der hulâsa-ı mezâmin-i defter-i dîvân* (Istanbul, 1280), 22–3.

foundations, the revenues of Yeni İl were also funneled into the inner private treasury of the sultan, which had a separate register that distinguished it from the outer public treasury that was under the supervision of the *defterdar*, or the minister of finance. An undated document noting the revenues that entered the private treasury of the sultan in the early 1620s recorded 2,000,000 *akçe*s (ca. £ 6,250 at the time) for the year 1029/1619–20, which it described as the surplus of the revenues of Nurbanu Sultan's endowment from Yeni İl.[15] The man who collected this money or who oversaw its collection was most probably Yusuf, the halberdier. The entry "Turkomans of Aleppo," with which Yusuf and his halberdier colleagues were associated in another archival record, was a similar source of revenue. It was collected from the areas occupied by nomads in the province of Aleppo and was earmarked for the private treasury of the sultan. At some time during the second reign of Mustafa I (1622–3), 2,143,893 *akçe*s (ca. £ 6,700) entered the coffers of the inner private treasury from the "Turkomans of Aleppo" for the years 1029–30/1619–21. The collectors whose names were recorded in the entry were a certain Murad Agha and Yusuf the halberdier, the latter of whom was also identified with the epithet of *hajı*, or pilgrim, suggesting that Yusuf the halberdier may have performed the pilgrimage in 1622.[16]

Yusuf seemed to be the perfect man for a top secret royal assignment. The inner private treasury (*hazine-i enderun*) of the sultan was separate from the outer treasury and functioned as his private purse. In contrast to tax collectors who worked for the finance department, collectors of revenues (*voyvoda*s) from the imperial demesne, such as Yeni İl and the "Turkomans of Aleppo," served the sultan or his immediate family. A contemporary source confirmed that Yusuf was trusted in court circles by stating that he was a protégé of the chief black eunuch.[17] Had the reign of Osman II been longer, Yusuf might well have followed in the footsteps of Nasuh Pasha, who started his career as a halberdier, served the queen mother Safiye Sultan as her *voyvoda* in the lands that were assigned to her for her endowment, and became grand vizier after recruiting a private army for himself.[18] Thus, Yusuf could well have been chosen to recruit soldiers for a new army. He was a man trusted by the court and experienced in dealing both with money and with nomads, an obvious source for army recruitment. However, his official assignment – to supply provisions in the province of Aleppo – could also have been taken as a cover for a secret mission to recruit a new army by people interested in creating such a rumor. Unfortunately, I have not come across any document that would help clarify which of the two possibilities was the case.

However, there is another clue in the narrative sources that lends support to the new army hypothesis. As mentioned earlier, Roe asserted, after the

[15] Topkapı Sarayı Arşivi, D. 7823; for the conversion of the *akçe* figure into pounds, see Chapter 1, n. 66.
[16] Topkapı Sarayı Arşivi, E. 7735/3.   [17] Aga Dede, *Ta'rîh-nâme*, f. 24a–b.
[18] See Chapter 4, 148–9.

uprising had already started, that Osman II had been planning to use the forces of Ibn Maʿn, the Druze ruler of Lebanon, in his new army. Fakhr al-Dīn belonged to a family whose history went back at least to the end of the fifteenth century.[19] His relationship with the Ottoman capital had its ups and downs, which necessitated his flight to the Medicis in Tuscany from 1613 to 1618 for refuge.[20] During the reign of Osman II, he did not create any problems for the Ottoman central government apart from continuing his struggle for power against Ibn Sayfā, a local magnate in Tripoli. In fact Ibn Maʿn seemed to be on good terms with officials in the Ottoman capital, where he sent part of his local revenues accompanied by appropriate amounts of money to be presented as gifts for people in power.[21]

Apparently Osman II was planning to meet Ibn Maʿn, as indicated by the fact that the grand admiral Halil Pasha, who had left the capital on the orders of the sultan right around the time of the uprising, arrived in Sayda in the summer of 1622 with soldiers on board.[22] The Ottoman navy usually cruised the Mediterranean in search of Spanish ships or corsairs and would not have been sent to the Levantine coast, especially with soldiers, unless military activity was planned there. The question is whether this activity was aimed at crushing the forces of Ibn Maʿn or joining with them in an alliance.

The way the contemporary author al-Khālidī, who must have been very close to Ibn Maʿn,[23] described Halil Pasha's arrival and stay at the ports of Sayda and Beirut did not suggest any tensions. Halil Pasha met Ali Ibn Maʿn and Husayn Ibn Maʿn, the sons of Fakhr al-Dīn, in Sayda and Beirut, respectively. The latter meeting must have been rather interesting as Husayn was less than a year old. Al-Khālidī stated that despite his age, Husayn neither cried nor peed in his pants. Halil Pasha apparently bestowed on him a robe of honor and wrote a petition to the capital asking for his appointment to the governorship of Ajlun; this request, supplemented by an appropriate monetary gift, was eventually honored in Istanbul.[24]

Thus one gets the impression that Halil Pasha's visit to Lebanon was a friendly one. Halil Pasha happened to be the right person to approach local rulers whose loyalties were uncertain. He had been the general of the janissary corps during Murad Pasha's campaign against Ibn Maʿn's former ally Canpoladzade Ali in 1607. After Canpoladzade surrendered, Halil Pasha used his good offices to spare the life of Canpoladzade's treasurer, Abaza Mehmed,

[19] See Salibi, "House of Maʿn."
[20] P. Paolo Carali, *Fakhr ad-Dîn II, principe del Libano, e la corte di Toscana, 1605–1635*, 2 vols. (Rome: Reale Accademia d'Italia, 1936–8), vol. II, 121–3; Ghazzī, *Lutf al-samar*, vol. II, 612–27; Kamal Salibi, "Fakhr al-Din," *Encyclopaedia of Islam, New Edition*, vol. II, 749–51.
[21] See, for instance, Ahmad al-Khālidī, *Lubnān fī ʿahd al-amīr Fakhr al-Dīn al-Maʿnī al-thānī: wa-huwa kitāb taʾrīkh al-Amīr Fakhr al-Dīn al-Maʿnī*, eds. Asad Rustum and Fuʾād Bustānī (Beyrut: Manshūrāt al-Jāmiʿa al-Lubnāniyya, 1969), 57, 89.
[22] Ibid., 109; anonymous, *Gazânâme*, f. 239.
[23] Khālidī, *Taʾrīkh*, 109–10; Muhibbī, *Khulāṣat*, vol. I, 297–8.
[24] Khālidī, *Taʾrīkh*, 110, 112, 117.

who later became an Ottoman governor and led a rebellion in the aftermath of the murder of Osman II, seeking justice for the murdered sultan. Moreover, it was also Halil Pasha who saved the steward of Ibn Maʿn from the Seven Towers in 1022/1613–14, at a time when the Maʿn family was not doing particularly well.[25] Thus Ibn Maʿn would have felt comfortable with Halil Pasha, and Osman II would have liked to ally himself with Ibn Maʿn, who might have been recommended to him by Abaza Mehmed Pasha, his trusted governor, or Canpoladzade Mustafa, his secretary of the internal treasury at the palace.

There is also evidence suggesting that Osman II was trying to create a secure zone for himself in Egypt and the Levant, an attempt that could be interpreted as yet another indication of the new army design. While orders were being sent to Egypt, the Hejaz, and Syria to prepare the logistics for the trip, Osman II appointed his most trusted men to administrative positions in those areas. His chief gardener Mehmed received the governorship of Egypt with the rank of vizier. His chief falconer Murtaza had already been appointed to the governorship of Damascus, and his brother-in-law Hafız Ahmed Pasha, who had been a close companion (*musahib*) of Osman II's father Ahmed I, held the governorship of Diyarbekir. The governorship of Aleppo was most probably held by Abaza Mehmed Pasha, the former treasurer of Canpoladzade Ali and a protégé of Halil Pasha.[26] Moreover, when the uprising started in Istanbul, Hafız Ahmed Pasha was in the vicinity of the capital. He was apparently scheduled to meet Osman II and then accompany him during his campaign. Later on Ahmed Pasha corresponded with Abaza Mehmed Pasha, exploring possibilities for a concerted provincial move against the capital to avenge the regicide.[27]

Finally, some of the contemporary sources suggested that Osman II was planning to move the capital of the empire to the Levant.[28] Although this idea may not sound plausible, because having a Levantine capital would make the Balkans too vulnerable to eastern European powers, the sultan may have planned to stay in the Levant until he could put together an army strong enough to return to Istanbul and confront the central Ottoman army.

All of the circumstantial evidence presented in this section supports the scheme of recruiting a new army better than it does that of a simple pilgrimage

---

[25] Ibid., 31.
[26] Karaçelebizade, *Ravzatü'l-ebrâr*, 545; Katib Çelebi, *Fezleke*, vol. II, 8, 10; BOA, KK 257, 58, 63, 84, 86, 88; Abdülkadir, *Tarih*, vol. II, 757; Khālidī, *Ta'rīkh*, 111; Ghazzī, *Lutf al-samar*, vol. I, 202; A. Mingana, "List of the Turkish governors and high judges of Aleppo from the Ottoman conquest to A.D. 1747," *Bulletin of the John Rylands Library* 10 (1926): 515–23, at 518.
[27] Bostanzade Yahya, [*Vak'a-i Sultân 'Osmân Hân*], Topkapı Sarayı Kütüphanesi, Revan 1305, f. 34a [for a modern Turkish edition of this work, see "II. Sultan Osman'ın şehadeti," tr. Orhan Şaik Gökyay, in *Atsız Armağanı*, ed. Erol Güngör et al. (Istanbul: Ötüken, 1976), 187–256]; Karaçelebizade, *Ravzatü'l-ebrâr*, 549–50; Peçevi, *Ta'rîh*, vol. II, 391.
[28] See, for instance, Peçevi, *Ta'rîh*, vol. II, 380.

or an attack against Ibn Maʿn. Thus the rumors circulating in the capital right around the time of the rebellion that the sultan was planning to crush his own army seem to have had a sound basis.

The uprising

On May 9, 1622, Roe, the English ambassador in Istanbul, wrote the following in a letter home: "The emperour [is] persisting stiffly in his purpose to visitt Mecha (as penance I thinke for his late shamefull retreat) contrary to the councell and instance of all his viziers and capteynes, and even to the hazard of a generall revolt."[29]

The French ambassador de Césy also recorded serious signs of resentment. On April 17, for instance, de Césy informed Paris that the "men of law, who have an unbelievable authority here and all over the empire," had urged the sultan on the previous day that he should give up his trip to Mecca.[30] The jurists were not alone in their opposition; they were joined by the members of the military corps. After abolishing the retirement benefits of high-ranking jurists on the eve of his campaign against the Polish-Lithuanian Commonwealth, Osman II was now intending to do the same to the central army by removing janissaries and cavalry soldiers who were exempt from campaign duty from the payroll registers.[31]

While the atmosphere was becoming increasingly tense, Osman II was growing more adamant than ever. The preparations for the trip were continuing despite the protests that a contemporary Ottoman observer found too inappropriate to mention.[32] On May 15, 1622, de Césy claimed that even the closest advisers of the sultan – the grand vizier, the mufti, his preceptor, and his chief black eunuch – were now trying to dissuade him from the trip, reminding him of the opposition both of the lords of the law and the central army corps. Moreover the peace treaty with the Commonwealth of Lithuania and Poland was not signed yet, and the Cossacks continued to pose a threat to the Black Sea coast. According to De Césy, Osman II stated that "even if the king of Poland were at the gates of Constantinople with an army and the Cossacks had taken Galata, he would not postpone the journey he has embarked upon for a day." Apparently the sultan also received letters alerting him that if he were to leave the capital despite these remonstrances, his uncle or his younger brother was to be enthroned in his place. In response, Osman II apparently decided to take them along on his pilgrimage campaign.[33]

What seemed to trigger the opposition forces to move was the sultan's reported decision to take the imperial treasury with him during the pilgrimage campaign. One cannot verify this decision independently, as evidence for it

---

29 NA, SP 97/8, f. 157Aa; Roe, *Negotiations*, 34; see also SP 97/8, f. 154.
30 BnF, fr. 16150, f. 118a.   31 BnF, fr. 16149, f. 321a; Tugi, [*Hikâyet*], ff. 7b–8a.
32 Abdülkadir, *Tarih*, vol. II, 762.   33 BnF, fr. 16150, f. 120a.

only appears retrospectively after the uprising already took place, yet it fit well with the sultan's designs to recruit a new army. Apparently the lords of the law and the central army corps submitted another plea to dissuade the sultan from his trip after they found out that the treasury was to leave the capital, yet it was of no avail.[34] Osman II seemed to think that he could do whatever he wanted, no matter what the lords of the law were telling him.

According to a unique manuscript, which is the only copy of a slightly modified version of the first recension of Tugi's chronicle, on Tuesday, May 17, 1622, the mufti Es'ad, who had recently become the father-in-law of Osman II, sent a note to the generals of the six divisions that made up the central cavalry troops. Apparently this note informed them that once the sultan had crossed over to Anatolia for his pilgrimage campaign, they would no longer receive salaries as he was taking the treasury with him. Moreover, Es'ad allegedly advised the cavalry troops to stop the sultan, who was following the advice of hypocrites, while they could still do so. It was this note that moved the cavalry soldiers to go to the barracks of the janissaries the next morning to persuade them to undertake a joint action.[35] Another contemporary source claimed that the kapı ağası, or the superintendent of the palace, sent a note to the soldiers on the morning of Wednesday, May 18, informing them of the plan to recruit a new army and to move the capital.[36] A later source mentioned a similar note, but did not ascribe it to any individual. According to this later source, the note that the soldiers received stated that, among other things, Osman II was also planning to burn the house of records (defterhane), which would have meant the abolition of all salaries, fiefs, and privileges.[37] These unverifiable stories may well have been fabricated in the aftermath of the rebellion to legitimize it retrospectively, but their substance fits with the scheme of things that Osman II was thinking about.

Many janissaries and cavalry soldiers met on the morning of Wednesday, May 18, 1622, the day on which the imperial pavilion was to be transported to Üsküdar, the starting point of campaigns in Asia. According to Tugi, they met at the Et Meydanı, literally the Meat Square, of the New Barracks around Aksaray (see Fig. 16).[38] Then they passed through the neighborhood of Karaman and walked toward the Square of Horses (At Meydanı), located on the site of the

[34] BnF, fr. 16149, f. 365.
[35] Osman bin Derviş and Hüseyin Tugi, [no title], Universiteitsbibliotheek Leiden, or. 917, f. 78.
[36] Anonymous, [Fasl], Dār al-kutub al-qawmiyya (Cairo), 212 M. Ta'rīkh Turkī, vol. II, appendix (ff. 237b–247b), at 238b–239a. This short text, which did not have a title and was appended to the end of a manuscript copy of Rumi's Nuhbetü't-tevârîh, seemed to constitute a part of a longer work; hence, my title choice, fasl.
[37] Hibri, Defter, f. 10b.
[38] For these barracks and their location, see İsmail Hakkı Uzunçarşılı, Osmanlı Devleti Teşkilâtından Kapukulu Ocakları, 2 vols. (Ankara: Türk Tarih Kurumu, 1943–4), vol. I, 238, 241, 247–9.

The Imperial
Palace   The Ayasofya

At Meydanı
(the ancient hippodrome)

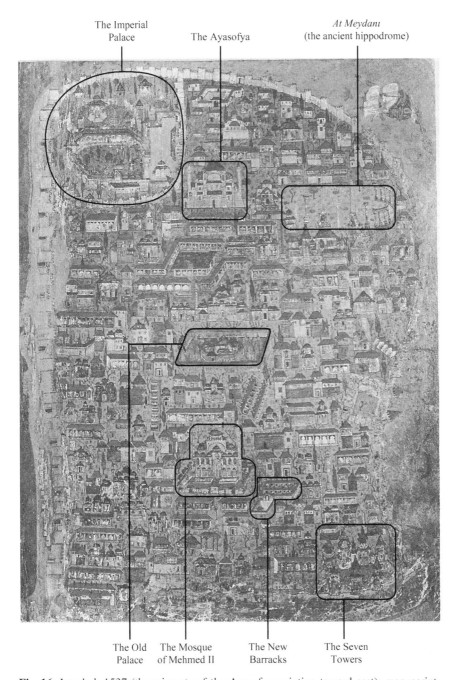

The Old   The Mosque   The New   The Seven
Palace   of Mehmed II   Barracks   Towers

Fig. 16. Istanbul, 1537 (the minarets of the Ayasofya pointing toward east); manuscript illustration from Matrakçı Nasuh, *Beyân-ı Menâzil-i Sefer-i 'Irakeyn*, İstanbul Üniversitesi Kütüphanesi, T. 5964, f. 8b.

ancient hippodrome.[39] Along the way, they were joined by some low-ranking members of the ulema. A Capuchin preacher who was in Istanbul at the time suggested that some 8,000 soldiers were gathered there.[40]

According to Tugi, at this point some soldiers were sent to the mufti to secure a legal opinion that would support their grievances. These soldiers apparently got the response they wanted from Es'ad, who was supposed to have stated that the appropriate punishment for those advisers of the sultan who had instigated his pilgrimage campaign was execution. Although this part of the story is difficult to verify because there is no record of a legal opinion to this effect, it would be hard for Tugi to have fabricated it because Es'ad was well and alive when Tugi's narrative was being circulated in the city and could have easily contradicted it. Another significant point to note about the soldiers' demand of a legal opinion from the grand mufti was their awareness of the power of the law. Instead of addressing the royal authority directly with their grievances, they first gathered legal support for their cause. They knew very well that jurists' law was the most appropriate formal mechanism to challenge royal authority. According to a contemporary chronicler, an experienced member of the military corps said that, without the help of the jurists in articulating their grievances in accordance with the law, they could not have put their affairs in order.[41]

After arriving at *At Meydanı*, the crowd went to the residences of the grand vizier Dilaver Pasha and the sultan's tutor Ömer, asking them to act as intermediaries to cancel the pilgrimage campaign and to secure the execution of Süleyman Agha, the incumbent chief black eunuch. They first went to see Ömer, who, upon seeing the crowd, left his residence in haste. The soldiers entered it by force and pillaged the place. They then went to the palace of Dilaver Pasha where Dilaver Pasha's men apparently attacked them with arrows.[42] Although the crowd consisted of soldiers, no one was armed, as the Ottoman soldiers did not usually carry arms, which were kept by the armorers in peacetime.[43] Accordingly the crowd moved toward the "Cavalry Bazaar (*sipahiler çarşusı*)" where one could buy arms. The shopkeepers, afraid of pillage, dissuaded the crowd from entering the market area. The persuasive power of the shopkeepers is very important to note, as it reflected the close relationship between the urban middle class and the members of the army

---

[39] *At Meydanı*, the site of the Byzantine hippodrome, is called Sultanahmet Square today. Karaman was apparently an Armenian neighborhood that must have been in the vicinity of Aksaray; see Antoine Galland's note in his translation of Tugi's chronicle (BnF, turc 227), *La mort du sultan Osman, ou le retablissement de Mustapha sur le throsne, traduit d'un manuscrit turc, de la Bibliotheque du Roy* (Paris, 1678), 28.

[40] Pacifique de Provin, *Lettre du pere Pacifique de Provin, predicateur capucin, estant present à Constantinople, enuoyee au R. P. Ioseph le Clerc, Predicateur du mesme ordre, & deffiniteur de leur Prouince de Tours, sur l'estrange mort du grand Turc, Empereur de Constantinople* (Paris: François Hvby, 1622), 8.

[41] Anonymous, [*Fasl*], f. 239a.   [42] Peçevi, *Ta'rîh*, vol. II, 382, did not refer to the arrow attack.

[43] Uzunçarşılı, *Kapukulu*, vol. I, 366.

corps, which I elaborate upon in the next chapter. As evening was approaching, the crowd dispersed. Another important point to note is that on the first day of the rebellion, the soldiers demanded the execution of only one man, Süleyman Agha.[44]

Osman II, having heard of the events going on in the city, apparently asked some of the lords of the law to come to the palace that evening. Bostanzade Yahya, a member of the *mevali* himself, suggested that the sultan was holding the lords of the law responsible for instigating the events and was using a threatening tone toward them.[45] Although Osman II might well have threatened the lords of the law, the fact that he dismissed the grand vizier Dilaver Pasha and appointed Hüseyin Pasha in his stead suggests that he was ready to negotiate.[46] Moreover, the earliest recension of Tugi's chronicle suggested that Osman II decided to cancel the pilgrimage that evening. This very important concession to the soldiers was edited out of the later revisions of Tugi's work.[47]

On the morning of Thursday, May 19, 1622, the crowd that met at the *Et Meydanı* was much larger and was now armed. They went first to the Mosque of Mehmed II where they prayed. Then they moved to the Mosque of Sultan Ahmed at the *At Meydanı*, where they were joined by members of the ulema (see Map 5). Whereas Tugi, the retired janissary, presented the arrival of the ulema as a voluntary affair, Bostanzade claimed that small groups of soldiers went to their residences and forced them to come to the *At Meydanı*.[48] Although it is quite plausible that members of the army corps used force to bring about the participation of jurists in their cause, it is nevertheless very important to note that they really seemed to care to legitimize their act of protest. This is a clear indication that legalism, if not constitutionalism, was a concern shared by the members of the central army corps just as much as it was shared by some of the jurists.

At the *At Meydanı*, the soldiers presented a petition to the grand mufti Es'ad to be conveyed to Osman II. According to Tugi, the soldiers were asking for the execution of six men: Ömer Efendi, the mentor of the sultan; Süleyman Agha, the chief black eunuch; Dilaver Pasha, the (former) grand vizier; Ahmed Pasha, who had been the deputy grand vizier in Istanbul during the military campaign against Poland in 1621; Baki Pasha, the minister of finance; and Nasuh Agha, a janissary officer. Ömer and Süleyman Agha were held responsible for instigating the pilgrimage campaign. Dilaver Pasha was apparently added to the list because his men had attacked the crowd with arrows the previous day. Baki Pasha was accused of using alloyed and clipped

---

[44] Tugi, [*Hikâyet*], ff. 2b–3a; compare BnF, fr. 3794, f. 16b.
[45] Bostanzade, [*Vak'a*], f. 12a.
[46] Although most of the sources presented Hüseyin Pasha's appointment to the grand vizierate in the aftermath of the execution of Dilaver Pasha later on Thursday, he must have been given this position on Wednesday evening as Bostanzade presented Hüseyin Pasha as grand vizier on Thursday morning; [*Vak'a*], f. 17a.
[47] Tezcan, "Searching for Osman," 284.   [48] Tugi, [*Hikâyet*], f. 7a; Bostanzade, [*Vak'a*], f. 13a.

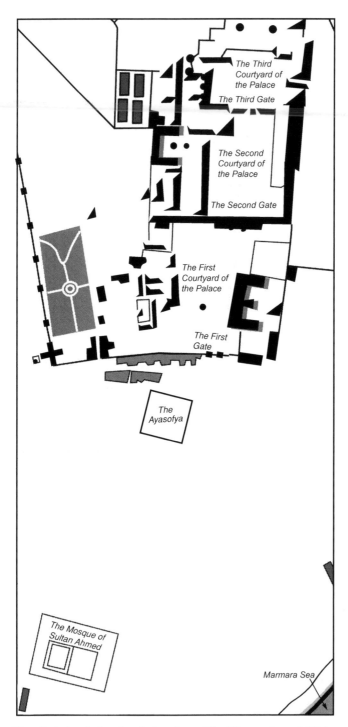

Map 5. A sketch showing the locations of the Ottoman Imperial Palace, the Ayasofya, and the Mosque of Sultan Ahmed, which was built to the immediate east of *At Meydanı* in the 1610s and is thus missing in Fig. 16.

coinage in salary payments. Ahmed Pasha was blamed for not paying the salaries of retired janissaries in 1621. Nasuh Agha, whom the janissaries had refused to accept as an officer in the past, was held responsible for allying himself with Ahmed Pasha to persuade the sultan to cut the salaries of retired janissaries.[49]

Bostanzade presented a slightly different list of men who were the targets of the soldiers. In addition to Ömer Efendi, Süleyman Agha, Dilaver Pasha, and Baki Pasha, he wrote that the soldiers were aiming at Ali Efendi and Musa Efendi, the chief justices of the European, and Asian and African provinces, respectively, and Abdullah Efendi, the judge of Istanbul, who was the son of Ömer.[50] These latter three men may have been the target of the constitutionalists among the ulema, as all three were much more closely connected to the court and its absolutist policies than they were to the *mevali*.

Apparently Hüseyin Pasha, the new grand vizier, sent a letter to the Mosque of Sultan Ahmed, inviting the higher ranking members of the ulema to the palace. The lords of the law and the viziers met at the hospital building within the palace compounds. Meanwhile two respected preachers were sent to the soldiers to quiet them down. Yet the crowd was getting restless, and the soldiers started to move toward the palace.[51] Because the soldiers were afraid that the gardener corps (*bostancıs*) at the palace might be armed and thus ready to offer resistance, one climbed up one of the minarets of the Ayasofya. When he saw no one around, the soldiers decided to move on. Tugi claimed that the gate of the palace was open. Yet Pacifique de Provin's account suggested that some janissaries climbed the walls and opened the door for the others. When they entered the first courtyard of the palace, which must have been around noon, the viziers and the *mevali* were still discussing their options. The unarmed people in the crowd, that is the cadets, the armorers, the artillerymen, and the civilians who joined them, helped themselves to the firewood in front of the armory.[52] After the viziers and the *mevali* had performed the noon prayer, they were received by Osman II. While they were discussing how to respond to the demands of the soldiers, the crowd moved from the first courtyard of the palace to the second one where the meetings of the imperial council used to be held.

It is at this point in his narrative that Tugi, the ultimate Ottoman source for the events of this uprising, skipped a very important detail that changed the overall interpretation of the events that followed. According to Bostanzade, while the crowd was in the second courtyard of the palace, the grand vizier Hüseyin Pasha brought an imperial rescript of Osman II and read it aloud. The sultan was announcing that Dilaver Pasha was to be arrested, and most of the

---

[49] Tugi, [*Hikâyet*], ff. 7b–8a.
[50] Bostanzade, [*Vak'a*], f. 14b, *Defter*, ff. 10b–11a, supports Bostanzade's presentation.
[51] Bostanzade, [*Vak'a*], f. 17.
[52] Ibid., ff. 18–20; Tugi, [*Hikâyet*] ff. 8b–9b; Provin, *Lettre*, 12.

other persons targeted by the soldiers were to be dismissed and exiled from the capital. However, Osman II was not giving over Süleyman Agha, his chief black eunuch. The crowd was not satisfied and attacked the grand vizier, who could only escape thanks to the help of a sheik. This was a significant attempt at a compromise on the part of the sultan. Yet Tugi did not relate this important episode in his narrative, presenting Osman II as unresponsive to the demands of the crowd until the last moment.[53]

While consultations were going on around the sultan, who was still reluctant to sacrifice Süleyman Agha, the crowd entered the third courtyard and reportedly started shouting, "[In accordance] with the law (*şer' ile*) we want Sultan Mustafa!"[54] An anonymous source explained the reasoning of the rebels in asking for the enthronement of Mustafa:

> From now on, Sultan Osman Khan being an emperor for us is thousand stages away from the frontiers of a possibility. Had he been our remedy-providing emperor, he would come out, sit on the throne of exalted fortune, and intend paying attention to our situation in accordance with the ancient and customary practice.[55]

Thus this source presented the members of the military corps who were asking for the enthronement of Mustafa as a group making a legitimate case for a new sultan.

Upon learning of Mustafa's whereabouts from a member of the palace staff, some soldiers apparently climbed to the roof of the harem, opened a hole, descended to Mustafa's room, and pulled him up to the roof with ropes. A contemporary English account of these events referred to the men who descended to Mustafa's room as "these new Electors," once again emphasizing the politically powerful role that the members of the military corps were assuming for themselves.[56] At this point Dilaver Pasha, who had taken refuge in the convent of Sheik Mahmud in Üsküdar, was brought to the palace. Upon hearing the news of Mustafa's deliverance, Osman II finally gave up on saving his chief black eunuch. Both Dilaver Pasha and Süleyman Agha were handed over to the crowd and thus killed instantly. Earlier rebellions, some of which are described in the second half of this chapter, used to end at this point, as soldiers had never gone any farther after receiving the heads that they wanted.

This time, however, killing the two most powerful men in the imperial administration did not satisfy the soldiers. The lords of the law tried to persuade the soldiers to disperse now that their demands had been met. But the crowd had found a new sultan, Mustafa I, and asked the lords of the law to take an oath of allegiance to him. Although the jurists who were present resisted for a while, they finally recognized Mustafa I as the new sultan because the soldiers

---

[53] Tugi, [*Hikâyet*], ff. 9b–10a; Bostanzade, [*Vak'a*], f. 23; anonymous [*Fasl*], f. 242a.
[54] Tugi, [*Hikâyet*], f. 10a.   [55] Anonymous, [*Fasl*], f. 241a.
[56] Anonymous, *A true and faithfull relation, presented to His Maiestie and the Prince, of what hath lately happened in Constantinople, concerning the death of Sultan Osman, and the setting up of Mustafa his uncle* (London: Bartholomew Downes, 1622), f. B(1)b.

were threatening to use force.[57] The only one who did not yield to threats was Es'ad, the grand mufti, whose refusal to take an oath of allegiance to Mustafa cost him his position.[58] This very moment is quite telling in reflecting the different interests held by the jurists and the army corps members. As noted by Cemal Kafadar, the coalitions between these two groups had nothing to do with "a common ideological commitment."[59] Most of the jurists, despite their opposition to Osman II, were satisfied once he gave up his pilgrimage campaign and sacrificed his chief black eunuch Süleyman Agha and his grand vizier Dilaver Pasha. The aim of their protests was to weaken the power centered at the court, and that aim was achieved. For the members of the army corps, however, the continuing rule of Osman II could bring back ideas about deleting soldiers' names from payroll registers or recruiting a new army, which would be detrimental to them. Mustafa I was going to be their guarantee that no such things were ever going to happen.

Even though the lords of the law had sworn an oath of allegiance to Mustafa I, the situation was still unclear. Instead of occupying the imperial palace and ousting Osman II, the soldiers put their new sultan Mustafa I into a cart and carried him to the Old Palace.[60] The general of the janissaries Ali Agha, whom Mustafa I confirmed in his position upon the recommendation of the soldiers, had declined Mustafa I's invitation for a royal audience. He was not going to take sides until it became clear who was to be sultan. Osman II was still in the imperial palace, and he still had some viziers and some lords of the law around him. After weighing different options that included leaving the capital and joining the governor of Diyarbekir, Hafız Ahmed Pasha, who was around Maltepe, today an Asian suburb of Istanbul, Osman II decided to stay in his capital. He was hoping to draw at least some of the janissaries to his side.[61]

Late in the afternoon, the soldiers heard rumors that Osman II was planning to attack the Old Palace with his gardeners and kill Mustafa. Therefore they went to the Old Palace, put Mustafa and his mother, who must have been residing at the Old Palace during the reigns of Ahmed I and Osman II, into a cart, and carried them to the mosque of the janissary barracks, the Orta Mosque.[62] Thus there were two sultans in the city: one in the palace and the other at a mosque under the protection of the janissaries.

---

[57] Tugi, [Hikâyet], ff. 10a–12a.   [58] Anonymous, [Fasl], f. 242b; Hibri, Defter, f. 12a.
[59] Kafadar, "Yeniçeri – esnaf relations," 90.
[60] The Old Palace was the first Ottoman royal residence in Istanbul. After the construction of the New Palace later in the reign of Mehmed II, the Old Palace continued to host the female members of the royal family. During the reign of Süleyman the Magnificent the Old Palace lost its importance as the royal family gradually moved to the New Palace, and part of the Old Palace grounds was used to build the Süleymaniye complex; Gülru Necipoğlu, Architecture, Ceremonial, and Power: The Topkapı Palace in the fifteenth and sixteenth centuries (Cambridge, MA: MIT Press, 1991), 159–63.
[61] Tugi, [Hikâyet], ff. 12b–15a; Bostanzade, [Vak'a], ff. 31b–32b.
[62] This mosque was located at the New Barracks, Uzunçarşılı, Kapukulu, vol. I, 241, 251–3.

Osman II and his grand vizier Hüseyin Pasha decided to bribe the janissaries to remain loyal to him. Pitting infantry soldiers against the cavalry forces had been a successful method in the past. So late at night on Thursday, May 19, they went to the residence of Ali Agha, the general of the janissaries; however, he had just left, after several invitations, to see Mustafa at the Orta Mosque. When he returned home he found another sultan waiting for him. Ali Agha agreed to Osman II's suggestion to try to win the loyalty of the janissaries against the cavalry troops. During that night, he met with some of the janissary officers. The next morning, on Friday, May 20, Ali Agha went to the Orta Mosque to persuade the janissaries to support Osman II. Yet some of the janissary officers had already alerted the cavalry troops of the latest developments. Thus Ali Agha was murdered outside the Orta Mosque that morning.

Once the soldiers learned that Osman II and Hüseyin Pasha were at the residence of Ali Agha, a group of men went there to arrest them. Hüseyin Pasha tried to run away but was killed. The soldiers put Osman II on a horse and brought him to the Orta Mosque. On the way to the mosque, Osman II, who was dressed rather poorly, was subjected to verbal harassment by the soldiers surrounding him.[63] A member of the Ottoman dynasty had never been treated with such disrespect in public. Once Osman II was brought to the mosque, the mother of Mustafa I was finally reassured about the sultanate of her son, so she started to discuss with the janissary officers in the mosque whom to appoint to the grand vizierate while Mustafa I seemed indifferent to the developments. The officers sensed her wish to appoint her son-in-law Davud Pasha and confirmed it. Then she asked them whether there was anybody who was literate among them. They pointed to Kara Mezak, one of the sergeants. Thus Kara Mezak wrote the imperial rescript, which was supposed to be in the sultan's own handwriting, appointing Davud Pasha to the grand vizierate. Kara Mezak wrote eighteen other letters of appointment, including one for his own promotion.

According to Kara Mezak's testimony, Mustafa I was not really aware of what was happening around him. His mother and foster mother were trying to make sure that he sat and did not move around. Osman II, who was also there, took off the old turban someone had put on his head and started to cry, apparently lamenting his fate. Davud Pasha appeared with the general of the armorers, who threw his lasso at Osman, ostensibly to strangle him. The deposed sultan caught it in the air, and the officers in the mosque intervened.[64]

In the afternoon, after Davud Pasha took Mustafa I to the palace, he returned to the Orta Mosque, put Osman in a wagon, and took him to the Seven Towers, which was tantamount to his execution. Mustafa I was kept at the imperial palace after his deposition in 1618, and if anyone intended to keep Osman alive, he could have been imprisoned in the palace. Not long after Osman was brought to the Seven Towers, he was murdered there on the orders of Davud

[63] Tugi, [Hikâyet], ff. 15a–19a.   [64] Peçevi, Ta'rîh, vol. II, 385–7.

Pasha, who was acting as the political delegate of Mustafa I, the new sultan.[65] Osman's corpse was brought to the palace that evening. The funeral took place the next morning, on Saturday, May 21. Yahya, the new grand mufti, led the funeral prayer. Osman was buried in the tomb of his father, Ahmed I. Thus happened the first regicide of Ottoman history.

The deposition and regicide did not cause any tumult around the city. It was only after a provincial rebellion led by Abaza Mehmed Pasha began in Erzurum later in the year that the members of the army corps started to feel some pressure to distance themselves from the regicide. As a former treasurer who worked for Canpoladzade Ali, Abaza knew how to raise *sekbans*. From the fall of 1622 onward, relying on his *sekbans*, he targeted the soldiers of the central army in the provinces and challenged the central government. Abaza presented his rebellion as an act of vengeance for the murder of Osman II: the soldiers were responsible for the regicide and they had to pay for it. Some other Ottomans agreed with and supported Abaza.[66] Under this pressure, the soldiers had to rewrite the history of their rebellion to emphasize how much they actually cared for Osman II. This task fell upon the shoulders of Tugi, the retired janissary chronicler of the uprising and its aftermath. In his revised edition, Tugi adopted a more sophisticated language on behalf of his comrades that included powerful references to law and legitimacy. He also added newly constructed details to the chronicle, distancing the soldiers from responsibility for the regicide and putting all the blame on Davud Pasha. In 1622 his comrades had made history by deposing a sultan. During the following months, Tugi molded the way in which that history was going to be remembered. As a storyteller-turned-propagandist, he did a great job of public relations for the janissary corps as the version of the events that came to be remembered turned out to be his revised narrative.[67]

The role of Davud Pasha in the murder of Osman II cannot be denied. Yet the regicide was ultimately the work of the soldiers just as much as the deposition had been. They could have stopped when Osman II canceled his pilgrimage, or when Hüseyin Pasha came out and announced to them that the sultan had ordered the arrest of Dilaver Pasha and the exile of many others, or after they killed both Dilaver Pasha and Süleyman Agha. Yet they went all the way and became king-makers. In the aftermath of the re-enthronement of Mustafa I,

[65] Ibid., 388; Hibri, *Defter*, f. 13a; Anonymous, *Vak'a-ı merhûm ve magfûr Sultân 'Osmân Hân*, Beyazıt Kütüphanesi, Veliyüddin 1963/4, ff. 48b–49a; on the latter text, see Tezcan, "The history of a 'primary source,'" 48–9.
[66] For an anonymous Jewish author who was very sympathetic toward Osman II as well as Abaza Mehmed Pasha, see Aryeh Shmuelevitz, "Ms Pococke no. 31 as a source for the events in Istanbul in the years 1622–1624," *International Journal of Turkish Studies* 3/2 (1985–86): 107–21; for an Arab emir's elegy for Osman II, in which the emir anticipated divine vengeance for the murder of the sultan, see M. A. Danon, ed. and tr. "Contributions à l'histoire des sultans Osman II et Mouçtafâ I," *Journal Asiatique* 11ème Série, 14 (1919): 69–139, 243–310, at 127–39, 296–305.
[67] Piterberg, *Ottoman Tragedy*, 114–32.

the soldiers continued to display hostility toward Osman II as evidenced in the way they publicly treated the former sultan when he was brought to the Orta Mosque and also later at a crucial moment at the Orta Mosque where soldiers raged against him:

Sultan Osman Khan . . . opened a window at the spot where he was standing [inside the mosque] and said: "My soldier servants, don't you want me?" Upon this, all of the men shouted together: "May God not want those who want you." The hearts of mankind, the soldiers, and the whole of the world had indeed suffered from Sultan Osman.[68]

Finally, by letting Davud Pasha take Osman II to the Seven Towers instead of the palace, where Mustafa I had been kept after his deposition in 1618, the soldiers were giving the new grand vizier a blank check to do whatever he saw fit to secure the new reign of Mustafa I.[69] Davud Pasha cashed this check by executing Osman II with the approval of Mustafa I.

As suggested by the diplomatic dispatches referred to earlier, the soldiers began preparing to move against the sultan several months before the uprising, after Osman II's decision to cut their retirement salaries. What made them take an action as drastic as enthroning a new sultan was probably the news that Osman II was taking the treasury with him on his pilgrimage. This news must have left no doubt in their minds that the sultan was going to recruit a new army. They knew that Osman II was quite dissatisfied with them. During the military campaign against the Polish-Lithuanian Commonwealth, the sultan made a number of inspections to find out how many soldiers there were in the army. Those who did not show up did not receive any campaign bonuses although the soldiers were used to skipping campaigns and receiving their salaries anyway, which they regarded as an entitlement. Moreover, the sultan started making the rounds of the city at night, checking the taverns for janissaries who were drinking. Instead of handing them over to their own officers, the sultan was apparently having his gardeners throw them into the sea.[70] Whether or not this story is true, it was definitely a reflection of the fact that the soldiers were feeling threatened about their privileges, one of which was to be judged and punished by their own peers.[71]

If Osman II were to recruit *sekban*s in Anatolia and create a new army, the contemporary connotation of which was discussed in the last chapter, the soldiers were going to lose a large number of privileges in addition to their salary and status. Thus the stakes were much larger than they had been in previous uprisings. They acted accordingly. It was not their first rebellion, but it turned out to be the one with the most radical results. They showed the whole world that they were going to be the guardians of their own privileges, which they represented as part of Ottoman law; this is reflected in an account

[68] Tugi, [*Hikâyet*], f. 19a–b. In later recensions of Tugi's chronicle this critical section was presented in a very different light; see Tezcan, "The history of a 'primary source,'" 57–8.
[69] Anonymous, *Vak'a*, 49a–b.
[70] Tugi, [*Hikâyet*], f. 5; BnF, fr. 16150, f. 57.   [71] Uzunçarşılı, *Kapukulu*, vol. I, 355–62.

of a contemporary Bosnian janissary sympathizer of the words of Mustafa I to Osman II while they were together at the Orta Mosque: "You overthrew the laws of the Ottoman dynasty; you established other laws and ruled [with them]."[72] The assumption of such a political role by the members of the Ottoman military corps did not happen overnight. This process and its links to the socioeconomic developments of the late sixteenth century are the focus of the remainder of this chapter.

The development of the Ottoman central army into a force of political opposition

Six times in fifteen years (in 1589, 1593, 1595, 1600, 1601, and 1603) the Ottoman cavalry troops of the central army – that is, the members of the "six divisions" (*altı bölük halkı*) – engaged in uprisings in Istanbul (see Fig. 17). Although some of these rebellions were triggered by issues related to their pay or benefits, these economic grievances were closely connected with political ones as I argue in this section. That these rebellions were directed against the court is clear from the fact that the rebels were mostly appeased only after the dismissal or execution of a court favorite.[73] In 1589, Murad III had to sacrifice his favorite vizier and personal companion (*musahib*), Mehmed Pasha; in 1593, Murad III had to replace Siyavuş Pasha, who was a more loyal grand vizier, with Sinan Pasha, who was favored by the rebels; in 1600, Esperanza Malchi, an influential Jewish woman who was known for her close relationship with the court, was murdered; in 1601, Mehmed III had to dismiss his chief gardener; and in 1603, the sultan had to give up the heads of both his chief white eunuch and chief black eunuch.[74] While the members of the six divisions were becoming major political actors, they were also getting increasingly involved in economic activities and expanding their size alongside other units of the Ottoman central army.

In this section I first question the widely held assumption that the expansion of the central army was a consequence of the need for more infantry soldiers equipped with firearms during the Habsburg wars. I suggest an alternative explanation that takes into account the political rivalry both among the viziers and between the viziers and the lords of the law on the one hand, and the court on the other. Finally, I place these developments in the context of an economy in the process of monetization.

---

[72] Aga Dede, *Ta'rîh-nâme*, 26b.
[73] See Cemal Kafadar, "A case and a source," unpublished paper presented at the Middle East Studies Association annual meeting in 1984.
[74] I do not offer detailed descriptions of these uprisings here. Only one of these six events, the uprising of 1589, has been studied in some detail; see Cemal Kafadar, "When coins turned into drops of dew and bankers became robbers of shadows: The boundaries of Ottoman economic imagination at the end of the sixteenth century," PhD diss. (McGill University, 1986), 76–80; and Kafadar, "A case and a source." For the uprisings in 1600, 1601, and 1603, see Chapter 2, 65–7. I touch upon the 1593 and 1595 incidents later.

Fig. 17. The commanders of the six divisions of the Ottoman imperial cavalry troops, late sixteenth century; Österreichische Nationalbibliothek, Cod. 8615, ff. 48b–49a: courtesy of the Austrian National Library.

176

The increasing size of the Ottoman army: Just a military phenomenon?
One of the most commonly accepted explanations for the increase in the number of soldiers in the Ottoman central army identifies the military requirements of the wars with the Habsburgs:

> During the wars against Austria from 1593 to 1606, the need to send into battle infantry troops equipped with firearms resulted in a significant increase in the number of Janissaries (7,886 in 1527 and 37,627 in 1610) and, in Anatolia, in the enrollment of large numbers of *sekban* mercenaries (mostly of peasant origin) – all with firearms.[75]

Whereas the expansion of the janissary corps led to their domination of the political life of the Ottoman capital and the provincial towns, the recruitment of mercenaries of peasant origin, or *sekban*s, whose services were not needed in peacetime, was the source of many troubles, such as the Jalali uprisings.[76]

In the last chapter, I showed that the increasing employment of *sekban*s had started independently from the Habsburg wars and that it had as much, if not more, to do with internal political dynamics as it did with wars.[77] The expansion of the Ottoman central army needs to be evaluated within a similar context. To start with, if the Ottoman army expanded because the war had generated a need for more infantry troops, one would expect the size of the noninfantry divisions to have remained the same. Yet that was not the case. Although the growth in the number of janissaries from 16,905 in 1583 to 37,627 in 1609, an increase of 122.5 percent, could be explained by the increasing need for infantry troops during the war against the Habsburgs, the same explanation cannot be used for the rise in the number of central cavalry troops from 8,346 to 20,869, an increase of 150 percent, nor for that of the armorers (*cebeciyan*) from 1,382 to 5,730, an increase of 314.6 percent.[78] Thus we have to look elsewhere for an explanation.

Another reason why one needs to question the relationship between military campaigns and the increasing number of Ottoman infantry soldiers is that most of those soldiers were not engaged in the war effort. An examination of the salary payments made to the army from the Hungarian campaign treasury from 1599 to 1601, a period during which the grand vizier İbrahim Pasha undertook major attacks against Uyvar (Nové Zámky in modern Slovakia) and Kanije

---

[75] İnalcık, "The Ottoman state," 24.

[76] Ibid., 24–5, and also İnalcık, "Military and fiscal transformation," 283–97.

[77] Caroline Finkel, who studied these wars in great detail, implicitly agrees: "the evidence available for *sekban* participation shows that rather small numbers were involved," *The Administration of Warfare: The Ottoman Military Campaigns in Hungary, 1593–1606* (Vienna: Verband der Wissenschaftlichen Gesellschaften Österreichs, 1988), 46; see also Rhoads Murphey, *Ottoman Warfare, 1500–1700* (London: UCL Press, 1999), 190.

[78] For the figures of 1582–3, see Halil Sahillioğlu, "III. Murad dönemine ait 1582–83 (hicrî 990) tarihli bütçe – çeviriyazı," in *Osmanlı Maliyesi: Kurumlar ve Bütçeler*, eds. Mehmet Genç and Erol Özvar, 2 vols. (Istanbul: Osmanlı Bankası Arşiv ve Araştırma Merkezi, 2006), vol. II, 45; for those of 1609, see Ayn Ali, "Risâle-i vazîfe-hᵛârân ve merâtib-i bendegân-ı âl-i 'Osmân," in *Kavânîn*, 82–104.

(Kanjiža in modern Serbia) in 1599 and 1600, reveals that the size of the active army had not changed much since the early 1580s. In the fiscal year 1582–3, when the janissaries numbered only 16,905, they received 44,788,104 *akçes*.[79] From 1599 to 1601, the janissaries and their cadets (*acemiyan*) who took part in the Hungarian campaign received 88,790,668 *akçes* in salaries or 44,395,334 *akçes* per year.[80] Thus the number of the janissaries who were actually fighting in Hungary at that time was probably around 17,000.[81] This number accords well with the fact that in 1597 the commander-in-chief in Hungary, Saturcı Mehmed Pasha, was assigned 15,000 janissaries. In 1598, Mahmud Pasha was assigned 3,000 janissaries for a separate campaign in Wallachia, 1,500 of whom were new graduates of the janissary cadets.[82] These 18,000 janissaries employed in the Balkans cannot have represented the whole of the janissary corps, which comprised around 35,000 soldiers in 1006/1597–8 according to Mustafa Âli, a contemporary who as a former secretary of the janissary corps should have had a sound idea of the size of the janissaries.[83] Thus it seems plausible to state that only half of the janissary corps was actually employed in active fighting in the Balkans.

What, then, did the other half of the janissary corps do? At this time the Safavid frontier was at peace. One might assume, however, that some of them may have been employed against the Jalalis. In 1599, Mehmed Pasha, the son of the former grand vizier Sinan Pasha, was ordered to lead a military campaign against the former governor and recent Jalali leader, Hüseyin Pasha. According to Selaniki, a contemporary in Istanbul, Mehmed Pasha actually enlisted new recruits for this campaign and was accompanied by only 1,000 janissaries, who seemed to have joined the corps very recently.[84] If there were 18,000 janissaries fighting in the Balkans and 1,000 in Anatolia, and there were altogether 35,000 janissaries, 16,000 are still unaccounted for. These janissaries might have been stationed at fortifications, but the salaries of the soldiers in the central army who were stationed at provincial fortifications were generally paid by provincial treasuries and were not reflected in aggregate sums in the central treasury accounts.[85] Most probably, the unaccounted janissaries were attending to their private business somewhere else. Whatever they may have been doing, if they were not fighting, they had clearly not been recruited in response to an increasing demand for infantry troops.

In short, the increase in the number of soldiers – the royal cavalry troops and armorers as well as the janissaries – is hard to account for simply by the hypothesis that the exigencies of the war against the Habsburgs created an

---

[79] Sahillioğlu, "1582–83 tarihli bütçe," 45.   [80] See Finkel, *Administration*, Appendix: 6.
[81] See also Selaniki, *Tarih*, vol. II, 844–5, 847, 849.   [82] Ibid., 718, 770.
[83] Âli, *Künhü'l-ahbâr*, TY 5959, f. 92a.   [84] Selaniki, *Tarih*, vol. II, 819.
[85] An anonymous treasury account, which may be dated to ca. 1602, suggested that the salaries of the soldiers stationed in the fortifications of Georgia, for instance, were paid by the provincial treasury of Aleppo and Tbilisi; BnF, ms turc 123, ff. 5a, 6b.

increasing demand for infantry troops. Moreover, it was not only in the army that there was such growth. The number of *müşahere-horan*, "receivers of monthly wages," a category that included the heralds (*çavuş*) and elite officers (*müteferrika*s), for instance, rose from 660 in 1583 to 1,196 in 1609, an increase of 81 percent; porters (*bevvab*) and halberdiers (*baltacı*, or *teberdar*) increased by 242 percent from 716 to 2,451.[86] Thus there was a general increase in the number of personnel receiving salaries, not just in the infantry or the army.

What is even perhaps more striking is the fact that the new personnel seemed to have been recruited in an unusual fashion from among the Muslim commoners. During the reign of Süleyman (1520–66), the number of cadets, the number of converted Christian boys, who were the primary source of recruitment for the main body of personnel both in the army and at the palace, had risen by 118 percent from 3,553 in 1527 to 7,745 in 1567. In that same period, the total number of janissaries and royal cavalry troops increased by 84 percent, from 12,974 to 23,842.[87] Whereas the enlargement of the central army more or less followed that of the cadets in this period, suggesting that the cadets indeed formed the main source of recruitment, the growth of personnel in the period 1583–1609 was of a different nature. The number of cadets in this period increased by a negligible 2 percent, from 9,220 to 9,406.[88] Therefore, one can claim with confidence that most of the newly recruited soldiers and other personnel with salaries who joined the Ottoman payroll registers in the late sixteenth century had *not* entered the Ottoman system through the channels of the *devşirme*, or the levy of Christian boys with a view to converting them into loyal servants of the sultan. The end of the sixteenth century must, then, have witnessed a heavy infiltration of "outsiders" (*ecnebi*s), or commoners, into the various levels of the privileged class, the *askeri*, an observation made so frequently by contemporary Ottoman authors.[89] An increasing demand for infantry troops, however significant a factor it may have been, fails to provide an explanation for this development as a whole.

War as a political opportunity

An alternative context in which to evaluate the increase in the number of Ottoman personnel is that of a new kind of power struggle at the imperial center, both between the viziers and the court and among the viziers themselves. This power struggle took place within the framework of the increasingly monetized

---

[86] See n. 78.
[87] Ömer Lûtfi Barkan, "H. 933–934 (M. 1527–1528) malî yılına ait bir bütçe örneği," *İstanbul Üniversitesi İktisat Fakültesi Mecmuası* 15 (1953–54): 251–329, at 300; Ö. L. Barkan, "H. 974–975 (M. 1567–1568) malî yılına âit bir Osmanlı bütçesi," *İstanbul Üniversitesi İktisat Fakültesi Mecmuası* 19 (1957–58): 277–332, at 305–6.
[88] See n. 78.
[89] See, for instance, Anonymous, "Kitâb-ı müstetâb," 2–4; Koçi Bey, *Risale*, 24.

Ottoman economy. The motivation for war, at least partially, may well be found in the same context.

As argued earlier, the need to supply the Habsburg front with infantry soldiers does not entirely explain the expansion of the whole army, including the cavalry divisions, and of the palace staff. Yet, it is a fact that this expansion took place during the long wars at the end of the sixteenth century. Thus the two are somehow related. The war presented the viziers with an opportunity to enhance their political power in a number of ways, such as by placing their supporters on the payroll of the sultan. The dramatic expansion of the army and the palace personnel was thus, at least partially, a product of internal political dynamics. As discussed elsewhere, the period between 1550 and 1650 witnessed the development of an aristocracy in the judicial hierarchy, the *mevali*, who gained considerable independence from the court.[90] Moreover, a similar development was underway among the viziers up to the end of the sixteenth century when it was curbed by the transformation of the court into a new center of power, as argued in Chapter 3. It was not a coincidence that the series of long wars in the east and the west, extending from 1578 to 1606, took place at exactly the same time that the court had a new absolutist thrust.

The expansion of the army around the same time that the court was flexing its muscles in response to the growing power of vizier households may well be seen as the viziers' answer to the dynasty's attempt to create networks of power centered at the court. When Murad III reasserted his privileges in making appointments, the viziers were left empty-handed. A new form of political patronage was in the making that could cut the ties between the viziers and their imperial networks. As long as one remained in the capital, the position of the monarch as the sole source of favors could not be challenged. In contrast, a commander-in-chief with extraordinary powers could make appointments and dismissals and control a number of provincial treasuries. The death of the Safavid Shah Tahmasp in 1576, which brought about a series of internal troubles in Persia, provided such an opportunity for ambitious viziers to gain power. Victory would not just bring fame; the leadership of a military campaign meant extraordinary powers of appointment, dismissal, and tax collection, as well as a large supplementary income from the "gifts" that new appointees were expected to present to the commander-general in charge.

A contemporary source showed well what the leadership of a military campaign could bring with it. At a later stage during the Safavid wars, when Ferhad Pasha had been commander-in-chief for almost four years between 1586 and 1590, the appointments he made and the "market values" of these appointments, which the grand vizier Sinan Pasha claimed Ferhad Pasha must have received from the appointees, were the following:

[90] Tezcan, "The Ottoman *mevâlî*."

28 provincial governors (@ 10,000 gold coins each)	= 16,800,000 *akçes*
331 district governors (@ 200,000 *akçes* each)	= 66,200,000 *akçes*
36 finance directorates (@ 200,000 *akçes* each)	= 7,200,000 *akçes*
447 palace officers and secretaries (@ 100,000 *akçes*)	= 44,700,000 *akçes*[91]

This added up to 134,900,000 *akçes*, more than the total of the central treasury revenues from the central lands of the empire for the fiscal year of 1582–3.[92] Most probably the grand vizier Sinan Pasha exaggerated the values of the offices because he saw Ferhad Pasha as a serious rival. Yet a certain Hızır did indeed bid for a position in supervising Ferhad Pasha's campaign treasury accounts and claimed that he could find some 140,000,000 *akçes* worth of irregularities.[93] Sinan Pasha also noted that Ferhad Pasha did not give him the records of the appointments he made for timars and the men he enlisted for the central army, which would probably have revealed an increase in the number of men enrolled.

Despite his apparent bias, Sinan Pasha's estimates of the extent of the fortunes a commander-in-chief could make suggested that leading a campaign could be a lucrative business both because of the fortunes one could make in "gifts" and the opportunities it offered for building networks of political clients. Some five years later, in 1595, in the midst of the wars against the Habsburgs in Hungary, Selaniki noted that commander-in-chiefs did not leave for their assignments unless they were given the opportunity to enlist "outsiders" in the cadres of palace officers, such as those of *müteferrika*s and *çavuş*es, as well as central cavalry troops, armorers, and artillery soldiers.[94] Thus commander-in-chiefs were enlisting not only soldiers but also men who would not be of any use at the Habsburg front, indicating that the expansion of salary-receiving personnel during the long wars was not just a matter of military necessity. War became an opportunity for a vizier to enlarge his power base through new recruits and to sell certain positions that normally remained under the control of the grand vizier or the sultan himself.

I must reiterate here that in the final analysis, it was still the socioeconomic transformation of the Ottoman Empire in the sixteenth century that made all this expansion possible. It seemed to be mainly connected to an intra-elite power struggle that encouraged each vizier to place as many of his clients as possible in the payroll of the sultan. Yet considering that the clients had to pay

---

[91] Sinan Pasha, [*Telhîsât*], ff. 64b–65a. Although Sinan Pasha should have used an exchange rate of 120 *akçes* per gold coin, he used the pre-1585 exchange rate of 60 *akçes*. His total was 135,000,000 *akçes*, 100,000 more than the actual total of the items he listed.

[92] The total of the revenues of the provinces of Anatolia and Rumelia in 1582–3 was 134,272,006 *akçes*; see Sahillioğlu, "1582–83 tarihli bütçe," 35, 38.

[93] Selaniki, a contemporary, noted that Hızır failed to find anything, yet one must remember that it would be quite difficult to find evidence for sale of offices because this practice was not officially recorded; *Tarih*, vol. I, 240.

[94] Ibid., vol. II, 533.

for their positions and were to receive their salaries in cash, it becomes clear that this political power struggle was closely related to the monetization of the Ottoman economy and the development of new social forces that excelled in manipulating monetary resources.

War provided Ottoman viziers with yet another opportunity, that of extracting funds from the inner treasury, which was the private treasury of the sultan. The finances of the Ottoman government were usually run by the outer treasury, which received the revenues of the central provinces and contributions sent from the outlying provinces. The revenues of the imperial demesne, or *hasses* – that is, the lands the tax revenues of which went directly to the sultan – entered the inner treasury. So did the revenues of the province of Egypt, which in the late sixteenth century provided some 600,000 gold ducats a year. It was during the late sixteenth and early seventeenth centuries that these reserves started to be used, in the midst of an ongoing scarcity of money. Despite the heavy demands of the wars on the private treasury of the sultan, the pocket of the sultan proved to be undepletable. The Ottomans never sought to take out loans in the financial markets of Europe in this period, which was supposed to be one of the most dire they went through. Thus the reserves in the inner treasury must have been immense.

The monetary troubles of this period were complex and were, at least partially, a consequence of the developing market economy.[95] The growth of this increasingly monetized economy required that millions of gold and silver coins leave the inner treasury of the Ottoman sultan to be invested in the economy. The high military expenditures during this period had the effect of doing just that.[96] Thus both from the perspective of internal politics and from an economic viewpoint, the best way to deal with an emperor who controlled vast resources was to induce him to wage a war in which he would remain in the capital but his money would be spent elsewhere. War, then, was not only an opportunity to build networks of political clients for viziers but was also a way of tapping the wealth of the sultan by channeling it out of the inner treasury.

The evolution of the army into a political pressure group

Some of the men who joined the Ottoman military forces and contributed to the great enlargement of the army in the late sixteenth century were political clients of viziers. As argued earlier, the viziers, as commander-in-chiefs with powers to enlist new men into the cadres of the army as well as the palace, made quite a fortune. In addition to amassing a fortune, they also created networks of clients who owed their salaries to them; yet some of these clients did not take part in the campaigns. The narrative histories of the period were

---

[95] See Tezcan, "The Ottoman monetary crisis," 500–2.
[96] Only between June 1604 and January 1605, the inner treasury supplied the army with 110,600,000 *akçes*; Finkel, Appendix: 4.

filled with complaints that the enlisted soldiers simply did not show up on the battlefield. These soldiers, however, were ready when political action was required.

Reflecting on the bouts of military unrest in the Ottoman capital caused by the central cavalry troops in April 1589, January 1593, and April 1595, Âli suggested that many of the troublemakers were men who had entered the imperial cavalry regiments in a certain way. According to Âli, these regiments were made up of men who had entered them in four distinct ways: the first group were the graduates of the palace school, the second comprised those who were promoted from the janissary corps, the third was made up of the sons of the soldiers in these cavalry regiments, and the fourth consisted of those who had been promoted from the artillery and the armorer regiments, as well as men who were originally *kuls* (servants, soldiers) of grandees (*ekabir*) or *kuls* in distant provinces such as Egypt, Syria, and central Iraq.[97] Âli claimed that the troublemakers were mostly from the fourth group many of whom had personal connections with high-ranking administrators.[98]

Selaniki made a similar observation about the cavalry unrest of April 1595: "They said [that] most of those who made trouble were [Sinan Pasha]'s followers (*tevabi*)." Sinan Pasha had just arrived back from the Habsburg front where he had been the commander-in-chief of the Ottoman forces and the grand vizier of Murad III. Yet, the new sultan Mehmed III, who succeeded his father in January 1595, had dismissed Sinan Pasha in February, prior to his arrival in Istanbul. Despite being ordered into exile in Malkara as soon as he arrived at the outskirts of the city in April, Sinan Pasha had not complied with the order. After the unrest he instigated was crushed with the help of the janissaries, he left for Malkara in haste.[99] Similarly, Cıgalazade Sinan Pasha, who had become the third vizier after the dismissal of Sinan Pasha, was dismissed in March 1595. After the unrest in April, Cıgalazade was forced to leave the city on the charge that his men had taken part in it, as well.[100] According to Âli, this was not the first time that Sinan Pasha had orchestrated an uprising of the cavalry regiments. In 1593, Âli claimed that Süleyman Agha, the general of the first cavalry division (*ebna-ı sipahiyan*) and a follower of Sinan Pasha, was actively involved in stirring up unrest, as a result of which Siyavuş Pasha was dismissed and Sinan Pasha was made grand vizier.[101]

It was not just the cavalry regiments that were infiltrated by the followers of grandees. When questioned about an incident in which the house of a governor closely connected to the court was pillaged and burnt in 1591, the janissaries

[97] Âli, *Künhü'l-ahbar*, Esad Efendi 2162, f. 611a; Atsız, ed., "Ek: *Künhü'l-Ahbâr*'ın Osmanlı Tarihi bölümünden III. Mehmed çağına ait parçanın sadeleştirilmiş şekli," in Atsız, *Âlî Bibliyografyası* (Istanbul: Süleymaniye Kütüphanesi Yayınları, 1968), 60, n. 1, suggests that in another manuscript the categorization was slightly different.
[98] Âli, *Künhü'l-ahbâr*, Esad Efendi 2162, f. 611b.
[99] Selaniki, *Tarih*, vol. II, 466–7, 473.
[100] Ibid., 462–3, 473; Hasanbeyzade, *Târîh*, vol. III, 444–55.
[101] Âli, *Künhü'l-ahbâr*, Esad Efendi 2162, f. 588b.

claimed that it was led by "*At Meydanı devşirmesi*," referring to the "outsider" janissaries who were tied to the households of grandees.[102] Similarly, in 1603, Yemişçi Hasan Pasha used janissaries who had been loyal to him in securing his position when he was threatened by the imperial cavalry troops.

All of these cases suggest that the increasing numbers of salary-receiving personnel at the end of the sixteenth century might have been related to the need of the Ottoman viziers to develop a power base in the capital, which they could use against other viziers or the court. The efforts of the court to reduce the concentration of power in the hands of relatively autonomous grand viziers by strengthening court figures and their client networks resulted in the long series of rebellions in the late sixteenth and early seventeenth centuries. In 1589, the cavalry troops secured the execution of the emperor's favorite, who was probably going to be the next grand vizier. In 1591, the janissaries attacked İbrahim Pasha, the brother of an influential courtier, Canfeda Hatun. In 1593, Sinan Pasha secured the grand vizierate for himself with the help of his supporters among the members of the six divisions. In 1595, the janissaries helped the incumbent grand vizier keep his position by suppressing the cavalry soldiers who supported another candidate. In 1600, the soldiers executed an influential Jewish woman who was closely connected to the palace and whose family ran important tax-farms. In 1601, the cavalry forces secured the dismissal of the chief gardener. In 1603, when the soldiers apparently talked about replacing the sultan with the grand mufti, the two highest ranking palace officers were executed.[103] The Ottoman army had evolved into a political pressure group through its expansion in the hands of the viziers.

This is not to say that the members of the army corps did not have their own interests or that there were no other social pressures on the army corps to expand, such as urbanization and opportunities for upward mobility sought by men who would otherwise consider serving Jalali leaders. As argued earlier, the deposition and regicide of Osman II were very much a consequence of the specific interests of the corps members. I dwell upon some of these interests and pressures in the next chapter, which focuses specifically on the janissaries. Below, I dwell on men who wanted to buy their way into sociopolitical privilege by entering the army, especially the cavalry corps. These cavaliers, however, excelled at other things than war.

Soldiers or financial entrepreneurs?

The new members of the central army corps quickly developed their own businesses, both commercial and financial. Narrative sources suggested that

[102] In 1591, the janissaries had attacked the house of İbrahim Pasha, the governor of Diyarbekir, who was the brother of Canfeda Hatun, a powerful woman at the court; Selaniki, *Tarih*, vol. I, 248.

[103] For more details on the last three incidents, see Chapter 2, 65–7.

the soldiers were engaged in business in the capital,[104] and financial records showed that they were also heavily involved in tax-farms.[105] Thus they grew increasingly independent of the grandees who had enlisted them in the army corps, developing into an economic interest group that was based not on private property, but again, as in the case of the *mevali*, on their "private offices."

A soldier in the central cavalry troops was entitled to pass part of his salary to his son by way of his own retirement – a portion of the father's full time salary would become the son's entry level salary.[106] Practically, such a position was a "private office," in the sense that the tenure of the position was almost inviolable and mostly inheritable, just as the right to private property was inviolable and inheritable. Although the infantry troops did not have this privilege, many of them did inherit their positions from their fathers.[107] Moreover, an infantry soldier could be promoted to the cavalry troops,[108] after which he would be able to pass on his status. Finally, later in the seventeenth century, this right was officially granted to the janissaries, the infantry troops of the Ottoman central army.[109] Thus, the Ottoman army evolved into a "third estate" parallel to the viziers and the *mevali* – especially the members of the latter group had their own retirement benefits and could pass their status to their sons as well.[110] In addition to securing certain privileges, the soldiers of the Ottoman central army even produced their own grand viziers in the seventeenth century, such as Bayram Pasha and Kemankeş Mustafa Pasha.[111]

Although the exigencies of war played an important role in the expansion of the Ottoman "third estate," as Count Luigi Ferdinando Marsigli (d. 1730) seemed to regard the central army corps,[112] war in and of itself could not create such a politically powerful institution. In addition to the need of the viziers to build a power base, other dynamics played a role in the expansion of the army. The monetization of the Ottoman economy and finances had an important impact in this process, just as similar processes empowered third estates elsewhere in the world.

As was suggested in the first chapter, investors of capital had seen the Ottoman army as an institution that provided financial security and social status since at least the mid-sixteenth century. Whereas some tax-farmers required entry into the salaried military-administrative personnel as a reward

[104] See, for instance, Selaniki, *Tarih*, vol. II, 732, 784.
[105] Darling, *Revenue-Raising*, 178–85.   [106] For instance, see, BOA, KK 1767, f. 31a, 50a.
[107] Anonymous, "Kavânîn-i yeniçeriyân-ı dergâh-ı âlî," ed. A. Akgündüz, in *Osmanlı Kanunnâmeleri*, vol. IX, 127.
[108] See, for instance, BOA, KK 1767, f. 59b.
[109] Norman Itzkowitz, "Eighteenth century Ottoman realities," *Studia Islamica* 16 (1962): 73–94, at 92.
[110] Tezcan, "The Ottoman *mevâlî*," 393–5.
[111] See Yusuf Halaçoğlu, "Bayram Paşa," *İA2*, vol. V, 266–7; Abdülkadir Özcan, "Kemankeş Mustafa Paşa," *İA2*, vol. XXV, 248–50.
[112] Timur, *Osmanlı Çalışmaları*, 121.

for their services,[113] other investors preferred receiving fiefs in return for their tax-farm bids.[114] In addition to complaining about tax-farmers who oppressed their subjects to compensate themselves for their initial outlays, which they had to pay to the treasury in advance of their actual collection of taxes, Aşık Çelebi, a sixteenth-century man of letters, suggested that these people were farming out taxes in order to receive *askeri* status.[115] This claim brings a whole new dimension to the expansion of the central army in the late sixteenth century. Unfortunately it is quite difficult to determine the number of people who may have entered the ranks of the central army in this way. However, it seemed that the practice was prevalent; otherwise it would have been impossible in 1618 to come across a Jewish Ottoman subject in the central army, which was supposed to consist exclusively of Muslims, born or converted.[116]

The examples provided in the discussion of the timar in Chapter 1, which suggested that one could buy a timar as an investment, trading with its yield,[117] and these cases parallel each other. In both cases we see men, who had apparently accumulated some capital, looking for an investment opportunity that would also bring them some social status. Becoming part of the Ottoman administrative-military apparatus was the only available form of privileged status in the empire, as the main social stratification distinguished the imperial rulers from those who were ruled. Those who were socially privileged were the *askeri*s, a term that literally meant military but conceptually applied to the whole ruling class,[118] and those who did not have any such privileges were the *re'aya*, or subjects. By buying timars and enlisting in the central army corps, the investors were both making a sound investment and achieving a privileged status. The members of the old elite referred to them as "outsiders," but soon the outsiders took over: by the end of the seventeenth century, the Ottoman *askeri* came to be made up almost exclusively of local Muslims as opposed to *devşirme*s who were handpicked by the imperial administration from among the Christian population and then converted to Islam.

In the absence of quantified data, it is not possible to determine whether the tax-farmer-turned-soldiers accounted for a significant portion of the expansion in the size of the Ottoman army. But they must have played a role in the process.

---

[113] For examples, see Chapter 1, 16, n. 4.

[114] See, for instance, İ. Hakkı Uzunçarşılı, "Buyruldı," *Belleten* 5/19 (1941): 289–318, at 292–4, pl. lxxxviii.

[115] Aşık Çelebi, *Mi'râcü'l-iyâle*, f. 146a.

[116] Kadı Sicilleri, Bursa, B-118, f. 117, no. 769. I must admit that, in theory, this man might be one of the Jewish blacksmiths employed at the Istanbul foundry, but it is highly unlikely.

[117] Around 1595, a secretary at the imperial council, Abdi Çelebi, sent a report in rhyme to the grand mufti, claiming, among other things, that the large timars called *ze'amet*s were being sold and that those who bought them engaged in trade with their produce; Selaniki, *Tarih*, vol. II, 520; see also Chapter 1, 22.

[118] Legally speaking, the *askeri* included the less powerful affiliates of the ruling class as well, such as imams, preachers, and secretaries. Therefore it is somewhat problematic to use the term interchangeably with the ruling class. However, politically speaking, the primary conceptual connotation of the term was the ruling class.

What is beyond doubt, however, is that, whether or not they had initially entered the central cavalry regiments through their bids for tax-farms, many cavaliers (*sipahis*) collected taxes and successfully bid for tax-farms. Various studies in the last sixty-five years have noted this financial function of the *sipahis* as tax collectors and tax-farmers.[119] The available evidence suggests that this practice was in place in the mid-sixteenth century and became more prevalent in the late sixteenth century, so much so that, around 1603, 64 percent of the tax-farmers recorded in a register were from the *askeris*, "mainly standing cavalry forces and palace servants." Later in the seventeenth century this figure increased to 85 percent.[120] Unfortunately it is not possible to determine whether these men were the same as those who entered the *askeri* class as a result of their tax-farm bids but they may well have been.

Although a large number of cavalry soldiers were tax-farmers, an even larger number were involved in the collection of the poll tax levied on non-Muslims (*cizye*). According to Darling's figures, whereas 78 percent of the collectors listed in a register from 1571–2 were members of the central cavalry forces, this proportion increased to 90 percent by 1615–16.[121] Both in the collection of the poll tax and in obtaining tax-farms, the central cavalry forces became ascendant in the late sixteenth and early seventeenth centuries.

Whether these cavalry soldiers were tax-farmers who turned into soldiers and continued with tax-farming or had originally been soldiers who later became tax-farmers, one thing is certain: these men were not making war. The tax-farm contracts under which the cavaliers accepted tax-farms usually specified that they were not expected to take part in military campaigns.[122] Some of them were also not engaging in actual tax collection, as it was possible for them to farm out their tax-farms to third parties.[123] One wonders how accurate it would be to call such men "soldiers." They should rather be conceived of as members of a privileged group that happened to be called the cavalry corps of the central army.

Although one may assume that as servants of the sultan, the cavalry "soldiers" would be more diligent in tax collection and more willing to return the funds they collected to the capital, and therefore the assignment of these tax collection duties to the cavalry forces may have been an intentional policy,[124] the historical record suggests that this was not the case. First, the government did not seem to have much control over the process. For instance, in late June 1593 poll tax registers were to be distributed among the central cavalry troops. The established custom was to assign a register to two soldiers, who would collect the taxes and keep a certain amount for themselves. The grand vizier

[119] Uzunçarşılı, *Kapukulu*, vol. II, 156–61; Mustafa Akdağ, *Türkiye'nin İktisadî ve İçtimaî Tarihi*, 2 vols. (Ankara: Ankara Üniversitesi Dil ve Tarih-Coğrafya Fakültesi Yayınları, 1959–71), vol. II, 283–4, 295; Darling, *Revenue-Raising*, 169–85.
[120] Darling, *Revenue-Raising*, 179.   [121] Ibid., 169–70.
[122] See BOA, İbnülemin, Maliye 219; Darling, *Revenue-Raising*, 150.
[123] Akdağ, *Türkiye*, vol. II, 283–4.   [124] Darling, *Revenue-Raising*, 170, 183.

Sinan Pasha and other viziers tried to distribute the registers in this way, but it proved to be impossible. Five to ten soldiers ended up sharing a register, which meant more extortion from the taxpayers. Selaniki's comments suggested that the government had lost control over the process and that the soldiers were asserting themselves.[125]

The rebellion of the central cavalry troops in 1600 was another example of those dynamics at work. The cavalry troops were expecting a certain number of poll tax and sheep tax registers to be distributed among them, but instead found out that some registers had already been sold among the grandees. The excluded registers were apparently the "better" ones, meaning they would yield higher income. According to Selaniki, the soldiers asked the general of one of the central cavalry troops: "What happened to the registers you brought? Are they given to the women and the eunuchs inside?" Then the soldiers attacked and killed Esperanza Malchi, the Jewish *kiera* (lady in Greek) who was known to have been very close to the queen mother and was allegedly acting as an intermediary in the sale of the "better" registers. The soldiers stopped short of asking for the execution of the chief gardener and the chief white eunuch.[126]

The rebellion of 1600 and most of the others described in this chapter were directed against a court that had become the center of an alternative network of financial entrepreneurs. Thus the increase in the number of central cavalry troops involved in tax collection duties and tax-farms at the end of the sixteenth and the beginning of the seventeenth centuries seemed to result from a confrontation between these "soldiers" and the court, rather than from an intentional policy of the government.

Moreover, the argument that as royal servants these men would be more loyal and return the funds they collected to the capital does not seem to hold. Both narrative and archival sources suggested that the poll tax was increased quite a few times in the late sixteenth and early seventeenth centuries.[127] Yet the total poll tax revenues actually seem to have decreased sharply during this period. Sheep tax and tax-farm revenues, in the collection of which the central cavalry troops played an important role, declined similarly.[128] Apparently the

---

[125] Selaniki, *Tarih*, vol. I, 319 [read "... leşker saltanat üstüne...," instead of "... leşker-i saltanat üstûne..."].

[126] Ibid., vol. II, 854–6.

[127] Selaniki, *Tarih*, vol. I, 292–3; Mustafa Akdağ, "Osmanlı İmparatorluğunun kuruluş ve inkişafı devrinde Türkiye'nin iktisadî vaziyeti," *Belleten* 13 (1949): 497–571, at 558–9, n. 108, 559–60; Darling, *Revenue-Raising*, 110–1.

[128] For the figures in 1582–3, see Sahillioğlu, "1582–83 tarihli bütçe," 35, 37, 38; for the figures in 1613–14, see Rhoads Murphey, "The functioning of the Ottoman army under Murad IV (1623–1639/1032–1049): Key to the understanding of the relationship between center and periphery in seventeenth-century Turkey," PhD diss. (University of Chicago, 1979), 440; the large poll-tax revenue from Transylvania recorded in the latter source should be excluded from the comparison as there was no comparative figure in the earlier one, and the difference in the value of the *akçe* in the two balance sheets has to be taken into account; see also Darling, *Revenue-Raising*, 239–40.

servants of the sultan were not really returning the collected funds to the capital.

Finally, tax collection was not the only economic activity in which the "soldiers" of the central army were taking part. They were also receiving appointments to the trusteeships of endowments and to the stewardships of guilds.[129] Moreover narrative and archival sources suggested their involvement in both local and international trade.[130] When one takes into consideration all these economic and financial activities of the members of the central army corps, it becomes quite difficult to see them as "soldiers." Not surprisingly, contemporaries complained about the many soldiers who were enlisted in the army corps but simply did not show up for military campaigns.[131] In short the Ottoman central army by the late sixteenth and early seventeenth centuries became a hub for commercial and financial entrepreneurs whose main interest lay in monetary activities rather than in military ones.

In an evolving market-driven economy in the process of monetization, as the Ottoman economy was in this period, monetary activities were coming to matter more than land per se. One should not therefore be surprised that the structure of the ruling elite went through a transformation at this time that almost mirrored the economic one. The frontier *ghazi* who conquered new lands and came to control resources tied to land in a timar could no longer constitute the backbone of the ruling elite in a society that was operating within the framework of a monetized economy on an imperial scale, one in which the developments in Aleppo had an impact on the Danube basin. This new socioeconomic configuration was to produce its own ruling elite, such as Baki Pasha, who started his life as the son of an Aleppan merchant, became a janissary, bid for tax-farms in the Balkans, and was appointed to the finance ministry after serving in the financial directorate of the Danube basin.[132]

The likes of Baki Pasha were not interested in timar assignments, except for investment purposes. The Ottoman central army that provided its members with both status and an advantageous position in which to acquire control of monetary resources was the place to be for such men. Thus they entered it as "outsiders" and transformed its function from a military institution to a

---

[129] See, for instance, İstanbul Müftülüğü Arşivi, İstanbul Mahkemesi 5, ff. 19b, 21b.
[130] Selaniki, *Tarih*, vol. II, 732; Halil Sahillioğlu, "Kuruluştan XVII. asrın sonlarına kadar Osmanlı para tarihi üzerinde bir deneme," PhD diss. (İstanbul Üniversitesi, 1958), 234, n. 28. A very telling example is found among the contracts that were recorded in "A Journall of all the Courts Actes, Contracts, Sentences, Ends of Controversies, and other Business concerning the English Nation . . . at the Port of Constantinople, begunne the first of January 1621 [January 11, 1622]," NA, SP 105/102. It seems the Ottoman merchants who dealt with their English counterparts were mostly non-Muslim, yet the handful of Muslim merchants whose transactions with the English were recorded in this book included a certain Mustafa who was described as a janissary; f. 48a. Another, or perhaps the same, janissary called Mustafa appeared among the large group of almost exclusively Muslim merchants who were trading with Venice around the same time; BOA, D. BŞM, 8/62.
[131] Selaniki, *Tarih*, vol. II, 519; Anonymous, "Kitâb-ı müstetâb," 16.
[132] See Chapter 1, 15.

financial one, at least partially. This new function of the central army, especially of the cavalry troops, also explains why most of the "military rebellions" of the late sixteenth and early seventeenth centuries had an economic agenda, such as the debasement of currency, the distribution of tax-farms through the intermediacy of the Jewish *kiera*, or the empowerment of palace officers who assigned tax-farms to their own clients. These "military rebellions" were responses to the absolutist policies of the court that aimed at centering all imperial networks of political and economic power in the palace just as much as they were articulations of the rebels' economic interests.

It was this kind of an army that deposed Osman II. In previous rebellions the "soldiers" had sometimes threatened the reigning sultan, but they had never gone this far.[133] This time they showed that they could realize their ultimate threat. In short, the Ottoman army that brought about a regicide in 1622 has to be seen as a political interest group with economic privileges that could well have been abolished had Osman II been able to recruit a new army. Thus they prepared to move when the sultan intended to cut their retirement benefits and acted more radically than ever before when they were persuaded that he was leaving the capital to create a new army.

In summary, the men who made up the Ottoman central army of the late sixteenth and early seventeenth centuries should be seen as political actors behaving in accordance with their economic and political interests, rather than as undisciplined soldiers of an army in decay. Just as the sultan was trying to assume full control of the imperial markets and the expanded political nation, the new members of the political nation were doing their best to protect their autonomy in this new polity, the Second Empire.

[133] The narrative sources suggested that both in 1589 and 1603 the cavalry troops threatened the sultan by implying that they could depose him; Selaniki, *Tarih*, vol. I, 211; Hasanbeyzade, *Târîh*, vol. III, 692.

CHAPTER 6

The Second Empire goes public

The age of the janissaries

In this chapter, I first paint a broad picture of the polity that was consolidated in the aftermath of the regicide, as I address this question: what did the Second Empire mean politically after the contestation for its control was over – or at least after the first round of this contestation? Then I paint in some details of this picture with a sharp focus on the janissaries, the leading actors of the Second Empire. In the last chapter my discussion of the political role of the central army concentrated on the cavalry troops because they were the ones who started the chain of revolts in the late sixteenth century. Although the cavalry troops were also active in the deposition of Osman II and a number of other incidents in the seventeenth century, it was the janissaries who ultimately ended up being recorded in twentieth-century Ottoman historiography as one of the two main culprits responsible for the Ottoman decline, the other being the ulema. The janissaries surpassed the cavalry troops in the political capital they accumulated throughout the seventeenth century. They eventually became the symbol of the Ottoman *ancien régime* in the eyes of those who chose to call the order they instituted in the late eighteenth and nineteenth centuries the "New Order."

The janissaries were indeed the symbol of the new political dynamics in what I call the Second Empire, which I cast as the imperial political system that replaced the patrimonial empire of the sixteenth century. However, to see them as such, we need to stop considering them, at least primarily, as an army. Thus I first discuss the janissaries as a sociopolitical organization and then focus on their political role in limiting the power of the monarch during the Second Empire by offering short analyses of some of the rebellions they took part in during the rest of the seventeenth century.

The Second Empire (1580–1826)

Andrews and Kalpaklı liken the murder of Osman II to the murder of the beloved by the lover in the context of early modern Ottoman cultural and literary history and suggest that it was the symbol of a fissure "that even has some of the underlying characteristics of the very modern notion of the separation of church and state."[1] A similar fissure opened up with this regicide in the bonds that held together the patrimonial empire. Elsewhere, I discussed how this murder destroyed the conceptual ties that bound Ottoman notions of government.[2] Here my focus is on more tangible bonds.

The murder of Osman II by his slaves marked the opening of a breach in the continuity between the sultan, his household, and his dominion – the patrimonial empire. The Ottoman Empire of the mid-sixteenth century was the ultimate embodiment of this continuity, as the larger polity was imagined as an expansion of the monarch's household. The political structures of the empire that were constructed during the reign of Mehmed II (1451–81) and perfected by Süleyman (1520–66) were based on the principle that the whole empire was the emperor's patrimony and that he ruled it all personally with the help of his household slaves who were handpicked by his agents. One of these handpicked slaves could first serve the sultan's person as his sword-bearer at the court and then become the next governor of Egypt, whereas a lesser page at the palace could ascend to be the district governor of a small provincial town. The sultan was personally in charge of his household, sitting on top of a pyramid-like organization, the power structures of which extended throughout the entire empire.

This structure grew out of the feudal political practices of the formative period of the Ottoman Empire (ca. 1300–1453), as the relationship between the suzerain and his vassals was transformed into that between the patriarch and his slaves. Thus, essentially, the pyramid-like political structure of the empire had not changed from its inception to the late sixteenth century.[3] As demonstrated earlier, however, the sultan had been losing his agency in picking his slaves for a while as an increasing number of "outsiders" entered his political organization. What happened in 1622 extended this loss one step further: his slaves then picked their new master and murdered the old one. The sultan had lost all control in his own household and, by extension, in his empire.

What the murder of Osman II symbolized was a much more radical transformation than the mid-fifteenth-century change from a feudal kingdom to a patrimonial empire. It represented a near rupture in the Ottoman political tradition as it came close to destroying the pyramid of political control. The various military rebellions of the late sixteenth and early seventeenth centuries that culminated in the deposition of Osman II in 1622 opened the way for a fundamentally different political system from both the one that had been in place and the one that was going to replace it; hence, my suggestion to call the period of ca. 1580–1826 the Second Empire. If the political structures

---

[1] Andrews and Kalpaklı, The Age of Beloveds, 323.
[2] I refer to the ties that held together ethics, economics, and politics in the Greco-Islamic intellectual tradition of governance; see Tezcan, "The Second Empire," 566.
[3] See Chapter 3, 90. Colin Imber makes a similar point in his The Ottoman Empire, 1300–1650: The Structure of Power (Hampshire: Palgrave Macmillan, 2002), 319–20.

of the feudal kingdom and the patrimonial empire could be represented by a pyramid at the apex of which stood the sultan, the Second Empire would best be symbolized by a spider web with the monarch at the center but not on top of anyone else. Some people were closer to the center and others were farther away, and yet the web provided links to get closer to power even for those who were farthest away.

Moving along this imperial web, coming closer to the center, were the representatives of social forces that were gradually taking over the military-administrative institutions of the empire. The very institutions that had been used to consolidate the political hegemony of the patrimonial empire over Ottoman society in the past were now being used to limit the royal authority of the dynasty and its agents. The best representative of these social forces were the *ecnebis*, or the "outsiders," who were not themselves descendants of the emperor's slaves but had bought their way into the imperial administration from the ranks of commoners. In contrast to the patrimonial empire, which was a polity run mostly by slaves of non-Muslim origin who were positioned at the top of the ruling class over a majority Muslim population, the Second Empire gradually came to be run predominantly by Muslims who previously had been mostly excluded from the administrative-military ruling class. The subjects, or the *re'aya*, were now becoming part of the ruling group, or the *askeri*,[4] yet another indication of the gradual destruction of the old ruling class' ideal model of governance in which the classes of society were to be kept in their places lest the commoners "whose appetites are not well-refined" take over the government.[5]

Whereas the appropriation of patrimonial political structures by newly emerging social forces constituted the defining characteristic of the Second Empire, the "New Order" (*nizam-ı cedid*), which was promulgated by Selim III in the late eighteenth century but could only be instituted in full force after the annihilation of the janissaries in 1826, represented the revenge of the state on those social forces.[6] The modernizing autocratic government that developed in the New Order, both in response to *and* hand in hand with European imperialism, fostered the development of new political elites whose members eventually took over the leadership of the empire and oversaw its dismemberment; this was as much their own making as that of European imperialism – hence the modern Middle East.

Just as the modern Middle East is a product of the Ottoman New Order of the nineteenth century, our understanding of pre-nineteenth-century Ottoman

---

[4] This process led to a transformation in the meaning of the term *re'aya*, which eventually came to denote the empire's non-Muslim subjects, who remained more excluded from the ruling class than their Muslim counterparts, as is touched upon in the conclusion of the present study.
[5] Kınalızade, *Ahlâk-ı 'Alâ'î*, book II, 73.
[6] Although the New Order usually refers to the reform program of Selim III (1789–1807), in this study I use it in a larger sense to refer to the regime gradually instituted in the Ottoman Empire after the destruction of the janissaries in 1826.

history is very much shaped by the perspectives fostered by that same order.
What I call the Second Empire is the *ancien régime* (*nizam-ı kadim*, or *atik*; i.e.,
old order) of the Ottoman New Order.[7] The Ottoman learned men of the early
nineteenth century were themselves very aware of the novelty of the New Order
and as early as 1804 referred to the order of the past as the *ancien régime*.
Some of these men actually preferred the Old Order to the new in several
respects,[8] and yet the dynamics of nineteenth-century history marginalized
them and brought the harbingers of the New Order to the forefront of Ottoman
historiography.[9] It was the historians of the New Order who held the Ottoman
ancien régime responsible for the decline of the Ottoman Empire.[10] Thus later
Ottoman historiography on the seventeenth and eighteenth centuries developed
with an agenda that was already set by the historians of the nineteenth century:
blaming the Ottoman decline on the *ancien régime*.

Another significant impact of the New Order on our understanding of
Ottoman history was its growing preoccupation with social engineering. This
interest was based on the assumption that the commoners could not be trusted
to shape their own future: the well-educated new elite were expected to lead
them there. Historians who held this assumption came to associate all political processes in which the commoners, or people who claimed to represent
them, played an active role with corruption and decay. Consequently, the *relative* democratization of the Ottoman ruling classes as a result of the entry of
*ecnebi*s was destined to be associated with the decline of the Ottoman Empire.
If we were to take off our social engineering glasses that carry the mark of the
Ottoman New Order, we might actually find a very different Old Order than
the one we are accustomed to see. I call this new conceptualization of the Old
Order, which aims at analyzing it for what it was rather than approaching it as
a deficient version of the patrimonial empire of Süleyman, the Second Empire.

The Second Empire corresponds to that period in Ottoman history in which
the limits of the political power of the emperor and his court were questioned,
challenged, and eventually redrawn by those members of the Ottoman society
who managed to enter the ruling classes through their own efforts, as opposed
to by royal will through the *devşirme* levy, which was based on the right of
conquest. Although it is always very problematic to decide on dates for political eras, as sociopolitical change does not happen overnight, for the sake of

[7] M. Tayyib Gökbilgin, "Nizam-ı cedid," *İA*, vol. IX, 309.
[8] See Ömer Fa'ik, "Nizâmü'l-atîk (İstanbul Üniversite Ktb. TY nr. 5836)," ed. Ahmet Sarıkaya,
    senior thesis (İstanbul Üniversitesi, 1979), which is a prime example for a eulogy of the Old
    Order from 1804.
[9] A recent study attempts to represent the voice of such marginalized men; see the editor's
    introduction to Ubeydullah Kuşmani and Ebubekir Efendi, *Asiler ve Gaziler: Kabakçı Mustafa
    Risalesi*, ed. Aysel Danacı Yıldız (Istanbul: Kitap Yayınevi, 2007), 7–27.
[10] See Baki Tezcan, "The New Order and the fate of the old: The historiographical construction
    of an Ottoman *ancien régime* in the nineteenth century," in *Empires in Contention: Sociology,
    History, and Cultural Difference*, eds. Peter F. Bang and Chris A. Bayly, forthcoming from
    Palgrave.

chronology, I propose 1580 and 1826 as the years limiting the lifespan of the Second Empire. I chose 1580 as the starting date because the last surviving vizier from Süleyman's patrimonial empire in the Ottoman council of ministers, Semiz Ahmed Pasha, died in 1580 after holding the grand vizierate for about six months. Upon the death of Ahmed Pasha, Murad III entertained the possibility of ruling directly, without a grand vizier.[11] The object of political power had changed. In a patrimonial empire in which feudal economic relations were still dominant, the emperor could delegate his political authority to his slaves as he theoretically enjoyed the right to land in most parts of the empire, which he saw as his own personal patrimony. As market relations started to gradually transform Ottoman society, the emperor's "slaves" became engaged in a contest with the emperor to control the empire-wide web of clients. Thus the emperor had to find creative ways of regaining his position of supreme authority, which was only possible by concentrating power at his court; hence, Ottoman absolutism.

During the period from 1580 to 1703 there was a fierce struggle between absolutists and constitutionalists in defining the boundaries of royal authority.[12] The year 1703 divides the history of the Second Empire into two, as the last major absolutist attempt to recapture the reins of power by Mustafa II came to a disastrous end that year. This year is also recorded as the one in which the last *devşirme* levy took place,[13] which is an appropriate symbol for the end of the dynasty's attempts to sustain a patrimonial empire run by the slaves of the emperor.

The second half of the life of the Second Empire began in 1703 and ended in 1826, the year in which Mahmud II destroyed the janissaries, the ultimate guardians of the Ottoman political order in the Second Empire. Notwithstanding its close association with military and territorial decline, I regard this period as the golden age of the Second Empire. During its golden age, the Second Empire was functioning much more smoothly as the royal authority had finally accepted the power of the web that surrounded it. With the exception of the 1730 rebellion, which included new features that did not exist in earlier rebellions,[14] the eighteenth century was more peaceful *internally* than the formative period of the Second Empire (1580–1703). What was most striking about it, however, was its political leadership. Grand viziers like Nişancı Mehmed Pasha (1717–18), Naili Abdullah Pasha (1755),

---

[11] Selaniki, *Tarih*, vol. I, 37, 128.
[12] While I was completing the final version of the present study, I noticed the publication of Hüseyin Yılmaz's "Constitutionalism in the Ottoman Empire before Westernization," *Dîvân: Journal of Interdisciplinary Studies* 13/24 (2009): 1–30, which might shed further light on the political landscape of the seventeenth century.
[13] Donald Quataert, *The Ottoman Empire, 1700–1922* (Cambridge: Cambridge University Press, 2000), 45.
[14] The lifestyle of the court and its powerful supporters was very much a target in 1730, which makes it a more complicated sociopolitical event that needs to be analyzed from a variety of perspectives.

Yirmisekizçelebizade Mehmed Sa'id Pasha (1755–6), Mehmed Ragıb Pasha (1757–63), Hamid Hamza Pasha (1763), Silahdar Mahir Hamza Pasha (1768), and Yağlıkçızade Mehmed Emin Pasha (1768–9) were unheard of in the sixteenth century. The first one was the son of a Muslim merchant from a village in Kayseri; the second, third, fourth, fifth, and last ones were professional bureaucrats; the fifth one's father was a Muslim merchant in a town around Niğde; the sixth one was the son of a wealthy Muslim man from Karahisar; and the father of the last one was a rich Muslim merchant from Istanbul who traded with India.[15] Unlike most of their predecessors during the age of the patrimonial empire, these grand viziers had not been handpicked by the *devşirme* collector representing the authority of the sultan but instead came from the ranks of the socioeconomic elite.

The relatively smooth functioning of the Second Empire in the eighteenth century was the result of the fine balance that the various representatives of Ottoman social classes had reached after a long period of political struggles. As demonstrated elsewhere, this balance was well reflected in the historiography of that era. In contrast to earlier periods of Ottoman history when chronicles commissioned by the court generally failed to draw any attention outside the court, this era was marked by a wider acceptance of the official historiography produced by the state.[16] This acceptance became possible because in the eighteenth century the government of the empire came to represent a much broader spectrum of social interests than ever before. Rather than limiting the ruling class as the dynastic institution of rule in the patrimonial empire tried to do, the eighteenth-century Ottoman state encompassed a larger ruling class and thus consolidated its legitimacy: the royal authority and its delegates had finally learned to share power. The social interests represented by the eighteenth-century Ottoman state included merchant classes in the cities whose members had infiltrated the janissary corps, as well as agricultural landlords who had secured official status for themselves as provincial notables, or *a'yan*. Yet, Mehmed Ragıb Pasha reportedly noted the fragility of the balance among the various interest groups, noting, "I am afraid that we shall be unable to re-establish order if we once break the harmony of the existing institutions,"[17] a prophecy that came to realization in the century following 1826.

One of the key political features of the Second Empire was the regularization of Ottoman succession, as discussed in length in Chapter 2. Because the sultan did not acquire the throne by virtue of his *devlet* (fortune), his legitimacy no longer depended on his personal charisma, but rather was contingent upon his recognition of and respect for the law and the rights and privileges of jurists

---

[15] Osmanzade Ta'ib Ahmed, Dilaverağazade Ömer Vahid, Ahmed Cavid, and Bagdadi Abdülfettah Şevket, *Hadîkat ül-vüzerâ [ve zeyilleri]* (Istanbul, 1271), part II, 27–9, 81–3, 84–6, part III, 4–8, 8–10, 16–18, 18–19, respectively.

[16] Tezcan, "Ottoman historiography."

[17] Niyazi Berkes, *The Development of Secularism in Turkey* (Montreal: McGill University Press, 1964), 53.

and established political corporations such as the janissaries. Gradually, the personage of the sultan lost so much of the semi-sacred qualities of the past that he was regarded as powerless without his office. Although Osman II and İbrahim were killed after their depositions in 1622 and 1648 because their deposers perceived them to be political threats, later deposed sultans were deemed incapable of plotting any potential comebacks and were allowed to remain alive, as if they were merely retired state officials.[18]

Another important feature of the Second Empire was the gradual demilitarization of the upper ruling class, or its *civilization* – civil in the sense of being nonmilitary. In the long term there occurred the transformation of a polity in which men with military power used to dominate the political process, changing the form of government to one in which civilian power holders increasingly came to control the central political apparatus. This transformation had *some* democratic implications to the extent that men with military power were either born or conscripted into the ruling class, whereas civilian power holders could come from more modest political backgrounds and make their way into the ruling class by virtue of their socioeconomic capital. In contrast, the New Order of the nineteenth century was eventually hijacked by the members of the military elite as the Ottoman autocratic modernization effort made its greatest investment in the armed forces and the education of their officers. Modern Turkey is dealing with the long-term implications of this legacy to this very day.

Although this study is mainly focused on imperial political structures, it is important to note that power sharing and proto-democratization were also visible at the local level. Starting from the late seventeenth century, local notables assumed gradually increasing political functions that transformed them into effective intermediaries between localities and the imperial center. Both the expansion of commercial agriculture in large farms, or *çiftliks*, throughout the seventeenth century and the introduction of lifelong inalienable tax-farms, the *malikane*s, in 1695 were influential factors in the economic empowerment of local notables who used their socioeconomic status to gain political authority by acquiring from the state formal recognition of their status as *a'yan*. The first local elections that determined the identity of the *a'yan* in a given locality likely took place in the 1680s, although little is known about the particular processes followed in these elections. In the eighteenth century, some Ottoman *a'yan* were to grow into regional dynasties that gained widespread support, from Muslims and non-Muslims alike.[19]

---

[18] Both Mehmed IV (1648–87) and Ahmed III (1703–30) lived for six more years after their depositions and died in 1693 and 1736, respectively; for the former, see this chapter, 218.

[19] One of the earliest studies in English on the political role of the *a'yan* was Deena R. Sadat's "Rumeli Ayanlari: The eighteenth century," *Journal of Modern History* 44 (1972): 346–63; for a recent review of the scholarship on the *a'yan*, see Khoury, "The Ottoman centre versus provincial power-holders;" for an introduction to the relevant scholarship in Turkish, see Özcan Mert, "Âyan," *İA2*, vol. IV, 195–8.

Yet power sharing and proto-democratization in the provinces went well beyond the formally recognized institution of the *a'yan*. Balkan historians and others who have focused on non-Muslim communities of the Ottoman Empire have shown the existence of communal corporations that were de facto accepted by Ottoman courts despite the absence of the category of the corporation in jurists' law. Eleni Gara observes "a close link between the extension of the tax-farming system, collective liability for the payment of taxes, and the emergence of communal institutions," which led to the evolution of "an institutional framework regulating collective representation and internal administration" beginning from the early seventeenth century.[20] In the same period neighborhood cash wakfs, which were trusts founded by well-to-do neighbors the yields of whose donated funds would be used to ease the payment of certain taxes assessed on Muslim neighborhoods, proliferated, suggesting that similar developments were taking place in Muslim communities as well.[21] Thus the proto-democratization brought about by the monetization of Ottoman economy in the sixteenth century was not limited to imperial structures centered in Istanbul but permeated local communities, encouraging them to develop mechanisms of self-government.

When the Ottoman dynasty stopped pushing for its own empowerment and acknowledged the power of such institutions as the janissaries and the *a'yan*, as well as the representational authority of local structures of self-government, the Ottoman state emerged as an institution that attracted respect from the representatives of emerging Ottoman social forces. It was then that the Ottomans could create an imperial currency to be used all over the empire, and it was also then that a relatively secular official historiography started to be read outside the court circles.[22]

In the remainder of this chapter I substantiate some of these theses about the proto-democratization of Ottoman politics and the limitation of royal authority during the Second Empire by focusing on the janissary corps. In the following section, I treat the janissaries not simply as an army but rather as a sociopolitical corporation that was open to the lower levels of Ottoman society. The last section discusses some of their rebellions in the seventeenth century and their political implications in terms of the limitation of royal authority.

The janissary corps as a sociopolitical corporation

Did Osman II fall victim to a military rebellion or a sociopolitical transformation? The response to this question depends, among other things, on our

---

[20] Eleni Gara, "In search of communities in seventeenth century Ottoman sources: The case of the Kara Ferye district," *Turcica* 30 (1998): 135–62, at 139.

[21] Çizakça, "Cash *waqfs*," 326–9.

[22] For the development of an imperial currency, see Chapter 1, 18; for the historiography, see Tezcan, "Ottoman historiography," 184–97; for secular implications of the way in which the Ottoman state of the Second Empire imagined itself, see Tezcan, "The Second Empire," 569–70.

understanding of the janissaries. Ottoman historiography in the twentieth century was quite united in approaching the janissary corps of the seventeenth century as an army in decay. I do not challenge this observation in its entirety for there is no question about the relative decay of the janissary corps as a fighting force. A comparison of Ottoman military history in the sixteenth century with that in the seventeenth century would easily confirm this observation.[23] My objection is of a different nature. When we look at the janissaries in the seventeenth century and simply see a military force, we actually miss a great deal of Ottoman history. The janissary corps of the seventeenth century was one of the most dynamic sites for cultural, economic, political, and social history of the Ottoman Empire in the early modern period. A very significant development was their growth into a heavyweight political actor in opposition to the court and its absolutist policies in the seventeenth century as exemplified by a number of rebellions. However, the political significance of the corps went well beyond these rebellions.

What is much more striking than the janissary rebellions themselves is the gradual appropriation of the corps by the larger society that it was designed to keep suppressed politically. The barrier constructed between the rulers (*askeri*) and the subjects (*re'aya*) had been one of the central tenets of the patrimonial empire in the period from 1453 to 1580. Politics was meant to be the domain of the *askeri*, who exploited the economic resources produced by the *re'aya*. The janissary corps was one of the most visible sites for the infiltration of the subjects (*re'aya*) into the ruling strata (*askeri*) as "outsiders," thus destroying this barrier and with it the *askeri*'s monopoly on politics. In short, a look at the janissary corps offers us the opportunity to witness the Ottoman society claiming its state, one janissary at a time.

The increasing involvement of the janissaries in economic activities is significant evidence indicating a growing presence of "outsiders" in the corps. As Cemal Kafadar reminds us, this involvement was not new; the janissaries had been involved in nonmilitary activities much before the late sixteenth century.[24] In the late sixteenth century, however, the proportion of janissaries who were *primarily* involved in such activities increased in relation to the number of fighting forces. If the absence of the janissaries from the city was directly reflected in the absence of grocers in the marketplace at a time when the size of the janissary corps was growing, then it is not difficult to argue that some of the new janissaries came from the ranks of the grocers.[25] The number of men enrolled in the janissary corps exploded in the 1580s and 1590s in parallel to the explosion in the number of cavalry soldiers and most other salary-receiving personnel that was discussed earlier.[26] The size of the janissary corps seemed to decrease around 1610, most probably during the

---

[23] See Murphey, *Ottoman Warfare*; Aksan, *Ottoman Wars, 1700–1870*.
[24] Kafadar, "On the purity," 278.   [25] See Selaniki, *Tarih*, vol. II, 615–6.
[26] See Chapter 5, 177–9; the enrollment numbers of 1609 were already reached in the late 1590s; see the figures for 1006/1597–8 in Âli, *Künhü'l-ahbâr*, TY 5959, f. 92a–93a, reproduced in Murphey, *Ottoman Warfare*, 45.

Fig. 18. A janissary in his uniform, drawn by Gentile Bellini, ca. 1480; British Museum, Prints & Drawings, Pp, 1.19; courtesy of the Trustees of the British Museum.

grand vizierate of Murad Pasha who might have successfully pressured the corps to cut down their numbers, as he was known for his iron fist.[27] In the aftermath of 1622, the size of the corps resumed its growth for the long term, and the admission of "outsiders" into the corps continued as a consequence of the janissaries' success in consolidating their political power by the deposition they staged.[28]

Clearly, the essence of the corps was changing (see Figs. 18 and 19 contrasting fifteenth and eighteenth century janissaries). As noted by Quataert,

[27] According to Ayn Ali, in 1609 the number of janissaries and their cadets exceeded 47,000, and they received a total salary of more than 100,000,000 akçes; Ayn Ali, "Risâle," 88–9; in the fiscal year of 1613–14, however, the total salary paid to them dropped to 83,883,911 akçes – I assume that the latter figure included the salaries of the cadets because there was no salary item devoted to them in the treasury balance sheet of 1613–14; see Murphey, "The functioning of the Ottoman army," 443.

[28] In the fiscal year 1661–2, 54,222 janissaries, excluding their cadets, received 148,477,020 akçes in salary; see Ömer Lûtfi Barkan, "1070–1071 (1660–1661) tarihli Osmanlı bütçesi ve

Fig. 19. A janissary in his daily attire, eighteenth century; from an album entitled *Les portraits des differens habillemens qui sont en usage a Constantinople et dans tout la Turquie*, f. 92; courtesy of the Deutsches Archäologisches Institut, Abteilung Istanbul.

"These one-time professional soldiers had become a group who first of all were artisans and guildsmen and only incidentally were on the military

bir mukayese," *İstanbul Üniversitesi İktisat Fakültesi Mecmuası* 17 (1955–56): 304–47, at 305, 310; the dating of the document published by Barkan has been corrected to 1661–2; see Erişah Abdurrahimoğlu, "1621–1680 yılları arasında Osmanlı devletinin merkezi hazine gelir ve giderleri," MA thesis (Marmara Üniversitesi, 1988), 42.

payroll."[29] The engagement of the janissaries in crafts and trades became highly visible in the late sixteenth century and increased throughout the seventeenth century such that, as suggested by Kafadar, in the eighteenth century "most of the *Yeniçeri*s pursued non-military trades and most artisans were affiliated with the corps."[30]

It is admittedly difficult to quantify the increasing involvement of the janissaries in nonmilitary activities. Fortunately, however, Ottoman court records include detailed estate records for the people who had *askeri* (military) status, including the janissaries. Legally speaking, those with *askeri* status were not limited to military personnel and officers but also included secretaries, servants, professors, judges, imams, preachers, and many others who were receiving salaries from the imperial administration or other public sources supervised by it. In addition, the wives, children, and freed slaves of the *askeri* were also included in this group. It is consequently hard to define this legal group as a social class even though it was inclusive of the ruling class, as it comprised both the governor-general of Egypt and the preacher of a small mosque.[31] Thus an unequal distribution of wealth among them might well be expected. One would also expect that all of these people would have depended for their livelihood on their salaries rendered for their professional services and thus would have accumulated their wealth in cash. A look at their estate records indicates that the first expectation is met exactly. The distribution of wealth among the *askeri* was as unequal as it was in the society at large. As for the second expectation, however, it is proven wrong. A considerable proportion of their wealth was invested in commercial goods, suggesting that they were also engaged in trade and did not live off the salaries they received for their professional services. Most importantly, the janissaries seemed to have had a special place among these *askeri*-merchants.

A detailed study of *askeri* estates in the seventeenth century conducted recently by Said Öztürk suggests that the distribution of wealth within this group was drastically unequal. Öztürk studied around 1,000 estate records from the period 1595 to 1668.[32] His sample includes every record found in the six surviving registers from this period in Istanbul. His findings clearly demonstrate that the legal category of *askeri* did not constitute a monolithic group but instead included people from a wide range of income groups. My reinterpretation of his data suggests, for instance, that the distribution of wealth among the *askeri* was just as unequal as it was in the rest of the Ottoman society. Whereas the richest 20 percent of the *askeri* controlled more than 80 percent of all wealth held by the members of the Ottoman *askeri*, the poorest fifth of the group had access to less than one percent of it in the first half of the seventeenth

---

[29] Donald Quataert, "The age of reforms, 1812–1914," in *An Economic and Social History of the Ottoman Empire*, 764.

[30] Cemal Kafadar, "*Yeniçeri – esnaf* relations," 85.   [31] See Chapter 5, n. 118.

[32] Said Öztürk, *Askeri Kassama ait Onyedinci Asır İstanbul Tereke Defterleri: Sosyo-ekonomik tahlil* (Istanbul: Osmanlı Araştırmaları Vakfı, 1995).

century. The findings of Hüseyin Özdeğer, who studied commoners' estates in Bursa in late fifteenth century, are similar in suggesting that there was a concentration of wealth in the richest quintile of the population.[33]

Table. Wealth distribution among the *askeri*, 1636–51[34]

Groups	Number of estates	The value of the smallest estate in the group	The value of the largest estate in the group	The value of the median estate in the group	The average value of estates in the group	The total value of estates in the group (TVEG in akçes)	TVEG divided by the total value of all estates (× 100)
1st quintile	52	380	9,262	4,638	4,802	249,713	0.6 %
2nd quintile	51	9,350	25,559	16,184	16,802	856,908	2.2 %
3rd quintile	51	26,010	51,109	35,900	36,921	1,882,948	4.7 %
4th quintile	52	51,200	161,408	80,808	87,054	4,526,817	11.4 %
5th quintile	52	164,856	2,801,984	391,796	621,014	32,292,740	81.1 %
Total	258	380	2,801,984	36,126	154,299	39,809,126	100.0 %

Although the distribution of wealth among the Ottoman *askeri* mirrored that in the larger society, among the various groups constituting the *askeri*, the janissaries seemed to be closest to the urban commoners in two important respects. First, they were much more involved in trade than other significant *askeri* groups, and second, the sizes of their estates were comparable to those of the commoners. Öztürk found that on average, more than 6 percent of the *askeri* estates consisted of commercial goods.[35] Yet, more than twice this percentage of the janissaries' estates consisted of commercial goods.[36] Thus, in this way the janissaries resembled the merchant population of the city, and the distribution of wealth among their ranks made them an almost exact match to a comparable sample of commoners. The datasets that could form the basis of a comparison between the estates of the commoners and those of the *askeri* come from the first half of the seventeenth century in Bursa and Istanbul. Özdeğer provides summary data for a register of commoners' estates from 1639–40 in Bursa, and Öztürk's study includes a detailed inventory of *askeri* estates found in a register dating from 1636–46 in Istanbul. What is striking to observe is that, although the estates of the *askeri* were on average much larger than those of the commoners, the janissary estates recorded in Istanbul on average were actually slightly smaller than those of Bursa's commoners if two

[33] Hüseyin Özdeğer, *1463–1640 Yılları Bursa Şehri Tereke Defterleri* (Istanbul: İstanbul Üniversitesi İktisat Fakültesi Yayınları, 1988), 135–42.
[34] Based on Öztürk's reproduction of his raw data, *İstanbul Tereke Defterleri*, 450–65.
[35] Ibid., 145.   [36] See the rows "beşe," "racil," and "solak-yesari," in ibid., 155.

unusually large estates are excluded from the estates of janissaries.[37] To sum up, among the Ottoman *askeri* in the first half of the seventeenth century, the janissaries seemed to be economically most involved in mercantile activities and much closer to the commoners than they were to other groups within the *askeri* in the amount of wealth they managed to accumulate.

This striking closeness between the composition and size of the estates of janissaries and commoners was primarily brought about by the infiltration of commoners into the janissary corps, made possible by its relative autonomy. Unlike in other segments of the Ottoman army and the administrative apparatus, entry into the janissary corps was to a large extent handled by janissary officers themselves. An early-seventeenth-century treatise on the traditions that governed the janissary corps drew attention to the uniqueness of the corps in producing its own payroll registers.[38] Although the sultan could theoretically check the growth of the corps from one payday to the next, which were usually every three to six months, in practice very few sultans seemed to do so.[39] Thus the janissaries were able to increase their numbers and also control to a considerable degree the choice of their new recruits.

Although part of the ease with which the janissaries were able to legitimize their growth was related to the increasing use of infantry in warfare, as argued in the last chapter, this reason does not sufficiently explain the corps' expansion. The growth in the number of the cadets (*acemiyan*) in the late sixteenth and early seventeenth centuries did not parallel that of the janissaries, suggesting that most of the new recruits came from among the Muslim population as opposed to the *devşirmes*.[40] Had the need for more infantry soldiers been the driving force for the expansion of the corps, one would have expected the Ottoman administration to increase the number of cadets with a view to training more infantry soldiers capable of using firearms. Yet, the number of cadets seemed to remain constant or decline during the seventeenth century.[41] That is why I argue for the primacy of socioeconomic factors in bringing "outsiders" into the corps rather than reasons related to wars.

The available evidence suggests that the social groups represented in the growing numbers of janissaries were diverse and included, among others,

---

[37] The average size of estates left behind by a sample of 163 commoners in Bursa in 1639–40 was 27,907 *akçes*; see Özdeğer, *Bursa Tereke Defterleri*, 141, the last two lines of Table 36. Öztürk, *İstanbul Tereke Defterleri*, 450–7, lists 133 estates from 1636–46, 31 of which may be identified as belonging to janissary-related families (estate numbers 7, 13, 22, 23, 27, 33, 34, 35, 37, 44, 46, 50, 51, 53, 56, 70, 75, 81, 86, 90, 94, 95, 99, 101, 104, 106, 108, 121, 125, 129, and 132). The average estate size for this group of thirty-one individuals was 142,090 *akçes*. However, if one excludes two unusually large estates from the sample (estate numbers 22 and 56) and takes the average of the remaining 29 estates, one reaches the figure of 25,540 *akçes*.
[38] Anonymous, "Kavânîn-i yeniçeriyân," 250.
[39] For reports submitted to an unidentified sultan who was closely supervising all payroll registers, see Topkapı Sarayı Arşivi, E. 1730/1–7.
[40] See Chapter 5, 179.
[41] Compare Ayn Ali, "Risale," 89, with Barkan, "1070–1071," 311.

members of the upper classes, such as the sons of the *mevali*, or the lords of the law.[42] But the lower segments of the middle classes stand out as the chief source of the new recruits. Ottoman narrative sources from the late sixteenth and early seventeenth centuries included several references to commoners of Muslim origin buying their way into the janissary corps.[43] They either managed to bribe the *devşirme* collector to accept their son into the corps of cadets, or adult Muslim males themselves bribed janissary officers to allow them to directly enter the janissary corps. For the janissaries to increase in numbers, then, the first necessary ingredient was the growth of a social class that could afford to pay the entry fee to the corps, which Ottoman sources regarded as a bribe and opposed ardently. According to a senior janissary who complained of the practice in the early seventeenth century, the average bribe that commoners paid to enter the corps was around 55 gold ducats – or, at the contemporary exchange rate of 120 *akçe*s per gold coin, the equivalent of 6,600 *akçe*s.[44] Although a peasant would have found it difficult to save this amount, for someone working in the city, the sum was manageable. A skilled worker made around 23 *akçe*s per day around this time;[45] thus the entry fee to the corps was less than a year's salary for a skilled worker.

The next question to ask is what one would gain from entry into the janissary corps in, let us say, the early seventeenth century. The only certain answer is a negative one: the salary may *not* have been the reason. The salaries of most janissaries were lower than the wages of unskilled workers who, on average, made 14 *akçe*s a day in the 1610s.[46] In addition, for a married man with children, some of the fringe benefits, such as housing at the barracks, did not mean much. So why would a city dweller join the janissary corps if the pay, which started around 3 *akçe*s a day in the early seventeenth century, would not even decently cover one's daily food (that amount would purchase a loaf of bread, three eggs, and three pounds of apples around 1600)?[47] Yet people were ready to pay the equivalent of 6,600 *akçe*s as a bribe to place themselves in the corps. There must have been other incentives, then, that made the corps such an attractive place for the commoners.

One very important incentive for joining the corps, particularly for someone who wanted to start a business or expand an existing one, must have been the availability of credit. According to Paul Rycaut, the British ambassador to the Ottoman Empire in the second half of the seventeenth century, "a Treasury

---

[42] Uzunçarşılı noted that the imperial administration permitted the entry of the sons of the *mevali* and other judges into the janissary corps in 1592; *Kapukulu*, vol. I, 152.
[43] Anonymous, "Kitâb-ı müstetâb," 11; Koçi Bey, *Risale*, 45.
[44] Anonymous, "Kavânîn-i yeniçeriyan," 252.
[45] Süleyman Özmucur and Şevket Pamuk, "Real wages and standards of living in the Ottoman Empire, 1489–1914," *Journal of Economic History* 62 (2002): 292–321, at 301.
[46] Ibid.
[47] Uzunçarşılı, *Kapukulu*, vol. I, 411; Mübahat S. Kütükoğlu, "1009 (1600) tarihli narh defterine göre İstanbul'da çeşidli eşya ve hizmet fiatları," *Tarih Enstitüsü Dergisi* 9 (1978): 1–85, at 22, 27, 29.

of unknown sums which have descended to the Common Bank" was one of the sources of wealth that made the janissaries rich and powerful. Although Rycaut did not explain the "Common Bank" in great detail, he believed that its funds grew as the estates of the deceased janissary aghas, or generals, were folded into it.[48]

Contemporary Ottoman sources suggested that there were two kinds of treasuries within the janissary corps. The one at the headquarters (*ağa kapusı*), called the "black coffer (*kara sandık*)," functioned as a safe rather than a bank. If a janissary died while his inheritors were still minors, his estate would be sold and the money thus raised would be kept in this "black coffer" for the minor to claim it upon his maturity.[49]

Although it is quite plausible that the general of the janissaries and other high-ranking officers may have used the funds in the "black coffer" for safe investments so that an inheritance would not lose its value against inflation, there also was a different type of treasury that was meant to be used as a bank. Each janissary company (*orta*) had one of these banks, which lent money both to its members and to outsiders. The capital of these banks must have been large enough to finance long-distance traders, such as a certain Jovan of Dubrovnik, who disappeared with 180,000 *akçes* that he borrowed from the sixty-sixth company of the janissaries around 1618.[50] Certainly, janissaries, such as the ones who traded with England and Venice, could use these banks as well.[51] Some of the capital came from the estates of janissaries who did not have any inheritors, some was held in trust until an inheritor would reach full age, and some was money bestowed by the well-off janissaries for the food supply of their comrades and the upkeep of their barracks.[52] The last source of money confirms that the janissaries did not constitute an economically monolithic group. Some probably did live in the barracks and made use of some fringe benefits, such as subsidized meat. But a married janissary, such as a certain Ferhad who lived in a house that was sold for 76,000 *akçes* in 1621,[53] most probably dropped in to the barracks rarely and instead minded his own business, which made it possible for him to purchase that house, which he could never have afforded had he lived off his janissary salary only. It must have been the likes of Ferhad who made it possible for the less fortunate janissaries to enjoy decent food, lighting, and heat at the barracks by donating sums of money to the bank of their company. Thus, the janissary corps attracted both people who needed credit and those who could use that credit to make money and then invest part of their proceeds into their companies.

There is also some evidence suggesting that the capital of the banks in the janissary companies were used for purposes other than lending. Some eighteenth-century documents dealing with janissaries of North Africa clearly

---

[48] Paul Rycaut, *The Present State of the Ottoman Empire* (London: John Starkey and Henry Brome, 1668), 193, 197.
[49] Anonymous, "Kavânîn-i yeniçeriyân," 180, 254.
[50] Yıldırım, *82 Numaralı Mühimme*, 184–5.   [51] See Chapter 5, 189, n. 130.
[52] Anonymous, "Kavânîn-i yeniçeriyân," 179–80, 254.   [53] BOA, D. BŞM 9/9.

suggested that these janissaries could create partnerships with their company banks, matching the funds of their common treasury with their labor.[54] Partnerships involving janissaries were to be found in the seventeenth century as well. In most of these cases the janissaries provided the capital, which they could easily borrow from their company's bank, whereas others did the trading.[55] Akif Aydın's research suggests that, by the eighteenth century, the janissary company bank had evolved to assume what would later be called a corporate identity.[56]

The corps provided other benefits for potential small businessmen. The immunity of janissaries from regular procedures of prosecution applied to everyone else, which secured them a trial by their elders and peers as opposed to a court of law, proved to be an invaluable advantage in business. If one were protected by the immunity of membership in the corps, then judicial authorities or market inspectors could not interfere with one's business. Thus a merchant who became a janissary could engage in a broader variety of business practices than could a regular merchant, such as breaking the price ceilings in their dealings with others. In the Ottoman marketplace, which continued to try to keep the appearance of a tightly controlled market in the late sixteenth and early seventeenth centuries, price ceilings were supposed to be enforced by market inspectors, or *muhtesib*s. But neither the market inspectors nor the local judges apparently intervened in the business of janissary merchants, leading others to raise complaints about them and the central authority to issue orders prohibiting janissaries to engage in trade. That these prohibitions did not mean much is clear from their frequent repetitions.[57]

Small businessmen also enjoyed the benefits of the immunity provided by membership at the janissary corps in relation to guild regulations. The Ottoman urban economy was not only controlled by market inspectors but also several self-enforcement mechanisms built around the guilds supervised the activity of people engaged in a certain trade. In the late sixteenth century, for instance, officers of the metalworkers guild complained about the noncompliance of their "soldier" members with certain regulations. Interestingly enough, the response of the central authority in this particular case was not to prohibit

54 Fethi Gedikli, *Osmanlı Şirket Kültürü: XVI—XVII. Yüzyıllarda Mudârebe Uygulaması* (Istanbul: İz, 1998), 137–8, no. 431.

55 Ibid., 96, 136; see also F. Gedikli, "İstanbul'da para vakıfları ve *mudârebe*," *Hak-İş Dergisi* (November 1999): 68–73; I would like to thank the author for providing me with an electronic version of this piece; for a slightly different case involving janissaries, see Murat Çızakça, *A Comparative Evolution of Business Partnerships: The Islamic World and Europe, with Specific Reference to the Ottoman Archives* (Leiden: E. J. Brill, 1996), 79.

56 M. Akif Aydın, "Eyüp şeriye sicillerinden 184, 185 ve 188 numaralı defterlerin hukuki tahlili," in *18. Yüzyıl Kadı Sicilleri Işığında Eyüp'te Sosyal Yaşam*, ed. Tülay Artan (Istanbul: Türkiye Ekonomik ve Toplumsal Tarih Vakfı, 1998), 71. Islamic law did not formally recognize corporate identity.

57 There are two from 1584 reproduced in Ahmed Refik [Altınay]'s *On Altıncı Asırda İstanbul Hayatı (1553–1591)* (Istanbul: Devlet Basımevi, 1930), 130–1, no. 50; and Uzunçarşılı, *Kapukulu*, vol. I, 695–6; see also Kafadar, "*Yeniçeri – esnaf* relations," 82.

commercial activities by soldiers, but rather to condemn the soldiers for not following the established customs of their guild.[58]

Janissary tradesmen eventually found very effective ways of circumscribing the guild regulations. Thirty years after the case of the metalworkers guild cited earlier, a new complaint was filed by a member of the guild of sesame oil sellers. The petitioner Hacı Mehmed stated that their officers used to be from among the elders of the guild, who were all commoners. Thus when new supplies arrived, they would purchase them together; and when taxes were levied, they would pay them together. But their current officers were all janissaries. They were purchasing most of the supplies that arrived in the city, but when taxes were levied, they were not sharing the burden with the rest of the guild members. Hacı Mehmed had apparently petitioned about this case earlier with no avail. Now he was trying once again, hoping that the central authority would intervene in his guild and change its leadership.[59]

This case reflected the rising socioeconomic leverage of "soldier" businessmen in Istanbul. Unfortunately it is not clear whether the new leadership of Hacı Mehmed's guild was chosen by the members of the guild or appointed by the central authority. Eunjeong Yi's detailed study of Istanbul guilds in the seventeenth century suggests that, whereas some guilds chose their own officers, in others the guild leaders were appointed.[60] As noted in the previous chapter, members of the imperial cavalry troops were indeed appointed to guild offices in this period, but there is no evidence of janissary appointments. Thus in this case what we are observing might well be the rise of janissary merchants to governing positions in their guilds through their own devices, such as building a following that would support them. It is significant to note that Hacı Mehmed came alone to complain and was not accompanied by other sesame oil sellers who were as adversely affected by the janissary leadership as he was. Therefore one may assume that some members of the guild were actually on the side of the janissary leadership.

The janissary connection continued to help the aspiring small businessmen of Istanbul and encouraged more to join the corps. According to Yi, the involvement of janissaries in the guilds of Istanbul increased notably during the seventeenth century. Whereas less than 20 percent of cases involving guild matters referred to "soldier" members in the 1610s, by the 1660s this percentage had almost reached 50 percent. Thus the janissaries who started infiltrating certain guilds in the late sixteenth century came to lead some of them and enter many more during the seventeenth century. As Yi notes, some of these "soldier" businessmen were janissaries originally and entered trades later, whereas others were commoners who joined the corps to increase their prospects in business.[61]

---

[58] [Altınay], On Altıncı Asırda, 134–5, no. 57.   [59] Yıldırım, 82 Numaralı Mühimme, 20–1.
[60] Eunjeong Yi, Guild Dynamics in Seventeenth-century Istanbul: Fluidity and Leverage (Leiden: Brill, 2004), 74.
[61] Ibid., 133, 139.

The impression one gets from the contemporary sources is that the commoners who joined the janissaries were more numerous than the members of the corps who entered trades. In a petition from 1649, for instance, the cadets sarcastically asked while waiting for their graduation whether they should quit and become porters so that they could actually enter the janissary corps by bribes as so many grocers and porters did.[62] Although the authors of the political treatises of the time, which enumerated the factors that contributed to what they called the social disorder, did mention the janissaries who picked up trades as one of those factors, their factor of choice, the ultimate evil, was the entry of commoners into the corps. For instance, when Koçi Bey, the most well known of the Ottoman authors who wrote on these issues, discussed the decay of the janissaries, his critique concentrated on the various practices that made it possible for commoners to buy their way into the corps.[63]

In contrast to the janissary corps that expanded with the entry of commoners, the imperial cavalry troops – the major actors of the late-sixteenth-century rebellions – were in eclipse during the seventeenth century. Part of the reason for this development was the structural rigidity of the cavalry troops. They were supposed to be elite troops receiving high salaries and, later, lucrative tax collection assignments. Because of the finite nature of economic resources, membership in such an expensive body could not be expanded beyond a certain limit, unlike the janissaries whose daily wages were negligible when compared with those of the cavaliers. A closely related reason for the decline of the imperial cavalry was the growth of the political power of the janissaries. As the janissaries grew in numbers and, more importantly, developed relationships with the people of Istanbul through the large number of commoners who joined their ranks, their political capital became much larger than that of the cavalry troops. In addition, the Ottoman administration cut the number of soldiers in the cavalry forces during the seventeenth century as the significance of the cavalry in military operations dwindled. By the second half of the seventeenth century, the janissaries and their urban allies had practically marginalized the cavalry troops in Ottoman politics.[64]

It is important to note, however, that the relationship that the janissaries built and developed with the people of Istanbul, whom they gradually came closer to represent in their makeup, was complex and not devoid of problems. To start with, the Ottoman city dweller was not a monolithic category. As pointed out earlier, Özdeğer's study of the estates of commoners in Bursa in the late fifteenth and early sixteenth centuries demonstrates that the distribution of wealth in Ottoman society was far from equal. Twenty percent of the population seemed to control 80 percent of the wealth. One would expect the economic interests of the rich to be at some variance with those of the middle

---

[62] Kafadar, "*Yeniçeri – esnaf* relations," 80.   [63] Koçi Bey, *Risale*, 44–5.
[64] Uzunçarşılı, *Kapukulu*, vol. I, 511; Murphey, *Ottoman Warfare*, 52.

classes. Similarly, the "soldier" businessmen did not constitute a monolithic body and had quite varying sizes of capital at their disposal. For instance, Fethi Gedikli's study of partnership records belonging to people of *askeri* status in court registers suggests that, of twenty-three cases, eight had capital of 3,000 *akçes* or less, and seven operated with capital ranging between 3,000 and 20,000 *akçes*. The other eight cases were partnerships that had 20,000 *akçes* or more invested, with 150,000 and 60,000 *akçes* ranking as the two largest partnerships.[65] It is quite plausible that a janissary with a capital of 2,000 *akçes* might find his interests to be at times opposed to another whose capital was 20,000 *akçes*. The same would be the case for their "civil" partners as well. Thus one might expect that some economic problems faced in the marketplace might have evoked different responses from different janissaries, as they did from different businessmen.

For example, at times the janissary officers who had access to larger capital thanks to their powerful position within the corps engaged in monopolistic practices that were resented by the tradesmen of the city who included rank-and-file janissaries. A clear reflection of this conflict of interest was seen during the 1651 protests, as described in Yi's detailed study. Representatives of guilds were protesting about several issues in 1651. One of their major complaints was that they "had to buy copper, hazelnuts, salt, soap, resin, fustian, Diyarbakır cotton cloth, alum, morocco leather, and so on brought in through the connections of janissary officers and imposed by the government at three times 'normal' prices." As Yi notes, the officers were all the more outraged because many janissaries whom "they had considered to be on their side, had also participated in the protest."[66] Clearly not every janissary was on the side of their officers. To the contrary, as the example of 1651 indicates, the janissaries acted in accordance with their specific economic interests, which at times were different from those of their officers.

The political groups of the Ottoman imperial capital, then, were not necessarily stratified along the lines of such corporate bodies as janissaries or tradesmen. Just as the janissary officers who at times could impose prices on the market must have had their collaborators in the imperial market network, the guildsmen who protested against them had their allies among the janissaries who were themselves small tradesmen. Thus the lines that divided the sociopolitical groups were not easy to draw. The most plausible one seemed to be the size of economic capital to which an individual had access. The 1651 protests by the guildsmen suggested that the big capital's alliance with the janissary officers enabled them to set prices in the market and thus turn the relatively pluralistic market into a monopoly. This monopolistic tendency seemed to be opposed by the smaller merchants who preferred an open and competitive market in which some janissaries were also involved. The paucity of records and the current state of research on the available material do not

---

[65] Gedikli, *Şirket*, 136–7.   [66] Yi, *Guild Dynamics*, 217, 223.

allow one to assert stronger claims at this point. However, Robert Brenner's *Merchants and Revolution*, which argues that some of the better established merchants were royalists during the English Revolution while some of the newer ones supported the parliament, may well find its counterpart in two opposing groups of merchants in the Ottoman capital.[67]

Having said that the janissaries did not always share common interests, especially with regard to their economic investments, I must emphasize that there were times when they acted in unison, such as in most of the depositions of the seventeenth century. Yet even at these times there may well have been dissidents to the common course of action adopted by the majority of the janissaries. However, these dissidents were either persuaded to join the majority during the consultation session the janissaries took part in before major uprisings or simply remained in their houses. In such instances when the majority acted in consensus, what usually was at stake was their ability to have an impact on the policies of the court. They acted together when they felt that their political power that helped them draw the boundaries of royal authority was threatened. They knew all too well that without their political privileges, they would also lose their economic advantages, whether they were janissary magnates with large amounts of capital or others allied with small-scale businessmen. Thus, for instance, in the deposition of Osman II in 1622 the janissaries did not have any difficulty in coming together, and in the aftermath of the regicide, they quickly developed a sophisticated political language to retell the history of their rebellion.[68]

The basic conclusion one can draw from the seventeenth-century janissary rebellions, which I discuss briefly in the next section, is that the janissaries proved to be invincible and enforced their political autonomy, notwithstanding the designs of others aimed at limiting their political power. Despite the autocratic politics of Murad IV during the latter half of his reign and the attempts of the Köprülü viziers to suppress the political power of the janissaries in the second half of the seventeenth century, the janissaries survived into the eighteenth century. The fact that they had become something very different from what was originally intended was acknowledged with the end of the *devşirme*-based conscription. In the eighteenth century the janissaries assumed full control over new membership. Most of the new members were adult men who had their own jobs.[69] As was the case in the seventeenth century, most seemed to come from the middle classes.

The connections between the corps and the tradesmen of the imperial capital that had been developing since the late sixteenth century seemed to evolve into an almost virtual identification in some cases; hence the observation of a contemporary that "many of the *orta*s or companies" had virtually become

---

[67] Robert Brenner, *Merchants and Revolution: Commercial Change, Political Conflict, and London's Overseas Traders, 1550–1653* (Princeton: Princeton University Press, 1993).

[68] Tezcan, "The history of a 'primary source,'" 62.   [69] Uzunçarşılı, *Kapukulu*, vol. I, 153–4.

"guilds of bakers, butchers, glaziers, boatmen, armorers, and so forth."[70] Thus
if one was hard-pressed to determine the economic class distinctions among
the janissaries, one could assert that the lower segments of the middle classes
continued to make up the majority of the corps.[71] Perhaps the question of
capital formation in the Ottoman Empire may benefit from a reconsideration
based on this observation. The resilience of the janissaries may have created
a more "democratic" distribution of capital among the economically active
urban population engaged in business. What is beyond any doubt, however, is
that the political power of the janissaries was at its height at the beginning of
the eighteenth century. When Sarı Mehmed Pasha made recommendations to
reform the corps so as to make its members more obedient to royal authority
in the early eighteenth century, he did not forget to add that "it is impossible to
put an end to these conditions by action from outside the corps." It was only
in consultation with janissary officers that the corps might be reformed; any
other attempt would simply fail.[72]

Let me emphasize that the rising political profile of the janissaries in the
seventeenth and eighteenth centuries was an empire-wide phenomenon. It was
not just in Istanbul that the janissary corps established firm control over the
political process. Contemporary examples from Aleppo, Baghdad, Belgrade,
Damascus, Mosul, and Tunis suggested that local corps of janissaries had
grown into significant players in local politics all over the empire.[73] The close
connections between the janissaries and middle-class commoners, especially
in trade, seemed to exist in these localities as well. Dina Khoury's discussion
of janissaries in Mosul is instructive: "The janissaries were no longer an elite
fighting force stationed in the city; they had become part of the population
and taken on a variety of occupations ranging from artisanal production to tax
farming and trade."[74] However, although the janissaries had become significant
economic and political actors throughout the empire, it was in Istanbul that
they engaged in their most high-profile activities, the subject of the remainder
of this chapter.

---

[70] Walter Livingston Wright, Jr., "Introduction," in Sarı Defterdar Mehmed Pasha, *Ottoman
Statecraft: The Book of Counsel for Vezirs and Governors (Nasā'ih ül-vüzera ve'l-ümera)
of Sarı Mehmed Pasha, the Defterdār*, ed. and tr. W. L. Wright, Jr. (Princeton: Princeton
University Press, 1935), 41, citing an Ottoman contemporary, Ignatius Mouradgea D'Ohsson,
Tableau general de l'empire othoman, 7 vols. (Paris, 1788–1824), vol. VII, 342–3.
[71] See Quataert, "Janissaries, artisans," 264–8.
[72] Mehmed Pasha, *Ottoman Statecraft*, 114–5.
[73] See Herbert Luther Bodman, *Political Factions in Aleppo, 1760–1826* (Chapel Hill: University
of North Carolina Press, 1963), 55–78; Uzunçarşılı, *Osmanlı Tarihi*, vol. III, part I, 158–62;
Deena R. Sadat, "Âyân and ağa: The transformation of the Bektashi corps in the eighteenth
century," *Muslim World* (1973): 206–19; Karl K. Barbir, *Ottoman Rule in Damascus, 1708–
1758* (Princeton: Princeton University Press, 1980), 89–97; Asma Moalla, *The Regency of
Tunis and the Ottoman Porte, 1777–1814: Army and Government of a North-African Ottoman
eyâlet at the End of the Eighteenth Century* (London: RoutledgeCurzon, 2004), 3–24.
[74] Khoury, *State and Provincial Society*, 133.

The janissary rebellions of the seventeenth century

In this section I draw a portrait of the janissaries as a major political power that effectively limited the royal authority of the sultan, more often than not in an uneasy alliance with the lords of the law. Rather than discussing every single act of protest, I focus on a few rebellions and contextualize them as responses to absolutist policies, taking into account the contemporary representations of these events as well.[75]

Ten years after the deposition of Osman II, the janissaries once again intervened in the political process in defense of their vested interests. In 1632, Murad IV had just dismissed his grand vizier Husrev Pasha, who was leading a military campaign against Safavid Persia to regain Baghdad, which had been lost to the Safavids during the second reign of Mustafa I (1622–3). The apparent cause of Husrev Pasha's dismissal was his failure to recapture Baghdad. Although contemporary Ottoman sources did not condone all of the actions of the soldiers in response to the dismissal of Husrev Pasha, some clearly suggested that this dismissal was unwarranted, as he had shown some progress on the Safavid front. It is also clear from the sources that the soldiers of the central army, especially the janissaries, were very loyal to Husrev Pasha, who had been their general during the Anatolian civil war that followed the regicide of Osman II. Later as grand vizier, Husrev Pasha had captured Abaza Mehmed Pasha and brought that civil war to an end. He was also a strong supporter of the autonomy of the janissary corps and opposed Murad IV's efforts to take control of their payroll registers, which would have checked their growth. Thus the members of the central army corps were correct in perceiving his dismissal as an action undertaken against their interests. To appease their protests, Murad IV had to give up his next grand vizier, Hafız Ahmed Pasha, whom the protesters executed at once. Incidentally, Hafız Ahmed had been another one of Osman II's close allies.[76]

Murad IV, however, was adamant about taking the army corps under his control as a means of establishing his absolute authority over the empire. That is why he ordered the execution of Husrev Pasha, thereby dealing a heavy blow to the janissaries. When the news of his execution reached the imperial capital, the soldiers staged a second round of protests. As with their revolt ten years earlier in 1622, their targets were individuals who were some of the closest men to the sultan. They asked for the execution of three men, two of whom were close confidants of Murad IV. The sultan had just appointed one of them, Hasan Halife, to the command of the janissaries, which was

---

[75] For the problematic relationship between the janissaries and the ulema, see Kafadar, "*Yeniçeri – esnaf* relations," 90–3; for a more complete list of janissary rebellions than the one offered here, see Kafadar, "Janissaries and other riffraff," 123.

[76] Peçevi, *Ta'rîh*, vol. II, 419–20; Uzunçarşılı, *Osmanlı Tarihi*, vol. III, part I, 183–8; see Chapter 5, 162, 173.

clearly an attempt to bring their corporation under closer control. The soldiers also stated that they did not trust Murad IV to maintain the well-being of his brothers as he might execute them to secure his throne by eliminating all possible alternative candidates. They were only appeased after the princes were brought out of the palace and shown to them; and the grand vizier and the grand mufti promised that they would be the guarantors of their lives. In the next few days, the three men whose executions were demanded by the soldiers were murdered, including Murad IV's personal companion Musa Çelebi, whose death apparently caused the sultan to cry.[77]

Even though the central army corps won this round in their political struggle against Murad IV's absolutism, the sultan did not give up. In the next eight years of his reign he executed three of his four brothers, many soldiers, statesmen, and the grand vizier and the grand mufti who had volunteered to become guarantors for the lives of his brothers. Murad IV thus became the first Ottoman sultan to order the execution of a grand mufti. He strengthened his authority during the two military campaigns he commanded in person against Safavid Persia; in the second campaign, he recaptured Baghdad. Along with the Köprülü era in the later seventeenth century, historians generally regard the second part of his reign (1632–40) as one of the short-lived restorations of Ottoman grandeur in an era of decay.[78] The praise for this restoration usually overshadows the critique of Murad IV's absolutist rule, which is a historiographical tendency that may also be observed in the assessments of the Köprülü era, as described later.

The tension between the supporters of absolutist politics and those who wanted limitation of royal authority continued during the reign of Murad IV's only surviving brother, İbrahim (1640–8). İbrahim's reign ended with a deposition, which was the product of a grand coalition between the central army corps and large segments of the ulema in 1648. Ottoman historiography in the twentieth century did not regard this deposition as a political action taken against absolutism as İbrahim was regarded as a mentally unstable ruler, deserving the epithet "Deli (mad)." Yet most of İbrahim's actions that were used to substantiate the mental incapacity argument may well be interpreted quite differently. For instance, his levy on sable fur on all the major officials of the empire, which created strong reactions from all corners, could well be seen as a tax on the political magnates rather than the capricious request of a mentally unstable ruler. Such a tax would be a natural continuation of the frequent appropriations that İbrahim executed on the properties of the political magnates during his reign. Similarly, the allocation of appanages (lands the tax resources of which were assigned to royal family members) for his

---

[77] Katib Çelebi, *Fezleke*, vol. II, 140–1; Peçevi, *Ta'rîh*, vol. II, 420–5; Na'ima, *Ta'rîh*, vol. III, 92–105.

[78] For a short and recent biography of Murad IV, see Ziya Yılmazer, "Murad IV," *İA2*, vol. XXXI, 177–83.

eight favorite concubines, which was usually seen as an irresponsible waste of public resources, could be regarded as a royal appropriation of resources that might otherwise be assigned to political magnates.[79]

If one were to interpret İbrahim's actions not as signs of madness but as attempts to centralize the control of economic resources at the court, his deposition becomes yet another successful defense of the privileges held by the major actors on the Ottoman political stage. The contemporary sources, many of which were produced by authors who would stand to lose from an absolutist consolidation, were in agreement in their positive depiction of the deposition. In addition, they generally noted with understanding the regicide of İbrahim that followed the deposition within less than a month. One must remember that these sources were produced by the likes of Karaçelebizade Abdülaziz, who personally accused the sultan of wrongdoing and argued for his deposition in a face-to-face encounter with him at the palace right after his son Mehmed IV was enthroned.[80]

Ottoman historiography has by and large regarded the thirty years of political tranquility from the mid-1650s to the mid-1680s as an era of recovery.[81] However, it was a time of autocratic rule by the Köprülü family of grand viziers. There was not much room for dissent. Köprülü Mehmed Pasha (d. 1661) established close ties with the palace and managed to sustain a strong alliance with the court that survived a revolt of the imperial cavalry troops stationed in Anatolia under the leadership of Abaza Hasan Pasha in 1658. The political protests led by Abaza Hasan Pasha could have brought about a deposition or at least a change of grand viziers, but the iron fist of Köprülü managed to disperse his manpower by massacring around 1,000 cavalry troops who had come to Istanbul to claim their salaries.[82]

During the tenures of Mehmed Pasha's son Fazıl Ahmed Pasha and son-in-law Kara Mustafa Pasha, which lasted for twenty-two years altogether (1661–83), the political alliance between the court and the office of the grand vizier continued to the detriment of other political forces in the empire. Although mainstream Ottoman historiography presents Mehmed IV as a sultan who did not care about the rule of his empire, left Istanbul behind, and indulged in hunting instead, the itinerary of the royal court during his reign was the busiest

---

[79] For a recent biography that approaches İbrahim's depiction as a mentally unstable sultan critically, see Feridun Emecen, "İbrâhim," *İA2*, vol. XXI, 274–81.

[80] The most detailed and colorful account of İbrahim's deposition and later regicide is in Na'ima, *Ta'rîh*, vol. IV, 298–334; see also Karaçelebizade Abdül'aziz, *Ravzatü'l-ebrâr Zeyli: Tahlil ve metin*, ed. Nevzat Kaya (Ankara: Türk Tarih Kurumu, 2003), 2–12.

[81] "[T]he grand vezir [Köprülü] resumed the traditional style of reform developed by Murad IV, making the system work once again;" Stanford Shaw, *History of the Ottoman Empire and Modern Turkey*, vol. 1: *Empire of the Gazis: The Rise and Decline of the Ottoman Empire, 1280–1808* (Cambridge: Cambridge University Press, 1976), 209; Shaw's book has been a standard reference and continuously in print since the 1970s and thus represents the mainstream of Ottoman historiography.

[82] Na'ima, *Ta'rîh*, vol. VI, 373–8.

one since the time of Süleyman the Magnificent as Mehmed IV physically
followed the military campaigns of the Köprülüs, sometimes moving to a
relatively nearer location to the target of a campaign, and sometimes taking
an active part in them.[83] He was a partner in the Köprülü autocracy, albeit
a junior one. When Mehmed IV was not following Ottoman armies led by
Köprülü, his court was mostly in Edirne rather than in Istanbul, which may
be read as another indication of his support for the Köprülü autocracy. In
Edirne the traditional political forces of Istanbul were far away and much
less able to stage any effective opposition to the court. Most of the janissaries
and the cavalry troops were used to living in Istanbul and had their business
connections there. Thus moving the court to Edirne was one way of bypassing
any potential opposition. As for the fighting segments of the politically active
troops, they were occupied by international military engagements, which did
not leave them much breathing space for political action in the capital. Last
but not least, Köprülü Mehmed Pasha's reign of terror, an incidence of which
was mentioned earlier while touching upon the Abaza Hasan Pasha revolt of
1658, had pacified these organizations whose leaders were now being closely
supervised.

The absolutism of the Köprülü viziers and of their junior partner,
Mehmed IV, was strengthened by the puritanism of Mehmed Vani, a charismatic Kurdish preacher. Mehmed Vani was introduced to Mehmed IV by Fazıl
Ahmed Pasha in the mid-1660s and became the "sheik of the sultan (*hünkar
şeyhi*)," or the "Emperor's preacher." He revitalized the Kadızadeli movement, a fundamentalist movement that had taken over some of the mosques
and streets of Istanbul in the earlier decades of the seventeenth century, and he
used the prestige of the court to strengthen it. This movement had enjoyed the
support of Murad IV in the 1630s. A satisfactory treatment of this movement
and its political meaning in the context of Ottoman absolutism would require
a separate chapter, if not a monograph.[84] Suffice it to state here that the absolutist policies of the court and the puritan agenda of the Kadızadelis made a
perfect match, as the political authority of the former provided the latter with
access to the masses of the capital, whereas the authoritative discourse of the
latter legitimized the autocracy of the former. Not surprisingly, the janissaries
were one of the targets of the Kadızadelis.[85]

The last pillar of the Köprülü autocracy was made up of two jurists,
Minkarizade Yahya and his loyal pupil Çatalcalı Ali, who monopolized the

---

[83] For the mainstream view, see Abdülkadir Özcan, "Mehmed IV," *İA2*, vol. XXVIII, 414–
8; Marc David Baer offers an insightful analysis of the transformation of Mehmed IV's
reputation from a ghazi to a hunter: *Honored by the Glory of Islam: Conversion and Conquest
in Ottoman Europe* (Oxford: Oxford University Press, 2008), 231–44.

[84] See Öztürk, "Islamic orthodoxy;" Madeline C. Zilfi, "The Kadızadelis: Discordant revivalism
in seventeenth-century Istanbul," *Journal of Near Eastern Studies* 45 (1986): 251–74; Derin
Terzioğlu, "Sufi and dissident in the Ottoman Empire: Niyazi-i Mısri (1618–1694)," PhD
diss. (Harvard University, 1999); Baer, *Honored by the Glory of Islam*, 63–80, 109–19.

[85] Terzioğlu, "Sufi and dissident," 244–5.

position of the mufti in the imperial capital from 1662 to 1686. Both of these men came from lower origins among the *mevali*, the upper ranks of which had been monopolized by the descendants of Sa'deddin and their clients until recently. They were chosen to lead the *mevali* and kept their positions for so long because they were relatively independent of the close relations among many lords of the law. As noted by Derin Terzioğlu, they "acted in consort with Vani," the sultan's closest advisor in socioreligious matters. When Minkarizade was asked why he let the Kadızadelis have so much influence, he explained that in a time such as theirs it was "good to have people like them who put fear in people's hearts and instilled obedience in them."[86] In short, the absolutist alliance between the Köprülü family and Mehmed IV's court was supported by a charismatic puritan preacher who gathered popular support behind the Köprülü autocracy and by two jurists who were sympathetic both to the political agenda of the Köprülüs and the socioreligious agenda of their preacher. It is no wonder that the janissaries and other forces of political opposition had to be quiet in this period.

The Ottoman military defeat at the gates of Vienna in 1683 sealed the end of the Köprülü autocracy. Kara Mustafa Pasha was beheaded; Vani was exiled.[87] As suggested by Rifa'at Abou-El-Haj, Mehmed IV probably thought this was an opportune time to assume the reins of power on his own as opposed to being the junior partner in the Köprülü autocracy.[88] Yet the continuing defeats and incompetence of the political leadership created great dissatisfaction among the populace. Upon the fall of Buda, the capital of Ottoman Hungary, in 1686, Mehmed IV invited Çatalcalı Ali to the palace for consultation. The grand mufti responded that the ulema did not permit him to honor the royal invitation,[89] a clear sign of protest at the highest level of the lords of the law. Although Mehmed IV punished his grand mufti by exiling him, the protests continued and culminated in a major revolt. Unlike the earlier revolts, this one started in an army encampment in the Balkans and ended with the most peaceful change in government produced by any of the seventeenth-century Ottoman political protests. As with the English "Glorious Revolution" of 1688, this change in Ottoman government was a bloodless one.

The way in which Mehmed IV was replaced by his brother Süleyman II in 1687 was a clear sign of the maturity of the Ottoman system of limited government by the end of the seventeenth century. The Ottoman army in the Balkans petitioned the new grand mufti, Ankaravi Mehmed, stating that they did not want Mehmed IV as their sultan. They had unanimously decided that Mehmed IV be deposed and his brother Süleyman be enthroned in his stead. After consulting with the ulema, who expressed their agreement with the army,

[86] Ibid., 231.
[87] For a short account of the siege of Vienna and its aftermath, see Baer, *Honored by the Glory of Islam*, 210–27; for a short biography of Vani, see Öztürk, "Islamic orthodoxy," 271–81.
[88] Abou-El-Haj, *1703 Rebellion*, 45–6.
[89] Uzunçarşılı, *Osmanlı Tarihi*, vol. III, part I, 497.

218   The Second Empire goes public

the mufti notified the army of his approval of their plans. Mehmed IV tried to change the course of events by asking the army to winter in the Balkans, but the army did not stop its move toward the capital. Before the army even reached the capital, Mehmed IV gave up any hope and expressed his wish to abdicate in favor of his son Mustafa. But the representatives of the army and the ulema decided in favor of the incumbent sultan's brother Süleyman, whom they duly enthroned as Süleyman II. No blood was spilled during the deposition of Mehmed IV, quite unlike the deposition of Osman II. Mehmed IV clearly saw the limits of his monarchical powers and abode by the decision of the representatives of the army and the ulema.[90]

Another important sign indicating the effective functioning of the limits imposed upon Ottoman royal authority was the fate of Mehmed IV after his deposition. The former sultan was first installed in an apartment in the palace. Two years later when Süleyman II left the capital to join the military campaign against the Habsburgs who had captured Belgrade, Mehmed IV was brought to Edirne. When Süleyman II died in 1691, Mehmed IV was still alive, but it was his younger brother Ahmed who was enthroned as Ahmed II. Mehmed IV died in 1693 in Edirne.[91] Unlike Mustafa I, who was also kept alive after two depositions, Mehmed IV was never considered to be mentally incompetent. Thus in a moment of political turmoil he could well have turned into a liability for his successors when he might have emerged as a candidate for the throne. Yet unlike his uncle Osman II or his father İbrahim, Mehmed IV was not murdered. Ottoman sultans had now become symbolic leaders whose absolutist ambitions did not mean much unless they could become junior partners of powerful viziers. Because the sultan was now literally appointed to office by the representatives of the army and the ulema, there was no longer any pressing reason to murder a deposed sultan.

Some of the contemporary sources that dealt with the deposition of Mehmed IV were critical of the event. Sarı Mehmed, who served as minister of finance seven times in the early eighteenth century, regarded the supporters of the deposition as sources of disorder and sedition. A certain İsazade, probably the grandson of Karaçelebizade Abdülaziz, censured the deputy grand vizier Fazıl Mustafa Pasha, the younger son of Köprülü Mehmed Pasha, for his role in the deposition.[92] However, Fındıklılı Mehmed, the sword-bearer (*silahdar*) of Ahmed III in the early eighteenth century, faithfully reflected the critique of Mehmed IV by the representatives of the army and the ulema.[93] Later in the eighteenth century, Mehmed Raşid, the official chronicler of the Ottoman

---

[90] For a summary of the events leading to the deposition in English, see Caroline Finkel, *Osman's Dream: The History of the Ottoman Empire* (New York: Basic Books, 2005), 293–8.
[91] Baer, *Honored by the Glory of Islam*, 239–40.
[92] Defterdar Sarı Mehmed Paşa, *Zübde-i Vekayiât: Tahlil ve metin, 1066–1116/1656–1704*, ed. Abdülkadir Özcan (Ankara: Türk Tarih Kurumu, 1995), 252; İsazade, *'Îsâ-zâde Târîhi: Metin ve Tahlil*, ed. Ziya Yılmazer (Istanbul: İstanbul Fetih Cemiyeti, 1996), 205.
[93] Silahdar, *Ta'rîh*, vol. II, 281.

Empire, created his own synthesis of the deposition in which he emphasized the role of the deputy grand vizier, Fazıl Mustafa Pasha, who was the grand vizier during the reigns of Süleyman II and Ahmed II. Yet in this version too, Fazıl Mustafa voiced a critique of the reign of Mehmed IV similar to that of the army and the ulema.[94] Thus at least some of the Ottoman chroniclers regarded the actions of the army that led to the deposition, as well as the agreement of the ulema with them, as understandable – if not legitimate.

The attitude of Ottoman contemporaries to another major intervention in the political process by the army and the ulema in 1703 was very similar. Upon the death of Ahmed II in 1695, Prince Mustafa, the son of Mehmed IV, was enthroned as Mustafa II. During his reign there was a clear attempt to establish royal absolutism, as discussed in some detail by Abou-El-Haj. Mustafa II had a strong relationship with his private tutor, Seyyid Feyzullah, which was quite reminiscent of the close ties that Osman II had with his tutor Ömer. Instead of agreeing to become the junior partner in another vizier's autocracy, however, Mustafa II created his own junior partner by appointing his tutor Feyzullah to the office of the grand mufti soon after his enthronement. Feyzullah remained in this position until the end of Mustafa II's reign and represented his own interests as well as those of his patron Mustafa II during the tenure of Amcazade Hüseyin Pasha as grand vizier (1697–1702). Hüseyin Pasha was another Köprülü and was appointed grand vizier at a low moment in the Ottoman war effort in the Balkans. He ended the long war that was started in 1683 by Kara Mustafa Pasha, the son-in-law of his uncle Köprülü Mehmed Pasha, with the Peace of Carlowitz in 1699. Yet unlike the other members of the Köprülü family who ruled the empire during the reigns of Mehmed IV, Süleyman II, and Ahmed II, the independence of Amcazade Hüseyin was severely limited by the close supervision of Feyzullah, who was both mufti and the chief consultant of the sultan. This close supervision led Amcazade Hüseyin to resign in 1702.[95] Feyzullah's continually increasing political power after the resignation became the most important factor in the justifications for the deposition of Mustafa II in 1703 put forward by contemporary sources.

Although one cannot ignore Feyzullah's responsibility in provoking the army and the ulema to demand the deposition of the sultan, what is usually skipped over is the fact that Feyzullah ultimately represented his own patron, Mustafa II. The background of the last grand vizier of Mustafa II's reign, Rami Mehmed Pasha, who was handpicked by Feyzullah, was very illustrative of the imperial government that Mustafa II had in mind. Rami Mehmed was a professional bureaucrat of relatively humble Muslim origins the likes of whom had never been brought to such a high office. Although he had accumulated some political capital as the secretary of state who negotiated and signed the Peace of Carlowitz in 1699, this record alone would not have brought him to the grand vizierate – after all, the peace treaty was a disaster in terms of its

[94] Raşid, Ta'rîh, vol. II, 2–3.   [95] Abou-El-Haj, 1703 Rebellion, 55–7.

territorial losses – had the sultan and his chief consultant not been interested in running the empire themselves. Clearly, Mustafa II was interested in bringing the administration of his empire closer to his court at a time when the pasha households were taking it away from him.[96] Moreover, by placing Feyzullah on top of the ulema hierarchy, the sultan was hoping to suppress the power of the *mevali*. The appointments of Feyzullah's own family members and supporters to powerful positions among the upper ranks of the ulema were not simply examples of nepotism but also an attempt to extend the reach of royal absolutism into the ranks of the lords of the law.

That the lords of the law continued to be a powerful check on the political power of the Ottoman emperor throughout the seventeenth century was exemplified by the family of Abdürrahim, a man who was adopted by the all-powerful Sa'deddin family as a teacher for Mehmed Baha'i, the grandson of Sa'deddin. Abdürrahim became grand mufti in 1647 and in that capacity played one of the most important roles in the deposition of İbrahim in 1648, gave the legal opinion that legitimized the regicide, and oversaw the execution personally. His son Mehmed was the chief justice of the Asian and African provinces and hence a member of the imperial council during the deposition of Mehmed IV. In that capacity, he affirmed the army's request to depose the sultan. Mehmed's son Yahya was elected chief justice of the Asian and African provinces by the forces of opposition in Istanbul during the 1703 incident and took part in the deposition of Mustafa II. Thus, as noted in the introduction to this study, Mustafa II came to be deposed, among others, by a jurist whose father had deposed his father and whose grandfather had deposed and exe-cuted his own grandfather.[97] The political authority of Ottoman emperors of the seventeenth century was clearly circumscribed by their jurists who, in turn, were supported by the janissaries in most but not all critical instances.

Given the continuing role of the lords of the law in the limitation of royal authority throughout the seventeenth century, Mustafa II, an Ottoman sultan with an absolutist political agenda, had to attempt to suppress their power. Therefore, although the critique of Feyzullah's accumulation of power is well taken, it is at the same time misleading, as it does not address Mustafa II's complicity in and encouragement of Feyzullah's nepotism and other actions. It is because Mustafa II did not want to become a junior partner in the government of another vizier or the victim of another deposition legitimized by the lords of the law that he had turned to Feyzullah; the grand mufti's empowerment was his own making.

Another cause of the deposition of Mustafa II noted by contemporary sources was his unwillingness to move from Edirne back to Istanbul. Although the Istanbulites "blamed Feyzullah for the extended absence of the court from

---

[96] See Abou-El-Haj, "The Ottoman vezir and paşa households, 1683–1703."

[97] Abou-El-Haj, *1703 Rebellion*, 28; Şeyhi, *Vakâyi'ü'l-fudalâ*, vol. III, 235–6, vol. IV, 10–11, 363–4; İsazade, *Tarih*, 205.

the city,"[98] this absence was very much in line with Mustafa II's absolutist leanings. One has only to recall that Osman II also wanted to move the capital away from Istanbul, at least temporarily, and that Mehmed IV moved his court frequently during the Köprülü autocracy. As noted earlier, Istanbul was the center of established political opposition, and being away from the imperial capital where the janissaries and the ulema were powerful was a way of rendering political opposition powerless.[99] Thus it was not only Feyzullah who benefited from being far away from the complaints of his critics as his contemporaries argued but also Mustafa II himself chose to live in Edirne to form a government free from long-standing sources of political opposition.

The contemporary chroniclers' understanding attitude toward the deposition was most apparent in their faithful reproduction of the points advanced by the army and the ulema. One of the critical debates that took place during the events leading to the deposition concerned the legality of congregational Friday prayers under the rule of Mustafa II:

Some felt that the conduct of the government did not warrant holding public prayers on that day. Others were of the contrary opinion, reasoning that the grievances which united them were all directed against the [mufti] and not the sultan. The question was finally posed before the most eminent of the *ulema* present, Başmakcızade Ali, who had served until recently as the [chief justice of the European provinces]. This [jurist] answered in the customary abstract response of the canonical opinion (*fetva*) that one of the necessary principles of the propriety of holding the Friday prayers is the equity of the sultan, viz. his justice. Since the banner of revolt had been unfurled against the incumbent ruler on the assumption he had failed in maintaining the precepts of justice (*namus-ı adalet*), in what ways could the Friday prayers be deemed justified and proper?[100]

By including this debate in his chronicle without any further comment, Fındıklılı Mehmed was expressing his understanding, if not approval, of the motives that led the army and the ulema to depose Mustafa II.

As I have been arguing, the military rebellions, which modern Ottoman historiography usually considers to be examples of a general disorder, were regarded by many a contemporary as understandable – albeit troublesome – interventions into the political process. This is not to deny that most chroniclers often judged the rebels "to be involved in things that ought to be none of their business."[101] Yet even then, not only did their accounts reconstruct the grievances of the rebels but they also often displayed implications of approval, especially if the rebels sought the legitimizing support of the ulema, which they mostly did. Therefore, by the early eighteenth century an understanding had developed in the Ottoman polity that the interventions of the army and the

[98] Abou-El-Haj, *1703 Rebellion*, 19.
[99] For a discussion of moving the court around, see Na'ima, *Ta'rîh*, vol. VI, appendix, 46–52.
[100] Abou-El-Haj, *1703 Rebellion*, 24, paraphrasing Silahdar Fındıklılı Mehmet Ağa, *Nusretnâme*, ed. İsmet Parmaksızoğlu (Istanbul: Devlet Kitapları Müdürlüğü, 1962–9), vol. II, 150–1.
[101] Kafadar, "A case and a source."

ulema in the political process were an integral feature of the Ottoman political system. Na'ima, who wrote a chronicle of the first half of the seventeenth century and lived in the second half of it, either wrote about or witnessed most of the rebellions covered in this book. In a short appraisal of the 1703 incident that he wrote as a preface to the second volume of his chronicle in honor of the grand vizier Damad Hasan Pasha, which was written soon after the incident, he stated the following:

> The Islamic state, especially the Ottoman sultanate, has several qualities of the sort [which we may call] hidden secrets. Since great rebellions break out among soldiers now and then because of some important causes, a radical change in [all] affairs (*inkılab-ı umur*) is one of its fixed qualities as well.[102]

Although Na'ima was not as explicit as we might have liked him to be here, he clearly offered his own version of what was to become a Marxist dictum: sociopolitical change is inevitable. I am not suggesting that Na'ima was a Marxist who preceded Marx but rather that he regarded the military rebellions and the political changes brought about by them as inherent features of the Ottoman polity.

After the fierce political struggles of the seventeenth century that culminated in the most radical intervention into the political process in 1703, the Ottoman polity reached an important consensus in the eighteenth century, which was reflected in contemporary sources.[103] The timing of the consensus may well have been related to the severity of the 1703 incident. Of the political confrontations discussed in this chapter, the 1703 rebellion was the one that would most likely be followed immediately by a large civil war. In this rebellion, the forces of opposition gathered together an army of more than 20,000 men, consisting of soldiers and inhabitants of Istanbul, and proceeded toward Edirne; on the way there they were met by a force of roughly equal size led by Mustafa II. A military confrontation and civil war were avoided when the forces led by the sultan ended up joining the opposition forces.[104]

More importantly, according to the contemporary sources, the 1703 incident was the only one in which the forces of opposition entertained the idea of installing a completely different model of government. In earlier depositions, the rebels circulated names of alternative royal families, such as the Khans of Crimea, Ottoman vassals whose ultimate ancestor was Genghis Khan, as possible alternatives to the Ottoman dynasty.[105] But in 1703, they apparently put forward a different model of government. A very well-informed contemporary chronicler, Na'ima, suggested that Çalık Ahmed proposed a new design for government. Çalık Ahmed was brought to the leadership of the janissary corps by the forces of opposition in Istanbul and then confirmed by the new sultan

---

[102] Na'ima, *Ta'rîh*, vol. VI, appendix, 17.
[103] See the remarks of Mehmed Ragıb Pasha and Sarı Mehmed Pasha in this chapter, 196, 212.
[104] Abou-El-Haj, *1703 Rebellion*, 75–8.
[105] See Emecen, "Osmanlı hanedanına alternatif arayışlar."

Ahmed III in the aftermath of the deposition. He had such power that he felt comfortable inviting the sultan to his office for a feast.[106] A sultan's visit to the office of the general of the janissaries in the city was unprecedented, as Ottoman sultans received people and were not in the habit of paying visits. And even when receiving others, they were very selective as they had been keen on limiting access to themselves since the early sixteenth century. Thus by inviting Ahmed III to his office, Çalık Ahmed was testing the limits of his political power, which, as confirmed by Ahmed III's acceptance of the invitation and eventual visit, were quite wide in the aftermath of the deposition. If anyone had entertained the idea of a system change at this time, it would have been him.

According to Na'ima, Çalık Ahmed was waiting for the janissaries to recover from the turmoil of the deposition. Then, he had plans for them to take over the government and turn the sultanate into a *cumhur cem'iyeti ve tecemmü devleti*, which I translate freely as a people's – read janissaries' – republic. My suggestion is based on Na'ima's reference to Algeria and Tunis as examples of such a political system.[107] Algeria, Tunis, and Tripoli, all in North Africa, were Ottoman provinces nominally governed by governors sent from Constantinople. However, these provinces were run by systems that included some form of political representation for the interests of the janissaries. In Tunis the *deys* – from *dayı*, Turkish for maternal uncle – who were "plebiscited by the grass-roots janissaries" were the actual power holders in the first half of the seventeenth century. Although they lost their supremacy to other local officers in the second half of the century, the new power holders, the *beys*, were themselves soldiers, albeit from a different corps.[108] Political dynamics in Algeria and Libya were similar, with some differences arising from specific local conditions. For instance, in Algeria, which had a powerful navy, the *deys* occasionally were sea captains.[109]

What Çalık Ahmed might have had in mind for the Ottoman Empire could well have been a janissary oligarchy along the lines of the North African examples of Algeria, Libya, and Tunis. These three provinces were autonomous as suggested by the designation *garb ocakları*, the "western hearths," which distinguished them from the other provinces. The term *ocak*, literally hearth, was used to refer to autonomous political entities such as certain districts of Kurdistan ruled by Kurdish lords who inherited their positions from their fathers.[110] The western *ocaks* – that is the ones in North Africa to the west

---

[106] Mehmed Pasha, *Zübde-i Vekayiât*, 830.
[107] Na'ima, *Ta'rîh*, vol. VI, appendix, 34; see also Kafadar, "Janissaries and other riffraff," 133.
[108] Moalla, *Regency of Tunis*, 3–46.
[109] Mehmet Maksudoğlu, "Dayı," *İA2*, vol. IX, 59–60; Uzunçarşılı, *Osmanlı Tarihi*, vol. III, part II, 293–302.
[110] Nejat Göyünç, "Yurtluk-ocaklık deyimleri hakkında," in *Prof. Dr. Bekir Kütükoğlu'na Armağan* (Istanbul: İ.Ü. Edebiyat Fakültesi Yayınları, 1991), 271–3; see also Tezcan, "Kurdistan."

of Egypt – were principally elective although the ones in Algeria and Libya became hereditary in the eighteenth century. Çalık Ahmed himself was elected by the janissaries rather than being appointed by the sultan or his grand vizier. Thus the system he wanted to erect in Istanbul may have been one that was to be run by the janissaries who would elect their own leader. In this system, the sultan could keep his place as the man who provided legitimacy for the rule of the janissaries, not unlike the Ottoman governors of the *garb ocakları* whose political power was largely symbolic.

Although Çalık Ahmed's aspirations may have been unrealistic, among the Ottomans, autonomous rule with a certain degree of political representation was not limited to North Africa. Right around the time of Osman II's deposition in 1622, Baghdad was controlled by local forces in defiance of imperial orders. In eighteenth-century Egypt *mamlūk* households ran the political life of the country. In the late eighteenth century, the janissaries of the Balkans aspired to local rule and used the same title, *dey*, that their North African comrades had used in the seventeenth century.[111] In short, Çalık Ahmed's aspirations have to be taken seriously.

Conclusion

Çalık Ahmed's aspirations to establish a republic of janissaries were indeed taken seriously by his contemporaries. After 1703 the janissaries were treated with great care; special attention was paid not to hurt their economic interests. They were deemed so powerful that, as Lady Mary Montagu, who experienced Ottoman political life as the wife of a British ambassador in the early eighteenth century, put it, the sultan would tremble "at a Janissary's frown."[112] Thus a political consensus according to which the independence of the janissaries was to be recognized and not tampered with became the defining characteristic of the eighteenth century. The critical language of the seventeenth-century political advisers who complained about the expansion of the janissary corps and their lack of interest in military matters was replaced by a much more careful tone in the eighteenth century. Although reform of the corps was still a popular subject in political tracts, the authors advised caution, gradual action, deliberation, and most importantly, consultation with the representatives of the corps. For instance, Sarı Mehmed Pasha stated that reform of the corps might only be realized by commanders who are from the corps themselves. He was strongly against appointing janissary officers who were not themselves

---

[111] For Baghdad, see Uzunçarşılı, *Osmanlı Tarihi*, vol. III, part I, 158–62; for Egypt, see Hathaway, *The Rise of the Qazdağlıs*, and Jane Hathaway, *A Tale of Two Factions: Myth, Memory, and Identity in Ottoman Egypt and Yemen* (Albany: State University of New York Press, 2003); and for the use of *dey* in the Balkans, see Leopold von Ranke, *The History of Servia and the Servian Revolution*, tr. Mrs. Alexander Kerr (London: Henry G. Bohn, 1853), 66–7.

[112] Lady Mary Wortley Montagu, *The Complete Letters*, ed. Robert Halsband, 3 vols. (Oxford: Clarendon Press, 1965–7), vol. 1, p. 322.

of janissary origin.[113] The practice of *devşirme*, the levy of Christian children with a view to raising them as administrators and soldiers, which was already in decline in the seventeenth century, was totally abandoned at the beginning of the eighteenth century. The janissaries took care of their own recruitment and did not let anyone interfere with their payroll registers. As discussed earlier, many of the companies (*orta*s) virtually became "guilds of bakers, butchers, glaziers, boatmen, armorers, and so forth."[114] During the reign of Mahmud I (1730–54), an exemption from import duties was added to their numerous privileges, making membership in the corps even more attractive.[115] Later in the eighteenth century, the pay tickets of janissaries were sold in the market as a public investment option.[116] The janissaries had thus become an independent public corporation.

Although Ottoman historiography of the nineteenth and twentieth centuries presented the independence of the janissary corps as a major factor in the military decline, and hence the territorial reduction, of the Ottoman Empire in the eighteenth century, it glossed over a very significant point. The eighteenth century also happened to be one of the most peaceful periods of Ottoman history in terms of political protests. Both in the imperial capital and the provinces, there were far fewer rebellions than in the sixteenth and seventeenth centuries. Six depositions took place in Istanbul from 1618 to 1703, in contrast to only one in the eighteenth century: in 1730, that of Ahmed III, during whose reign there was a tendency for absolutism.[117]

The eighteenth-century peace in the provinces was the product of a development similar to that which happened with the janissaries. As the Ottoman government came to recognize the independence of the janissary corps, it also came to cede more local political power to the notables, the *a'yan*, whose self-interests lay in the peace and prosperity of the regions they came to govern as, practically, a hereditary nobility.[118] Thus the political peace of the eighteenth century was not limited to the imperial center but also extended to the provinces. After the long struggles of the late sixteenth and seventeenth centuries, a consensus about the limits of royal authority was finally achieved when the court recognized the independence of the janissaries as a

---

[113] Mehmed Pasha, *Ottoman Statecraft*, 110–5.   [114] See this chapter, 212, n. 70.
[115] Porter, *Observations*, 308.
[116] Ahmed Cevad, *Tarîh-i 'Askerî-i 'Osmânî*, vol. I: *Yeniçeriler* (Istanbul: Kırk Ambar Matbaası, 1299), 52.
[117] Ahmed III consolidated the highest level of the imperial administration and the judiciary with two close allies who had unusually long tenures for the period: the grand vizier Nevşehirli İbrahim Pasha and the mufti Yenişehirli Abdullah, both of whom remained in office from 1718 to 1730. For a reassessment of the modern Turkish historiography on this era, which was retrospectively named the "Tulip Age" in the early twentieth century, see Can Erimtan, *Ottomans Looking West? The Origins of the Tulip Age and its Development in Modern Turkey* (London: Tauris, 2008).
[118] In addition to the sources cited in n. 19, see Ali Yaycıoğlu, "The provincial challenge: Regionalism, crisis, and integration in the late Ottoman Empire (1792–1812)," PhD diss. (Harvard University, 2008).

corporation and the local autonomy of the notables as representatives of legitimate sociopolitical interests in the provinces – at least until the late eighteenth century when the center tried to flex its muscles once again.

Why then, one could legitimately ask, is the hegemonic historical narrative of eighteenth-century Ottoman history so negative? The first factor that comes to mind is the territorial reduction of the empire. Yet, the territorial losses of the Ottoman Empire in the eighteenth century were not as significant as, for instance, the area lost by the British Empire in North America in the late eighteenth century.[119] Therefore it may be prudent to look for the answer elsewhere. I would argue that the short answer is the New Order of the nineteenth century. The definitive history of the Ottoman decline with its negative take on the seventeenth and eighteenth centuries came to be written in the aftermath of the consolidation of the Ottoman New Order, which began during the reign of Selim III (1789–1807) and then was completed by Mahmud II (1808–39) and Abdülmecid (1839–61). The New Order entailed a heavy dose of state centralization that attacked all sources of established political opposition. Ottoman histories produced in the late nineteenth century, such as Ahmed Cevdet's *History*, which had a defining influence on the way in which Ottoman historiography developed in the twentieth century, were written from the vantage point of the New Order that had annihilated the janissary corps in 1826 and weakened the ulema. Having no one to defend it, the Ottoman Empire of the seventeenth and eighteenth centuries became a corrupt *ancien régime* as opposed to a type of limited monarchy that had the potential to evolve and eventually become the subject of a history of democratization.[120]

---

[119] For Ottoman military engagements and territorial losses in the eighteenth century, see Aksan, *Ottoman Wars*.

[120] Baki Tezcan, "Lost in historiography: An essay on the reasons for the absence of a history of limited government in the early modern Ottoman Empire," *Middle Eastern Studies* 45 (2009): 477–505; B. Tezcan, "The New Order and the fate of the old."

Conclusion

Early modernity and the Ottoman decline

It is quite true what Philosophy says:
that Life must be understood backwards.
But that makes one forget the other saying:
that it must be lived – forwards.
Søren Kierkegaard (1843)[1]

Looking back at their recent history, several Ottoman authors of the seventeenth century must have felt that they had entered a new era at some point in the late sixteenth century. Although Ottoman chronicles of the sixteenth century generally started narrating events from the beginning of the reign of a particular sultan, a number of seventeenth-century chronicles began with the *hijri* year 1000 (1591–2 CE). In two such chronicles one reads how some people were expecting the apocalypse to occur in the year 1000 AH and how they were wrong. Both chronicles listed several calendars used by different people and gave the year corresponding to 1000 AH in each one,[2] displaying a pluralistic attitude toward timekeeping that reminded readers of the relativity of the Islamic way of reckoning time and at the same time ridiculed those who were expecting the apocalypse to occur in 1000 AH. This intellectual suspicion of millenarian movements aligned with a remarkable decrease in the frequency and intensity of Muslim messianic movements from the seventeenth century on. The end of times was slowly pushed to a distant future that did not have much of an impact on one's life, at least immediately. The Ottomans seemed to be moving toward secular modernity.[3]

---

[1] *The Diary of Søren Kierkegaard*, ed. Peter P. Rohde and tr. Gerda M. Andersen (New York: Wisdom Library, 1960), 111.
[2] Katib Çelebi, *Fezleke*, vol. I, 2; Na'ima, *Ta'rîh*, vol. I, 66, which is based on the former.
[3] For recent studies that identify the Ottoman Empire as an early modern one, see, among others, Cemal Kafadar, "The Ottomans and Europe," in *Handbook of European History, 1400–1600: Late Middle Ages, Renaissance and Reformation*, eds. Thomas A. Brady, Jr., Heiko A. Oberman, and James D. Tracy, 2 vols. (Leiden: E. J. Brill, 1994–5), vol. I, 589–635; Virginia Aksan, "Locating the Ottomans among early modern empires," *Journal of Early Modern History* 3 (1999): 103–34; and Virginia H. Aksan and Daniel Goffman, eds., *The Early Modern Ottomans: Remapping the Empire* (Cambridge: Cambridge University Press, 2007);

A change in perceptions of time was not the only significant development in the Second Ottoman Empire that reflected a modern sensibility. Several artistic, sociocultural, and literary developments together suggested that the expansion of markets, trade, and urbanization not only led to an expansion of the political nation but also created a preoccupation with the contemporary, the modern. About the developments in Ottoman music, for instance, Cem Behar states that "[t]he changes observable between the seventeenth and twentieth centuries are minor compared to those that occurred between the 1500s and 1600s."[4] The development of the coffeehouse as an urban secular public space also took place in this period (see Fig. 20).[5] This new urban social institution provided a stage for cultural activities, such as shadow plays.[6]

Not only were new institutions in the making during the seventeenth century but also older ones were being transformed. A significant example was Ata'i's quintet (*hamse*), which consisted of five narratives in verse (*mesnevis*). Although neither *mesnevi* nor *hamse* was a novel literary form, Ata'i's *mesnevis* took the genre to a new place. Whereas traditional narratives in verse told ideal stories from the past, Ata'i drew his heroes from contemporary Istanbul, celebrating the modern.[7] It was also in this period that storytelling performances expanded into the city.[8] Another novelty in seventeenth-century Ottoman literature was the development of first-person narratives, which, being quite suggestive of individuation, may be considered as a marker of modernity.[9]

During the age of the Second Empire, high art and culture did not belong exclusively to the court any longer. For instance, painting came down from the royal workshops to the marketplace in the form of albums that included, among other things, reflections of contemporary city life (see Fig. 20).[10]

for other indications of the secular nature of the Second Empire, see Tezcan, "The Second Empire," 569–70.

[4] Cem Behar, "The Ottoman musical tradition," in *The Cambridge History of Turkey*, vol. 3: *The Later Ottoman Empire, 1603–1839*, ed. Suraiya N. Faroqhi (Cambridge: Cambridge University Press, 2006), 394.

[5] Ralph S. Hattox, *Coffee and Coffeehouses: The Origins of a Social Beverage in the Medieval Near East* (Seattle: University of Washington Press, 1985).

[6] Andreas Tietze, *The Turkish Shadow Theater and the Puppet Collection of the L. A. Mayer Memorial Foundation* (Berlin: Gebr. Mann Verlag, 1977).

[7] The most detailed monograph on Ata'i's *hamse* is Tunca Kortantamer's *Nev'îzâde Atâyî ve Hamse'si* (Izmir: Ege Üniversitesi Edebiyat Fakültesi Yayınları, 1997); for earlier literary developments pointing in the same direction, see Kafadar, "The Ottomans and Europe," 622.

[8] On storytellers, see Ahmet Ö. Evin, *Origins and Development of the Turkish Novel* (Minneapolis: Bibliotheca Islamica, 1983), 28–37; the most detailed monograph on the topic is Özdemir Nutku's *Meddahlık ve Meddah Hikayeleri* (n.p.: İş Bankası Kültür Yayınları, c. 1976).

[9] Cemal Kafadar, "Self and others: The diary of a dervish in seventeenth century Istanbul and first-person narratives in Ottoman literature," *Studia Islamica* 69 (1989): 121–50; a sense of individual subjectivity is also discerned in some of the chronicles studied by Dana Sajdi, "Peripheral visions: The worlds and worldviews of commoner chroniclers in the 18th century Ottoman Levant," PhD diss. (Columbia University, 2002).

[10] Tülay Artan, "Arts and architecture," in *The Cambridge History of Turkey*, vol. 3: *The Later Ottoman Empire, 1603–1839*, ed. Suraiya N. Faroqhi (Cambridge: Cambridge University Press, 2006), 431.

Fig. 20. A coffeehouse; from an Ottoman album of painting and calligraphy dated to the sixteenth or seventeenth century; Chester Beatty Library, T.439, f. 9; courtesy of the Trustees of the Chester Beatty Library.

And classical court music managed to survive without any court support in the third quarter of the eighteenth century after two successive sultans dismantled the staff of palace musicians.[11] Alternative courts developed in palaces along the Bosporus, creating a growing group of patrons of the arts and culture who came from the urban middle and upper middle classes.[12] In short, the expansion of markets and investment opportunities in the sixteenth century led to the formation of social groups whose members not only bought their way into the politically privileged classes of society but also spent their money on arts and culture at a time when their temporal horizons were no longer limited by the notion of an ever-impending end of times. No wonder Sir Henry Blount, an Englishman who visited the Ottoman Empire in 1634, claimed that the "Turkes" were the "only moderne people" of his time.[13]

However, we should not take Sir Blount's word for it, but instead should ask ourselves what distinguishing features of modernity began appearing in this period. There are many answers to this question that concern different domains of individual and social life. Some of the examples from cultural and literary spheres of social life described earlier are generally regarded as markers of modernity. But there are other markers as well, some of which are deemed to be more central than others. Some argue that the most important development for modernity is the formation of nation-states. Yet if we were to use this as a marker of modernity, then early modernity would become a very limited historical experience, squeezed into western Europe. Even central and southern Europe, where states such as Germany and Italy did not exist until the nineteenth century, would be excluded from the experience of early modernity. Others propose that it is the Enlightenment that defines modernity. But then when did modernity begin in England, where it was hard to find the counterpart of a French or Scottish Enlightenment?[14]

Another feature strongly associated with modernity is the rise of capitalism, a concept I have shied away from throughout this study. The question of why capitalism did not take off in the Ottoman Empire has been asked far too many times, and the answers generated have not necessarily helped us understand the Ottoman Empire very much, as focusing on an absence – that of capitalism – has somewhat distracted us from the presence of many other things, such as the fundamental political transformation that this book is about. However, in

---

[11] Behar, "The Ottoman musical tradition," 396.
[12] On the residential developments alongside the Bosporus, see Tülay Artan, "Architecture as a theatre of life: Profile of the eighteenth century Bosphorus," PhD diss. (Massachusetts Institute of Technology, 1989); Shirine Hamadeh, *The City's Pleasures: Istanbul in the Eighteenth Century* (Seattle: University of Washington Press, 2008).
[13] Henry Blount, *A Voyage into the Levant* (London, 1636), 2. I am grateful to Karen Kupperman, Professor of American History at New York University, for bringing Blount to my attention.
[14] John G. A. Pocock, however, proposes a sort of Enlightenment for England as well, see his "Clergy and commerce: The conservative Enlightenment in England," in *L'Età dei Lumi: Studi Storici sul Settecento Europeo in Onore di Franco Venturi*, 2 vols. (Naples: Jovene Editore, 1985), vol. I, 523–62.

the context of world history, the question is still relevant, especially if one is interested in assessing whether capitalism is a feature of early modernity.

Arguably, capitalism is the product of two developments in England and parts of northwestern Europe: (1) the commercialization of agriculture and (2) long-distance trade.[15] Neither of these two developments is particularly English or unique to northwestern Europe, yet the way in which they unfolded there produced capitalism in Europe. The expansion of *çiftliks*, or large farms, in the seventeenth-century Ottoman Empire suggests that the commercialization of agriculture was on its way in the Ottoman Empire as well.[16] And yet independent peasant households continued to be an important operating unit in the Ottoman Empire. Even those local notables who came to practically own villages did not rent their lands out to tenants but rather let the peasants take care of them in return for keeping a certain percentage for themselves – not very different from a feudal landlord. Tenant farming that led to a competitive market in rents was not common in the Ottoman Empire. Similarly, Ottoman merchants engaged in long-distance trade very much like their northwestern European counterparts did, but they were not organized into institutions like the East India Company. Moreover, sociopolitical institutions like the janissaries constituted a bulwark against monopolistic tendencies in trade and kept the playing field level for small agents in the Ottoman Empire. In contrast, small agents in England had no protection against the monopolistic practices of English companies such as the East India Company to which Queen Elizabeth (1558–1603) granted exclusive trade rights between England and East India.

However, these differences between the consequences of similar processes in England and the Ottoman Empire had nothing to do with English or Ottoman cultures. Instead, they had a great deal to do with the medieval legacy of these two socioeconomic realms. Neither the concentration of unusually large land holdings that came to be worked by tenants in England, which was crucial for the development of agrarian capitalism, nor the existence of a legal category called the corporation in Europe, which facilitated the growth of long-distance trade companies, was related to anything cultural. For instance, the corporation had its origins in the Roman Empire and became a prevalent European institution during the Middle Ages, at least partially because of the absence of an imperial authority and the autonomous development of the Catholic Church.[17] It did not develop as a legal category in the Islamic world nor in the Byzantine Empire where an imperial authority continued to exist and the Orthodox Church remained under its close watch. Obviously, however,

[15] Ellen Meiksins Wood, *The Origin of Capitalism: A Longer View* (London: Verso, 2002); and Niels Steensgaard, "Violence and the rise of capitalism: Frederic C. Lane's theory of protection and tribute," *Review* 5/2 (Fall 1981): 247–73.
[16] Halil İnalcık, "The emergence of big farms, *çiftliks*: State, landlords, and tenants," in *Contributions à l'histoire économique et sociale de l'Empire ottoman*, eds. Jean-Louis Bacqué-Grammont and Paul Dumont (Louvain: Peeters, 1983), 105–26.
[17] Timur Kuran, "The absence of the corporation in Islamic law: Origins and persistence," *American Journal of Comparative Law* 53 (2005): 785–834, at 789–91.

the Catholic Church did not have the development of capitalism in mind when it adopted the Roman concept of corporation and gave it a wider use during the Middle Ages. Thus the development of capitalism can never be reduced to teleological explanations that posit a European aptness for business. And yet at the same time, the existence of this medieval legacy – the concept of corporation – in northwestern Europe helped long-distance trade develop in an innovative way in the late sixteenth and early seventeenth centuries, leading to the development of capital markets; for example, the first stock exchange was established by the Dutch East India Company in Amsterdam.

This brief analysis of the development of capitalism in northwestern Europe as a result of the particular consequences of the interaction between the legacy of the Middle Ages and the developments of the early modern period suggests that, although the modern period may be the logical continuation of the early modern era in northwestern Europe, it may not be so elsewhere in the world. Because different parts of the world inherited different historical legacies, the expansion of markets and trade that was experienced almost all over the world in the sixteenth century did not have the same impact in every region. That is why it may make sense to speak about an almost global early modern era followed by a form of modernity that originated in northwestern Europe in relation to the rise of capitalism. We may connect this form of modernity more closely with the rise of industrial capitalism, which came into being as a result of the interaction of early modern capitalist institutions with technological developments. This modernity was imposed upon or exported all over the world as there was practically no escape from capitalist markets once one entered into transactions with them; one could only delay their impact by closely controlling economic interactions with these markets. European colonialism provided the economic and institutional means for the expansion of capitalism. In short, capitalism and colonialism transformed early modernity to modernity. How about the aspect of continuity that makes the early *modern* period *modern*?

I argue that the early modern and modern periods had two very significant sociopolitical developments in common – the expansion of the political nation and the limitation of royal authority – both of which started in the early modern period and continued into the modern era. Economically speaking, the expansion of markets and global trade seems to be the common denominator of the early modern period. It was this common socioeconomic development that led to the expansion of the political nation and the limitation of royal authority in, at least, Europe and the Ottoman Empire. It is in relation to these common sociopolitical consequences that I define the early modern. This definition is not based on an urge to fit the Second Ottoman Empire into an artificial description of the early modern but rather on the revolutionary character of early modern political change, the results of which are still unfolding in the modern era. This definition thus builds on the most significant line of continuity between the early modern and modern periods.

Over the last four hundred years of history there was an unprecedented opening in the ranks of the ruling classes of the world. Most societies in

premodern history were obsessed with one form of social stratification or
another. Although the caste system may have been most pronounced in India,
the idea that society is divided into groups with unsurpassable barriers between
them was found almost all over the world. Since the early modern era, however, these barriers have been attacked continually. This obviously does not
mean that we are about to reach social equality, especially because as each new
group makes it to the other side of the barrier, many of the newly privileged
become the most staunch supporters of their recently acquired social distinctions. However, most of us live and function with the assumption that life is
a reasonably fair game in which upward mobility is a possibility, however
illusionary this assumption may be. This is a legacy of the socioeconomic and
political developments that started in the early modern era with the expansion
of markets and trade.

The conversion of socioeconomic capital into political power took different
forms in different societies. What seems to be common to many a society that
did not go through the experience of colonization in this period – which is a
qualification that excludes many societies in Africa, the Americas, Asia, and
Oceania – was either the opening up of privileged classes to many who would
never have belonged to them in the past or the relaxation of the requirements
of entry into the playing field of politics in such a way that commoners could
start having an impact on various political decisions. In either case, there was
a relative democratization of political privileges and a tightening of control
on the limits of royal authority, both of which facilitated the formation of
collective political identities, which many scholars regard as a cornerstone of
modernity.[18]

Throughout this book I have argued that the age of the Second Empire
witnessed an expansion of the political nation or a *relative* democratization
of political privileges. One may even claim that the Second Empire was constituted by this expansion. It is true that the Ottoman historical experience
did not include anything corresponding to Western Europe's barons and lords
whose political authority was challenged by the socioeconomic forces of a
bourgeoisie. Yet if we stop looking for identical charters of privileges and
other formal instruments that define a lord or an incorporated city, we may
actually see that European and Ottoman societies moved in a comparable
pace in several areas related to politics. Throughout the course of the seventeenth century, more and more commoners joined the political nation of the
Ottoman Empire either by buying their way into the privileged army corps,
farming taxes and securing a local notable status, or becoming jurists.[19] The
pressing question in terms of the early modern character of the Second Empire

---

[18] Shmuel N. Eisenstadt and Wolfgang Schluchter, "Introduction: Paths to early modernities –
a comparative view," *Daedalus* 127/3 (Summer 1998): 1–18.

[19] Although the higher ulema positions were almost monopolized by a limited number of
families constituting the lords of the law, or the *mevali*, who made and unmade emperors, the
lower ranks were open for newcomers. Denise Klein's path-breaking study of the Ottoman
ulema in the period 1630–1703 suggests that many low-ranking jurist-scholars came from the

is whether a collective Ottoman political identity was in the making during this process of the expansion of the Ottoman political nation. My answer is yes. Yet to recognize the development of that collective political identity, one first needs to understand that there was political development in the premodern Middle East.

One of the influential claims about Middle Eastern political history is its lack of political development. Collective political identities, which could bring together the ruling classes that governed the states in the region with members of their societies, are not supposed to have developed in this part of the world. One dynasty followed another in Middle Eastern history, with no noticeable political development throughout the centuries: "with the exception of the Prophet's time," Islamic civilization is supposed to have "failed to provide a satisfactory political system."[20] Patricia Crone and Martin Hinds locate the source of this failure in the strict autonomy of the field of the law: because "a ruler who has no say at all in the definition of the law by which his subjects have chosen to live cannot rule those subjects in any but a purely military sense."[21] If this was indeed the case, there would be no way, of course, for collective identities to develop that would bring the rulers and the ruled together.

In studies of jurists' law in the Ottoman Empire of the sixteenth century, this overemphasis on the autonomy of the law is reversed, leading to an overemphasis on the role of the political authority in the definition of jurists' law.[22] When one moves to the seventeenth century and beyond, however, we are expected to believe that things turned upside down all of a sudden. The "forces of religious fanaticism" were then rampant, taking over the "business of the state" in legal matters.[23]

Both sets of assumptions about the history of jurists' law, pertaining both to the pre-Ottoman and the Ottoman periods, may be revised in light of the present study. In the Ottoman period, something else seemed to be happening in the late sixteenth and seventeenth centuries that had some relevance to all the assumptions about jurists' law. The strict distinction that was supposed to exist between public – or administrative – and private law began to disappear as the political authority was drawn into the domain of private law, perhaps more deeply than ever, as a consequence of the sociopolitical changes described throughout this study. Yet at the same time, the political authority opened up its own domain to the scrutiny of jurists to an unprecedented degree. Thus the

provinces of the empire and had relatively modest backgrounds; *Die osmanischen Ulema des 17. Jahrhunderts: Eine geschlossene Gesellschaft?* (Berlin: Klaus Schwarz, 2007).
[20] Andrew Christie Hess, "Islamic civilization and the legend of political failure," *Journal of Near Eastern Studies* 44 (1985): 27–39, at 28.
[21] Crone and Hinds, *God's Caliph*, 109. Wael B. Hallaq hails more or less the same phenomenon as an indication of the supremacy of the "rule of law;" see his "'Muslim rage' and Islamic law," *Hastings Law Journal* 54 (2003): 1705–19.
[22] See, for instance, Imber, *Ebu's-Su'ud*.   [23] Barkan, "Türkiye'de din ve devlet," 91.

seventeenth-century predominance of jurists' law had more to do with the relative success of the institutional checks on the political authority than the religious fanaticism that allegedly tainted this period. Because the political authority felt hemmed in by the limitations imposed on it by jurists' law, it tried to abolish the *kanun* altogether in the late seventeenth century and to claim jurists' law as the sole domain of law. By so doing, the political authority was counting on having a more formative role in the articulation of jurists' law so that it could offset the politically limiting impact of that law.

One may even go one step further and start questioning whether the division between the domain of the political authority and that of the jurists ever existed as strictly as claimed by scholarship on the pre-Ottoman Islamic world. For instance, Muhammad Qasim Zaman's work on the early Abbasid period (749–833) suggests that the jurists and the state were in close contact and, many times, acted cooperatively.[24] More recently, Yossef Rapoport has argued that in the Mamluk period "the state and its jurists shared a common vision of the social good" and that "the state was more actively involved in the legal sphere than is commonly assumed."[25] Thus perhaps there had always existed a domain in which the interests of the administrative-military apparatus and those of the legal representatives of social forces, the jurists, were negotiated.[26] What may be distinctive about the Ottoman experience might be the enlargement of this common domain, the public sphere as opposed to both private and official spheres if you wish,[27] to such a degree that the administration and the society made some headway toward establishing a collective political identity. Given the fact that this domain did not seem to grow very much during the feudal age – between the end of the Late Antiquity and the beginning of the early modern period – in most of Europe and around the Mediterranean, the political history of the Islamic world, then, may not be as different as it has been claimed to be. Muslim societies were just as alienated from their rulers as the ones in Christian Europe where collective political identities developed on the eve of modernity.

Such a shared identity between the society and its rulers seemed to be emerging in the eighteenth-century Ottoman Empire when the connotation of the term *re'aya*, which literally means herd or flock, shifted from subjects or peasants in general to non-Muslim subjects in particular.[28] Around the same

---

[24] Muhammad Qasim Zaman, *Religion and Politics under the Early 'Abbasids: The Emergence of the Proto-Sunni Elite* (Leiden: Brill, 1997).
[25] Yossef Rapoport, "Legal diversity in the age of *taqlid*: The four chief *qadis* under the Mamluks," *Islamic Law and Society* 10 (2003): 210–28, at 227–8.
[26] Cemal Kafadar, "The Ottomans and Europe," 616.
[27] For the relevance of these three categories for a discussion of modernity, see Eisenstadt and Schluchter, "Introduction," 9–13.
[28] As late as the late seventeenth century, the term did not have any denominational connotations; see Franciszek Meninski, *Thesaurus linguarum orientalium turcicae, arabicae, persicae*, 4 vols. (Vienna, 1680), vol. 2, c. 2329–30. Yet "[f]rom the 12th/18th century onwards, the term is increasingly used for the Christian taxpayers only; 13th/19th century population counts

time, increased attention was paid to marking non-Muslim subjects in Ottoman court records with orthographic and vocabulary distinctions.[29] In contrast to the patrimonial past when the slaves who were handpicked mainly through the *devşirme* system by the administrative-military apparatus constituted the pool from which the ruling class emerged,[30] in the eighteenth century any free Muslim male – that is, any imperial subject endowed with the full legal rights granted to the individual under jurists' law – could *theoretically* rise up in the state hierarchy to the highest position.[31]

As suggested several times in this study, the early modern Ottoman state came into existence when it accepted its new role as the political representative of the ruling class, as opposed to being that class itself. By recognizing that any free Muslim male was *theoretically* entitled to be part of the ruling class, the state gave up its claims of political exclusivity. At the same time, the idea that all first-class subjects shared a common identity as Muslims enabled the ruling class to consolidate its economically dominant position in society without appearing to do so. The concept that every Muslim male could *theoretically* attain high sociopolitical status was the perfect fiction to keep the commoners from the lower classes content with their lower socioeconomic status. It was in this context that non-Muslims came to be associated with *re'aya* status while Muslims moved upward in the political hierarchy to a position that was somewhat akin to that of white settlers in colonial America, who "found a shared identity as white men by asserting their superiority defined against Indians and Africans."[32] Although it was race that became the marker of social privilege in colonial America, in the Ottoman Empire of the eighteenth century religion was being assigned that function.

Just as racism in the modern sense arose in a "democratic" society,[33] the subjection of non-Muslims to second-class status occurred in conjunction with proto-democratization in the Ottoman Empire. Needless to say, this emphasis on religion as a social marker was not the result of the resolution of class tensions but, to the contrary, a device to suppress them. I should also add that the ruling class continued to include many a non-Muslim in the provincial

distinguish between re'āyā and Islām"; Suraiya Faroqhi, "Ra'iyya – in the Ottoman Empire," *Encyclopedia of Islam, New Edition*, vol. VIII, 404.

29 Najwa al-Qattan, "Discriminating texts: Orthographic marking and social differentiation in the court records of Ottoman Damascus," in *Arabic Sociolinguistics: Issues and Perspectives*, ed. Yasir Suleiman (London: Curzon, 1994), 57–77; Cemal Kafadar, "A Rome of one's own: Reflections on cultural geography and identity in the lands of Rum," *Muqarnas* 24 (2007): 7–25, at 12–13.

30 The collective identity of the ruling class in this period – and even earlier, during the feudal kingdom – could perhaps be identified as *Rumi*, literally Roman, a category that gradually lost its significance and all but disappeared in the eighteenth century; see Salih Özbaran, *Bir Osmanlı Kimliği: 14.–17. Yüzyıllarda Rûm / Rûmî Aidiyet ve İmgeleri* (Istanbul: Kitap Yayınevi, 2004); Kafadar, "A Rome of one's own."

31 See, for instance, the grand viziers of commoner backgrounds in Chapter 6, 195–6.

32 Alan Taylor, *American Colonies: The Settling of North America* (New York: Penguin, 2001), xiii.

33 "Racism in the modern sense first arose in a 'democratic' society" in postrevolutionary France; see Colette Guillaumin, *Racism, Sexism, Power and Ideology* (London: Routledge, 1995), 56.

and imperial administrations – from *kocabaşıs*, or non-Muslim community leaders, to Phanariot princes who ruled Moldavia and Wallachia.[34] Yet it was the Muslims who finally graduated from constituting the *re'aya*, or the flock of rulers, and moved up to become citizens of sorts much before the autocratic political modernization of the Tanzimat era. The historical roots of the particular kind of "Muslim nationalism" that evolved into modern Turkish nationalism in the early twentieth century are to be found in this eighteenth-century development.[35]

When analyzed within the larger context of the slow but steady enlargement of a public sphere in which the administrative-military apparatus and new social groups negotiated the articulation of the law that would govern them both, the ability of a mufti (Es'ad) to *en*throne an Ottoman sultan (Mustafa I) and then deny another one (Osman II) the customary royal privilege to execute his brother becomes a very significant marker of profound political change. In the history of the Islamic world during the Middle Ages, a jurist's successful intervention into dynastic affairs was very uncommon, if not unheard of. Thus when Es'ad entered the political domain of the dynasty and told the sultan that he could not do everything he desired to do, even with respect to his own family members, he was taking an important step toward bringing the political authority into the same legal domain in which the social groups representing Ottoman society were negotiating their differences; that is, the domain of jurists' law. As demonstrated in Chapters 5 and 6, jurists' law came to be used in matters directly pertaining to succession, the legitimacy of a particular sultan, and the question of legitimate revolt against the government in a manner and frequency unmatched in the history of the Islamic world before the Ottomans.[36] Using the terminology adopted in this study, the constitutionalists had clearly won.

Therefore the key to understanding the longevity of the Ottoman dynasty, which ruled more or less uninterruptedly for more than six centuries, is this important legal-political development: subjecting the highest representative of the imperial political authority to the same law that judged everyone else. This development invested the dynasty with something quite close to popular

---

[34] On the latter, see Christine Philliou, "Communities on the verge: Unraveling the Phanariot ascendancy in Ottoman governance," *Comparative Studies in Society and History* 51 (2009): 151–81.

[35] Although modern Turkish nationalism takes pride in being secular, its history offers several examples that make it clear that its notion of "Turkishness" was very much predicated upon being a Muslim. The Greek-Turkish population exchange of the early 1920s is one these examples. During this exchange, Turkish-speaking Orthodox Christians had to leave Turkey for Greece, and Greek-speaking Muslims had to move to Turkey from Greece. The decision of who belongs where was made on the basis of religion. The most recent study on this exchange is Onur Yıldırım's *Diplomacy and Displacement: Reconsidering the Turco-Greek Exchange of Populations, 1922–1934* (New York: Routledge, 2006). For more examples of the centrality of Islam for the modern secular Turkish identity, see Soner Çağaptay, *Islam, Secularism, and Nationalism in Modern Turkey: Who is a Turk?* (London: Routledge, 2006).

[36] Middle Eastern history is actually full of revolutions that used Islamic principles to legitimize a new dynasty, such as the Abbasids, or a political group, such as the Kharijites. However, such revolutions rarely resulted in stable polities that endured for centuries.

legitimacy. If an emperor could be "recalled" and replaced by another one, not only was there no longer any need to challenge the dynasty but, more importantly, there was also a considerable incentive to keep the dynasty in operation to maintain its openness to political representation. If any state in the Islamic world ever "sat on top of society" as opposed to being "rooted in it," as Crone and Hinds claim Islamic states in general did, this state of affairs was no more. After the Ottomans, no more dynasties "came and went," in the words of Crone and Hinds; the Ottomans continued to rule the former lands of the Eastern Roman Empire until the arrival of European colonialism, which, incidentally, left a legacy of states that fit the description of "sitting on top of societies without forming any roots in them" much better than did their Ottoman predecessors.[37]

That the Second Ottoman Empire (ca. 1580–1826) was an early modern polity does not, however, necessarily mean that decline is a concept that was irrelevant to Ottoman history. After all, the seeds of the collapse of the Ottoman Empire must have been sown before 1922 when the empire formally ceased to exist with the abolishment of the sultanate by the Grand National Assembly in Ankara. Although the autocracy of the nineteenth-century Ottoman modernization and the heavy socioeconomic and political bill of European imperialism were surely very important factors that contributed to the collapse of the empire, I am not quite sure whether they were the only causes. Of course, one could also discard the question of decline without replacing it with an alternative grand narrative.[38] Ottoman history is not the only field of history in which grand narratives have become unpopular. Barbara Weinstein notes that "those historians involved in methodological innovation and current theoretical debates . . . have been accustomed to avoiding . . . macrohistorical questions."[39] Margaret Jacob states thus:

For my generation of historians [. . .] the big questions in Western or world history became strangely unfashionable. None is bigger than the question of what were the factors that made Western hegemony possible. Indeed, the very notion of Western hegemony, of the domination of much of the world by Western political or economic power from roughly 1800 to 1970, may be said to be so fraught with anger and guilt as to be almost untouchable.[40]

Western hegemony, however, does not disappear when we choose not to study it or decide to provincialize it,[41] just as the collapse of the Ottoman Empire in

---

[37] For the quotations from Crone and Hinds, see God's Caliph, 109.

[38] See Introduction, 9–10; a significant exception who chose not to discard the concept is Cemal Kafadar; see his "The question of Ottoman decline," Harvard Middle Eastern and Islamic Review 4 (1997–8): 30–75.

[39] Barbara Weinstein, "History without a cause? Grand narratives, world history, and the postcolonial dilemma," International Review of Social History 50 (2005): 71–93, at 82–3.

[40] Ibid., 83, citing Margaret Jacob, "Thinking unfashionable thoughts, asking unfashionable questions," American Historical Review 105 (2000): 494–500.

[41] Dipesh Chakrabarty, Provincializing Europe: Postcolonial Thought and Historical Difference (Princeton: Princeton University Press, 2000); see also Jacques Pouchepadass, "Pluralizing reason," History and Theory 41 (2002): 381–91.

the early twentieth century is not undone when we argue that the empire was doing well in the seventeenth century.

To adapt a phrase by my colleague Alan Taylor, a historian of colonial North America and the early republic, one cannot and should not treat the coming of the Ottoman decline as "utterly irrelevant" to the late sixteenth and seventeenth centuries – just as one "cannot and should not allow that knowledge to overwhelm the other possibilities in that past." In short, "the creative tension between teleology and contingency" in Ottoman history of the early modern period needs to be balanced.[42] The rest of this conclusion is devoted to some proposals on how this balance may be achieved.

Although the gradual formation of a collective Ottoman political identity around the category of Muslim in the eighteenth century established the early modern credentials of the Second Empire, it also led toward the path to the eventual dissolution of the Ottoman Empire. Even though the Ottoman polity was a multireligious one, it had always been governed by Muslim rulers. Yet the fact that the dividing line separating the rulers from the ruled had not run along sectarian divisions had made things relatively fair for the ruled. A Muslim peasant belonged just as much to the *re'aya*, or the flock of the sultan, as the non-Muslim one; they were both outsiders, or *ecnebis*, as far as the ruling class was concerned. Once certain paths that were closed for the *re'aya* started opening up only for upwardly mobile Muslim subjects of the sultan, however, non-Muslim subjects had a legitimate ground for resentment, which the Ottoman state failed to address adequately before it was too late. Non-Muslim Ottoman subjects' expression of political resentment eventually took the form of withdrawal of their political loyalties.

Had the Ottoman Empire been located in a place like the Americas, far away from any other political entity that could capitalize on the resentment of some of its subjects, non-Muslim Ottomans might have gained their political emancipation and equality gradually over many years, not unlike the nonwhite inhabitants of the United States whose fight for civil rights predated the Civil War and is arguably not over yet. However, the Ottoman Empire was located in the midst of the Old World where several imperialist powers were competing with each other for new markets and for strategic allies along routes to other markets. As a result, Ottoman internal political issues became European diplomatic problems that came to constitute the Eastern Question, with its solution coming to be seen as the dissolution of the Ottoman Empire, the long term implications of which are with us to this day.[43]

The failure of the Ottoman state to address the political grievances of its non-Muslim subjects in a timely fashion and the exploitation of this failure by European imperialist powers were not the only causes of the collapse of the Ottoman Empire. The early-nineteenth-century Ottoman state also did not

---

[42] Taylor, *American Colonies*, xv.
[43] For a classic study on the Eastern Question, see M.S. Anderson, *The Eastern Question, 1774-1923: A Study in International Relations* (London: MacMillan, 1966).

treat its Muslim subjects well. With the destruction of the janissary corps in 1826, the subsequent disempowerment of the ulema, and the heavy blow dealt by the central authority to provincial notables, various social groups lost their representation in the government and thus their "protection against the most terrible riots of bureaucratic despotism."[44] The sociopolitical consensus that created the early modern Ottoman state after a long series of political struggles in the seventeenth century was lost again at the beginning of the nineteenth century, especially after the enthronement of Mahmud II who moved first against the local notables, then the janissaries, and finally the jurists.

It is for all of these reasons that the question of decline is relevant. Why did the Second Empire, which was a major improvement in terms of state–society relations when compared with the patrimonial empire that had preceded it, collapse in 1826? One could place all of the blame on the shoulders of Mahmud II and other modernizing autocrats of the nineteenth century as some Islamist critics do.[45] The analysis offered in this book, however, suggests two answers in addition to the one proposed earlier related to the formation of a collective Ottoman political identity. Whereas during the Second Empire there was significant progress in many spheres of life, such as the easing or opening of a relatively rigid system of upward mobility in the imperial political structures and the limitation of royal authority, there were other spheres in which developments were not as positive, such as the military and scientific fields. Not surprisingly, the sociopolitical progress in upward mobility and limitation of royal authority, on the one hand, and the setbacks in the military and scientific fields, on the other, were closely related. Some of the ways in which the political nation expanded, by which new social groups came to have an impact on the political process, proved to be hazardous for the military power of the empire. The empowerment of jurists and their law, which contributed to the gradual limitation of royal authority, created unexpected setbacks in the production of scientific knowledge.

Some of the expansion of the political nation took place within the ranks of the army as the central infantry army – the janissary corps – was transformed into a public corporation representing the interests of certain segments from the middle and lower middle classes. However, this transformation contributed to the territorial losses the Ottoman Empire suffered in the seventeenth and eighteenth centuries. The janissaries were not categorically against the development of a new fighting force that would do the job their predecessors used to do.[46] Yet they could see that such a development would eventually bring their privileges and political power to an end. The absolutist ambitions of sultans like Osman II who wanted to get rid of old institutions that had acquired

---

[44] A. D. Mordtmann, *Stambul und das moderne Türkenthum: Politische, sociale, und biographische Bilder von einem Osmanen*, 2 vols. (Leipzig: Duncker & Humblot, 1877–8), vol. I, 134.
[45] See, for instance, D. Mehmet Doğan, *Batılılaşma İhaneti* (Istanbul: Dergah Yayınları, 1975).
[46] Timur, *Osmanlı Çalışmaları*, 133–4, 157, n. 50.

constitutional privileges upset the janissaries. Thus the whole question of military reform was a very political question on which hinged the sociopolitical privileges of large masses. The janissaries defended their political position of opposition to the absolutist designs of sultans and others at the expense of military defeats that cost the Ottomans dearly. At the end, the sultans decided to acknowledge the janissary corps as a public corporation and in effect granted it almost unlimited autonomy. In consequence, the eighteenth century was the most peaceful one in terms of political conflicts between the janissaries and the court; yet at the same time, it was also a century of major territorial losses, contributing to the long-term territorial decline. Not surprisingly, an army centered upon a public corporation of middle and lower middle class merchants and craftsmen failed to perform successfully as a professional military organization. The long-term result of this failure was a weakened military that left the Ottomans vulnerable against the forces of Russian and, later, western European imperialism. A similar fate awaited the ulema, the Ottoman scholars who became more and more focused on law at the expense of other fields of inquiry.

If the janissaries constituted the physical guardians of the limits of royal authority in the Second Ottoman Empire, the ulema functioned as the sociopolitical body that safeguarded the intellectual foundations of these limits. Constitutionalist claims aimed at the limitation of royal authority, whether developed by jurists or others, tended to tap into legalistic thought that drew on arguments that, more often than not, took their claim to truth from tradition – both invented and received. However, some of the earliest absolutist sultans of the period, such as Murad III and Osman II, patronized scholars like the astronomer Taqī al-Dīn, the geographer Su'udi, and the jurist Mullah Ali, who used arguments based on experiment and reason in their works. As argued elsewhere, this patronage should be interpreted as an attempt on the part of the court to destabilize the epistemological supremacy of traditionalist knowledge and thereby take control of the field of jurists' law by reconstituting it primarily on reason rather than tradition. For the constitutionalists, giving away the epistemological ground could lead to giving away their political leverage arising from their monopoly on traditional knowledge, which was the basis of jurists' law. Therefore the progress of scientific thought slowed down in the Ottoman Empire as most scholars remained suspicious of the absolutist political implications of an epistemology that emphasized reason and experience at the expense of tradition. For instance, consider the destruction of the Imperial Observatory in 1580 or the exclusion of rational sciences from the curricula of law schools.[47]

Therefore the historical processes that made the Ottoman Empire an early modern one also laid the grounds for its decline. This should not be surprising because, as indicated earlier, although the socioeconomic impact of the

---

[47] See Tezcan, "Ottoman science," and Tezcan, "Law in China."

early modern period was similar in most of the world, the way in which this impact interacted with the medieval legacy of each region produced different outcomes. For instance, a site for the political representation of new social forces emerged in both England and the Ottoman Empire. Yet where this site was located differed because the medieval legacies of these two polities were different: England had inherited a medieval institution called parliament, whereas the Ottomans had a military corporation, the janissary corps, which transformed itself into a political organization.

Even though this study sees the Second Empire as much more than a cause of future decline – in that period there was an unprecedented level of proto-democratization in Ottoman political structures as well as the development of a fairly constitutional monarchy – one may still ask what exactly is the difference between the Ottoman decline proposed here and the one that has recently been discarded by Ottoman historiography.[48] The first and obvious difference is this study's categorical rejection of "cultural" explanations. Second, the present study privileges local dynamics and identifies the actors of change primarily within the Ottoman Empire. Third, this study does not single out an institution or a people to unload responsibility for "failure." Fourth, according to this study, the Ottoman Empire did not decline because it was too conservative to adapt to the requirements of a new age. To the contrary, the empire was truly transformed during the seventeenth century under the impact of the socioeconomic changes brought about by the expansion of an imperial market economy. Last but not least, the framework presented in this study as a tool to approach Ottoman history between the late sixteenth and early nineteenth centuries is not centered on decline but rather on socioeconomic and political transformation. As such, decline is at once marginalized but also recognized.

Each society's future is shaped by a conversation between its past and present. The late medieval past of the Ottoman Empire, which this study calls the patrimonial empire (1453–1580), had created certain institutions that constituted the legacy inherited and then transformed by the Second Empire. Some of these medieval institutions were so truly transformed in the early modern era that they could not carry out some of their older functions appropriately; for example, the janissaries who quit fighting and became a sociopolitical corporation that came to represent lower and middle classes of Ottoman society or the jurist-scholars who became much more juridical than scholarly in their endeavors to limit royal authority. This does not mean, however, that the janissaries and the jurists were *responsible* for the Ottoman

---

[48] For the classic formulation of the case for the Ottoman decline, see Lewis, "Some reflections;" the decline paradigm has been approached critically since, at least, the 1970s; see Roger Owen, "The Middle East in the eighteenth century – an 'Islamic' society in decline: A critique of Gibb and Bowen's *Islamic Society and the West*," *Review of Middle East Studies* 1 (1975): 101–12. For more recent responses, see Hathaway, "Problems of periodization;" Darling, "Another look at periodization;" Donald Quataert, "Ottoman history writing and changing attitudes towards the notion of 'decline,'" *History Compass* 1 (August 2003).

decline. If anything, the way in which they transformed their late medieval selves and their relationship with each other as well as with the dynasty was truly revolutionary, leading to the proto-democratization of Ottoman political structures and the development of an unwritten constitution about the limits of Ottoman royal authority. Taking the epigraph of this conclusion as a model, this study suggests that the Second Ottoman Empire was moving forward in all senses of the word. It is only when we look backward with a view to understanding its eventual disappearance that we detect structural problems in the relationship between its past and present that weakened it in the long term.

Bibliography

Archival and Manuscript Sources

Başbakanlık Osmanlı Arşivleri, İstanbul
D. BŞM 8/62, 9/9
İbnülemin, Maliye 219.
Kamil Kepeci 257, 1767, 1807, 1808, 1909, 1911, 1914
Maliyeden Müdevver 4695, 6147
Kadı Sicilleri*
    Bursa, no. B-41, B-118.
    Manisa, no. 48.
    Rodoscuk, no. 1570.

Topkapı Sarayı Arşivi, İstanbul
D. 73, 7823
E. 7735/1–7

İstanbul Müftülüğü Arşivi, İstanbul
İstanbul Mahkemesi, no. 5.

Bibliothèque nationale de France, Paris
MS Collection Dupuy 429
MS fr. 3794, 16148, 16149, 16150
MS turc 123
Tugi, Hüseyin. [*Ta'rîh*]. MS turc 227

The National Archives, London
State Papers 97/4, 97/7, 97/8, 105/102

Süleymaniye Kütüphanesi, İstanbul
Aşık Çelebi. *Mi'râcü'l-iyâle ve Minhâcü'l-'adâle*. Reisülküttab 1006.
Âli, Mustafa. *Künhü'l-ahbâr*. Esad Efendi 2162.

* These records have recently been moved to the Başbakanlık Osmanlı Arşivleri where they have not yet been cataloged. Their identification numbers refer to the ones assigned to them while they were housed at the Milli Kütüphane in Ankara where I consulted them.

246   Bibliography

Es'ad bin Sa'deddin. *Fetâvâ*. Kasidecizade 277.
El-Habeşi, Ali. *Râfi'ü'l-gubûş fî fezâyili'l-hubûş*. Fatih 4360.
Kadızade Mehmed. *Kitâb-ı makbûl der hâl-i huyûl*. Kadızade Mehmed 420.
Kadızade Mehmed (Sofyalı). *Nushü'l-hükkâm ve sebebü'n-nizâm*. Aşir Efendi 327
_____. *Mesmû'atü'n-nakâyih mecmû'atü'n-nasâyih*. Husrev Paşa 629.
Kınalızade, Ali. *Ahlâk-ı 'Alâ'î*. Hamidiye 626.
Rumi, Mehmed bin Mehmed. [*Ta'rîh*]. Lala İsmail Efendi 300.
Sinan Pasha. [*Telhîsât*]. Esat Efendi 2236/2.

Topkapı Sarayı Kütüphanesi, Istanbul
Anonymous. *Gencîne-i 'adâlet*. Bağdat 348.
Bostanzade, Yahya. [*Vak'a-i Sultân 'Osmân Hân*]. Revan 1305.

Beyazıt Kütüphanesi, Istanbul:
Anonymous. *Vak'a-ı merhûm ve magfûr Sultân 'Osmân Hân*. Veliyüddin 1963/4 (ff. 44a-54a).
Hibri, Abdurrahman. *Defter-i Ahbâr*. Veliyüddin 2418.
Katib Çelebi. *Fadhlakat al-tawārīkh*. MS 10318.

İstanbul Üniversitesi Kütüphanesi, Istanbul
Âli, Mustafa. *Künhü'l-ahbâr*. TY 5959.
Hasanbeyzade, Ahmed. *Usûlü'l-hikem fî nizâmi'l-âlem*. TY 6944.

Dār al-kutub al-qawmiyya, Cairo
Anonymous. [*Fasl*]. 212 M. Ta'rīkh Turkī, vol. II, appendix (ff. 237b-247b).
Anonymous. [*Ta'rîh-i Sultân Murâd Hân*]. 191 Ta'rīkh Turkī.

Nuruosmaniye Kütüphanesi, Istanbul:
Bidlīsī, Idrīs. *Hasht bihisht*. MS 3209.

İzzettin Koyunoğlu Kütüphanesi, Konya
Tugi, Hüseyin. [*Hikâyet-i Sultân 'Osmân Hân*]. MS 13316.

British Library, London
Rumi, Mehmed bin Mehmed. *Nuhbetü't-tevârîh ve'l-ahbâr*. Or. 31.

Princeton University Library, Princeton
Âli, Mustafa. *Fusûl-i hall u 'akd fî usûl-i harc u nakd*. Islamic Manuscripts 106B.
Kadızade. *Câmi'ü'l-'akâ'id*. 2012Y

Gazi Husrev-begova Biblioteka, Sarajevo
Aga Dede. *Ta'rîh-nâme*. R-9724.

Österreichische Nationalbibliothek, Vienna
Anonymous [attributed to Vasfi]. *Gazânâme-i Halîl Paşa*. H. O. 72.

Universiteitsbibliotheek, Leiden
Osman bin Derviş and Hüseyin Tugi. [no title]. Or. 917.

Milli Kütüphane, Ankara
Âli, Mustafa. *Künhü'l-ahbâr.* A 68.

Private collection
Kafadar, Cemal. "A Case and a Source." Unpublished paper presented at the Middle East Studies Association annual meeting in San Francisco, 1984.

Published Archival Sources

Akgündüz, Ahmed, ed. *Osmanlı Kanunnâmeleri ve Hukukî Tahlilleri.* 9 vols. Istanbul: Osmanlı Araştırmaları Vakfı, 1990–6.

[Altınay], Ahmed Refik. *On Altıncı Asırda İstanbul Hayatı (1553–1591).* Istanbul: Devlet Basımevi, 1930.

Barkan, Ömer Lûtfi. *XV ve XVI ıncı asırlarda Osmanlı İmparatorluğunda Ziraî Ekonominin Hukukî ve Malî Esasları.* Vol.I: *Kanunlar.* Istanbul: İstanbul Üniversitesi Edebiyat Fakültesi Yayınları, 1945.

_____. "H. 933–934 (M. 1527–1528) malî yılına ait bir bütçe örneği." *İstanbul Üniversitesi İktisat Fakültesi Mecmuası* 15 (1953–4): 251–329.

_____. "954–955 (1547–1548) Malî Yılına âit bir Osmanlı bütçesi." *İstanbul Üniversitesi İktisat Fakültesi Mecmuası* 19 (1957–8): 219–76.

_____. "H. 974–975 (M. 1567–1568) malî yılına âit bir Osmanlı bütçesi." *İstanbul Üniversitesi İktisat Fakültesi Mecmuası* 19 (1957–8): 277–332.

_____. "1070–1071 (1660–1661) tarihli Osmanlı bütçesi ve bir mukayese." *İstanbul Üniversitesi İktisat Fakültesi Mecmuası* 17 (1955–6): 304–47.

_____. "İstanbul Saraylarına ait Muhasebe Defterleri." *Belgeler* 9/13 (1979): 1–380.

_____, and Ekrem Hakkı Ayverdi. *İstanbul Vakıfları Tahrîr Defteri – 953 (1546) Târîhli.* Istanbul: İstanbul Fetih Cemiyeti – İstanbul Enstitüsü, 1970.

Barozzi, Nicolo, and Guglielmo Berchet, eds. *Le relazioni degli stati europei lette al senato dagli ambasciatori veneziani nel secolo decimosettimo: Turchia.* 2 vols. Venice, 1871–2.

Calendar of State Papers and manuscripts relating to English affairs, existing in the archives and collections of Venice, and in other libraries of northern Italy. 38 vols. [in 40]. London: H. M. Stationery Office, 1864–1947.

Ebussu'ud. "Zur Anwendung des islamischen Rechts im 16. Jahrhundert: Die "juristischen Darlegungen" (Ma'rūżāt) des Schejch ül-Islam Ebū Su'ūd (gest. 1574)." Edited by Paul Horster. PhD diss. Friedrich-Wilhelms-Universität, 1935.

[Eldem], Halil Edhem. "Sultân 'Osmân Hân-ı Sânînin Leh seferine dâ'ir Türkce bir kitâbesi." *Ta'rîh-i 'Osmânî Encümeni Mecmû'ası* 1 (1329/1911): 223–32.

_____. "Bir atın mezâr taşı kitâbesi." *Türk Ta'rîh Encümeni Mecmû'ası* 15/9 [86] (1341/1925): 196–9.

Gontaut Biron, Jean de. *Ambassade en Turquie de Jean de Gontaut Biron, Baron de Salignac, 1605 à 1610: Correspondance diplomatique & documents inédits.* Edited by Comte Théodore de Gontaut Biron. 2 vols. Paris: H. Champion, 1888–9.

İnalcık, Halil. "Adâletnâmeler." *Belgeler* 2/3–4 (1965): 49–145.

Kânûn-ı Esâsî – Meclis-i Meb'ûsân Nizâmnâme-i Dâhiliyesi – Meclis-i A'yân Nizâmnâme-i Dâhiliyesi – İntihâb-ı Meb'ûsân Kânûnu. Istanbul: Matba'a-ı 'Âmire, 1328.

Lello, Henry. *The Report of Lello: Third English Ambassador to the Sublime Porte – Babıâli nezdinde üçüncü İngiliz elçisi Lello'nun muhtırası.* Edited and translated by

248   Bibliography

Orhan Burian. Ankara: Ankara Üniversitesi Dil ve Tarih-Coğrafya Fakültesi Yayınları, 1952.

Lugal, Necati, and Adnan Erzi, eds. *Fâtih Devrine âit Münşeat Mecmuası*. Istanbul: İstanbul Enstitüsü Yayınları, 1956.

Orhonlu, Cengiz, ed. *Osmanlı Tarihine Âid Belgeler: Telhîsler, 1597–1607*. Istanbul: İstanbul Üniversitesi Edebiyat Fakültesi Yayınları, 1970.

Özcan, Abdülkadir, ed. *Fatih Sultan Mehmed: Kānunnâme-i Âl-i Osman (Tahlil ve Karşılaştırmalı Metin)*. Istanbul: Kitabevi, 2003.

Özcan, Tahsin. "Para Vakıflarıyla ilgili önemli bir belge." *İLAM Araştırma Dergisi* 3/2 (1998): 107–12.

Pedani-Fabris, Maria Pia, ed. *Relazioni di ambasciatori veneti al senato*. Vol. XIV: *Constantinopoli, Relazioni inedite (1512–1789)*. Padova: Bottega d'Erasmo, 1996.

Sahillioğlu, Halil. "III. Murad dönemine ait 1582–83 (hicrî 990) tarihli bütçe – çeviriyazı." In *Osmanlı Maliyesi: Kurumlar ve Bütçeler*, edited by Mehmet Genç and Erol Özvar. 2 vols. Istanbul: Osmanlı Bankası Arşiv ve Araştırma Merkezi, 2006, vol. II, 31–79.

Tietze, Andreas. "A document on the persecution of sectarians in early seventeenth-century Istanbul." *Revue des Études Islamiques* 60 (1992): 161–6.

Uzunçarşılı, İsmail Hakkı. "Gazi Orhan Bey vakfiyesi, 724 Rebiülevvel – 1324 Mart." *Belleten* 5 (1941): 277–88.

Yıldırım, Hacı Osman, et al., eds. *82 Numaralı Mühimme Defteri (1026–1027 1617–1618): Özet – Transkripsiyon – İndeks ve Tıpkıbasım*. Ankara: Başbakanlık Devlet Arşivleri Genel Müdürlüğü, 2000.

Published Literary Sources

Abdülkadir. *Topçular Kâtibi 'Abdülkādir (Kadrî) Efendi Tarihi (Metin ve Tahlil)*. Edited by Ziya Yılmazer. 2 vols. Ankara: Türk Tarih Kurumu, 2003.

Akbar, ʿAlī. *Khitāynāme*. Edited by İraj Afshār. 2nd edition. Tehran, 1372.

———. *Tercüme-i Ta'rîh-i Nevâdir-i Çîn-i Mâçîn*. Anonymous translation. Istanbul, 1270.

Akhisari, Hasan Kafi. "Hasan Kâfî el-Akhisarî ve devlet düzenine ait eseri Usûlü'l- hikem fî nizâmi'l-âlem." Edited by Mehmet İpşirli. *Tarih Enstitüsü Dergisi* 10–11 (1979–80): 239–78.

Âli, Mustafa. *Künhü'l-ahbâr*. 5 vols. Istanbul, 1277–86.

———. *Künhü'l-ahbār, c. II: Fātih Sultān Mehmed devri, 1451–1481*. Edited by M. Hüdai Şentürk. Ankara: Türk Tarih Kurumu, 2003.

———. "Ek: *Künhü'l-Ahbâr*'ın Osmanlı Tarihi bölümünden III. Mehmed çağına ait parçanın sadeleştirilmiş şekli." Edited by Atsız. In *Âlî Bibliyografyası*. Istanbul: Süleymaniye Kütüphanesi Yayınları, 1968, 52–121.

———. *Mustafâ ʿÂlî's Description of Cairo of 1599: Text, Transliteration, Notes*. Edited and translated by Andreas Tietze. Vienna: Verlag der österreichischen Akademie der Wissenschaften, 1975.

———. *Mustafâ ʿÂlî's Counsel for Sultans of 1581*. Edited and translated by Andreas Tietze. 2 vols. Vienna: Verlag der österreichischen Akademie der Wissenschaften, 1979–82.

———. *The Ottoman Gentleman of the Sixteenth Century: Mustafa Âli's Mevâ'idü'n-nefâ'is fî Kavâ'idi'l-mecâlis – Tables of Delicacies Concerning the Rules of Social Gatherings*. Translated by Douglas S. Brookes. Cambridge, MA: Harvard University, Department of Near Eastern Languages and Civilizations, 2003.

Anonymous. *The Book of Dede Korkut*. Translated by Geoffrey Lewis. Harmondsworth: Penguin, 1974.

Anonymous. *L'Entrevue du sultan Hibraïm, empereur des Turcs et du roi d'Angleterre aux Champs Elysées*. Paris, 1649.

Anonymous. "Hırzü'l-mülûk." In *Osmanlı Devlet Teşkilâtına Dair Kaynaklar: Kitâb-ı Müstetâb – Kitabu Mesâlihi'l Müslimîn ve Menâfi'i'l-Mü'minîn – Hırzü'l-Mülûk*, edited by Yaşar Yücel. Ankara: Türk Tarih Kurumu Yayınları, 1988, 143–207.

Anonymous. "Kavânîn-i yeniçeriyân-ı dergâh-ı âlî." Edited by A. Akgündüz. In *Osmanlı Kanunnâmeleri ve Hukukî Tahlilleri*. 9 vols. Istanbul: Osmanlı Araştırmaları Vakfı, 1990–6, vol. IX, 127–268.

Anonymous. "Kitâb-ı müstetâb." In *Osmanlı Devlet Teşkilâtına Dair Kaynaklar: Kitâb-ı Müstetâb – Kitabu Mesâlihi'l Müslimîn ve Menâfi'i'l-Mü'minîn – Hırzü'l-Mülûk*, edited by Yaşar Yücel. Ankara: Türk Tarih Kurumu Yayınları, 1988, 1–40.

Anonymous. "Kitâbu mesâlihi'l-müslimîn ve menâfi'i'l-mü'minîn." In *Osmanlı Devlet Teşkilâtına Dair Kaynaklar: Kitâb-ı Müstetâb – Kitabu Mesâlihi'l Müslimîn ve Menâfi'i'l-Mü'minîn – Hırzü'l-Mülûk*, edited by Yaşar Yücel. Ankara: Türk Tarih Kurumu Yayınları, 1988, 91–129.

Anonymous. "The Strangling and Death of the Great Turk." Reprint of the original edition of July 15, 1622, with revised spelling. In *The Harleian Miscellany*. Vol. IV. London: T. Osborne, 1745, 32–40.

Anonymous. *A true and faithfull relation, presented to His Maiestie and the Prince, of what hath lately happened in Constantinople, concerning the death of Sultan Osman, and the setting up of Mustafa his uncle*. London: Bartholomew Downes, 1622.

Aşık Paşa. *Garib-nâme: Tıpkıbasım, Karşılaştırmalı Metin ve Aktarma*. Edited by Kemal Yavuz. 2 vols. Istanbul: Türk Dil Kurumu, 2000.

Aşıkpaşazade, Ahmed. "Tevârîh-i Âl-i Osman." Edited by Çiftçioğlu N. Atsız. In *Osmanlı Tarihleri*, edited by Ç. N. Atsız. Istanbul: Türkiye Yayınevi, 1949, 77–319.

Ata'i, Nev'izade. *Hadâ'iku'l-hakâ'ik fî tekmîleti'ş-şakâ'ik*. 2 vols. Istanbul, 1268 [reprinted with indices in *Şakaik-ı Nu'maniye ve Zeyilleri*, ed. Abdülkadir Özcan, 5 vols. (Istanbul: Çağrı Yayınları, 1989), vol. II].

Ayn Ali. *Kavânîn-i âl-i 'Osmân der hulâsa-ı mezâmin-i defter-i dîvân*. Istanbul, 1280.

———. "Risâle-i vazîfe-hᵛârân ve merâtib-i bendegân-ı âl-i 'Osmân." In *Kavânîn-i âl-i 'Osmân der hulâsa-ı mezâmin-i defter-i dîvân*. Istanbul, 1280, 82–104.

Ayvansarayi, Hüseyin. *Hadîkatü'l-cevâmi'*. Edited [with additions] by Ali Sati, 2 vols. Istanbul, 1281.

———. *Mecmuâ-i Tevârih*. Edited by Fahri Ç. Derin and Vâhid Çubuk. Istanbul: İstanbul Üniversitesi Edebiyat Fakültesi Yayınları, 1985.

Blount, Henry. *A Voyage into the Levant*. London, 1636.

Bosnavi, Hüseyin (called Koca Mü'errih). *Bedâyi'ü'l-vakâyi'*. Edited by A. S. Tveritinova. 2 vols. Moscow: Izd-vo vostochnoi lit-ry, 1961.

Bostanzade, Yahya. "II. Sultan Osman'ın şehadeti." Translated by Orhan Şaik Gökyay. In *Atsız Armağanı*, edited by Erol Güngör et al. Istanbul: Ötüken, 1976, 187–256.

Būrīnī, al-Ḥasan ibn Muḥammad. *Tarājim al-aʿyān min abnā' al-zamān*. Edited by Ṣalāḥ al-Dīn al-Munajjid. 2 vols. [incomplete] Damascus: al-Majmaʿ al-ʿIlmī al-ʿArabī bi-Dimashq, 1959–63.

Danon, M. A., ed. and trans. "Contributions à l'histoire des sultans Osman II et Mouçtafâ I." *Journal Asiatique* 11ème Série 14 (1919): 69–139, 243–310.

Della Valle, Pietro. *Reiss-Beschreibung in unterschiedliche Theile der Welt*. Genff, 1674.

Evliya Çelebi. *Evliya Çelebi Seyahatnamesi*. 10 vols. Istanbul, 1314–1938.

Feridun Bey, et al., eds. *Münşe'ât-ı Selâtîn*. 2nd edition. 2 vols. Istanbul, 1274.

Fontanier, Victor. *Voyages en Orient, entrepris par ordre du gouvernement français*, vol. I: *Turquie d'Asie*. Paris: Mongie aîné, 1829.

Georgius de Hungaria. *Tractatus de moribus condictionibus et nequicia Turcorum: Traktat über die Sitten, die Lebensverhältnisse und die Arglist der Türken*. Edited and translated by Reinhard Klockow. Köln: Böhlau, 1993.

Ghazzī, Najm al-Dīn. *Al-kawākib al-sā'ira bi-a'yān al-mi'a al-'āshira*. Edited by Jibrā'il Sulaymān Jabbūr. 3 vols. Beirut: American University of Beirut, 1945–59.

————. *Lutf al-samar wa qatf al-thamar min tarājim a'yān al-tabaqa al-ūlā min al-qarn al-hādī 'ashar*. Edited by Mahmūd al-Shaykh. 2 vols. Damascus, 1981–2.

Gregoras, Nikephoros. *Rhomäische Geschichte*. Translated by Jan Louis van Dieten. Stuttgart: A. Hiersemann, 1973–.

Halisi, Mehmed. *Zafer-nâme*. Facsimile edited by Yaşar Yücel. Ankara: Ankara Üniversitesi Dil ve Tarih-Coğrafya Fakültesi Yayınları, 1983.

Hamadānī, 'Alī. *Dhakhīrat al-mulūk*. Edited by Mahmūd Anwārī. Tebriz: Mu'assasa-i Ta'rīkh wa Farhang-i Īrān, 1358/1980.

————. *Zahîratü'l-mülûk: Hadisler ışığında yönetim ilkeleri, yönetici nitelikleri*. Translated by Muhammed b. Hüseyin. Edited by Necdet Yılmaz. Istanbul: Dârulhadis, 2003.

Hasanbeyzade, Ahmed. *Hasan Bey-zâde Târîhi*. Edited by Nezihi Aykut. 3 vols. Ankara: Türk Tarih Kurumu, 2004.

Ibn Abī al-Surūr, Muhammad. *Al-minah al-rahmāniyya fī al-dawla al-'uthmāniyya*. Edited by Laylá al-Sabbāgh. Damascus: Dār al-Bashā'ir, 1995.

Ibn Jum'a, Muhammad. "Al-bāshāt wa'l-qudāt." In *Wulāt dimashq fī al-'ahd al-'uthmānī*, edited by Salāh al-Dīn al-Munajjid. Damascus, 1949, 1–69.

İsazade. *'Îsâ-zâde Târîhi: Metin ve Tahlil*. Edited by Ziya Yılmazer. Istanbul: İstanbul Fetih Cemiyeti, 1996.

John VI Cantacuzenus. *Geschichte*. Translated by Georgios Fatouros and Tilman Krischer. Stuttgart: A. Hiersemann, 1982–.

Juchereau de Saint-Denys, Antoine de. *Histoire de l'empire ottoman depuis 1792 jusqu'en 1844*. 4 vols. Paris: Au comptoir des imprimeurs-unis, 1844.

Kadızade, Mehmed. *Kitab-ı Makbul: Atalarımızın Gözüyle At*. Edited by Tahir Galip Ser'atlı. Istanbul: Uğur Yaraman, 1986.

Karaçelebizâde, Abdül'aziz. *Ravzatü'l-ebrâr*. Bulak, 1248.

————. *Ravzatü'l-ebrâr Zeyli: Tahlil ve metin*. Edited by Nevzat Kaya. Ankara: Türk Tarih Kurumu, 2003.

Katib Çelebi. *Fezleke*. 2 vols. Istanbul, 1286–7 AH.

————. *The Balance of Truth*. Translated by G. L. Lewis. London: George Allen and Unwin, 1957.

Khālidī, Ahmad. *Lubnān fī 'ahd al-amīr Fakhr al-Dīn al-Ma'nī al-thānī: wa-huwa kitāb ta'rīkh al-Amīr Fakhr al-Dīn al-Ma'nī*. Edited by Asad Rustum and Fu'ād Bustānī. Beyrut: Manshūrāt al-Jāmi'a al-Lubnāniyya, 1969.

Kınalızade, Ali. *Ahlâk-ı 'Alâ'î*. Bulak, 1248.

Knolles, Richard, and Edward Grimston. *The Generall Historie of the Turkes*. 3rd edition. London: Adam Islip, 1621.

Koçi Bey. *Koçi Bey Risalesi*. Edited by Ali Kemali Aksüt. Istanbul: Vakit, 1939.

Kuşmani, Ubeydullah, and Ebubekir Efendi. *Asiler ve Gaziler: Kabakçı Mustafa Risalesi.* Edited by Aysel Danacı Yıldız. Istanbul: Kitap Yayınevi, 2007.

Lutfi Pasha. "Lütfi Paşa Âsafnâmesi: yeni bir metin tesisi denemesi." Edited by Mübahat S. Kütükoğlu. In *Prof. Dr. Bekir Kütükoğlu'na Armağan.* Istanbul: İstanbul Üniversitesi Edebiyat Fakültesi Tarih Araştırma Merkezi, 1991, 49–99.

Marsigli, Luigi Ferdinando. *Stato militare dell'imperio ottomanno / L'état militaire de l'empire ottoman.* La Haye: Gosse, 1732.

Mehmed Pasha, Sarı Defterdar. *Ottoman Statecraft: The Book of Counsel for Vezirs and Governors (Nasā'ih ül-vüzera ve'l-ümera) of Sarı Mehmed Pasha, the Defterdār.* Edited and translated by Walter Livingston Wright, Jr. Princeton: Princeton University Press, 1935.

_____. *Zübde-i Vekayiât: Tahlil ve metin, 1066–1116/1656–1704.* Edited by Abdülkadir Özcan. Ankara: Türk Tarih Kurumu, 1995.

Mingana, A. "List of the Turkish governors and high judges of Aleppo from the Ottoman conquest to A.D. 1747." *Bulletin of the John Rylands Library* 10 (1926): 515–23.

Montagu, Lady Mary Wortley. *The Complete Letters.* Edited by Robert Halsband. 3 vols. Oxford: Clarendon Press, 1965–7.

Moryson, Fynes. *An Itinerary.* London, 1617.

Muhibbī, Muhammad Amīn. *Khulāṣat al-athar fī a'yān al-qarn al-ḥādī 'ashar.* 4 vols. Cairo, 1284.

Muntaner, Ramón. *The Chronicle of Muntaner.* Translated by Lady Goodenough. 2 vols. London: Hakluyt Society, 1920–1.

Nadiri, Ganizade. "Ganî-zâde Nâdirî: Hayâtı, Edebî Kişiliği, Eserleri, Dîvânı ve Şehnâmesinin Tenkidli Metni." Edited by Numan Külekçi. PhD diss. Atatürk Üniversitesi, 1985.

Na'ima. *Ta'rîh-i Na'îmâ.* 6 vols. Istanbul, 1281–3.

Neşri, Mehmed. *Kitâb-ı Cihan-nümâ: Neşrî Tarihi.* Edited by Faik Reşit Unat and Mehmed A. Köymen. 2 vols. Ankara: Türk Tarih Kurumu, 1949–57.

Osman II. "Bütün şiirleri." Edited by Esra Keskinkılıç. In *Sultan II. Osman.* Istanbul: Şûle Yayınları, 1999, 63–149.

Osmanzade, Ta'ib Ahmed, Dilaverağazade Ömer Vahid, Ahmed Cavid, and Bağdadi Abdülfettah Şevket. *Hadîqat ül-vüzerâ [ve zeyilleri].* Istanbul, 1271.

Ömer Fa'ik. "Nizâmü'l-atîk (İstanbul Üniversite Ktb. TY nr. 5836)." Edited by Ahmet Sarıkaya. Senior thesis. İstanbul Üniversitesi, 1979.

Pachymérès, George. *Relations historiques.* Vol. IV (Livres X–XIII). Edited and translated by Albert Failler. Paris: Institut français d'études byzantines, 1999.

Peçevi, İbrahim. *Ta'rîh-i Peçevî.* 2 vols. Istanbul, 1281–3.

Porter, James, Sir. *Observations on the Religion, Law, Government, and Manners of the Turks.* 2nd edition. London: J. Nourse, 1771.

Provin, Pacifique de. *Lettre du pere Pacifique de Provin, predicateur capucin, estant present à Constantinople, enuoyee au R. P. Ioseph le Clerc, Predicateur du mesme ordre, & deffiniteur de leur Prouince de Tours, sur l'estrange mort du grand Turc, Empereur de Constantinople.* Paris: François Hvby, 1622.

Raşid, Mehmed. *Ta'rîh-i Râşid.* 2nd edition. 5 vols. Istanbul, 1282.

Resmi, Ahmed. *Hamîletü'l-kübera.* Edited by Ahmet Nezihi Turan. Istanbul: Kitabevi, 2000.

Roe, Thomas, Sir. *The Negotiations of Sir Thomas Roe in His Embassy to the Ottoman Porte.* London, 1740.

Ruhi. "Rûhî Tarihi." Edited by Halil Erdoğan Cengiz and Yaşar Yücel. *Belgeler* 14/18 (1989–92): 359–472.

Rumi, Mehmed bin Mehmed. *Nuhbetü't-tevârîh ve'l-ahbâr.* Istanbul, 1276.

Rycaut, Paul. *The Present State of the Ottoman Empire.* London: John Starkey and Henry Brome, 1668.

Sa'deddin. *Tâcü't-tevârîh.* 2 vols. Istanbul, 1279–80.

Safi, Mustafa. *Mustafa Sâfî'nin Zübdetü't-Tevârîh'i.* Edited by İbrahim Hakkı Çuhadar. 2 vols. Ankara: Türk Tarih Kurumu, 2003.

Schütz, E., ed. *An Armeno-Kipchak Chronicle on the Polish-Turkish Wars in 1620–1621.* Budapest: Akadémiai Kiadó, 1968.

Selaniki, Mustafa. *Tarih-i Selânikî.* Edited by Mehmed İpşirli. 2 vols. Istanbul: İstanbul Üniversitesi Edebiyat Fakültesi Yayınları, 1989.

Silahdar, Fındıklılı Mehmed Ağa. *Silahdâr Ta'rîhi.* 2 vols. Istanbul, 1928.

Şükrullah. *Bahjat al-tawārīkh.* Excerpt edited and translated by Theodor Seif. In "Der Abschnitt über die Osmanen in Šükrüllāh's persischer Universalgeschichte." *Mitteilungen zur osmanischen Geschichte* 2 (1923–6): 63–128.

[Tugi.] *La mort du sultan Osman, ou le retablissement de Mustapha sur le throsne, traduit d'un manuscrit turc, de la Bibliotheque du Roy.* Translated by Antoine Galland. Paris, 1678.

Studies

Abdullaeva, Firuza. "A Turkish prose version of Firdawsi's Shahnama in the manuscript collection of the St. Petersburg University Library." *Manuscripta Orientalia: International Journal for Oriental Manuscript Research* 3 (1997): 49–57.

Abdurrahimoğlu, Erişah. "1621–1680 yılları arasında Osmanlı devletinin merkezi hazine gelir ve giderleri." MA thesis. Marmara Üniversitesi, 1988.

Abou-El-Haj, Rifa'at Ali. "The Ottoman vezir and paşa households, 1683–1703: A preliminary report." *Journal of the American Oriental Society* 94 (1974): 438–47.

———. *The 1703 Rebellion and the Structure of Ottoman Politics.* Leiden: Nederlands Instituut voor het Nabije Oosten, 1984.

———. "The Ottoman nasihatname as a discourse over 'morality'." In *Mélanges Professeur Robert Mantran,* edited by Abdeljelil Temimi. Zaghouan: Publications du Centre d'Etudes et de Recherches Ottomanes, Morisques, de Documentation et d'Information, 1988, 17–30 [*Revue d'histoire maghrébine* 47–48 (1987): 17–30].

———. "Power and social order: The uses of the kanun." In *The Ottoman City and Its Parts: Urban Structure and Social Order,* edited by Irene A. Bierman, Rifa'at A. Abou-El-Haj, and Donald Preziosi. New Rochelle, NY: Aristide D. Caratzas, 1991, 77–99.

———. *Formation of the Modern State: The Ottoman Empire, Sixteenth to Eighteenth Centuries.* 2nd edition. Syracuse: Syracuse University Press, 2005 [first ed., 1991].

Ágoston, Gábor. *Guns for the Sultan: Military Power and the Weapons Industry in the Ottoman Empire.* Cambridge: Cambridge University Press, 2004.

Ahmed Cevad. *Tarîh-i 'Askerî-i 'Osmânî.* Vol. I: *Yeniçeriler.* Istanbul: Kırk Ambar Matbaası, 1299.

Akarlı, Engin Deniz. "Review of Colin Imber's Ebu's-Su'ud: The Islamic legal tradition." *Islamic Law and Society* 6 (1999): 284–8.

Akdağ, Mustafa. "Osmanlı İmparatorluğunun kuruluş ve inkişafı devrinde Türkiye'nin iktisadî vaziyeti." *Belleten* 13 (1949): 497–571.

_____. *Celâlî İsyanları, 1550–1603.* Ankara: Ankara Üniversitesi Dil ve Tarih-Coğrafya Fakültesi Yayınları, 1963.

_____. *Türkiye'nin İktisadî ve İçtimaî Tarihi.* 2 vols. Ankara: Ankara Üniversitesi Dil ve Tarih-Coğrafya Fakültesi Yayınları, 1959–71.

Akman, Mehmet. *Osmanlı Devleti'nde Kardeş Katli.* Istanbul: Eren, 1997.

Aksan, Virginia H. "Locating the Ottomans among early modern empires." *Journal of Early Modern History* 3 (1999): 103–34.

_____. *Ottoman Wars, 1700–1870: An Empire Besieged.* Harlow: Longman/Pearson, 2007.

_____, and Daniel Goffman, eds. *The Early Modern Ottomans: Remapping the Empire.* Cambridge: Cambridge University Press, 2007.

Alderson, A. D. *The Structure of the Ottoman Dynasty.* Oxford: Oxford University Press, 1956.

Alexander, John Christos. *Toward a History of Post-Byzantine Greece: The Ottoman kanunnames for the Greek Lands.* Athens, 1985.

Anderson, M. S. *The Eastern Question, 1774–1923: A Study in International Relations.* London: MacMillan, 1966.

Andrews, Walter, and Mehmet Kalpaklı. *The Age of Beloveds: Love and the Beloved in Early-Modern Ottoman and European Culture and Society.* Durham: Duke University Press, 2005.

Arjomand, Said Amir. *The Shadow of God and the Hidden Imam: Religion, Political Order, and Societal Change in Shi'ite Iran from the Beginning to 1890.* Chicago: University of Chicago Press, 1984.

Artan, Tülay. "Architecture as a theatre of life: Profile of the eighteenth century Bosphorus." PhD diss. Massachusetts Institute of Technology, 1989.

_____. "Arts and architecture." In *The Cambridge History of Turkey.* Vol. III: *The Later Ottoman Empire, 1603–1839,* edited by Suraiya N. Faroqhi. Cambridge: Cambridge University Press, 2006, 408–480.

Aydın, M. Akif. "Eyüp şeriye sicillerinden 184, 185 ve 188 numaralı defterlerin hukuki tahlili." In *18. Yüzyıl Kadı Sicilleri Işığında Eyüp'te Sosyal Yaşam,* edited by Tülay Artan. Istanbul: Türkiye Ekonomik ve Toplumsal Tarih Vakfı, 1998, 65–72.

Ayhan, Aydın, and Tuncer Şengün. "Anadolu Beyliklerinin ve Osmanlı Beyliği'nin İlhanlılar adına kestirdiği sikkeler." In *XIII. Türk Tarih Kongresi, Ankara, 4–8 Ekim 1999: Kongreye sunulan bildiriler.* 3 vols. in 5. Ankara: Türk Tarih Kurumu, 2002, vol. III, part 2, 1161–71.

Baer, Marc David. *Honored by the Glory of Islam: Conversion and Conquest in Ottoman Europe.* Oxford: Oxford University Press, 2008.

Baltacı, Cahid. *XV-XVI. Asırlarda Osmanlı Medreseleri: Teşkilat – Tarih.* Istanbul, 1976.

Barbir, Karl K. *Ottoman Rule in Damascus, 1708–1758.* Princeton: Princeton University Press, 1980.

Barkan, Ömer Lûtfi. "Essai sur les données statistiques des registres de recensement dans l'Empire Ottoman aux XVe et XVIe siècles." *Journal of the Economic and Social History of the Orient* 1 (1957): 9–36.

_____. "Timar." *İA.* Vol. XII/I, 286–333.

_____. "Feodal düzen ve Osmanlı timarı." *Hacettepe Üniversitesi Türkiye İktisat Tarihi Semineri* (Haziran 1973): 1–32.

_____. "Türkiye'de din ve devlet ilişkilerinin tarihsel gelişimi." *Cumhuriyetin 50. Yıldönümü Semineri: Seminere Sunulan Bildiriler.* Ankara: Türk Tarih Kurumu, 1975, 49–97.

Barkey, Karen. *Bandits and Bureaucrats: The Ottoman Route to State Centralization.* Ithaca: Cornell University Press, 1994.

Baştav, Şerif. *Bizans İmparatorluğu Tarihi: Son Devir (1261–1461).* Ankara: Türk Kültürünü Araştırma Enstitüsü, 1989.

Behar, Cem. "The Ottoman musical tradition." In *The Cambridge History of Turkey.* Vol. III: *The Later Ottoman Empire, 1603–1839,* edited by Suraiya N. Faroqhi. Cambridge: Cambridge University Press, 2006, 393–407.

Berkes, Niyazi. *The Development of Secularism in Turkey.* Montreal: McGill University Press, 1964.

Berktay, Halil. "The feudalism debate – the Turkish end: Is 'tax-vs.-rent' necessarily the product and sign of a modal difference?" *Journal of Peasant Studies* 14 (1986–7): 291–333.

Bilgin, Vejdi. *Fakih ve Toplum: Osmanlı'da sosyal yapı ve fıkıh.* Istanbul: İz, 2003.

Birnbaum, E. "Vice triumphant: The spread of coffee and tobacco in Turkey." *Durham University Journal* (December 1956): 21–7.

Blaskovics, Jozef. "XVII. asırda beylerbeyi hassaları ve tebaanın hayatı." *VI. Türk Tarih Kongresi (Ankara, 20–26 Ekim 1961): Kongreye Sunulan Bildiriler.* Ankara: Türk Tarih Kurumu, 1967, 294.

Bloch, Marc. *Feudal Society.* Translated by L. A. Manyon. 2 vols. Chicago: Chicago University Press, 1961.

Bodman, Herbert Luther. *Political Factions in Aleppo, 1760–1826.* Chapel Hill: University of North Carolina Press, 1963.

Börekçi, Günhan. "İnkırâzın eşiğinde bir hanedan: III. Mehmed, I. Ahmed, I. Mustafa ve 17. yüzyıl Osmanlı siyasî krizi." *Dîvân: Disiplinlerarası Çalışmalar Dergisi* 14/26 (2009): 45–96.

Brenner, Robert. "The agrarian roots of European capitalism." In *The Brenner Debate: Agrarian Class Structure and Economic Development in Pre-industrial Europe,* edited by T. H. Aston and C. H. E. Philpin. Cambridge: Cambridge University Press, 1985, 213–327.

_____. *Merchants and Revolution: Commercial Change, Political Conflict, and London's Overseas Traders, 1550–1653.* Princeton: Princeton University Press, 1993.

Bryer, Anthony. "Greek historians on the Turks: The case of the first Byzantine-Ottoman marriage." In *The Writing of History in the Middle Ages: Essays Presented to Richard William Southern,* edited by R. H. C. Davis and J. M. Wallace-Hadrill. Oxford: Clarendon Press, 1981, 471–93.

Caferoğlu, Ahmet. "Türk tarihinde 'nöker' ve 'nöker-zâdeler' müessesesi." *IV. Türk Tarih Kongresi – Ankara, 10–14 Kasım 1948.* Ankara: Türk Tarih Kurumu, 1952, 251–61.

Carali, P. Paolo. *Fakhr ad-Dîn II, principe del Libano, e la corte di Toscana, 1605–1635.* 2 vols. Roma: Reale Accademia d'Italia, 1936–8.

Chakrabarty, Dipesh. *Provincializing Europe: Postcolonial Thought and Historical Difference.* Princeton: Princeton University Press, 2000.

Chamberlain, Michael. *Knowledge and Social Practice in Medieval Damascus, 1190–1350.* Cambridge: Cambridge University Press, 1994.

Cook, Michael A. *Population Pressure in Rural Anatolia, 1450–1600.* London: Oxford University Press, 1972.

_____. *Commanding Right and Forbidding Wrong in Islamic Thought.* Cambridge: Cambridge University Press, 2000.

Coşgel, Metin M. "Agricultural Productivity in the Early Ottoman Empire." *Research in Economic History* 24 (2006): 161–87.

Crone, Patricia, and Martin Hinds. *God's Caliph: Religious Authority in the First Centuries of Islam.* Cambridge: Cambridge University Press, 1986.

Cvetkova, Bistra A. "L'évolution du régime féodal turc de la fin du XVIe jusqu'au milieu du XVIIIe siècle." *Etudes historiques* 1 (Sofia, 1960): 171–206.

Çağaptay, Soner. *Islam, Secularism, and Nationalism in Modern Turkey: Who is a Turk?* London: Routledge, 2006.

Çizakça, Murat. "Cash waqfs of Bursa, 1555–1823." *Journal of the Economic and Social History of the Orient* 38 (1995): 313–54.

_____. *A Comparative Evolution of Business Partnerships: The Islamic World and Europe, with specific reference to the Ottoman Archives.* Leiden: E. J. Brill, 1996.

Danon, M. A. "Un interrogatoire d'hérétiques musulmans (1619)." *Journal Asiatique* 11ème Série 17 (1921): 281–93.

Darling, Linda T. *Revenue-Raising and Legitimacy: Tax Collection and Finance Administration in the Ottoman Empire, 1550–1660.* Leiden: E. J. Brill, 1996.

_____. "Another look at periodization in Ottoman history." *Turkish Studies Association Bulletin* 26/2 (2002): 19–28.

Değirmenci, Tülün. "Resmedilen siyaset: II. Osman devri (1618–1622) resimli elyazmalarında değişen iktidar sembolleri." PhD diss. Hacettepe Üniversitesi, 2007.

Doğan, D. Mehmet. *Batılılaşma İhaneti.* Istanbul: Dergah Yayınları, 1975.

Eisenstadt, Shmuel N., and Wolfgang Schluchter. "Introduction: Paths to early modernities – a comparative view." *Daedalus* 127/3 (Summer 1998): 1–18.

Emecen, Feridun. "Osmanlı Hanedanına Alternatif Arayışlar: İbrahimhanzadeler Örneği." In *XIII. Türk Tarih Kongresi, Ankara, 4–8 Ekim 1999: Kongreye sunulan bildiriler.* 3 vols. in 5. Ankara: Türk Tarih Kurumu, 2002, vol. III, part III, 1877–86.

Ergene, Boğaç A. "On Ottoman justice: Interpretations in conflict (1600–1800)." *Islamic Law and Society* 8 (2001): 52–87.

Erimtan, Can. *Ottomans Looking West? The Origins of the Tulip Age and its Development in Modern Turkey.* London: Tauris, 2008.

Evin, Ahmet Ö. *Origins and Development of the Turkish Novel.* Minneapolis: Bibliotheca Islamica, 1983.

Faroqhi, Suraiya. *Approaching Ottoman History: An Introduction to the Sources.* Cambridge: Cambridge University Press, 1999.

_____. "Crisis and change, 1590–1699." In *An Economic and Social History of the Ottoman Empire, 1300–1914,* edited by Halil İnalcık with Donald Quataert. Cambridge: Cambridge University Press, 1994, 411–636.

_____. *Pilgrims and Sultans: The Hajj under the Ottomans, 1517–1683.* London: Tauris, 1994.

_____. "Ra'iyya – in the Ottoman Empire." *Encyclopedia of Islam, New Edition.* Vol. VIII, 404–6.

Fine, John V. A., Jr. *The Late Medieval Balkans: A Critical Survey from the Late Twelfth Century to the Ottoman Conquest.* Ann Arbor: University of Michigan Press, 1987.

256   Bibliography

Finkel, Caroline. *The Administration of Warfare: The Ottoman Military Campaigns in Hungary, 1593–1606.* Vienna: Verband der Wissenschaftlichen Gesellschaften Österreichs, 1988.

———. *Osman's Dream: The History of the Ottoman Empire.* New York: Basic Books, 2005.

Fleet, Kate. "Early Ottoman self-definition." *Journal of Turkish Studies* 26/1 (2002): 229–38.

Fleischer, Cornell H. *Bureaucrat and Intellectual in the Ottoman Empire: The Historian Mustafa Âli (1541–1600).* Princeton: Princeton University Press, 1986.

Fodor, Pál. "State and society, crisis and reform, in 15th-17th century Ottoman mirror for princes." *Acta Orientalia Academiae Scientiarum Hungaricae* 40 (1986): 217–40.

Gara, Eleni. "Moneylenders and landowners: In search of urban Muslim elites in the early modern Balkans." In *Provincial Elites in the Ottoman Empire*, edited by Antonis Anastasopoulos. Rethymno: Crete University Press, 2005, 135–47.

———. "In search of communities in seventeenth century Ottoman sources: The case of the Kara Ferye district." *Turcica* 30 (1998): 135–62.

Gaunt, Peter. *Oliver Cromwell.* Oxford: Blackwell, 1996.

Gedikli, Fethi. *Osmanlı Şirket Kültürü: XVI.-XVII. Yüzyıllarda Mudârebe Uygulaması.* Istanbul: İz, 1998.

———. "İstanbul'da para vakıfları ve mudârebe." *Hak-İş Dergisi* (November 1999): 68–73.

Gibb, Hamilton A. R. "Lutfī Paşa on the Ottoman Caliphate." *Oriens* 15 (1962): 287–95.

Goffman, Daniel. *The Ottoman Empire and Early Modern Europe.* Cambridge: Cambridge University Press, 2002.

Goldstone, Jack A. *Revolution and Rebellion in the Early Modern World.* Berkeley: University of California Press, 1991.

Gökbilgin, M. Tayyib. "Nizam-ı cedid." *İA.* Vol. IX, 309–18.

Göyünç, Nejat. "Yurtluk-ocaklık deyimleri hakkında." In *Prof. Dr. Bekir Kütükoğlu'na Armağan.* Istanbul: İ.Ü. Edebiyat Fakültesi Yayınları, 1991, 269–78.

Greene, Molly. "An Islamic experiment? Ottoman land policy on Crete." *Mediterranean Historical Review* 11 (1996): 60–78.

Griswold, William J. *The Great Anatolian Rebellion, 1000–1020/1591–1611.* Berlin: Klaus Schwarz, 1983.

Guillaumin, Colette. *Racism, Sexism, Power and Ideology.* London: Routledge, 1995.

Hallaq, Wael B. "The 'qadi's diwan (sijill)' before the Ottomans." *Bulletin of the School of Oriental and African Studies* 61 (1998): 415–36.

———. *Authority, Continuity and Change in Islamic Law.* Cambridge: Cambridge University Press, 2001.

———. "'Muslim rage' and Islamic law." *Hastings Law Journal* 54 (2003): 1705–19.

Hamadeh, Shirine. *The City's Pleasures: Istanbul in the Eighteenth Century.* Seattle: University of Washington Press, 2008.

Hanna, Nelly. *Making Big Money in 1600: The Life and Times of Isma'il Abu Taqiyya, Egyptian Merchant.* Syracuse: Syracuse University Press, 1998.

———. *In Praise of Books: A Cultural History of Cairo's Middle Class, Sixteenth to the Eighteenth Century.* Syracuse: Syracuse University Press, 2003.

Hathaway, Jane. "Problems of periodization in Ottoman history: The fifteenth through the eighteenth centuries." *Turkish Studies Association Bulletin* 20/2 (Fall 1996): 25–31.

_____. *The Politics of Households in Ottoman Egypt: The Rise of the Qazdağlıs*. Cambridge: Cambridge University Press, 1997.

_____. *A Tale of Two Factions: Myth, Memory, and Identity in Ottoman Egypt and Yemen*. Albany: State University of New York Press, 2003.

Hattox, Ralph S. *Coffee and Coffeehouses: The Origins of a Social Beverage in the Medieval Near East*. Seattle: University of Washington Press, 1985.

Hess, Andrew Christie. "Islamic civilization and the legend of political failure." *Journal of Near Eastern Studies* 44 (1985): 27–39.

Heyd, Uriel. *Kānūn and Sharī'a in Old Ottoman Criminal Justice*. Jerusalem: Israel Academy of Sciences and Humanities, 1967.

_____. *Studies in Old Ottoman Criminal Law*. Edited by V. L. Ménage. Oxford: Oxford University Press, 1973.

Howard, Douglas A. "The Ottoman timar system and its transformation." PhD diss. Indiana University, 1987.

_____. "Ottoman historiography and the literature of 'decline' of the sixteenth and seventeenth centuries." *Journal of Asian History* 22 (1988): 52–77.

_____. "Ottoman administration and the tîmâr system: ṣûret-i ḳânûnnâme-i 'Osmânî berây-ı tîmâr dâden," *Journal of Turkish Studies* 20 (1996): 46–125.

_____. "Genre and myth in the Ottoman advice for kings literature." In *The Early Modern Ottomans: Remapping the Empire*, edited by Virginia H. Aksan and Daniel Goffman. Cambridge: Cambridge University Press, 2007, 137–66.

Imber, Colin H. *Ebu's-su'ud: The Islamic Legal Tradition*. Stanford: Stanford University Press, 1997.

_____. *The Ottoman Empire, 1300–1650: The Structure of Power*. Hampshire: Palgrave Macmillan, 2002.

_____. "Die Thronbesteigungen der osmanischen Sultane: die Entwicklung einer Zeremonie." In *Investitur- und Krönungsrituale: Herrschaftseinsetzungen im kulturellen Vergleich*, edited by Marion Steinicke and Stefan Weinfurter. Köln: Böhlau Verlag, 2005, 291–303.

İnalcık, Halil. "Ottoman methods of conquest." *Studia Islamica* 2 (1954): 103–29.

_____. "The Ottoman succession and its relation to the Turkish concept of sovereignty." Translated by Douglas Howard [translation of "Osmanlılarda saltanat verâseti usûlü ve Türk hakimiyet telâkkisiyle ilgisi," *Siyasal Bilgiler Fakültesi Dergisi* 14 (1959): 69–94]. In *The Middle East and the Balkans under the Ottoman Empire: Essays on Economy and Society*, edited by H. İnalcık. Bloomington: Indiana University Turkish Studies, 1993, 37–69.

_____. "Kanun, iii.-Financial and public administration." *Encyclopedia of Islam, New Edition*. Vol. IV, 558–62.

_____. "Mehemmed II," *Encyclopedia of Islam, New Edition*. Vol. VI, 978–81.

_____. *The Ottoman Empire: The Classical Age, 1300–1600*. Translated by Norman Itzkowitz and Colin Imber. London: Weidenfeld & Nicolson, 1973.

_____. "Military and fiscal transformation in the Ottoman Empire, 1600–1700." *Archivum Ottomanicum* 6 (1980): 283–337.

_____. "The emergence of big farms, çiftliks: State, landlords, and tenants." In *Contributions à l'histoire économique et sociale de l'Empire ottoman*, edited by Jean-Louis Bacqué-Grammont and Paul Dumont. Louvain: Peeters, 1983, 105–26.

_____. "Comments on 'sultanism': Max Weber's typification of the Ottoman polity." *Princeton Papers in Near Eastern Studies* 1 (1992): 49–72.

258   Bibliography

————. "The Ottoman state: Economy and society, 1300–1600." In *An Economic and Social History of the Ottoman Empire, 1300–1914*, edited by H. İnalcık with Donald Quataert. Cambridge: Cambridge University Press, 1994, 9–409.

————. "Foundation of the Ottoman state." Translated by Metin Yeğenoğlu. In *The Turks*, edited by Hasan Celal Güzel, C. Cem Oğuz, and Osman Karatay. 6 vols. Ankara: Yeni Türkiye, 2002, vol. III, 46–73.

Irwin, Robert. "Factions in medieval Egypt." *Journal of the Royal Asiatic Society* (1986): 228–46.

Itzkowitz, Norman. "Eighteenth century Ottoman realities." *Studia Islamica* 16 (1962): 73–94.

İzgi, Cevat. *Osmanlı Medreselerinde İlim.* 2 vols. Istanbul: İz, 1997.

Johansen, Baber. "Sacred and religious elements in Hanafite law – function and limits of the absolute character of government authority." In *Islam et politique au Maghreb*, edited by Ernest Gellner and Jean-Claude Vatin. Paris: Éditions du centre national de la recherche scientifique, 1981, 281–303.

————. "The claims of men and the claims of God: The limits of government authority in Hanafite law." In *Pluriformiteit en verdeling van de macht in het Midden-Oosten.* [Nijmegen]: Vereniging voor de Studie van het Midden-Oosten en de Islam, 1980, 60–104.

Jorga, Nicolae. *Geschichte des osmanischen Reiches.* 5 vols. Gotha: Perthes, 1908–13.

Kafadar, Cemal. "Yeniçeri – esnaf relations: Solidarity and conflict." MA thesis. McGill University, 1981.

————. "When coins turned into drops of dew and bankers became robbers of shadows: The boundaries of Ottoman economic imagination at the end of the sixteenth century." PhD diss. McGill University, 1986.

————. "Self and others: The diary of a dervish in seventeenth century Istanbul and first-person narratives in Ottoman literature." *Studia Islamica* 69 (1989): 121–50.

————. "On the purity and corruption of the Janissaries." *Turkish Studies Association Bulletin* 15 (1991): 273–80.

————. "Eyüp'te kılıç kuşanma törenleri." In *Eyüp: Dün / Bugün (Sempozyum, 11–12 Aralık 1993)*, edited by Tülay Artan. Istanbul: Tarih Vakfı Yurt Yayınları, 1994, 50–61.

————. "The Ottomans and Europe." In *Handbook of European History, 1400–1600: Late Middle Ages, Renaissance and Reformation*, edited by Thomas A. Brady, Jr., Heiko A. Oberman, and James D. Tracy. 2 vols. Leiden: E. J. Brill, 1994–5, vol. I, 589–635.

————. *Between Two Worlds: The Construction of the Ottoman State.* Berkeley: University of California Press, 1995.

————. "The question of Ottoman decline." *Harvard Middle Eastern and Islamic Review* 4 (1997–8): 30–75.

————. "A Rome of one's own: Reflections on cultural geography and identity in the lands of Rum." *Muqarnas* 24 (2007): 7–25.

————. "Janissaries and other riffraff of Ottoman Istanbul: Rebels without a cause?" In *Identity and Identity Formation in the Ottoman World: A Volume of Essays in Honor of Norman Itzkowitz*, edited by Baki Tezcan and Karl Barbir. Madison: University of Wisconsin Center of Turkish Studies, 2007, 113–34.

Kaplan, Mehmet. *Namık Kemal: Hayatı ve eserleri.* Istanbul, 1948.

Kassis, Riad Aziz. *The Book of Proverbs and Arabic Proverbial Works.* Leiden: Brill, 1999.

Kastritsis, Dimitris J. "Çelebi Mehemmed's letter of oath (sevgendnāme) to Ya'kūb II of Germiyan: Notes and a translation based on Şinasi Tekin's edition." *Şinasi Tekin'in Anısına: Uygurlardan Osmanlıya.* Istanbul: Simurg, 2005, 442–4.

Khoury, Dina Rizk. *State and Provincial Society in the Ottoman Empire: Mosul, 1540–1834.* Cambridge: Cambridge University Press, 1997.

_____. "The Ottoman centre versus provincial power-holders: An analysis of the historiography." In *The Cambridge History of Turkey.* Vol. III: *The Later Ottoman Empire, 1603–1839,* edited by Suraiya N. Faroqhi. Cambridge: Cambridge University Press, 2006, 135–56.

Klein, Denise. *Die osmanischen Ulema des 17. Jahrhunderts: Eine geschlossene Gesellschaft?* Berlin: Klaus Schwarz, 2007.

Kortantamer, Tunca. *Nev'îzâde Atâyî ve Hamse'si.* Izmir: Ege Üniversitesi Edebiyat Fakültesi Yayınları, 1997.

Köprülü, M. Fuad. "Alp." *İA.* Vol. I, 379–84.

_____. "Bey." *İA.* Vol. II, 579–81.

Kunt, İ. Metin. *The Sultan's Servants: The Transformation of Ottoman Provincial Government, 1550–1650.* New York: Columbia University Press, 1983.

Kuran, Timur. "The absence of the corporation in Islamic law: Origins and persistence." *American Journal of Comparative Law* 53 (2005): 785–834.

Kütükoğlu, Bekir. *Osmanlı-İran Siyâsî Münâsebetleri, 1578–1612.* 2nd edition. Istanbul: İstanbul Fetih Cemiyeti, 1993.

Kütükoğlu, Mübahat S. "1009 (1600) tarihli Narh Defterine göre İstanbul'da çeşidli eşya ve hizmet fiatları." *Tarih Enstitüsü Dergisi* 9 (1978): 1–85.

Lambton, Ann K. S. *State and Government in Medieval Islam: An Introduction to the Study of Islamic Political Theory – the Jurists.* London: Oxford University Press, 1981.

Lapidus, Ira Marvin. *Muslim Cities in the Later Middle Ages.* Cambridge: Harvard University Press, 1967.

Lewis, Bernard. "Some reflections on the decline of the Ottoman Empire." *Studia Islamica* 9 (1958): 111–27.

_____. *The Emergence of Modern Turkey.* London: Oxford University Press, 1961.

_____. "Slade on Turkey." In *Social and Economic History of Turkey, 1071–1920: Papers Presented to the First International Congress on the Social and Economic History of Turkey (Hacettepe University, Ankara, 11–13 July 1977),* edited by Osman Okyar and Halil İnalcık. Ankara: Meteksan, 1980, 215–26.

Lin, Yih-Min. *Ali Ekber'in Hitayname adlı eserinin Çin kaynakları ile mukayese ve tenkidi.* Tai-Pei, 1967.

Liske, Xaver. "Der türkisch-polnische Feldzug im Jahre 1620: nach gedruckten und handschriftlichen Quellen dargestellt." *Archiv für österreichische Geschichte* 41 (1869): 353–97.

Lowry, Heath W. "The Ottoman Liva Kanunnames contained in the Defter-i Hakani." *Osmanlı Araştırmaları / Journal of Ottoman Studies* 2 (1981): 43–74.

_____. *The Nature of the Early Ottoman State.* Albany: State University of New York Press, 2003.

Mandaville, Jon E. "Usurious piety: The cash waqf controversy in the Ottoman Empire." *International Journal of Middle East Studies* 10 (1979): 289–308.

Mardin, Şerif. "Freedom in an Ottoman perspective." In *State, Democracy, and the Military: Turkey in the 1980s,* edited by Metin Heper and Ahmet Evin. Berlin: W. de Gruyter, 1988, 23–35.

260   Bibliography

Metcalf, D. M. *Coinage in the Balkans, 820–1355*. Thessaloniki: Institute for Balkan Studies, 1965.

Moalla, Asma. *The Regency of Tunis and the Ottoman Porte, 1777–1814: Army and Government of a North-African Ottoman eyâlet at the End of the Eighteenth Century*. London: Routledge Curzon, 2004.

Moravcsik, Gyula. "Türklüğün tetkiki bakımından Bizantolojinin ehemmiyeti." In *İkinci Türk Tarih Kongresi (İstanbul, 20–25 Eylül 1937)*. Istanbul: Türk Tarih Kurumu, 1943, 483–98.

Mordtmann, A. D. *Stambul und das moderne Türkenthum: Politische, sociale, und biographische Bilder von einem Osmanen*. 2 vols. Leipzig: Duncker & Humblot, 1877–78.

Mordtmann, J. H. "Das Observatorium des Taqī ed-dīn zu Pera." *Der Islam* 13 (1923): 82–96.

———. "Die jüdischen Kira im Serai der Sultane." *Mitteilungen des Seminars für orientalischen Sprachen* 32 (1929): 1–38.

Murphey, Rhoads. "The Functioning of the Ottoman Army under Murad IV (1623–1639/1032–1049): Key to the Understanding of the Relationship between Center and Periphery in Seventeenth-Century Turkey." PhD diss. University of Chicago, 1979.

———. *Ottoman Warfare, 1500–1700*. London: UCL Press, 1999.

Mutafcieva, Vera P. "Sur le caractère du timar ottoman." *Acta Orientalia Academiae Scientiarum Hungaricae* 9 (1959): 5–61.

Müderrisoğlu, M. Fatih. "Osmanlı İmparatorluğu'nun Doğu Akdeniz'deki iskelesi Payas ve Sokullu Mehmed Paşa Menzil Külliyesi." In *9th International Congress of Turkish Art – 23–27 September 1991, Istanbul*. 3 vols. Ankara: Kültür Bakanlığı, 1995, vol. II, 513–24.

Necipoğlu, Gülru. *Architecture, Ceremonial, and Power: The Topkapı Palace in the fifteenth and sixteenth centuries*. Cambridge: MIT Press, 1991.

Nicol, Donald M. *The Last Centuries of Byzantium, 1261–1453*. 2nd edition. Cambridge: Cambridge University Press, 1993.

Nutku, Özdemir. *Meddahlık ve Meddah Hikayeleri*. n.p.: İş Bankası Kültür Yayınları, c. 1976.

Owen, Owen. "The Middle East in the eighteenth century – an 'Islamic' Society in decline: A critique of Gibb and Bowen's *Islamic Society and the West*." *Review of Middle East Studies* 1 (1975): 101–12.

Öz, Mehmet. *Osmanlı'da "Çözülme" ve Gelenekçi Yorumcuları*. Istanbul: Dergah Yayınları, 1997.

Özbaran, Salih. *Bir Osmanlı Kimliği: 14.–17. Yüzyıllarda Rûm / Rûmî Aidiyet ve İmgeleri*. Istanbul: Kitap Yayınevi, 2004.

Özcan, Tahsin. *Osmanlı Para Vakıfları: Kanûnî Dönemi Üsküdar Örneği*. Ankara: Türk Tarih Kurumu, 2003.

Özdeğer, Hüseyin. *1463–1640 Yılları Bursa Şehri Tereke Defterleri*. Istanbul: İstanbul Üniversitesi İktisat Fakültesi Yayınları, 1988.

Özmucur, Süleyman, and Şevket Pamuk. "Real wages and standards of living in the Ottoman Empire, 1489–1914." *Journal of Economic History* 62 (2002): 292–321.

Öztürk, Necati. "Islamic Orthodoxy among the Ottomans in the seventeenth century with special reference to the Qadi-Zade movement." PhD diss. University of Edinburgh, 1981.

Öztürk, Said. *Askeri Kassama ait Onyedinci Asır İstanbul Tereke Defterleri: Sosyo-ekonomik tahlil*. Istanbul: Osmanlı Araştırmaları Vakfı, 1995.

Pakalın, Mehmet Zeki. "Kadı." In *Osmanlı Tarih Deyimleri ve Terimleri Sözlüğü*, edited by M. Z. Pakalın. 3 vols. Istanbul: Milli Eğitim Bakanlığı, 1946, vol. II, 119–25.

Pamuk, Şevket. *A Monetary History of the Ottoman Empire*. Cambridge: Cambridge University Press, 2000.

Pedani, Maria Pia. "Safiye's household and Venetian diplomacy." *Turcica* 32 (2000): 9–31.

Peirce, Leslie. *The Imperial Harem: Women and Sovereignty in the Ottoman Empire*. Oxford: Oxford University Press, 1993.

Petrushevsky, I. P. "The socio-economic condition of Iran under the Il-khans." In *The Cambridge History of Iran*. Vol. 5: *The Saljuq and Mongol Periods*, edited by J. A. Boyle. Cambridge: Cambridge University Press, 1968, 483–537.

Philliou, Christine. "Communities on the verge: Unraveling the Phanariot ascendancy in Ottoman governance." *Comparative Studies in Society and History* 51 (2009): 151–81.

Piterberg, Gabriel. *An Ottoman Tragedy: History and historiography at play*. Berkeley: University of California Press, 2003.

Pocock, John G. A. "Clergy and commerce: The conservative Enlightenment in England." In *L'Età dei Lumi: Studi Storici sul Settecento Europeo in Onore di Franco Venturi*. 2 vols. Naples: Jovene Editore, 1985, vol. I, 523–62.

_____. *The Ancient Constitution and the Feudal Law: A Study of English Historical Thought in the Seventeenth Century, a Reissue with a Retrospect*. Cambridge: Cambridge University Press, 1987.

Pouchepadass, Jacques. "Pluralizing reason." *History and Theory* 41 (2002): 381–91.

Qattan, Najwa. "Discriminating texts: Orthographic marking and social differentiation in the court records of Ottoman Damascus." In *Arabic Sociolinguistics: Issues and Perspectives*, edited by Yasir Suleiman. London: Curzon, 1994, 57–77.

Quataert, Donald. "The age of reforms, 1812–1914." In *An Economic and Social History of the Ottoman Empire, 1300–1914*, edited by Halil İnalcık with Donald Quataert. Cambridge: Cambridge University Press, 1994, 759–943.

_____. "Janissaries, artisans, and the question of Ottoman decline, 1730–1826." In *17° Congreso Internacional de Ciencias Historicas, Madrid – 1990*. Vol. I: *Sección Cronológica*, edited by Eloy Benito Ruano and Manuel Espadas Burgos. Madrid: Comité International des Sciences Historiques, 1992, 264–8.

_____. *The Ottoman Empire, 1700–1922*. Cambridge: Cambridge University Press, 2000.

_____. "Ottoman history writing and changing attitudes towards the notion of 'decline.'" *History Compass* 1 (August 2003).

Ranke, Leopold von. *The History of Servia and the Servian Revolution*. Translated by Mrs. Alexander Kerr. London: Henry G. Bohn, 1853.

Rapoport, Yossef. "Legal diversity in the age of *taqlid*: The four chief *qadi*s under the Mamluks." *Islamic Law and Society* 10 (2003): 21028.

Repp, Richard C. *The Müfti of Istanbul: A study in the Development of the Ottoman Learned Hierarchy*. London: Ithaca Press, 1986.

_____. "Qānūn and sharīʿa in the Ottoman context." In *Islamic Law: Social and Historical Contexts*, edited by Aziz al-Azmeh. London: Routledge, 1988, 124–45.

Robertson, William. *History of the Reign of the Emperor Charles V*. 3 vols. London, 1769.

Röhrborn, Klaus. "Die Emanzipation der Finanzbürokratie im osmanischen Reich (Ende 16. Jahrhundert)." *Zeitschrift der deutschen morgenländischen Gesellschaft* 122 (1972): 118–39.

———. "Osmanlı İmparatorluğunda müsadere ve mutavassıt güçler." In *I. Milletlerarası Türkoloji Kongresi, İstanbul, 15–20.X.1973: Tebliğler.* Vol. I: *Türk Tarihi.* Istanbul: Tercüman, 1979, 254–60.

Sadat, Deena R. "Rumeli Ayanlari: The eighteenth century." *Journal of Modern History* 44 (1972): 346–63.

———. "Âyân and ağa: The transformation of the Bektashi corps in the eighteenth century." *Muslim World* (1973): 206–19.

Sahillioğlu, Halil. "Kuruluştan XVII. asrın sonlarına kadar Osmanlı para tarihi üzerinde bir deneme." PhD diss. İstanbul Üniversitesi, 1958.

Sajdi, Dana. "Peripheral visions: The worlds and worldviews of commoner chroniclers in the 18th century Ottoman Levant." PhD diss. Columbia University, 2002.

Salibi, Kamal S. "The secret of the House of Ma'n." *International Journal of Middle East Studies* 4 (1973): 272–87.

———. "Fakhr al-Dīn." *Encyclopedia of Islam, New Edition.* Vol. II, 749–51.

Salzmann, Ariel. "An ancien régime revisited: 'Privatization' and political economy in the eighteenth-century Ottoman Empire." *Politics & Society* 21 (1993): 393–423.

Shaw, Stanford. *History of the Ottoman Empire and Modern Turkey.* Vol. I: *Empire of the Gazis: The Rise and Decline of the Ottoman Empire, 1280–1808.* Cambridge: Cambridge University Press, 1976.

Shmuelevitz, Aryeh. "Ms Pococke no. 31 as a source for the events in Istanbul in the years 1622–1624." *International Journal of Turkish Studies* 3/2 (1985–6): 107–21.

Slade, Adolphus. *Turkey Greece and Malta.* 2 vols. London: Saunders and Otley, 1837.

———. *Turkey and the Crimean War: A Narrative of Historical Events.* London: Smith, Elder and Co., 1867.

Staffa, Susan Jane. *Conquest and Fusion: The Social Evolution of Cairo, A.D. 642–1850.* Leiden: E. J. Brill, 1977.

Steenbergen, Jo Van. *Order out of Chaos: Patronage, Conflict and Mamluk Socio-Political Culture, 1341–1382.* Leiden: E. J. Brill, 2006.

Steensgaard, Niels. "Violence and the rise of capitalism: Frederic C. Lane's theory of protection and tribute." *Review* 5/2 (Fall 1981): 247–73.

Stone, Lawrence. *The Crisis of the Aristocracy, 1558–1641.* Abridged edition. London: Oxford University Press, 1967.

———. *The Causes of the English Revolution, 1529–1642.* 2nd edition. London: Routledge, 1986, p. 55.

Şeyhi, Mehmed. *Vakâyi'ü'l-fudalâ.* 2 vols. Beyazıt Kütüphanesi, Veliyüddin 2361–2. Facsimile edition with indices in *Şakaik-ı Nu'maniye ve Zeyilleri,* edited by Abdülkadir Özcan, 5 vols. Istanbul: Çağrı Yayınları, 1989, vols. III–IV.

Taylor, Alan. *American Colonies: The Settling of North America.* New York: Penguin, 2001.

Tayşi, Mehmet Serhan. "Şeyhü'l-islâm Seyyid Feyzullâh Efendi ve Feyziyye Medresesi." *Türk Dünyası Araştırmaları* 23 (April 1983): 9–100.

Teschke, Benno. "Geopolitical relations in the European Middle Ages: History and theory." *International Organization* 52 (1998): 325–58.

Tekin, Şinasi. "Fatih Sultan Mehmed devrine ait bir inşa mecmuası." *Journal of Turkish Studies* 20 (1996): 267–311.

Tekindağ, Şahabettin. "Şah Kulu Baba Tekeli İsyanı." *Belgelerle Türk Tarihi Dergisi* 1/3 (December 1967): 34–9, 1/4 (January 1968): 54–9.

Terzioğlu, Derin. "Sufi and Dissident in the Ottoman Empire: Niyazi-i Mısri (1618–1694)." PhD diss. Harvard University, 1999.

_____. "Bir tercüme ve bir intihal vakası: Ya da İbn Teymiyye'nin Siyāsetü'ş-şer'iyye'sini Osmanlıcaya kim(ler), nasıl aktardı?" *Journal of Turkish Studies* 31/2 (2007): 247–75.

Tezcan, Baki. "The definition of sultanic legitimacy in the sixteenth century Ottoman Empire: The *Ahlâk-ı Alâ'î* of Kınalızâde Ali Çelebi (1510–1572)." MA thesis. Princeton University, 1996.

_____. "The development of the use of 'Kurdistan' as a geographical description and the incorporation of this region into the Ottoman Empire in the 16th century." In *The Great Ottoman-Turkish Civilisation*, edited by Kemal Çiçek et al. 4 vols. Ankara: Yeni Türkiye, 2000, vol. III, 540–53.

_____. "The 'Kânûnnâme of Mehmed II:' A different perspective." In *The Great Ottoman-Turkish Civilisation*, edited by Kemal Çiçek et al. 4 vols. Ankara: Yeni Türkiye, 2000, vol. III, 657–65.

_____. "Ethics as a domain to discuss the political: Kınalızâde Ali Efendi and his *Ahlâk-ı Alâî*." In *Proceedings of the International Congress on Learning and Education in the Ottoman World, Istanbul, 12–15 April 1999*, edited by Ali Çaksu. Istanbul: IRCICA Publications, 2001, 109–20.

_____. "Searching for Osman: A reassessment of the deposition of the Ottoman sultan Osman II (1618–1622)." PhD diss. Princeton University, 2001 [for the notes, see http://docs.google.com/fileview?id=0B9ULJyAfRPyfMWM2MTQzY2YtZGYwNi00-MzZlLTkxODEtMDQwNjE3ZjQ4MjQ0&hl=en].

_____. "The 1622 military rebellion in Istanbul: A historiographical journey." *International Journal of Turkish Studies* 8 (2002): 25–43.

_____. "The politics of early modern Ottoman historiography." In *The Early Modern Ottomans: Remapping the Empire*, edited by Virginia H. Aksan and Daniel Goffman. Cambridge: Cambridge University Press, 2007, 167–98.

_____. "*Dispelling the Darkness*: The politics of 'race' in the early seventeenth-century Ottoman Empire in the light of the life and work of Mullah Ali." In *Identity and Identity Formation in the Ottoman World: A Volume of Essays in Honor of Norman Itzkowitz*, edited by Baki Tezcan and Karl Barbir. Madison: University of Wisconsin Madison Center of Turkish Studies, 2007, 73–95.

_____. "The question of regency in Ottoman dynasty: The case of the early reign of Ahmed I." *Archivum Ottomanicum* 25 (2008): 185–98.

_____. "The debut of Kösem Sultan's political career." *Turcica* 40 (2008): 347–59.

_____. "The history of a 'primary source:' The making of Tûghî's chronicle on the deposition of Osman II." *Bulletin of the School of Oriental and African Studies* 72 (2009): 41–62.

_____. "The multiple faces of the One: The invocation section of Ottoman literary introductions as a locus for the central argument of the text." *Middle Eastern Literatures* 12 (2009): 27–41.

_____. "Lost in historiography: An essay on the reasons for the absence of a history of limited government in the early modern Ottoman Empire." *Middle Eastern Studies* 45 (2009): 477–505.

_____. "Khotin 1621, or how the Poles changed the course of Ottoman history." *Acta Orientalia Academiae Scientiarum Hungaricae* 62 (2009): 185–98.

———. "The Ottoman monetary crisis of 1585 revisited." *Journal of the Economic and Social History of the Orient* 52 (2009): 460–504.

———. "The Ottoman *mevâlî* as 'lords of the law.'" *Journal of Islamic Studies* 20 (2009): 383–407.

———. "The Second Empire: The transformation of the Ottoman polity in the seventeenth century." *Comparative Studies of South Asia, Africa and the Middle East* 29 (2009): 556–72.

———. "Hanafism and the Turks in al-Ṭarasūsī's *Gift for the Turks* (1352)." *Mamluk Studies Review* 15 (2011): forthcoming.

———. "Law in China or conquest in the Americas: Competing constructions of political space in the early modern Ottoman Empire." Forthcoming in *Journal of World History*.

———. "Some thoughts on the politics of early modern Ottoman science." In *Beyond Dominant Paradigms in Ottoman and Middle Eastern/North African Studies: A Tribute to Rifa'at Abou-El-Haj*, edited by Donald Quataert and Baki Tezcan. Istanbul: İSAM, forthcoming.

———. "The New Order and the fate of the old: The historiographical construction of an Ottoman *ancien régime* in the nineteenth century." In *Empires in Contention: Sociology, History, and Cultural Difference*, edited by Peter F. Bang and Chris A. Bayly. Hampshire: Palgrave, forthcoming.

Tietze, Andreas. *The Turkish Shadow Theater and the Puppet Collection of the L. A. Mayer Memorial Foundation*. Berlin: Gebr. Mann Verlag, 1977.

Timur, Taner. *Osmanlı Çalışmaları: İlkel feodalizmden yarı sömürge ekonomisine*. Ankara: Verso, 1989.

Togan, Ahmet-Zeki Validi. "Economic conditions in Anatolia in the Mongol period." Translated by Gary Leiser [translation of "Mogollar devrinde Anadolu'nun iktisadî vaziyeti," *Türk Hukuk ve İktisat Tarihi Mecmuası* 1 (1931): 1–42]. *Annales Islamologiques* 25 (1991): 203–40.

Turan, Şerafettin. *Kanuni Süleyman Dönemi Taht Kavgaları*. 2nd edition. Ankara: Bilgi, 1997.

Uluçay, Çağatay. "Yavuz Sultan Selim nasıl padişah oldu?" *Tarih Dergisi* 6/9 (1954): 53–90, 7/10 (1954): 117–42, 8/11–12 (1955): 185–200.

Uzunçarşılı, İsmail Hakkı. "Buyruldı." *Belleten* 5/19 (1941): 289–318.

———. *Osmanlı Devleti Teşkilâtından Kapukulu Ocakları*. 2 vols. Ankara: Türk Tarih Kurumu, 1943–4.

———. *Osmanlı Tarihi*. 4 vols. Ankara: Türk Tarih Kurumu, 1947–59.

———. *Osmanlı Devletinin İlmiye Teşkilâtı*. Ankara: Türk Tarih Kurumu, 1965.

Vatin, Nicolas and Giles Veinstein. *Le sérail ébranlé: Essai sur les morts, dépositions et avènements des sultans ottomans, XIVᵉ–XIXᵉ siècle*. Paris: Fayard, 2003.

Weinstein, Barbara. "History without a cause? Grand narratives, world history, and the postcolonial dilemma." *International Review of Social History* 50 (2005): 71–93.

Weiss, Bernard G. *The Spirit of Islamic Law*. Athens: University of Georgia Press, 1988.

Wong, R. Bin. *China Transformed: Historical Change and the Limits of European Experience*. Ithaca and London: Cornell University Press, 1997.

Wood, Ellen Meiksins. *The Origin of Capitalism: A Longer View*. London: Verso, 2002.

Woods, John E. *The Aqquyunlu: Clan, Confederation, Empire, a Study in 15th–/9th Century Turko-Iranian Politics*. Minneapolis: Biblioteca Islamica, 1976.

[Yaşar], Hüseyin Hüsameddin. *Amasya Ta'rîhi*. 4 vols. Istanbul, 1328–1928.

_____, and Mahmud Kemal. *Evkâf-ı hümâyûn nezâretinin ta'rîhçe-i teşkîlâtı ve nuzzârın terâcim-i ahvâli*. Istanbul, 1335.

Yaycıoğlu, Ali. "The provincial challenge: Regionalism, crisis, and integration in the late Ottoman Empire (1792–1812)." PhD diss. Harvard University, 2008.

[Yazıksız], Necib Asım. "Fevâ'id-i gazâ: On birinci 'asrda hayât-ı cündiyâne." *Ta'rîh-i 'Osmânî Encümeni Mecmû'ası* 1 (1329/1911): 542–50.

Yi, Eunjeong. *Guild Dynamics in Seventeenth-century Istanbul: Fluidity and Leverage*. Leiden: Brill, 2004.

Yüksel, Hasan. *Osmanlı sosyal ve ekonomik hayatında vakıfların rolü (1585–1683)*. Sivas, 1998.

Zaman, Muhammad Qasim. *Religion and Politics under the Early 'Abbasids: The Emergence of the Proto-Sunni Elite*. Leiden: Brill, 1997.

Zilfi, Madeline C. "Elite circulation in the Ottoman Empire: Great mollas of the eighteenth century." *Journal of the Economic and Social History of the Orient* 26 (1983): 318–64.

_____. "The Kadızadelis: Discordant revivalism in seventeenth-century Istanbul." *Journal of Near Eastern Studies* 45 (1986): 251–74.

_____. *The Politics of Piety: The Ottoman Ulema in the Postclassical Age (1600–1800)*. Minneapolis: Bibliotheca Islamica, 1988.

_____, ed. *Women in the Ottoman Empire: Middle Eastern Women in the Early Modern Era*. Leiden: Brill, 1997.

Reference Works

Catalogue des manuscrits et xylographes orientaux de la Bibliothèque impériale publique de St. Pétersbourg. Edited by Boris Andreevich Dorn and Reinhold Rost. St. Pétersbourg: Imprimerie de l'académie impériale des sciences, 1852.

Encyclopaedia of Islam, New Edition. Edited by H. A. R. Gibb, et al. 13 vols. Leiden: Brill, 1954–2008.

İslâm Ansiklopedisi. Edited and translated by A. Adıvar, et al. 13 vols. Istanbul: Milli Eğitim Bakanlığı, 1940–88.

Meninski, Franciszek. *Thesaurus linguarum orientalium turcicae, arabicae, persicae*. 4 vols. Vienna, 1680.

Pedani-Fabris, Maria Pia and Alessio Bombaci, eds. *I "Documenti Turchi" dell'Archivio di Stato di Venezia*. Roma: Ministero per i beni culturali e ambientali, 1994.

Schmidt, Jan. *Catalogue of Turkish Manuscripts in the Library of Leiden University and Other Collections in the Netherlands*. Leiden: Leiden University Library, 2000–.

Tarama Sözlüğü. Edited by Ömer Asım Aksoy and Dehri Dilçin. 8 vols. Ankara: Türk Dil Kurumu, 1963–77.

Topkapı Sarayı Müzesi. *Topkapı Sarayı Müzesi Arşivi Kılavuzu*. 2 vols. Istanbul, 1938–40.

Türkiye Diyanet Vakfı İslâm Ansiklopedisi. Edited by İslâm Araştırmaları Merkezi. Istanbul: Türkiye Diyanet Vakfı, 1988–.

Index

Abaza Hasan Pasha, 215–216
Abaza Mehmed Pasha, 162, 173, 213
Abdülhalim Karayazıcı, 65, 66, 143–148,
    150–151
Abdullah Efendi, 169
Abdürrahim family, 5, 220
Abou-El-Haj, Rifa'at Ali, 9, 34, 217,
    219
absolutism, 80, 213
    appointments, royal power of, 55
    army and, 152, 180
    conservatives and, 49, 53
    constitutionalists and, 48–59
    court politics and, 114
    definition of, 54, 80
    divine law and, 29, 53, 157
    historiography and, 215
    liberals and, 49, 53
    long wars and, 180
    market economies and, 80
    Mehmed III, 65
    Murad III, 97
    Murad IV, 214
    Mustafa I, 77, 109
    Mustafa II, 43–44, 219
    Osman II, 80–81, 109, 116, 128–141, 153
    political authority and, 44
    public law and, 47, 48
    sciences and, 29, 241
    Second Empire and, 150
    social mobility and, 53, 54–55, 58
    ulema and, 29, 44, 169, 171
Age of Beloveds, The, 1, 4
agriculture, 17, 80, 88, 197, 231. *See also*
    timars
Ahizade Hüseyin, 74
Ahmed Bey. *See* Etmekcizade Ahmed Pasha
Ahmed Cevdet, 226
Ahmed I
    accession to throne, 72–73
    chief gardeners, 104
    dynastic succession, 47, 61–63

effects of survival of brother on, 71
fratricide, 64
Mehmed Pasha (Sokolluzade) and, 108
Mustafa Agha and, 110–111
Mustafa Efendi and, 118
Osman II and, 115
pious acts of, 70
rebellions and, 71, 120n22
Safavid wars, 131–132
Sun'ullah Efendi and, 70
warrior sultan tradition and, 120
Ahmed III, 197n18, 222–223, 225
Ahmed Pasha (deputy grand vizier), 167, 169
Ahmed Pasha (Etmekcizade). *See*
    Etmekcizade Ahmed Pasha
Akarlı, Engin, 41
alcohol, 66, 67(fig), 174
Aleppo, 15, 95, 104, 132, 148–149, 159–160,
    162, 178n85, 189, 212
Algeria, 223–224
Ali Agha, 171, 172
Ali Bey, 121
Ali Efendi (Sarı), 37–38, 121. *See also*
    Mullah Ali
Ali Pasha (d. 1511), 101
Ali Pasha (1581–1621), 110, 111, 132–136,
    137
*alp*s, qualities of, 84–85
ambassador reports, reliability of, 113
Amcazade Hüseyin Pasha, 219
ancien régime, 191, 194, 226
Andrews, Walter, 1, 4, 191
Ankara, Battle of (1402), 88
army
    absolutism and, 152, 180
    administrators of, 80
    cavalry soldiers. *See* cavalry soldiers
    decline narrative and, 4, 195, 240
    *devşirme*s. *See devşirme* system
    dynastic succession and, 47
    economic interests and, 190
    endowment trusteeships and, 189

268   Index

276   Index

Cambridge Studies in Islamic Civilization

Titles in the series:

POPULAR CULTURE IN MEDIEVAL CAIRO *Boaz Shoshan*

EARLY PHILOSOPHICAL SHIISM: THE ISMAILI NEOPLATONISM OF ABŪ YAʾQŪB AL-SIJISTĀNI *Paul E. Walker*

INDIAN MERCHANTS IN EURASIAN TRADE, 1600–1750 *Stephen Frederic Dale*

PALESTINIAN PEASANTS AND OTTOMAN OFFICIALS: RURAL ADMINISTRATION AROUND SIXTEENTH-CENTURY JERUSALEM *Amy Singer*

ARABIC HISTORICAL THOUGHT IN THE CLASSICAL PERIOD *Tarif Khalidi*

MONGOLS AND MAMLUKS: THE MAMLUK–ĪLKHĀNID WAR, 1260–1281 *Reuven Amitai-Preiss*

HIERARCHY AND EGALITARIANISM IN ISLAMIC THOUGHT *Louise Marlow*

THE POLITICS OF HOUSEHOLDS IN OTTOMAN EGYPT: THE RISE OF THE QAZDAĞLIS *Jane Hathaway*

COMMODITY AND EXCHANGE IN THE MONGOL EMPIRE: A CULTURAL HISTORY OF ISLAMIC TEXTILES *Thomas T. Allsen*

STATE AND PROVINCIAL SOCIETY IN THE OTTOMAN EMPIRE: MOSUL, 1540–1834 *Dina Rizk Khoury*

THE MAMLUKS IN EGYPTIAN POLITICS AND SOCIETY *Thomas Philipp and Ulrich Haarmann (eds.)*

THE DELHI SULTANATE: A POLITICAL AND MILITARY HISTORY *Peter Jackson*

EUROPEAN AND ISLAMIC TRADE IN THE EARLY OTTOMAN STATE: THE MERCHANTS OF GENOA AND TURKEY *Kate Fleet*

REINTERPRETING ISLAMIC HISTORIOGRAPHY: HARUN AL-RASHID AND THE NARRATIVE OF THE ʿABBĀSID CALIPHATE *Tayeb El-Hibri*

THE OTTOMAN CITY BETWEEN EAST AND WEST: ALEPPO, IZMIR, AND ISTANBUL *Edhem Eldem, Daniel Goffman, and Bruce Masters*

A MONETARY HISTORY OF THE OTTOMAN EMPIRE *Sevket Pamuk*

THE POLITICS OF TRADE IN SAFAVID IRAN: SILK FOR SILVER, 1600–1730 *Rudolph P. Matthee*

THE IDEA OF IDOLATRY AND THE EMERGENCE OF ISLAM: FROM POLEMIC TO HISTORY *G. R. Hawting*

CLASSICAL ARABIC BIOGRAPHY: THE HEIRS OF THE PROPHETS IN THE AGE OF AL-MAʾMŪN *Michael Cooperson*

EMPIRE AND ELITES AFTER THE MUSLIM CONQUEST: THE TRANSFORMATION OF NORTHERN MESOPOTAMIA *Chase F. Robinson*

What is the main Argument?
How does the Author's Argument
Compliment what we've read so
far

The question Sorrounding why
Ahmed I let mustafa live is
interesting

mustafa   was   constitutional
Osman II   was   absolutist.

OSman II Sekban Army meant
that he was using monetary + Absolute Power
The military   had   a lot   at stake
when they fought for mustafa
because of the Privilages that were
given to the Sekban.